Travis · Waldt

The SGML Implementation Guide

Springer
Berlin
Heidelberg
New York
Barcelona
Budapest
Hong Kong
London
Milan
Paris
Tokyo

Brian Travis *(left)* is the president of Information Architects, Inc., an SGML consulting group specializing in structured information. He has installed SGML systems for clients as varied as book publishers, airlines, and chemical manufacturers. He has been involved in all phases of SGML selection and implementation, from providing management with information necessary for the decision to writing SGML applications for conversion and end-user maintenance. He is a principal voting member of the ANSI X3V1 SGML committee.

Dale Waldt *(right)* has over ten years experience with SGML and electronic publishing and database system design and development. He is the Director of Data Development for Research Institute of America, a Division of Thomson Professional Publishing, a large legal publishing company, where he leads a team in the design and conversion of complex publications into a database system based on SGML.

Both authors are alumni of the Internal Revenue Service Publications Division that was instrumental in creating what is now called SGML. Dale Waldt is a founder and publisher, and Brian Travis is managing editor of <TAG> *The SGML Newsletter*, the only regular technical periodical on SGML and publishing database development.

Brian E. Travis Dale C. Waldt

The SGML Implementation Guide

A Blueprint for SGML Migration

With 97 Figures

Springer

Brian E. Travis
Information Architects
6360 S. Gibraltar Circle
Aurora, CO 80016
USA

Dale C. Waldt
Research Institute of America
90 Fifth Avenue
New York, NY 10011
USA

Library of Congress Cataloging-in-Publication Data

Travis, Brian E., 1958-
The SGML implementation guide : a blueprint for SGML migration / Brian E. Travis, Dale C. Waldt.
p. cm.
Includes bibliographical references and index.
ISBN 3-540-57730-0 (acid-free paper)
1. Hypertext systems. 2. SGML (Document markup language)
I. Waldt, Dale C., 1960- . II. Title.
QA76.76.H94T73 1995
005.7--dc20 95-21239
CIP

ISBN 3-540-57730-0 Springer-Verlag Berlin Heidelberg New York

Typesetting: Camera-ready by author
Cover design: Springer-Verlag, Design & Production
SPIN: 10131845 33/3142-543210 – Printed on acid-free paper.

To Deni, who puts up with these projects, and to Cooper and Miller, who can now have their dad back. —*B.E.T.*

I now know why so many books are dedicated to families who bear the brunt of absenteeism, preoccupation, and occasional grumpiness on the part of the authors. You do not know how much your support and love mean to me.

Thank you, Kelly, Max, and Miles. —*D.C.W.*

Table of Contents

Foreword xxi
Preface xxi
Conventions . . . . *xxiv*
About the Authors . . . . *xxv*
Acknowledgements xxv

Part I / The Business Issues* *1

Chapter 1 / Your Publishing System is Broken! 3

Introduction 3
Related Topics 4
The Problem with Unstructured Information 4
The Promise of SGML 5
Technology Changes *5*

Stating Problems with Publishing Systems in Business Terms 7
What are Goals of an SGML-Based System? 9
The Power of SGML Databases 11
Enabling Information Management Technologies 11
Problems Inherent in Existing Systems 12
Conceptual Configuration of the Solution System 13

Chapter 2 / Evolution of Publishing Systems 21

Introduction 21
Related Topics 22
Markup Systems 22
Punctuation, Capitalization, and Spacing 24
Presentational Markup 24
Procedural Markup 24
Generic Markup 25
Standardized Markup 26
Summary 28
Publishing Systems 28
Stand-alone Composition Systems 30
Linked Publishing Systems 31
Integrated Publishing Systems 31
Federated Publishing Systems 33
Publishing Process Flow 34
Summary 36

Chapter 3 / Desktop Publishing and Professional Publishing Systems 37

Introduction 37
Related Topics 37
Productivity and Flexibility - Which Tool is Right for the Job 38
Desktop Publishing 38
Professional Systems 39
Let Editors Edit 39
The Best of Both Worlds 40
Checklist for Selecting a System 41

Chapter 4 / The SGML Environment 43

Introduction 43
Related Topics 44
Working in an SGML Environment 44
The SGML Environment 44
SGML Parser 46

Translator 47
SGML Editorial Workstation 47
SGML Add-ins 51
Delivery Vehicles 51
Workflow Managers 57
Database Repositories 58
DTD Development Tools 59
Related Standards 59
What is an SGML Application? 60

Part II / The Project* *63

Chapter 5 / Document Analysis 65

Introduction 65
Related Topics 66
Documents and Document Models 66
The Document Analysis Team 67
The Evangelist 67
The Document Analyst 67
The Document Analysis Team 69
The Document Analysis Methodology 70
The Document Analysis Report 71
Preliminary Analysis 73
Expanded Group Analysis 73
The Document Model 75
Discovering the Information in Documents 76
Illustrating Information Structure 78
Documents and Databases 86
Formatting and Structure 87
Format Tagging 87
Structure Tagging 88
Content Tagging 89
Balanced Approach 89
Usability and Understandability 90
Reusability and By-products 90
Longevity of Data 91
Common Elements 91
System Issues 91
Performance 91
System Limitations 92
Degree of Automation 92
Defining a Markup Language — The Recipe 92
Elements in a Recipe 93

Chapter 6 / The SGML Application 101

Introduction 101
Related Topics 101
The Application Defined 102
The Application Development Team 103
Owner *103*
Managers *103*
Analysts *104*
Programmers *104*
Users *105*
Application Considerations 105
Capture *105*
Editorial Workstations *106*
SGML Browsers *110*
Databases *110*
Composition Engines *111*
Translation to non-SGML applications *111*
Publication-specific Development *111*
Vendor-Supplied Applications 117
Customizability *117*
SGML Features Supported *118*
Integratability *118*
System Compatibility and Resources *118*
Support *118*
Price *118*
SGML Application Integration Issues 118
Glue *119*
Cross-platform Compatibility *119*

Chapter 7 / Implementation Planning 121

Introduction 121
Related Topics 122
System Evaluation and Design 122
Project Scope *123*
Stating Business Objectives *124*
Using SGML to Restructure Processes and Information *124*
Functional Evaluation *127*
Conceptual Design *133*
Cost and Benefit Evaluation *133*
Quantifying Benefits *134*
System Development 139
Implementation Tasks *140*
Implementation Resources *144*

Chapter 8 / Information Conversion 151

Introduction 151
Related Topics 152
The Need for Conversion 152
Terms *153*
Anatomy of an SGML Conversion 153
The Basic Conversion Process *154*
Finding Clues in Source Data *155*
Creating a Conversion Spec *156*
Data Conversion Planning and Implementation 160
Planning *161*
Conversion Processing *163*
Managing DTD Change *163*
Data Cleansing and Validation *164*
Conversion Strategies *165*
Conversion Resources *169*
Existing Conversions that May be High-cost Areas *171*
Types of SGML Conversions *175*
Summary 181

Chapter 9 / SGML Data Management and Workflow 183

Introduction 183
Related Topics 184
The File System as Database Manager 184
Entity Management 184
Version Control 186
Version Control Basics *186*
Revision Numbering *187*
Versions *187*
Branching *188*
Reconciliation *188*
Editions *189*
Reporting *189*
Graphical Interface *191*
Implementation Factors *191*
Network Functionality 192
Database Managers 192
Relational Databases *192*
Full-text Databases *193*
Object-oriented Databases *195*
Choosing an SGML-enabled Database Manager 201
Document Assembly *201*
Granularity of Locking *201*

Version Management 201
Programmability 201
Tolerance of Invalid SGML 201
Transaction Processing 201
Query 202
Blobs 202
Direct Integration to System 202
Database Implementation Factors 202
Determine Granularity 202
Application Development 203
Workflow 205
Workflow in Action 206
Creating a Project 207
Assigning Tasks 209
User Authorities 211
System Management 211
Implementation Considerations 211

***Part III / The Language* 213**

Chapter 10 / Understanding SGML 215

Introduction 215
Related Topics 216
The SGML Document Model 216
SGML Declaration 217
SGML Document Instance Set 218
Versions of SGML 219
Markup 219
Start-Tag 221
End-Tag 221
General Entity Reference 221
Comment Declaration 222
Processing Instruction 222
Character Reference 223
Marked Section Declaration 223
Short Reference Use Declaration 223
LINK Set Use Declaration 223
Declarations 224
The SGML Declaration 225
The Document Type Definition 229
The Element Declaration 229
The Attribute Definition List Declaration 239
The Entity Declaration 250

The Comment Declaration 262
The Document Type Declaration 263
Link-related Declarations 264
Short Reference Use Declaration 264
Marked Section Declaration 264
Notation Declaration 265
Minimization Features 266
Omitted Tag Minimization 267
Short Reference Minimization (SHORTREF) 269
Short Tag Minimization (SHORTTAG) 271
Other Minimization Features 273

Chapter 11 / Building the DTD 275

Introduction 275
Related Topics 275
Organizing a DTD 276
Naming Conventions 276
Comment Your DTD 278
Sequence 279
Organizing Elements and Attributes 280
Grouping Element Declarations 280
Alphabetical or Sequential 281
White Space 281
Advanced Features 283
DTD Version Control 284
DTD Change Strategy 284
Specific vs. General DTDs 285
Test Your DTD Against Reality 286
DTD Documentation 286
Application Overview 287
Tag Documentation 287
Common Elements 288
Tables 288
Equations 292
Cross-references 293
Quotes 295
Graphics 297
Footnotes 298
Indexing 299
Warnings, Cautions, and Notes 300

Chapter 12 / Tipniques and Pratfalls 301

Introduction 301

Related Topics 302
Using Parameter Entity References 302
Naming Parameter Entity References *303*
Elements vs. attributes 304
Parameter Entities 307
DTD Fragments 308
Start-tag Omission 308
Recursion 311
Mixed Content 312
Ambiguous Content Models 315
Using CDATA and RCDATA Elements 316
Using Glue to Hold an SGML System Together. 316
Convert Prologues from One Form to Another *316*
Normalize SGML Instances *317*
Pre-process Files for a Future Step *318*
Entity Management *318*
Omitted Attribute Specifications 319
Uses for Empty Elements 321
External Graphics *321*
Cross-references *322*
Part Numbers *323*
Formatting Information *324*
Managing Documents using "Hub Files" 324
The Hub File Concept *325*
Generate Public Identifier Mapping Files 328
Using Short Reference Minimization 330
Quotes *330*
Tables *331*
Using Processing Instructions the "Right Way" 333
SGML Editorial Workstation *334*
SGML Data Pre-processor *334*
Typesetting System *335*
Using Marked Sections 335
Cautions When Using Nested Marked Sections *335*
Parameter Entities *336*
Using NOTATION for External Tables 338
Tracking Information about Elements During DTD Development . . . 340
Using Ambiguity for Maximum Benefit 341
A Tool to Assist in Accurate Document Analysis 342
Use Table of Contents First 343
The Problems with Politics 343
Dealing with Floating Elements 344
Using DOCTYPE ID to Fool Application 345
Using Both LIT and LITA in an Attribute 346

Embedding Notes During Conversion Clean-up 347
Use Processing Instructions for Inter-application Communication . . . 348
Using Attributes to Capture Essential Data for Processing 348
FOSI hints 350
Protect Comments from the Parser 350
Protect Entity Names 351
Using #CONREF to enable External Table Processing 352
Use Minimization to Keep Keyboarding Costs Down 353
Using a Comment to Avoid Entity Misinterpretation 354
Rendering Footnotes in Electronic Documents 356
Handling ID/IDREF when Deleting Elements 357
Using Nested Quotes 357
Three "Views" in one Branching DTD 359
Using Titles in Subordinate Elements 360
Use #CURRENT Attribute for Ease of Entry 362
Using Attributes to Specify Semantic Information 363
Creating a Conditional Processing Language with SGML 365

Appendices 369

Appendix 1 / Case Study: RIA TIGRE System 371

Introduction 371
Background 371
Issues Faced by RIA 372
Enabling Technologies Employed 372
System Components 373
Critical System Features 373
Seamless Access 374
Conflicting Concurrent Structures 374
Access by Element and Physical Views, and Ranges of Each 376
Master Databases 378
Batch Composition 379
Workflow and Work-in-progress 379
SGML-smart Editing 380
Successes and Difficulties 381
Critical Success Factors 383

Appendix 2 / Case Study: Kodak Technical Information Documentation 385

Introduction 385
Background 386
Scope and Goals 386

The Project 387
Future 389

Appendix 3 / Case Study: Douglas Aircraft Company 391

Introduction 391
The Need for SGML at Douglas Aircraft 392
Meeting Modern ATA Requirements *392*
Improve Customer Satisfaction *393*
Improve Customer Satisfaction *394*
Accomplishments To Date 395
Requirements Gathering 395
System Architecture and Design *396*
Proof-of-Concept System *396*
Implementation of Production Service Bulletin System *397*
Lessons Learned 397
Future 398
Summary 399

Appendix 4 / Colophon: How this Book was Produced 401

Data Gathering 401
Initial Authoring 402
SGML Conversion 403
SGML Production 403
Ventura Publisher Used for Output 403
Tables 404
Graphics 406
Valid SGML Examples 407
World Wide Web Access 408
Text as Data 409
Production Credits 409

Appendix 5 / Brian and Dale's Excellent DTD 411

Introduction 411

Appendix 6 / Fully Commented SGML Declaration 425

Introduction 425
Default SGML Declaration 426
Fully Defined SGML Declaration 427

Appendix 7 / Glossary of Terms and Acronyms 437

Appendix 8 / SGML Resources 445

Parsers 446
Editors 449
Document Modeling Tools 456
Browsers 459
Translators 464
Formatters/Paginators 470
Data Management Systems 473
World Wide Web Applications 478
Workflow Products 480
Consulting Services 481
Conversion Services 483
Periodicals 485
User Community 487
Standards Publications 488
Conferences 490
Organizations 492
Publications 494
Seminars 498
Miscellany 499

Appendix 9 / Addresses of SGML Companies 503

Appendix 10 / Index 509

The SGML Implementation Guide

Brian E. Travis • Dale C. Waldt

Foreword

SGML is misunderstood and underestimated. I have always wanted to write this book. I am pleased that two people with whom I have had the pleasure to work were finally able to do so. Since I have always been a bit of an evangelist, I feel pride when my "students" become recognized "teachers".

In the early years of SGML we struggled to define a language that would bring the information to its rightful place. We succeeded. Then we had to explain these idea to technical adoptors. Again, I think we have succeeded. We have learned much about SGML in the process of implementing it. These experiences must now also be shared, along with comprehensible information on the language itself. The word must move out of the lab and the computer center and reach the business people, the users, the movers and shakers. The next generation will do things with SGML that we can't even imagine yet— it is that versatile.

There really is a dramatic and fundamental change taking place in the world regarding the use and reuse of information. What was once science fiction is now taken for granted as part of everyday life. Two years ago the Internet was frequented by a select group of specialists. Now, it is nearly as ubiquitous as a fax machine. You cannot pick up a newspaper or mainstream magazine without reading about it, and the problems associated with identifying, accessing, and using information found in its vast "libraries". Through the use of enabling technology such as SGML and related standards, communication protocols, affordable powerful computers, and intelligent data management concepts, the real potential of the Internet, networking, and information and communication will be realized. Information will finally be freed of the constraints of the processing, and will enable critical thinking and information sharing.

SGML truly is changing the way we look at information and, as such, it is changing the world. It is nice to have been a part of this movement.

William W. Davis, Jr., Chairman,
ANSI X3V1.8, Computer Languages for Processing Text,
the Task Group responsible for developing SGML
Alexandria, Virginia, April, 1995

Preface

This is the book the authors needed when we were first implementing an SGML system. At that time, and up until this book, there has been no single source of information for the SGML implementor. We had to perform major research at every single phase of the process using time-honored systems analysis techniques. While this approach worked, we would have gladly embraced any help we could have found.

This book provides a set of guidelines for the following groups of users:

1. Managers who have been given the requirement for investigating SGML, whether by choice or by fiat,
2. Systems analysts who are in charge of providing a plan towards implementing SGML,
3. Developers actively involved in implementing an SGML system, and
4. Programmers and other technical people who are looking for a few tips.
5. Users who want to know more about this thing that will inevitably come to pass.

We have nearly two decades of combined experience in implementing SGML and related disciplines. Implementations ranging from simple to complex, small to large, in commercial, academic, and government organizations, have given us a rare combination of the practical knowledge needed to implement SGML systems that make technical and economic sense.

The philosophy behind this book is to provide a pragmatic working knowledge of SGML and the related disciplines and techniques needed to achieve a successful implementation. SGML cannot be implemented in a vacuum. It involves software development, project management, information analysis, and an awareness of the environment in which it will be applied. It requires a pragmatic use of its very powerful features. We provide this by capturing our collective experience in implementing SGML for dozens of applications, both in the commercial and government areas. This is a hands-on book, sprinkled with helpful tips.

We are not computer science academics, nor are we language or grammar specialists. Rather, we are businessmen with publishing and systems integration backgrounds, and have been involved in all phases of the SGML implementation process. The business issues are written from the standpoint of building the business case. The technical sections are written from the perspective of the implementor, not the language specialist. This is not a comprehensive treatise on the SGML standard; rather, it contains a detailed description of the areas of SGML that we feel have been helpful in performing our own SGML implementations. When there is an area of the language that we do not feel is necessary in a typical implementation, we will refer the reader to the standard itself, or to other books that specialize in such areas.

In the book there are many examples scattered throughout. There is a chapter titled Chapter 12, *Tipniques and Pratfalls* on page 301, which shows helpful tips, techniques, and practices we have learned to use, and pitfalls we have learned to avoid over the years. In addition to these, we have placed examples in-line with the technical and business sections of the books. We include these because they are helpful to the new user to see how the language works, and real-life applications of the syntax and markup. You might see the same topic more than once, but each time it comes from a different perspective and provides additional information.

In the appendicies, there are several case studies of real-life SGML implementations. One of the case studies is a description of how we created this book. We are calling it "The World's Longest Colophon", because it tells the story of the production of the book, using the techniques that are discussed in the book.

This book is not a review of products, but it does mention many products in order to illustrate the concepts presented in the book and to describe what types of products are available. It is not merely an executive briefing offering a high-level view of the advantages of implementing a structured approach to data, nor is it a nuts-and-bolts description of how to write SGML applications. Rather, it strikes a ground between those two extremes, offering to the people who must make the decision to implement, then the implementors, enough information to get well down the road to SGML.

We recognize a gaping void in the selection of books and literature about SGML when it comes to actually implementing it to solve business problems. Most information available is very technical and does not show how SGML fits into the big picture. Companies have struggled, sometimes unnecessarily, with SGML due to the lack of information that transcends academic understanding and is backed by practical experience in implementing SGML.

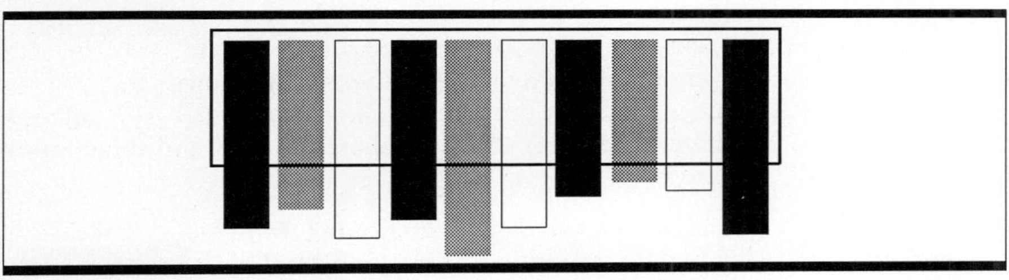

Figure 1. *The Scope of this Book*

The diagram above is an attempt to illustrate the scope of this book. The vertical rectangular boxes represent various topics in the SGML world, including information analysis, the SGML standard itself, database technology, workflow analysis, systems analysis, software development, project planning and management, and other business and technical subjects. The horizontal box arranged across the topics represents the depth of each topic that we feel an implementor of SGML needs to understand in order to succeed in most SGML implementations. This book is the physical manifestation of the body of knowledge needed to implement SGML represented by the horizontal box. We did leave out the esoteric information that is rarely needed, and often confusing. There might be circumstances when your implementation requires more in-depth knowledge about a particular subject. In that case, we have compiled a bibliography of works that you might find helpful to go further into depth on these subjects. What we believe we have built is the foundation for many successful SGML system implementations.

CONVENTIONS

Words in `courier` are usually the names of attributes or elements. Uppercase `COURIER` usually indicates an SGML keyword. We say "usually" because sometimes the conventions are broken for the sake of clarity.

This book contains many examples of SGML coding. These were produced by using an automated technique to assure all examples were correct (See *Valid SGML Examples* on page 407). We call this "Hot" validation, because the SGML coding is generated and parsed during the output-processing phase. All examples have been formatted on-the-fly by the translation programs, so adhere to some standard conventions. All SGML keywords are in uppercase letters. Everything in the SGML samples in lowercase are the author-defined words.

For some examples, the parsed output from the SGMLS parser is shown in the book. The format of this output is as follows:

1. The first character in each line indicates the type of line:
   a. `(` Start-tag. The name of the started element (generic identifier) follows
   b. `)` End-tag. The name of the ended element (generic identifier) follows.
   c. `-` Character content of the element.
   d. `&` Entity reference. The name of the entity follows.
   e. `?` Processing instruction. The data folows.
   f. `A` Attribute. The name of the attribute, its type, and value follow. Types are:
      i. `IMPLIED` The value of the attribute is implied.
      ii. `CDATA` The attribute is character data. This is used for attributes whose declared value is `CDATA`.
      iii. `NOTATION` The attribute is a notation name; nname will have been defined using a N command. This is used for attributes whose declared value is `NOTATION`.
      iv. `ENTITY` The attribute is a list of general entity names. Each entity name will have been defined using an I, E or S command. This is used for attributes whose declared value is `ENTITY` or `ENTITIES`.
      v. `TOKEN` The attribute is a list of tokens. This is used for attributes whose declared value is anything else.
   g. `N` Notation declaration. The name of the notation follows.
2. Newlines in the source are indicates with a `\n` in the text.
3. Backslashes (\) are indicated with two backslashes.
4. A `C` at the end of the file indicates a conformant SGML document (no SGML errors).
5. Sometimes, a line number is generated before each line for the purpose of discussion in the text.

In some cases, an SGML error stream is shown. This is the output from the parser used for the "hot" validation of SGML samples. This text is the actual text created by the "hot" validation process. It shows the name of the source file (almost always `valid.sgm`), followed by the line number and character position of the error. The text following describes the error. Because of the way the "hot" validation process works, the line and character numbers do not necesarily coincide with the line and character positions in the displayed example.

In the segments where SGML code is presented, sometimes a part of the total SGML document is suppressed. In the text, we have placed an ellipsis (...) to show that some material has been suppressed for clarity.

About the Authors

Brian Travis is the president of Information Architects, Inc., an SGML consulting group specializing in custom implementations. He has installed SGML systems for clients as varied as book publishers, airlines, and chemical manufacturers. Mr. Travis has been involved in all phases of SGML selection and implementation, from consulting with management to writing SGML applications for conversion and end-user production and maintenance. He is a principal voting member of the ANSI X3V1, Text Processing: Office and Publishing Systems, the committee responsible for the development of SGML.

Dale Waldt is the Director of Data Development for Research Institute of America, a Division of Thomson Professional Publishing, a large legal publishing company, where he leads a team in the design and conversion of complex publications into database systems based on SGML. He has over ten years of experience with SGML and electronic publishing and database system design and development.

Both authors are alumni of the Internal Revenue Service Publications Division that was instrumental in creating what is now called SGML. Mr. Waldt is a founder and Publisher, and Mr. Travis is Managing Editor of <TAG>, The SGML Newsletter, the only regular technical periodical on SGML and publishing database development. Both speak regularly at SGML conferences and events, have written articles and teach courses on SGML and related subjects extensively and are widely known and respected in the SGML industry.

Acknowledgements

This book would not have been possible without the help of many individuals throughout the extended SGML community. Any attempt to name everyone who has been there for us would inevitably be incomplete, but some that have to be mentioned include Bill Davis for showing us the light, Paul Jensen for his leadership, patience and support, Mike Metz for his pragmatism, Sharon Adler for her expert advice and mothering, John McFadden for his frankness and for being John, Yuri Rubinsky for his optimism and accessibility, and our reviewers, who have tried to keep us out of trouble: Paula Angerstein, Bob Goldberg, Chet

Ensign, Donna Harmon, Ed Covannon, and the invaluable Dr. Lynne Price. Even with their expert advice and opinions, we claim all errors, omissions, and opinions.

Then, at the risk of missing a few whose acquaintance has been beneficial and often entertaining, we would like to thank the following: Tom, Ludo, at least three Erics, two Daves, Wayne, Elliott, Tommie, Debbie, and, of course, Dr. Goldfarb and the many standards people who created SGML who are too numerable to list, but whose brilliant contributions will last beyond their lifetime.

We would also like to express our thanks to the many software developers who have provided insight, knowledge, and copies of their software that allowed us to illustrate this book with examples using their fine products. Please accept this as acknowledgement of your trademarks and copyrights. May you prosper.

We owe a debt of gratitude to all the wonderful contributors and subscribers to <TAG>, The SGML Newsletter over the last nine years, whose input, contact, constructive criticism, and support have been invaluable to us. Stay in touch.

We would be terribly remiss if we didn't mention our appreciation for the folks at GCA, especially Norman Scharpf, Marion Elledge, Joy Blake, and Tanya Bosse, for their continued support, generosity and patience throughout the years.

Finally, we would like to acknowledge the support we received from the staffs of the University of Wisconsin and the Rochester Institute of Technology for allowing us to conduct the courses that made us get our notes together and start this book two years ago (did it really take that long?), and to the brewmeister and pool sharks at the Breckenridge Brewery whose late-night presence kept those long days at the end bearable.

Brian Travis & Dale Waldt, Breckenridge, Colorado, USA February, 1995

PART • I

Part I / The Business Issues

CHAPTER • ONE

Your Publishing System is Broken!

Introduction

The publishing systems implemented in the last ten years are broken and need to be fixed. Unstructured publishing systems are being used in strategic environments, creating documents that have no future, and companies are putting themselves at risk because of it.

We have been seduced by the claims of word processors and desktop publishers into thinking that they can handle our publishing requirements.

In this age of information re-use, companies who have gambled on the whiz-bangery of desktop publishing technologies are finding it hard to distribute their beautiful pages on alternative media like CD-ROM and interactive network resources like the World Wide Web.

This Chapter discusses the business issues and goals that drive an organization to implement a publishing system based on SGML, including technological changes in publishing systems and the opportunities they present to a system designer. Concepts of SGML database publishing, and the goals of an SGML-based publishing system are discussed.

Related Topics

- Chapter 2, *Evolution of Publishing Systems* on page 23
- Chapter 3, *Desktop Publishing and Professional Publishing Systems* on page 37
- Chapter 4, *The SGML Environment* on page 43
- *Related Standards* on page 59
- Chapter 6, *The SGML Application* on page 101
- *Vendor-Supplied Applications* on page 117
- *Using SGML to Restructure Processes and Information* on page 124
- *System Evaluation and Design* on page 122
- Chapter 9, *SGML Data Management and Workflow* on page 183
- *Workflow in Action* on page 206
- Appendix 8, *SGML Resources* on page 445

The Problem with Unstructured Information

Desktop publishing and word-processing systems produce unstructured documents very efficiently. Even with a reliance on style sheets and other methods to assist in the identification of the structure and a consistency of these documents, it is possible, even likely, that the author will undermine the overall structure of the document in favor of making the page look "just right".

Developers using unstructured tools have had to struggle with many issues including:

1. difficulties in using unstructured text such as the need to use expensive and slow manual labor to clean-up text before it can be used in automated processes and electronic products.
2. expensive system integration, development or acquisition due to the proprietary data formats and the lack of effective data interchange mechanisms, and
3. performing expensive data conversion to new coding formats when new composition systems or other tools are implemented.

What was once viewed as a powerful composition system may now be viewed as a system limited to producing print pages at the expense of effectively producing alternative forms of delivery. What was once a suitable publishing environment for producing publications that meet the organization's business needs may now be inefficient compared to new alternatives that can meet the higher expectations of the organization.

The Promise of SGML

SGML-based systems are being developed and implemented an a furious rate around the world in many different types of organizations. The implementors of these systems have recognized the need to capture the benefits possible from using structured concepts in information management and processing. Although text is different than, perhaps accounting data, many of the same lessons learned in the more mainstream computer applications are now possible in text processing. Through the application of SGML, implementors can achieve:

1. reduced costs and production schedules through increased automation and processing efficiency,
2. improved interchange of information between diverse existing and replacement systems through the use of structured information concepts, and
3. improvements in data quality through the use of `smart` tools that assist the author in creating information that adheres to a desired structure.

Many of the concepts employed in an SGML-based publishing system were first employed in data processing systems. The major difference between these two types of systems is the nature of the data. Text is not as regular as business data, can have many levels of nesting or recursion, can be much more variable in length and requires much more sophisticated formatting and rendering capabilities to be performed on it.

Since its formal adoption as ISO 8879 in 1986, implementors' understanding of SGML has improved. Tools employing SGML have become more numerous and more sophisticated. Implementations of SGML have grown in number and sophistication as well. It is now much easier to implement SGML in a way that achieves business goals aimed at overcoming the problems with existing publishing systems.

This book discusses publishing systems issues and goals, SGML system implementation, and the SGML language itself sufficiently to assist you in implementing SGML in your organization. The following chapters describe the business issues being faced by developers of publishing systems and the management issues that need to be addressed as you evaluate and select your publishing system tools. SGML tools, their role and how they fit together, are described to improve understanding by managers, users, and developers.

TECHNOLOGY CHANGES

When a new technology comes along, the early adopters will rush to start using it any way they can, whether it makes financial sense to do so or not. But, more often than not it takes a long time for a really advanced technology to become feasible after it has become possible. Older, less elegant solutions may still make better financial sense to a competitively minded manager for some time. The trick is to determine what business benefits a new technology may bring before jumping on the bandwagon and investing in it.

In order for the mainstream to embrace a new technology, several things must be in place. The technology needs to be made very reliable, be well-documented, and be well packaged. The chart below[1] shows the difference between an older technology like full-text retrieval and the newer SGML-based technology. The curves approximate at what point in the evolution and adoption these technologies are at. The third line represents a hypothetical new technology that is still only in the lab.

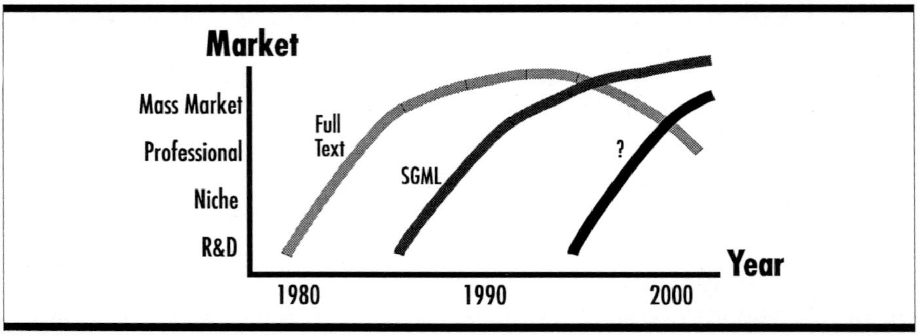

Figure 2. *Evolution of technology toward mass market.*

As a technology matures and understanding of it grows, tools improve, as does the support documentation and distribution of them. This allows the new technology to become more common in the mainstream. Other factors that increase the use of a technology are the simplification of its application, the reduction of costs (both in its implementation and its production use) achieved through economies of scale, and the demonstration of the technology providing benefits that meet business objectives such as reducing costs and schedules, improving data quality and value, and the ability to do desirable things that other technologies cannot do. SGML is rapidly approaching this level of maturity. The lines are not intended to be scientifically accurate, but rather to show increasing acceptance and "market share" that SGML is now enjoying. The third line is a technology that has yet to emerge, but will provide business benefit some day. These technologies are not necessarily mutually exclusive and may actually complement each other.

1 Presented by John McFadden, President of Exoterica Corporation, at an OmniMark Users' Group Meeting.

STATING PROBLEMS WITH PUBLISHING SYSTEMS IN BUSINESS TERMS

For years we have been hearing about the technical benefits of SGML: capturing the intelligent structure of information, making it more flexible, making it possible to validate a document for accuracy and completeness, easing translation to multiple output media, to name a few. But most discussions of SGML stop just short of the business reasons, such as cost savings. Perhaps this is so because many implementations of SGML have been done for other than strictly business reasons. For instance the requirement to adhere to U.S. Department of Defense (DoD) specifications requires little debate as to the merits of SGML for a contractor interested in selling to the Department of Defense.

This is not to say that a business case cannot be made for adopting SGML. SGML may not be the right tool for all systems development, but a clear case can be made in business terms, just as one can be made in any other form of MIS development. Either the benefits of the SGML-based system provide a better payback than the alternatives or they don't. There tends to be four work areas where benefits can be identified from SGML systems:

1. **Information capture**. Activities associated with keying, scanning, or electronically capturing source files for later editing. Capturing usually involves adding codes to identify the components of the information.
2. **Information creation**. The cerebral process of manually editing information or original authoring of new material.
3. **Information management**. Tracking work in progress, storing and accessing it, managing versions, and other processing.
4. **Information delivery processing**. Includes a wide range of possibilities such as composition, extraction, sorting, translating, indexing, and processing for use in alternative electronic publishing media.

The following discussion will illustrate ways in which applying SGML to complex publishing systems can provide tangible and intangible benefits to each of these three work areas.

It is very easy to state problems in terms that suggest a specific solution. For instance, you can say "If I just had a faster computer I can speed up the work I do on it." This assumes that the only solution is that you need a faster computer. Perhaps another solution could achieve the same results for less cost, or more results for about the same or slightly higher cost. Perhaps if your data had more detailed and consistent coding your programs would could be made simpler and run faster on the same processor.

When describing the problems existing in publishing systems, we find it difficult to not assume certain solutions before we fully understand the problems we face. Problems with publishing systems may not be related to the technology itself. It will serve you well to try to articulate the problems in your system in terms that relate to business issues. In doing this, you may find more complete solutions with farther reaching benefits. Simply speeding up the process, is called "paving over the cow path".

When re-engineering a process, the re-engineering team first lists the problems that need to be solved in business terms. Solutions must be justified on economic terms, how much benefit they bring to the company. When re-engineering, the scope of the analysis is not limited to the technology in use. The people involved, their skills, the flow of the information, and the assumptions guiding the specific systems in place are not sacred and can be challenged.

Evolution to a new publishing system may require much more than a new set of technological tools. It most likely will include changing personnel skills and roles, or at least their skills, and dramatically changing the process flow to achieve maximum benefit.

Changing and creating products can be time-consuming and expensive making it difficult to stay competitive and responsive to customer demands. You must consider the costs of not changing and compare it to the development costs of implementing SGML and the resulting savings that are possible. Iterative and outdated production steps cause high costs and long production times. Difficulty in controlling text due to working in an unstructured environment causes inconsistencies and poor quality that make reusing information and quality control a difficult and expensive process. Expected growth in volume of information and increased pressure to speed up the process will exacerbate these problems.

Information Access

Access to information may be limited by disparate systems in use that provide poor inter-connectivity. More specifically, issues can be related to author, editor, and reviewer access to information, as well as access by other systems.

The requirement for many people to handle information during an update process may not be supported, security and multiple user access control may be inadequate. Authors might be forced to track, manage, and perform work in many tasks simultaneously without adequate job tracking and management support.

Information stored in diverse unstructured forms makes it difficult to reuse without expensive conversion and limits the value of the information and reduces revenue generation or cost-avoidance potential.

Aging Systems

One of the most common reasons to invest in new technology is that the existing system is aging and many new opportunities exist in the market that should be adopted to improve costs and schedules associated with the system. Older technology, especially those that work with unstructured information, may require manual intervention that can be avoided with newer tools and structured information. Manual labor should be considered an expensive cost area, one that can almost always be made more cost effective if automated tools can instead be applied.

Newer workstations are generally cheaper for equivalent power. Often, much more powerful systems are available for less than the cost of maintaining existing older systems.

Data Inconsistency

If data is prepared without the value of structured tools, it will become very inconsistent. Inconsistency should be regarded as an unnecessary cost that can be avoided with newer structured editing and data management tools.

Inconsistency of data will usually mean that the programs that process them will have to support a variety of situations that could otherwise be avoided. These programs would therefore need to be more complicated and expensive to produce that programs designed to work with rigorously defined structured data. This complexity and processing time should be considered and avoidable cost.

A lack of detail and consistency in markup may cause programs to not work satisfactorily and may even create quality problems that can only be resolved manually. For instance, if headings are created using specific procedural markup (markup specific to a proprietary system's processing instructions), and only well-intended humans are used to enforce consistency of structure, then the resulting extracted table of contents may not be accurate enough to publish without human intervention and cleansing. Humans, no matter how well intended, will always be less consistent than computer programs designed to enforce consistency. Our strengths lie elsewhere.

Many publishing organizations enforce an editorial style to enhance reader understanding and the aesthetic appearance of the publication. Again, if left to humans, the consistency may never be enforced, and the usability of the information, from the reader's point of view, may not be sufficient.

Inconsistent data coding will make it difficult to reuse information in other publications due to the decreased ability to accurately locate and extract information using programs that read markup. Expensive humans, once again, would need to be employed to verify that the extracted information is complete and appropriate for the intended use, and nothing was missed. For instance, if two elements of information were marked-up using the same specific markup for bold, 12-point, flush left heading, perhaps a figure caption and a third level head, then the programs that try to extract the table of contents and the table of figures would not be able to determine what elements need to be extracted accurately for each specific table. Bring in the expensive humans.

WHAT ARE GOALS OF AN SGML-BASED SYSTEM?

A system is designed to improve the performance of a task and, hopefully, a new system will allow this task to be performed more easily, more rapidly, more accurately, or more frugally than in the prior system. Sometimes, when discussing SGML-based systems, the focus can be placed too heavily on the SGML portion of an overall system. SGML is a technology that is used in conjunction with several other technologies to provide a system. In general terms it is easy to make or refute claims that SGML provides certain benefits. Different combinations of the many SGML software tools available can provide different potential benefits, therefore, benefits are best discussed in specific terms, with a specific problem in mind. Just as in any project, specific goals should be identified and used to guide the design, development, and evaluation of the system. One man's treasure is another man's junk. An editorial organization probably does not have the same needs as a composition or conversion shop. Tools are neither good nor bad; they are simply better suited for different types of jobs.

With that said, let's now focus on a specific hypothetical example of a SGML-based system developed to provide functionality associated with all work areas. Company X, a large publishing firm, produces many very technical reference books each year. Hundreds of authors and editors work on many thousands of pages each year in several geographically distant offices. The technical information in these books has to be very accurate. Some of the books are hard bound volumes, some have supplements, others are loose-leaf, and many products appear as either CD-ROMs or on-line database services or both. Company X wants to move away from a system that is based on composition processing and is labor intensive. The current subsystems used to produce these products are so inter-dependent that new product development is complex and costly and cannot meet market demands. Also, the accuracy of the information is a little out-of-date and mistakes are frequent and need correcting due to the lack of enforced structure and detailed tagging. The products are very expensive to produce in an ever increasingly competitive market.

Notice that no assumption has been made that the new system must be SGML compliant. The first order of business is not to decide whether a new system needs to involve SGML or not. The first order of business is to clearly state your goals, for example:

1. Reduce costs to produce existing products, to make products more competitive in the market.
2. Speed production of existing products, especially electronic derivatives, to increase subscriptions revenue.
3. Increase accuracy of products to reduce correction costs and possibly reduce subscription cancellations.
4. Reduce costs and complexity associated with reusing information through derivative products to increase sales potential for information without dramatically increasing costs of developing that information.

These goals have been stated without presupposing any particular solution.

The Power of SGML Databases

ENABLING INFORMATION MANAGEMENT TECHNOLOGIES

It is difficult to consider the adoption of SGML without bringing into the fray the opportunities presented by other related enabling technologies. Database management is at the forefront of the list of functionality that, combined with richly-encoded structured text, can provide significant business advantages. To focus only on SGML, would mean missing an opportunity to implement the advantages these related technologies can provide in combination.

The problems associated with creating, maintaining, and producing technical documentation, to a large degree, are information management problems. SGML will provide a powerful means of expressing the structures of your information. Database technology will provide access and information management. Other tools offer benefits in related areas. SGML is at the core of these tools and their ability to provide these benefits since they rely on unambiguous, richly-encoded, content-oriented information.

The traditional document production processes are changing, sometimes dramatically, to enable new opportunities and efficiencies. Many steps can be automated or even eliminated. New tasks need to be performed. Organizations, roles and skills need to evolve in order for these efficiencies and opportunities to be realized.

The most dramatic example of the change in roles of the different departments involved in producing technical documentation is the diminished presence of production-oriented personnel and processes due to automation. Processes that once required many people and many steps can now be done entirely automatically on computers—not big, expensive mainframes, but rather on affordable PCs or workstations. Whole departments that entered the complex proprietary coding required by typesetting have given way to a small development staff producing automated formatting programs driven by SGML markup. These development personnel now have more sophisticated skills and are more expensive, but are so fewer in number and provide such significant time and quality improvements that the publisher can now run much more inexpensively and be more responsive to demands of the market.

Similarly, the editorial department will require new skills and maybe even new people. The most obvious change is the introduction of computer-based editing. Most existing editing workstations are merely word processing systems based on duplicating the old typesetting production processes. By merely transferring these activities to the editorial environment (whether they belong there or not) you may miss out on many streamlining and value-adding opportunities. Incremental gains in processing speeds are the net result, and, therefore, net benefits are constrained to modest incremental cost and time savings. Increasingly, this realization has been made by implementors of electronic publishing systems, and more emphasis is now being placed on the process of information management rather than electronic document production in order to achieve the significant gains that are possible.

The task of changing an organization from a production-oriented one to an information-management-oriented one is not always simple. It will cause upheaval and confusion, and it has other risks, but, dramatic results are possible through a combination of process re-engineering (redefining the business processes) and the use of enabling technologies such as open systems for inter-connectivity and inter-operability. SGML should be used to provide unambiguous "smart" information design, other official and *de facto* standards to provide flexibility, and database management to provide the access and control required to make it all work.

PROBLEMS INHERENT IN EXISTING SYSTEMS

The systems used currently to produce technical support documentation materials have many inherent problems that cause costs to be high, extended time frames for producing materials, and a lack of overall control of the materials. There may be multiple systems used to produce the same materials in one or more locations. If these systems are not "open" the result will be difficulty in integration and information exchange between them. For example:

- The work process may be fragmented into many departments. This fragmentation causes dependencies and delays to the flow of work through the organization.
- Tools used may not be not current with functionality provided by state-of-the-art equivalents causing extra steps, manual processes, and delays. Production time frames may be excessive due to a lack of automated functionality and the need for constant human intervention at various stages of production. Opportunities to streamline processes, reduce labor costs, and reduce operational and maintenance costs may exist.
- The data formats required by these systems may be proprietary and widely different making it difficult and extremely expensive to reuse the data for alternative publishing media such as CD-ROM.
- Documents may be inconsistent due to lack of style and structure enforcement. Inconsistent documents are harder to reuse for alternative formats and media (CD-ROM, etc.) and may be more confusing to the reader. Inconsistency is a problem that is exacerbated when documents have been around for a long time and have gone through several styles and technologies.
- Authors may have more than one task "on their plate" at one time and may not have tools to effectively manage their work load and flow. Improvements are needed in accessing files, submitting jobs to processing and output, and access to supporting processing results such as scanning output.

- Storage of multiple copies of graphic and textual information used in multiple places may use excessive disk space and make tracking, managing, and updating complex and time-consuming.
- Many people may be required to handle and update a document during the revision cycle. Improvements are needed in routing, tracking, and accessing the documents as they are passed to essential personnel. Also, non-value-adding steps such as manual transfer of files or change of status should be either eliminated or automated.

CONCEPTUAL CONFIGURATION OF THE SOLUTION SYSTEM

The type of environment that would provide efficiencies and better control must allow concurrent processing and controlled access to the information elements. The links between processes and platforms should be seamless to allow unimpeded access in order for editing of images and graphics to be done efficiently. Information needs to be stored in a single master database to manage multiple versions and revisions. Automatic process must be integrated to reduce labor costs and improve production throughput. Language translations should be run automatically and updated/reviewed as needed. Composition should be handled by automated routines and viewed, corrected, and/or output by the author on demand in a variety of formats and styles. All work must be performed on the data in the masterfile or in the applications that access this masterfile to prevent multiple draft versions from becoming unsynchronized. Below is a diagram that illustrates the concept of multiple access to a single master database being tracked and managed by a Database Management System (DBMS).

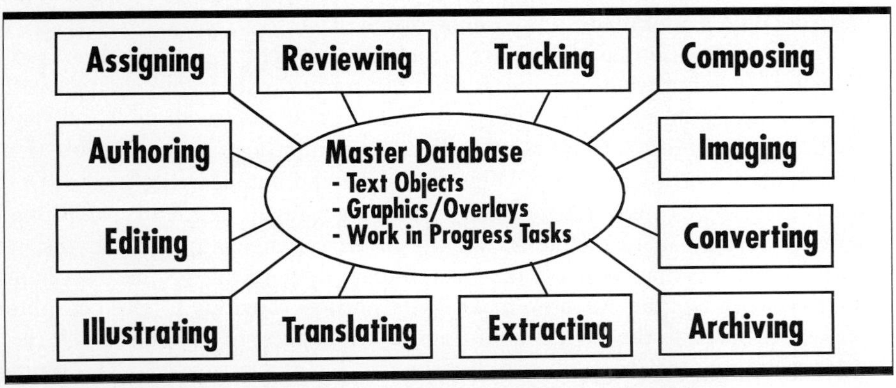

Figure 3. *Conceptual Configuration of a process-oriented SGML-based System*

This model is only possible through the application of content-oriented generic markup and customizable data management facilities. A traditional publishing system will not provide the linkages and breadth of automatic facilities to fulfill the entire model since they tend to deal with only selected processes. A typical commercially available composition-oriented publishing system will usually focus only on the composition, illustration, and extraction processes, and possibly the editing and review processes. If composition-specific systems are selected for use, capabilities (manual or automatic) must either already exist in the user's shop or be developed to handle the rest of these activities, including the data management system at the core of the overall process.

Data Definition Opportunities

Data turns into information once it is useful. By using a structured approach to defining data, we can take a collection of data and turn it into a body of valuable information. Conversion to a structured form, such as that described by SGML, is a value-adding process whereby information about the information is being added to make the data more usable and valuable.

A proper approach to defining information structures, *i.e.* SGML elements and markup, is to consider all of the uses of the information to determine what are the valuable parts, and then defining a language to describe those parts. Notice that we did not say to define a language that addresses the processing or data management semantics (actions or processes) to be enacted upon the data. All processing of the data belongs in the processing applications. SGML markup should be describing nouns, not verbs; should describe what things are, not what to do with them. This is called generic markup.

Generic markup can be structural or content-oriented. Structural markup describes elements in a very generic hierarchical relation ship, such as `<head1>` and `<head2>`. But, if every chapter in a training manual must start with an "overview" followed by a "lesson" followed by a "quiz", then you might want to call these elements `<overview>`, `<lesson>` and `<quiz>` instead of using the `<head1>` tag on each. This specific form of markup is content-oriented.

Content-oriented markup frees the data of specific processes. For example, when deciding what to do with what has traditionally been called an italic phrase, identify its underlying purpose. Why was it italicized? Is it a foreign word? A glossary term? Emphasis usually has an underlying purpose, more than just making the word stand out. Why should it stand out? If we define an SGML tag as `<italic>` we cannot capture that underlying value. If we identify all foreign words as foreign word elements, and all glossary items as glossary items, we capture what was once only obvious to a human. By marking-up these elements using content tagging we now make their purpose obvious to the computer software processing the data, enabling automatic process to be applied to it such as generating glossaries and lists of foreign words. Of course we can still render them in an italic font since more than one intellectual or logical element may use the same formatting.

Complexity Associated with Graphical Information

Graphics can be managed as separate elements and viewed in the context of where they are used. If a graphic is used in more than one place with different associated textual overlays, each portion of the graphic can be easily managed in a DBMS and even be called into the data stream on the fly during output processing or viewing. A single graphic can have many layers of varying information due to the high frequency of reuse and the many languages in which this documentation is published. A single graphic image can have many different graphic overlays as well that include arrows and other non-textual information that changes from one use to another. This complexity can best be managed by a DBMS. The DBMS will be most effective if it can interpret the SGML markup that is used to identify the specific graphics and overlays and data content types.

Also, if one graphic is prepared in the TIFF graphic format, and another in CGM, the system may be configured to instantiate the appropriate graphic editing tools or processing when that graphic is selected for enhancement or output.

Document Consistency

Document information consistency is critical to successful automatic processing of the data into the various output forms; composition, electronic delivery, and tables and cross reference extractions. An SGML editing system forces authors to adhere to rules when creating and editing information. Although this may be seen as restricting to an end user, it provides significant benefit when converting the resulting data to electronic product form. Until data is maintained in a consistent form, human intervention will most likely be required when converting text to other forms such as reuse in another publication style or delivery media. Data inconsistency can cause diminished accuracy of these outputs, increased timeframes, and higher costs due to the requirements of manual intervention to clean up inconsistent data. A database of SGML-encoded information that is regularly validated will provide the consistency needed to avoid these costs.

Database Management Opportunities

Most electronic publishing systems today provide functionality based on the linear production process traditionally used in publishing. This type of process is nearly a hundred years old and contains vestiges of antiquated technology. The emphasis is not on managing information, but rather the production of documents. Therefore the tendency is to be locked into a document format.

Many producers of technical documentation have found advantages from freeing their processes from the constraints of a linear production process. Some of these benefits include reduction in iterative steps that can increase costs and schedules and decrease accuracy and consistency of data content through the need to maintain different versions of the same data at different points of the production process.

The trend in technical documentation systems is toward a database management approach where information is organized and managed as logical units. A logical unit of text may resemble the physical data structures used to organize print publications but there are significant differences in the access, editing, and maintenance processes used in these paradigms.

First, in chronological order of work flow, authors do not always create information in a complete form. Instead, as they gather and prepare information content in the early stages of compiling a document, the information tends to be disorganized, incomplete, and may be in disparate or unstructured organizational forms. Writing to the specification of an intended publication may expedite the creation of that particular output product, but may sub-optimize the use of the same information content for other purposes, either alternative delivery media such as CD-ROM and on-line and their inherent design differences, or reuse in differently organized print publications. SGML, databases, alternative media and reuse of data present some opportunities for altering the organization and presentation of the information, and therefore, some potential design issues will need to be considered during the implementation of a logically organized data management strategy.

Database management opportunities include keeping related information together in a logical unit, even if these elements appear in different locations in the physical delivery forms. For instance, all the information about a copier's delivery system, could be managed as a single logical unit of information by an expert on that particular device even if that device is used in several different models of copiers. The advantage of this strategy is that a single expert does a better job at maintaining information about a particular device than a collection of more generalized editors working on products organized by copier model documentation. This strategy requires that the information be defined and encoded richly enough to facilitate the proper extraction and to accommodate the capture and maintenance of slightly different versions of that device (tasks for which SGML is well suited due to the ability to define elements and attributes based on content).

Indexing

Indexing provides some requirements that can be improved upon by the use of SGML and database management strategies. The first assumption being made here is that there is something to an index that cannot be duplicated entirely through the use of automated processes, such as logically grouping or linking the index items produced by a keyword extraction and adding `see also` lines to an index once assembled. Some cerebral activities are still better handled by a human. But a database manager can handle the logical components of an index in a similar fashion to the delivery system example above. This strategy allows index elements to be identified through detailed tagging and be stored with the text content to which it applies and later be extracted to create the index. The DBMS can assist in re-merging the index elements into the text as well after the index published.

For example, as an editor is updating material to be published, he can take a quick look at the index elements and add new topics if needed. Often, a hierarchically organized text will grow to the point where a passage is contained in a section under one heading, and an editor may choose to break that passage into two or more smaller sections covering different areas of focus. The index material will also need to be reorganized to reflect this change. Having it in the logical unit accessed by the editor allows the editor to perform some of the maintenance himself at the point the section was reorganized, expediting the implementation of the change and, perhaps, improving the execution of it by allowing it to be done while the changes are fresh in his mind. Putting off these changes for later, perhaps to be done by another person in another department, allows some of the thoughts and knowledge of the moment to be lost, and actually adds time to the overall process since the second person will have to read through the changes to determine what needs to be done; a start-up productivity "curve".

At some point, the people who are experts at indexing will want a shot at the accumulated index to perform their craft on it. At that point the index elements can be extracted (just as they would to produce the printed index), sorted, de-duped, etc. and made available to the indexers. Once they are done, the information can be sorted back into the logical order and reinserted into the database into the logical units of text. This approach depends on detailed tagging and enforcement and validation of consistency and markup.

Data Organization and Access

Under the current file management system there is little control, security, or support provided to the author. The data is stored in directories and sub-directories as files. Authors need to know which file and which directory they need to access. The author may need to consult with the file manager, a human, on occasion in order to determine this information, and also to have files made available for access when needed. This access and control could more effectively be handled by a DBMS.

Currently, the documents are stored in either complete document form, or as very large document fragments. Access to smaller document fragments concurrently by multiple authors could expedite editing speed and allow for easier reuse of information. Storing document information as logical elements, which may be very small portions of documents, will create a large number of units of information that will need to be managed. Again, the DBMS is designed to manage large numbers of smaller information elements.

By managing the document components in smaller, more numerous and granular units of information, the pieces of the document can more easily be grouped for editing and processing simultaneously to improve the editing schedule. If information is stored in larger units, an entire chapter might be checked out and made unavailable to other users even though a very small portion is being worked on by a user. Also, smaller units can be more flexibly organized and reordered for product assembly. Managing information in units small enough to support these types of processes is difficult to do without the aid of a DBMS.

Work Flow Management Opportunities

As information is captured, revised, processed, and distributed, management of these functions can become complex and cumbersome without the assistance of database and file management tools. Work flow and process design are often overlooked or trivialized during the system selection and implementation phases, but in reality can be at the heart of the documentation process development. Opportunities exist to change the way a document is created and the way the library of documents is managed and tracked that can produce significant business benefits.

Information Authoring and Revision

Computer technology can assist authors and editors in the creative processes they perform that cannot be handled by the computer itself, mainly the work of writing and editing textual information. Authors and editors familiar with simple word processing do not need to learn a whole new discipline of skills so that a documentation system can become more effective. For instance, many documentation systems fall short of expected efficiency and costs savings projections due to merely shifting tasks from an outside source to an inside source, specifically by moving composition related skills into the authoring environment. Although a gap between the two functional areas of writing and composition is bridged with tools such as desktop publishing, efficiencies and cost savings may not be incurred as a result.

The best way to achieve efficiency improvements and cost savings is to keep authoring and composition separate and build a better bridge between these two functional environments and to automate the composition functions as much as possible. This is one of the roles of a database management system (DBMS). Work can be performed in several "environments" and tracked and controlled using a data management application. The composition processing, although managed separately, can be integrated so that the author can submit the data to be processed, view it interactively, route the output to one of several devices for printing (or viewing), all without the assistance of (or dependence on) another human.

Consider the following scenario as an example of how a database manager can assist the multiple tasks involved in the overall documentation process. A revision is required due to changes in a copier system. An author is notified by his manager via the facilities of a DBMS as to which document, or portions of a document will be needing updating. The DBMS has automatically checked that information out of the master database and put a copy of it into the work environment of the author. The author then selects the work and kicks off an editing session, which starts up an SGML-smart editor. This software has rich editorial functionality and limited composition capabilities. There is enough composition functionality to assist the author in identifying different elements of text and to display tables, equations, graphics and other heavily format dependent information. Once the information has been updated, the author checks it back into the DBMS. The DBMS knows where to store it and to do two other things:

1. change its status to `revised`, and
2. notify the reviewing manager that it is now work for him to review.

A similar set of steps occur when the reviewer checks it and adds comments. When the reviewer checks it back into the DBMS, he must specify whether it has been approved or returned back to the author for additional work. The DBMS prompts for the appropriate status changes and other information along the way.

Specific authors and reviewers can be assigned to specific titles and/or versions and or tasks defined by the system administrator and available in the DBMS environment. The entire update cycle may involve many tasks, authors, reviewers, language translators, production specialists, and editorial assistants. Many different status codes may be applied along the way. An author for one title may in fact be the reviewer on another. All of these assignments can be made once during a configuration, either when implementing the system and as titles are added, and managed entirely by the DBMS. It is often difficult to manually track and manage this complex network of assignments especially when an organization chooses to manage information as a single piece of data and reuse it in many places (*e.g.*, graphic images). But, this complexity is easily managed by a DBMS.

A DBMS is usually integrated with many types of software. If one part of a book is text, when selected for editing, the DBMS can have a specific text editor associated with that part of the book and automatically kick off a session of that software when that data is selected. This is also true for graphics software, and for both interactive and batch software.

A DBMS may also provide information to each of these software packages that would otherwise need to be specified by the end user. When opening a desktop publishing package or a word processor, the end user needs to specify which templates or pre-defined formats they need to use. This information, and many other items, can automatically be provided by the DBMS. Considering how many authors there are, how many times they open files, and how many specific bits of information that may need to be provided, this level of integration can quickly add up to considerable time savings and even improvements in accuracy though elimination of mistakenly applied specifications.

If we continue the documentation update scenario, we may find that the reviewer approved the updates made by the author and sent it to the language translation program. The DBMS actually sends it to the batch program, and checks the error messages to determine whether to send it to the language translation person if it translated successfully, or back to the reviewer if it failed. Once the language translator has completed his work and has stored it in the database and indicated that it has been completed, the DBMS will allow the work to progress by notifying the person in the next step of its availability.

Data Capture

Processing associated with automated feeds during the capture of information may require several steps. Similar to the editing and production processes, these steps will require a mixture of manual and automated processing before the data can be loaded into a database in a consistent, validated form. Auto-tagging and cleansing tracking and processing can be managed by the DBMS and even initiated automatically by it. Return codes can be used to determine the placement of this work upon completion of an automated process such as auto-tagging.

Summary

This scenario allows many complex tasks to be managed and performed concurrently with as much control over the flow and progress as possible. The use of a computer-based DBMS makes the task of managing this process extremely affordable and precise.

CHAPTER • TWO

Evolution of Publishing Systems

Introduction

Publishing systems have evolved over time. In order to understand some of the seemingly confusing aspects of publishing systems, it is helpful to understand their evolution.

This chapter provides an overview of how today's publishing systems are a continuation of the types of electronic publishing systems that have been developed over the last twenty years or so. We have identified four classes based on the types of problems they were intended to solve, and describe the strengths and weaknesses of each

Related Topics

- *The Problem with Unstructured Information* on page 4
- *Formatting and Structure* on page 87
- *Defining a Markup Language — The Recipe* on page 92
- *Markup* on page 219
- Chapter 11, *Building the DTD* on page 275
- *Naming Conventions* on page 276

Markup Systems

Markup is the information we use to identify and classify information. In a computer-based publishing system, markup is the coding used to identify an information element or a process to be performed. This markup has evolved from the basic tools we use to communicate our ideas, punctuation and layout. As the systems we use to manage and process our information become more sophisticated, so must our markup systems.

Hidden beneath the formatted view of information prepared in tools that we commonly call WYSIWYG (What You See Is What You Get), or rich text, is data with buried coding that drives that same formatting. The coding may be stored in-line with the text, as done in WordPerfect files and which can be made visible by selecting Reveal Codes from the Edit menu. The following formatted view is what an author may see while editing in a WYSIWYG environment:

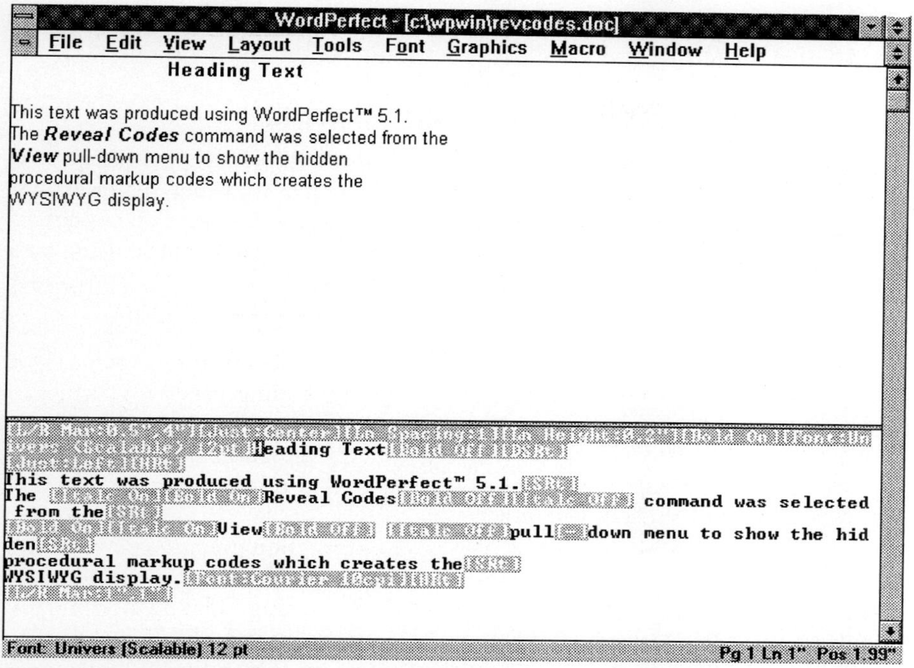

Figure 4. *Rich text created using a WYSIWYG editor*

"Behind" this formatted view is coding to allow the editor to create the rich view.

While editing, WordPerfect shows the author a formatted view that is really an on-the-fly rendering of the marked-up raw text and coding by the internal composition engine. Before word processors and desktop publishing systems were able to render type on the fly, authors were forced to enter the markup directly. Other systems in use today may not store coding in-line with the text, but actually may index the formatting associated with the text from a header or footer in the file. These systems, such as Microsoft Word, can resolve this indirect method of encoding to a coding structure that shows the coding in-line, RTF (Rich Text Format) in the case of Word. No matter how information is presented and coding is managed, there is always some sort of coding driving the presentation or processing of information being created and updated in authoring tools that perform formatting.

So much of the way we manage textual information is based upon processes and concepts that are centuries old. We have speeded these processes considerably during the last thirty years through the use of computers, but in many ways we have "paved over the cow path" by not changing the process of managing textual information more fundamentally.

What follows is a brief history of the evolution of markup (albeit with a bias toward Western languages). It is provided to illustrate that markup systems, like everything else, have undergone a continuous series of improvements. It is the natural process humans perform on everything they make, a continual search to improve the quality, value and/or effectiveness of their systems.

Punctuation, Capitalization, and Spacing

Punctuation, capitalization, and spacing are similar to markup in that it is information about the text designed to convey structure, meaning, relationships, and other attributes to the reader. These clues, however, are not rich enough to imply detailed structure or relationships needed to perform text processing on a computer. They are also often inconsistently applied.

```
Punctuation, Capitalization, and Spacing

The use of punctuation, capitalization,
and spaces make it easy for the powerful
human brain to locate and identify language
elements in text, but is insufficient for
use as a computer markup language.
```

Presentational Markup

Presentational markup involves the use of highlighting, position, and other formatting information to convey information about text to the reader. A bold line that is arranged slightly above the roman-faced paragraph can be interpreted as a heading for that text based on presentational markup clues. Presentational markup is richer than punctuation and spacing, adding more clues to the reader, but is often not sufficient to convey detailed structure and identification without ambiguity. Presentational markup is also often applied inconsistently.

Presentational Markup
Visual clues such as
  - type **weight** and *style*,
  - position,
  - formatting, and
  - *emphasis*
can assist and improve
human understanding of text.

Procedural Markup

Procedural markup languages consist of verbs that direct a specific device to format and image type. Procedural markup languages made it possible for humans to convey information about the appearance of the text to the computer, which would then execute these commands and produce a page image that carried clues in the form of presentational markup to the eventual reader of the information. Procedural markup languages are device-specific and are not usually easily ported to other devices with a different set of commands and functions. Procedural markup is often limited in the same way as presentational markup in that it addresses format and layout, not hierarchy and element identification, therefore it is often too ambiguous to be used to imply structure to text applications such as databases. The procedural coding may be complex and unwieldy to a human as well.

A popular typesetting program is TeX, which runs on many different computer platforms. The TeX code below

```
\hrule
\vskip 1in
\centerline{\bf Building The DTD}
\vskip 6pt
\centerline{\sl by Erskine von K\"oeningsvaldt}
\vskip .5cm
```

As you can see, procedural markup gets complex quickly, but allows for direct control over the look of the output.

As long as the author is only trying to create paper, procedural markup, as unwieldy as it was, was designed to drive typesetting devices was usually all that was needed. Eventually, may organizations realized that there may be other uses for or ways of dealing with text, such as automated processing to create electronic tools and databases to manage text.

GENERIC MARKUP

Another improvement was the simplification of the complex coding through the use of generic commands that were interpreted into several detailed procedural markup commands by the typesetter. This combining of several commands into a single generic code is sometimes referred to as macros or "gencodes". The use of generic markup also simplified the application and reading of markup since the markup could be made more readable and impart meaning. For instance, all the typesetting commands required to set a bold, centered head in 18 point Helvetica on 20 points of leading could be executed every time a single mnemonic code was encountered in text, such as:

```
:chapter. This is a chapter Heading
```

The style sheets features of many word processors and desktop publishing systems use a form of generic markup that simplifies the application of formatting information to an element of text in this same way, although the specific characters surrounding the generic code varies from system to system.

Generic markup can be designed to convey both formatting and structure. If done is such a way that is not tied to a particular processing command, the text can be "labled" or identified for more than one purpose. For instance, if instead of calling a line of text a "bold centered head" the generic markup label applied was "chapter", the same text could be formatted many different ways and used in a number of processes other than typesetting such as database loading and electronic product menuing and formatting. By freeing the information from a specific process, it is much more flexible, and therefore more valuable since it can be used for multiple purposes. The following sample shows a level-one heading that could be typeset to a specific type formatting style using typesetting quality formatting procedures. It also could be used to create on-line electronic publishing files where the headings are used to create menus that eventually lead into the text. Many older electronic publishing systems were based on mainframe character displays that had very limited formatting capabilities. But the same coding could be used to produce both sophisticated typeset output and computer displays through the use of two different interpreters.

```
:h1.Generic Markup
:p.Generic markup was designed to make
text more readable by reducing the
number of codes in text and more
:it.portable:eit. and reusable.
```

Unformatunately, generic markup languages are not often portable. The specific coding used in one system or organization may not be easily understood in another due to system, cultural, and other differences. Systems that employ generic markup often do not validate document structure to ensure that all required elements of data are present. For instance, if you required that all chapters start with a title heading, were followed by one or more paragraphs, and ended with a list of bibliographic references, you would have to build specialized tools to check that this rule is adhered to that is able to read your specific flavor of generic markup. Validation of content is often done manually and indirectly through the page inspection process.

Standardized Markup

Standardized markup using developed using the Standard Generalized Markup Language (SGML) is the most powerful and flexible means of encoding the structure of textual information that exists today. Standardized markup, or markup defined using SGML, can be efficient and mnemonic like generic markup, but can also be very portable and offer validation features. SGML encoded text can be as versatile as generic markup files and can be interpreted into typeset printed products or electronic products, or even text databases and other more sophisticated applications.

At the heart of SGML is the ability to create an application suited to meeting the business objectives of your information processing needs. SGML is not really a markup language, rather it is a language for creating markup languages (See Chapter 10, *Understanding SGML* on page 215). This is done in a way that is unambiguous to a computer in order to support extensive automated processing of textual information. It is done in a way that can greatly improve the ability to manage information in a logical form and manipulate it for use in many forms including print, electronic delivery, database applications, and many that we haven't come up with yet. SGML provides the ability to capture and interchange information between systems, between countries, between operating systems and application software, and for the data to outlive its current processing environment.

SGML is designed to allow implementors to create markup that has meaning and is mnemonic for ease of understanding. Rules can be written in SGML to manage name and information elements in the way we think, logically and hierarchically. Consequently, SGML markup can be very easy to read and understand for both humans and computers, as illustrated in the following example:

```
...
<topic id='i1234'>
<para t='1'>Text created in a system based on
 &sgml; has all the benefits of generic text and more since it
can be:
<list>
<item>validated, and
<item>processed using standardized tools, eliminating the need
for some aspects of tools development.
</list>
<para>This increases its transportability, processability, and
<emph>value
</emph>.
```

The custom definition created using SGML can be as detailed as needed to satisfy existing business needs for all processing requirements without sacrificing detail for one in favor of another. The order and occurrence of information elements can be enforced. If a training lesson requires at least one statement of objectives to appear at the very beginning of the lesson, it can be enforced electronically. If absent, it can be reported by the computer and corrected by the user, increasing the quality, consistency, and value of the information.

As an international standard, SGML (ISO ISO 8879:19868879 1986) is forced to be very stable. International standards are not changed whimsically. No single company or organization owns it and can steer it to their own advantage. Since SGML is so stable, software developers can safely build tools that employ the standard without the risk of having to constantly keep up with another company's dictums. Users benefit from tools that work in predictable ways and can use off-the-shelf tools instead of having to develop their own validation and transformation programs.

SGML markup is generic and can be used for more than just one purpose. The same data used to prepare composed and printed pages can also support hypertext applications, commercial on-line database services, and sophisticated database applications. The need to store the same information in numerous parallel document databases, and to attempt to keep all copies consistent, is eliminated. Data created for one publication can be easily reused in many others and still only be captured, edited, and managed in one place.

Processes that required manual intervention due to the ambiguities of early markup approaches can now be automated due to the ability to add as much detail and specific information as needed to support automatic processes. Extraction of information for use in index and finding table generation can be completely automated. So composition applications can be entirely automated with the elimination of manual page inspection and correction due to the level of detail of specific SGML applications. SGML adds value to a corporate information resource that translates into reduced production costs and/or increased revenue opportunities from new and improved products.

SUMMARY

We have been perfecting our methods for communicating in the written form for a very long time. The earliest forms of markup were based on the logical identification of the information content in text. Somewhere along the line the emphasis shifted to the expedient processing of machines at the expense of retaining the meaning, and therefore value, of our information resources. SGML is allowing us to regain the value of our information and still keep our machines running smoothly and cost-effectively.

Publishing Systems

Every publishing system supports most or all of the processes diagrammed below:

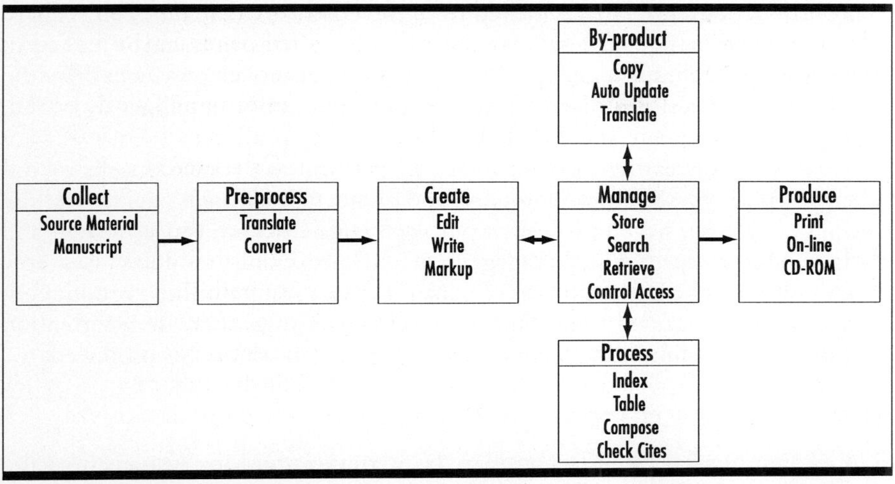

Figure 5. *The Publishing Process*[1]

The Collection process above deals with getting information from outside of the system into the domain of the system. This usually involves keying, scanning, and encoding information. The Pre-processing process involves adding value to the information in the form adding detailed markup designed to support the other processes. The Create process is the cerebral process best performed by humans, but which can be greatly assisted by smart editorial and research tools. The Manage process is the tracking, access, security, task initiation, integration, and distribution of information to the other processes. The by-producting process is the process of taking information prepared for a specific format or delivery vehicle and rearranging it or adding value to it to allow resale or reuse in another delivery form. Processing involves steps such as extracting information to produce cross-reference tables and other content, to prepare it for distribution by "composing" it into print and electronic delivery forms, or run validation and quality assurance checks against the data. Finally, the Produce process, what is typically thought of as printing books or magazines, duplicating CD-ROMs, or cutting tapes for electronic delivery.

This breakdown of the underlying processes in publishing has been very useful to illustrate the bias electronic publishing systems have traditionally had toward the composition process. What is clear from this diagram is that information management is central to the overall publishing process. Also, with the advent of non-print delivery of information, the output processes associated with

1 This section, adapted from "Evolution of Publishing Systems", Paul Jensen, 1994, appears with the permission of the author.

print production have been removed from the central driving function. Where once composition requirements dictated how other processes would be managed, now the complete information processing requirements of all processes drive the development of systems based on information that can be intelligently coded, managed, manipulated, and distributed.

If simply creating electronic tools to perform the same old tasks we did when we were typesetting with hot lead and photo-typesetting is paving over the cowpath, what we have today, with our sophisticated composition system and their added-on information management and processing modules, is a cow superhighway. The entire process of publishing, not just publishing production, needs to be reexamined to produce more effective ways to create information that will live beyond the functionality of the system in which it is produced.

STAND-ALONE COMPOSITION SYSTEMS

The earliest of what could be considered electronic publishing systems were the stand-alone composition systems that were based on proprietary computer equipment and software. In these systems, documents were encoded using the proprietary specific or procedural markup of that system.

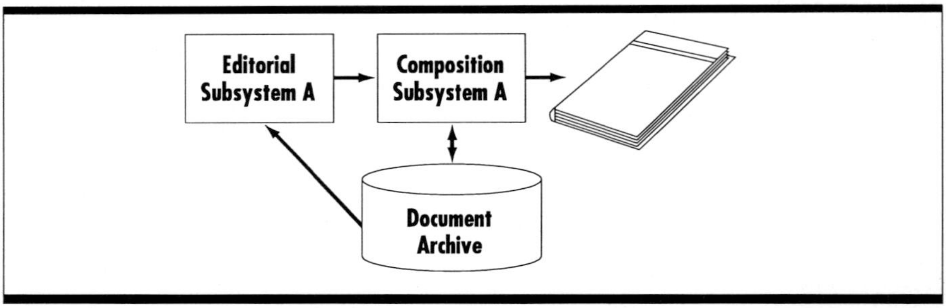

Figure 6. *Stand-alone Publishing System Flow*

The stand-alone systems worked very well to increase the productivity of the team producing the publications compared to hot-lead and mechanical photo-typesetting. At the time they were introduced users had not begun to reuse their information, or if they had, they were not expecting to have produced from a single source. The process was focused on specific delivery formats of products, not on the information. Maintaining multiple copies of the same information was a reasonable method of reusing information in more than one publication. Information was not identified logically, but rather was treated as page images. Markup tended to be format-oriented, could be either specific or, eventually, generic, and useable in more than one system.

The production process was detached from the information creation process. Authors and editors often worked from hard-copy manuscript. Information was often keyed several times during the entire publishing process: once by authors on typewriters, later by composition personnel, and maybe even again for use in alternative products and delivery formats. It was usually very difficult to connect any of theses processes due to the proprietary nature of the systems, the markup, and even the character sets.

LINKED PUBLISHING SYSTEMS

If a printed product in a stand-alone system were to be reproduced in, perhaps, electronic form on CD-ROM, a separate system would need to be developed to produce the CD-ROM version. It is obvious how the additional data management, keying and editing would cause the separate publishing systems to be costly and inefficient. Users sought to link these separate systems in order to eliminate duplicate keying and editing. Gains were made in data preparation efficiency, but additional production steps were needed to process the information due to the different specific markup required for each output process. Below you can see the separate data management and processing required in a linked publishing system:

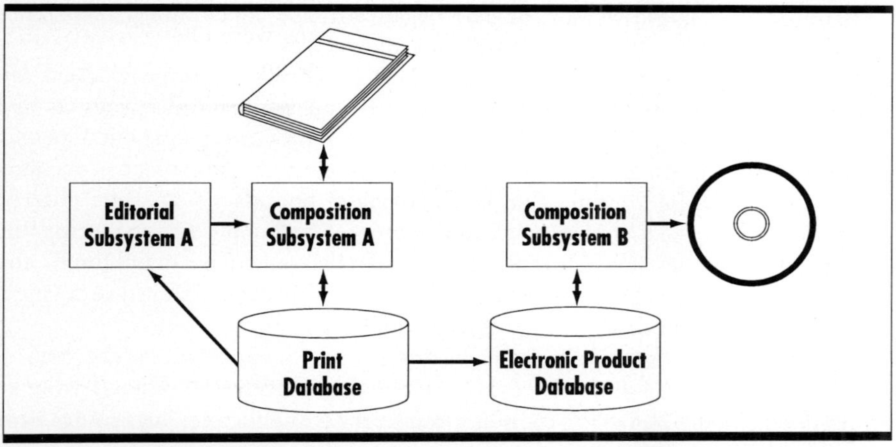

Figure 7. *Linked Publishing Systems*

Data flowing from the print database would need to be transformed to the markup of the electronic product database, or a normalized generic markup language would need to be developed to support both processes. Information reuse is supported in one-way flow. The focus of the system is still on the output products. The information is very dependent on its output formats.

INTEGRATED PUBLISHING SYSTEMS

Some of the more sophisticated publishing systems, both with and without SGML, have managed to allow single source files to be used in more than one delivery format.

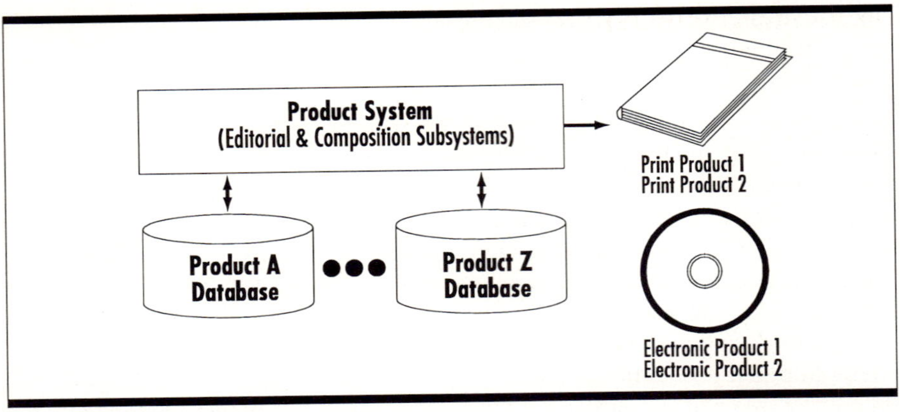

Figure 8. *Integrated Publishing Systems*

Integrated systems are the most common today. They can be developed and integrated by a single vendor, or user organizations may choose several independent tools and perform the integration themselves.

Functionality required to produce both print and electronic products can be provided in a single, integrated system. Producing multiple products and formats from a single source is accomplished by removing the product-specific information from the data and developing subsystems that introduce processing information during output. For instance, page boundaries are not entered directly into the text, but rather are determined for composition during the composition processing. Multiple product databases can be maintained, and information can be shared between publications. All data is stored in a single centralized location that manages the data and access to it.

One issue that is gradually becoming more important is the lack of detailed control over some processing that could affect overall costs of using an integrated system. If specific tools in use are very cost effective, but require page boundaries to be retained, for instance, to support demand printing repositories and loose-leaf page budgets, the page boundaries may be lost if the system cannot retain them after determining them during composition processing. Another example would be where the need to have remote offices work independently exists and the requirements for centralized data management would add complexity and cost to the system.

The focus of integrated systems is maintaining data independent of its output uses. This is done to remove the burden of maintaining product output specific information in the masterfile. Including this type of information in the master database is often referred to as polluting the database. But there may be pragmatic economic considerations that make it all but impossible to avoid using these work-arounds. Even so, for most applications, an integrated approach has provided significant cost and schedule reductions.

FEDERATED PUBLISHING SYSTEMS

Competitive pressures make it difficult to develop a single integrated system that meets all of the needs of all departments within an organization. The marketing people may have a different agenda and schedule in mind than the engineering department, or the technical documentation people. Marketing may require the use of more color and interactive workstation tools, while the engineering department needs precision drawings and data management of a database and can settle for batch-produced black-and-white pages. Meanwhile, the technical documentation people are expected to produce all of the above cost-effectively, on-time, and in fourteen languages.

Technological advancements in computing systems have provided interesting opportunities and problems to designers of publishing systems. Client/server applications, distributed systems, wide-area networking, the Internet, improvements in electronic delivery and research tools, and the proliferation of low-cost, powerful workstaions have made it clear that integrated systems have room for improvement.

A federated system is one that allows distributed autonomy for addressing localized concerns and constraints, but supports global information management methods to facilitate reuse of information throughout the entire system. Federated systems do not require data formats, operating systems, or application software to be consistent, only compatible or interchangeable in a client/server architecture.

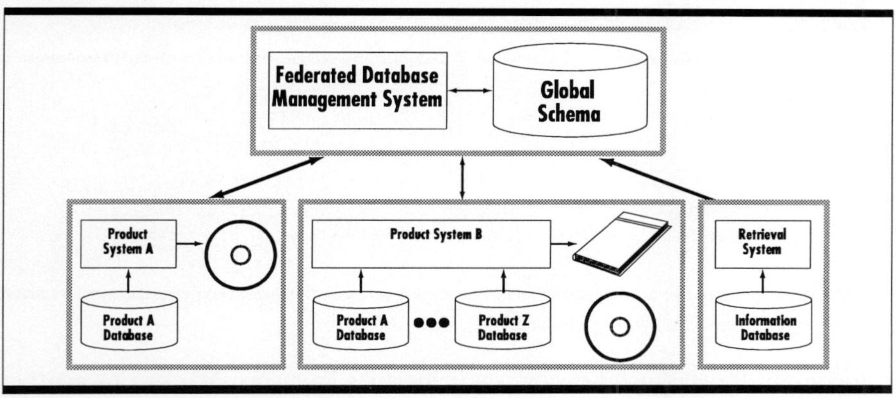

Figure 9. *Federated Publishing System*

A federated system may be comprised of several subsystems that may themselves be integrated, linked or stand-alone systems. The entire system is governed by a centralized global schema to ensure that requirements for reuse of information within a federated system is supported effectively. Meanwhile, data that is created and updated— and flows between elements of a federated system—can be managed in a variety of coding forms, and using a diverse set of tools.

A federated system could support a mixture of specific and generic data markup if there were no economic reasons dictating that all data be encoded consistently. For instance, if a marketing office chose to use a desktop publishing system to prepare certain materials, but depended on other organization for input to these materials, they would not be forced to use a more expensive integrated system. Conversely, if another department wanted to use the materials prepared by the marketing group, it might make economic sense for the marketing group to use more structured tools or develop a easy, cost-effective way to add structure information to their unstructured data.

Recently, many tools have been developed that make a federated system possible. The purists that have said that all data must be coded in s single monolithic format to support a global schema will need to revisit the problem. Auto-taggers and data transformation tools make transfer and reuse of information prepared in diverse forms economically feasible. Even so, when data structure needs to be rigorously enforced to ensure effective automated processing and validation, your best bet is going to be a structured approach such as SGML.

Publishing Process Flow

Most of the publishing systems in place today are based on the linear production processes design for use originally by Henry Ford when he invented the production line. Information (instead of cars) moves along a linear production line, from one set of hands to another, until the entire process is complete, as illustrated below:

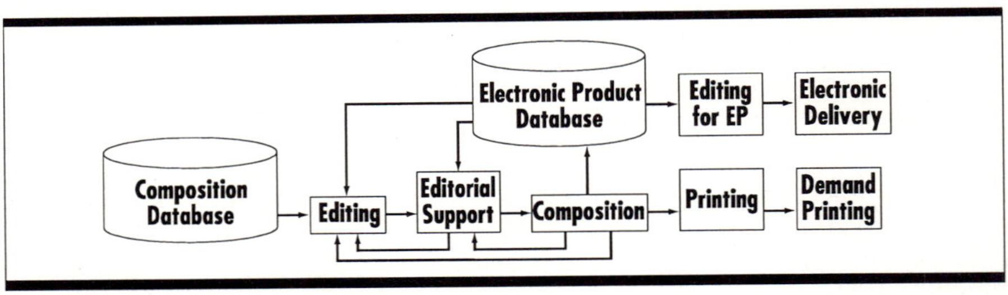

Figure 10. *Linear Publishing Production Process*

By constantly handing the work, and the files being worked on, to another department or system, the files are constantly duplicated and updated. Changes made in a later process may not be reflected in the earlier process' version of the data. Also, where a later process sends the file back to an earlier one, these iterations are indicated by arrows going backwards on the diagram above. Research done by process re-engineering experts suggests that these iterative tasks contain a significant amount of wasted time; up to 95% of the total process time may be dead time where the files are waiting to be worked on, and only 5% of the time work is actually being performed (these researchers also warn that most people find these numbers hard to believe)!. The real issue with this dead time is that the information contained in the files is not generally available to other users and processes while in the queue for a task. Subsequently, tasks may be extended and the entire publishing process may be unreasonably long.

This diagram also shows the add-on processes designed to create electronic products from the same data used to produced printed pages. Many variations on this theme have been developed to use data encoded with specific composition markup, transform it using automated and manual processes, and produce electronic products. One issue with adding on a parallel linear process for electronic products is the need to maintain a separate complete copy of the database, and try to keep it totally synchronized with the print database. The likelihood that the data will be 100% consistent is slim. Also, the data cannot be prepared for electronic products until the print product processes are completed, causing unnecessary delays in delivering data to customers of the electronic products. Users of electronic media expect the electronic versions to be the most up to date, especially those using large, commercial on-line databases services. The effectiveness of electronic delivery is diminished if it is dependent on print-oriented process.

The processes used to produce information that appears in print and electronic products needs to be re-engineered to eliminate these vestiges of the production line. A system based on database management systems can provide many benefits. A Database Management System (DBMS) can control multiple access to files, eliminating dead time, can manage many thousands of chunks of data, and can integrate all of the processes in the publishing system to provide the best flow and schedule possible. The following diagram shows, very simplisticly, multiple access and output to a single master database. The DBMS is central to the entire process and requires intelligently encoded data:

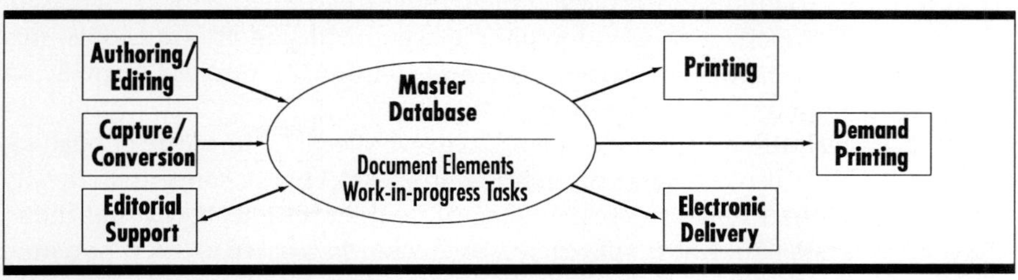

Figure 11. *Using a DBMS to integrate the Publishing Process*

The following figure shows how a database that can support multiple outputs from a single editing source can expedite the electronic product production by making the various production processes run concurrently instead of in parallel and reduce overall time and total effort:

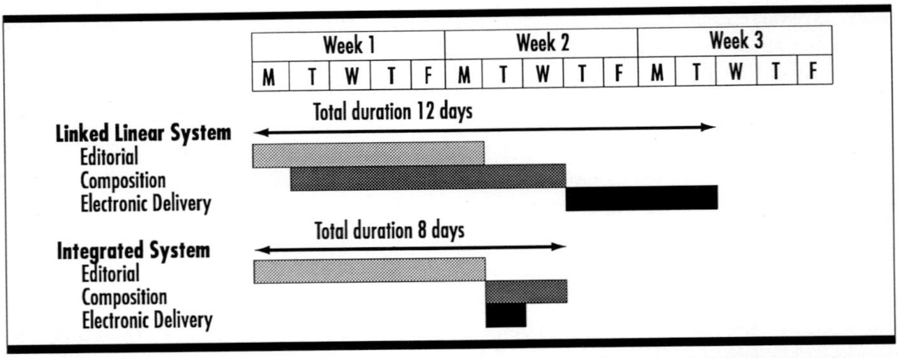

Figure 12. *Comparing the Linear Production Process and a Integrated DBMS-based Process when Applied to Publishing Efficiency.*

Significant efficiencies can be achieved by migrating from a linked, linear publishing process to an integrated one. By removing the dependence of electronic product production on print product production, the schedule for delivering electronic products may be reduced considerably. Also, by automating and integrating tasks, and allowing multiple user access to eliminate dead time, the schedule and total duration of the print production process may be reduced considerably as well.

Summary

SGML is just another step in the long line of systems designed to allow more effective communication. With the introduction of computers in the production processes used to publish information the complexity of markup was increased. Now through the effective use of generic markup and standardized tools, this complexity can be made more manageable and additional return can be made on investments in publishing technology.

New technologies provide opportunities to speed up the entire publishing process. But they also rearrange the existing processes, change some dramatically and eliminate others and can create upheaval in organizations that adopt them. Care must be taken to choose approaches and techniques based on their potential value to the organization, and not to adopt technology blindly simply because it can be done.

CHAPTER • THREE

Desktop Publishing and Professional Publishing Systems

Introduction

Desktop publishing provided (or at least promised) great improvements in productivity and accessibility for many users. The issues that will decide whether a desktop publishing system will deliver expected results, or whether a more sophisticated professional publishing system will do so, are discussed. A checklist for evaluating the effectiveness of these tools is provided.

- Chapter 9, *SGML Data Management and Workflow* on page 183
- Chapter 2, *Evolution of Publishing Systems* on page 23
- *Existing Conversions that May be High-cost Areas* on page 171
- *System Evaluation and Design* on page 122
- Chapter 9, *SGML Data Management and Workflow* on page 183
- *Object Database in Action* on page 199

Productivity and Flexibility - Which Tool is Right for the Job

Many organizations are faced with choosing between highly interactive Desktop publishing systems and more powerful workstation or professional publishing systems that include batch composition. At one end of the spectrum you have an inexpensive, yet somewhat powerful layout and composition environment that provides the graphics tools needed to produce professional looking documents. At the other end of the spectrum you also have the tools, but many processes have been automated to expedite production of pages, sometimes at the expense of limiting flexibility of design. Both types of systems can produce just about any type of book, the trick is which one, or what combination of the two, is best suited to produce the particular type of book required for a specific need.

These tools are similar to a hand-held coping saw and a motor-driven table saw in that one can provide intricacy at the expense of productivity, while the other is a workhorse designed to a more limited set of tasks, but to do them very efficiently. You could rip a sheet of plywood with a coping saw, but you probably would rather use a table saw for this task. Following is a brief description of the functions for which both types of publishing systems are well suited and, therefore, the types of tasks and publications to which they could best be applied. Hopefully it will become clear that these tools can be combined when needed to provide the best of both worlds.

Desktop Publishing

Desktop publishing gets its name from the desktop-based computer, usually a microcomputer, on which it resides. A desktop publishing system, such as Adobe PageMaker or Quark XPress, provides many powerful features such as page layout grids, a wide range of fonts, rules, and borders, automatic page numbering and running heads, automatic hyphenation and justification (H&J), and wrapping of text around irregular shaped objects, just to name a few.

These tools were not available on anything but sophisticated and expensive professional system just a few years ago. The problem with these tools is that they usually are time-consuming to utilize even in combination with style sheets and templates that perform many of these tasks automatically. This is due to the limited sophistication of these features on a desktop system. Since desktop publishing is largely a manual process, the creator of the document usually has to perform many tweaks to get a page to look just right. The benefit of desktop systems is that a document creator can do just that, spend a lot of time on each page making it look fresh and different. Ironically, using a desktop publishing system, a document creator can also make a page chaotic and disorienting, depending on his or her skill and training in graphic arts.

Documents that lend themselves to the desktop environment are newsletters, magazines, and smaller publications since they tend to be more flexible in their design and are not very large. Desktop systems are usually a one-way process, where data flows from editing, through page layout and does not go back to editing very easily. But this one-way flow may not be an issue for these types of publications if their content tends to be more prone to becoming obsolete in a short time and may not be reused in other products.

Professional Systems

Products that might be difficult to produce on a desktop system might be very large, require automatic features such as cross-references, have many tightly packed pages that require sophisticated H&J algorithms, or are accessed and updated by many editors on a regular basis. A large loose-leaf service would be difficult to produce on a desktop system since many people edit the content simultaneously and the composition and data management requirements can be pretty complicated. Also, desktop publishing systems do not usually offer some of the complex features available in professional systems, such as variable running heads based on content (*e.g.* dictionary running heads).

The speed of a large professional publishing system can handle more throughput in a given period than desktop machines as well due to the more powerful computers they tend to run on. But, professional systems do not come with a small price tag. A small stand-alone workstation could easily exceeds US$50,000. Throw in a few extras, like an RC film typesetter, some storage, etc., and the bill could easily start at US$100,000 with full-blown networked systems topping US$1 million. Training costs also must be added. But, since the performance is there, it may be worth this kind of investment for some applications.

Let Editors Edit

There is a debate going on as to whether an author or editor should have the ability to layout a page. One side says that authors should author and leave the typesetting development to the technical staff (with direction by the Editorial department). The other side says that, if an author really wants a paragraph to have a box around it, then, by golly, it should have a box around it. If the technical staff can't give it to them without a lot of development and hassle, well, let's use desktop. Of course, professional editors and authors, such as lawyers, securities analysts, engineers and scientists, are pretty expensive to be doing page layout, so the answer must be in the middle somewhere.

Our feeling is that they are both correct, that for most large publications, the system should take care of all the formatting, but that sometimes an author will **need** something, but only need it once, and to try to name that instance and write a typesetting program to handle that instance may be overkill when someone could have just gone in and adjusted the formatted output before it was printed. Many professional systems also allow interactive page layout to handle these instances, but then you have to analyze the frequency of which this interactivity will be needed. A goal of a professional publishing system should be to automate as much of the process as possible. Desktop systems will allow very little automation, but users of desktop publishing systems are probably cheaper labor than those of professional publishing systems.

If a publication has a lot of display advertising and changes in page appearance, then an interactive page layout system is needed, but it should not be run by a high-priced authors not trained in the aesthetics of typography and layout. Rather, a trained graphic artist may be better suited to take over after the content of the information is written.

The Best of Both Worlds

We believe the bottom line is that both desktop and professional publishing tools may continue to be needed for some time in a large publishing house with diverse product requirements. Until the speed and power of small computers increases enough, and the sophistication of composition tools improves, large systems will be better and more efficient for longer, more regular runs of pages. But, nothing can beat the price of a desktop system for intensely interactive page layout and simple graphics creation. A mix of the three technologies can provide the best features and solutions to the widest range of problems possible in a large publishing house.

The following graph shows complexity of page layout (requiring much manual manipulation) on one axis and volume of pages (prohibiting much manual manipulation) on the other.

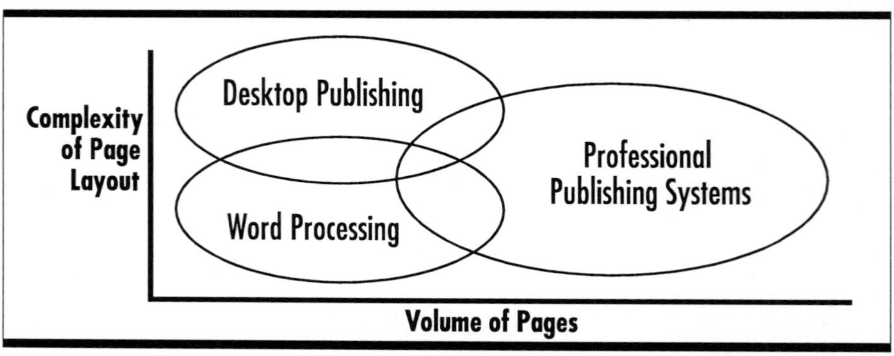

Figure 13. *Desktop/Word Processing/Professional Publishing*

Desktop or professional publishing systems may be better suited for particular products and/or production issues. Word processing offers little in either sophisticated layout or powerful processing, but may be useful in tasks in the overall publishing process such as initial editing.

Note that the worlds of desktop and professional publishing systems overlap in the middle (perhaps why there is any debate at all). The other thing to note is that as computers get smaller, faster and cheaper, this overlap will increase to the point of there being no distinction between the two technologies. A system that encompasses the best of both worlds will be the most productive.

Checklist for Selecting a System

To decide which type of system, desktop publishing or professional publishing, to use today ask your self the following questions:

1. **Will the information outlive this single issuance? Is it reusable? Do many people need controlled, on-going access to it?**. If the answer is yes to any or all of these concerns, for instance material that appears in a supplement to either a loose-leaf publication or a large bound service, then the information should be captured in a standardized form such as SGML markup supported by professional systems. Information in this form can easily be managed in a database and reused. If the information can be reused in a by-product or other related publications, standardized coding is a better choice than proprietary coding used in desktop systems.
2. **Are the page layouts regular and consistent in appearance? Are there hundreds of pages or more in this product?**. Larger publications tend to have very consistent looking pages, the type that can be managed very productively by professional systems. Smaller publications, such as newsletters and single volume books, can lend themselves to more varied styles and unusual features (sidebars, graphics, photos) and may require more interactive page layout, the strengths of desktop systems.
3. **Will the information be used in electronically electronic products published products? Is a rich coding format required for multiple uses and complex data management?**. Again, standardized coding schemes, such as SGML, allow data to be easily reused and therefore more income from the same resource. Desktop systems produce data that needs more difficult conversion to be reused in any form.

CHAPTER • FOUR

The SGML Environment

Introduction

There are four basic subsystems in an SGML environment:

1. Capture
2. Creation
3. Output, and
4. Database.

In order to implement an SGML system, you must have at least addressed each of these items.

In this chapter, you will learn about these four basic subsystems, and what tools are available to use in each one.

Related Topics

- *The Problem with Unstructured Information* on page 4
- *The Power of SGML Databases* on page 11
- *Federated Publishing Systems* on page 34
- *Documents and Document Models* on page 66
- *System Issues* on page 91
- Chapter 6, *The SGML Application* on page 101
- *Vendor-Supplied Applications* on page 117
- *System Evaluation and Design* on page 122
- *System Development* on page 139
- *Terms* on page 152
- Chapter 9, *SGML Data Management and Workflow* on page 183
- *Object Database in Action* on page 199
- Chapter 10, *Understanding SGML* on page 215
- Appendix 8, *SGML Resources* on page 445

Working in an SGML Environment

Working in an environment based on SGML is similar to working in any other publishing or database environment. This section covers various functions, and how they might be accomplished in an SGML environment.

The SGML Environment

SGML provides the means to put intelligence into the data, instead of relying on a particular application to provide it. We call this "smart data", and it is the central concept behind the SGML Environment.

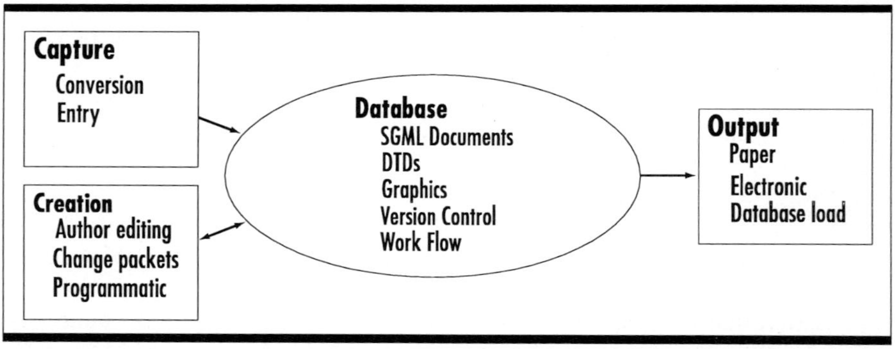

Figure 14. *The SGML Environment*

When we talk about the SGML environment, we mean a set of tools that exists to serve a central database of SGML-coded information and support files. All tools fall into four basic functions:

1. **Capture**. This is the task of getting information into the SGML database. Data can enter the database in several ways: conversion of data that is in another format, bulk keyboard entry from paper documents, or optical scanning of paper documents.
2. **Creation**. Once captured information is loaded into the database, it will be updated and managed over time. This is usually done by authors or editors making changes to text for revision packages or creating new related products. Automatic updating can also be accomplished as part of some external database modification, or wholesale change in certain parameters, such as a corporate acquisition or change of name.
3. **Output**. Most information in the database will need to go through some form of output transformation in order to be of use to anyone. Typical output forms are typesetting files for paper output, input files for electronic delivery tools, or loading for an external database.
4. **Database**. The database itself contains all user-maintained information. This includes the SGML instance files themselves, as well as the document type definition (DTD) that contains structural information about them. Other information, like graphics and sounds, that is referenced in the SGML documents can be in the database, as well.

   In addition to actual data that is maintained in the database, version control and workflow information can be kept in the database. While this is not actually part of the data that appears in deliverables, it provides information that the system can use to maintain the data.

Note that all processes are defined by the data, not the other way around. Traditional text processing systems have relied on a vendor to provide the tools to manipulate the data, which was maintained in a system-specific format. Once a company gets all of its information into this format, the company is beholden to the vendor to support the data by maintaining its systems and providing features the users need.

However, if a vendor does not support the product or raises prices, the users have a hard choice to make: either live 0with it or change systems. Usually, changing systems is expensive and resource-consuming, so there is really no choice. The company is being held hostage by its data.

On the other hand, if the model above is followed, the data becomes the king of the process, is said to be system-independent information, and individual vendor products can come and go as appropriate. Now, if a vendor raises prices or refuses to support the product satisfactorily, the owner of the data can replace that piece with another without converting any data.

SGML PARSER

The job of the SGML parser is to read all information about a particular SGML file, determine whether or not the file is valid, and report any errors. A parsing run consists of processing an instance of the SGML document model, described above. The standard defines two types of parsers:

1. **SGML parser**. A program (or portion of a program or a combination of programs) that recognizes markup in SGML documents[1], and
2. **Validating SGML parser**. A conforming SGML parser that can find and report a reportable markup error if (and only if) one exists.[2]

The main job of a validating SGML parser is to assure that the document conforms to the rules set forth in the standard. Most parsers produce a stream of information to an application. Some produce what is called the "element structure information set", or "ESIS". The ESIS contains information about each element, such as the values of its attributes, its content, and, by extension, where it is in the document (context).

In addition to ESIS, the validating parser outputs a separate stream of error information. Errors are generated whenever the instance does not conform to the SGML declaration or the DTD. Errors are for informational purposes only, and do not affect the parser. This is an important point; the parser will, upon finding an inconsistency in a document, attempt to discern what the author meant using the DTD as a guide.

If the parser can find a path in the tree structure defined by the DTD that makes sense, it usually will report the error, and list the steps it made internally to achieve consistency with the DTD. If it can't find a likely path, some parsers will issue a fatal error and give up. Others will assume the offending element is an undeclared inclusion, issue the appropriate error, and continue on. Continuing sometimes has the effect of rendering the remainder of the parsing process of little value, because the instance is out of "synch" with the DTD and error messages will not provide relevant information until the original error is resolved.

There has been much talk about conformance testing since the standard was published. There has been some work by various committees and standards organizations, but a standardized conformance test suite has not, at the time of

1 ISO 8879:1986 4.285 SGML parser

2 ISO 8879:1986 4.329 validating SGML parser

this writing, been made available to the industry or the users. There is an effort by the U.S. National Institute of Standards Technology (NIST) to develop an objective conformance test suite by utilizing an independent testing laboratory to conduct the tests. A board of industry experts will oversee the effort and keep everyone honest. Until this happens, there is no guarantee that the parser you are using conforms to the rules set forth in the standard. We have found, however, that most parsers are accurate enough to do real work. For critical applications, we usually use two or more parsers when doing initial development to assure that they give the same results.

Translator

The term "translator" is used very broadly. Some call them auto-taggers, converters, text-processors, or transformers. All are a type of translator. The purpose of a translator is to convert one form of input to another form of output. In the SGML world, translators can be placed in three general categories:

1. those that take non-SGML input and create an SGML file
2. Those that convert from one SGML form to another SGML form
3. Those that take SGML input and create something else as output

For the purpose of discussion, the process of creating SGML files from non-SGML input will be called "information conversion" or "conversion". The process of creating SGML or non-SGML files (such as typesetter code or CD-ROM input data) from SGML will be called "translation".

Other words used in the industry are: auto-tagging, tree-to-tree translation, and downward translation.

For more information on conversion and translation, see Chapter 8, *Information Conversion* on page 151.

SGML Editorial Workstation

SGML in its native form is difficult to work with. The markup can be quite ugly, and it is easy for the casual user to lose track of his location while editing a document. SGML can be edited using any text editor that can read sequential files from a file system. However, for most users, this is not a welcomed means of editing SGML data.

Fortunately, there is a class of software called SGML Editorial Workstationss[1]. These are tools that assist a user in the creation and maintenance of SGML documents. They provide an intelligent "shield" to protect the user from the

1 The tools described in this section are commonly called "SGML Editors". Since this term can also be applied to a person in charge of editing SGML documents, we have chosen to use the term "SGML Editorial Workstation" to describe the software tools.

markup, and provide a means to validate that the document conforms to all the rules set forth in the implementation.

Most of these workstations run in a graphical operating environment (Microsoft Windows, Unix X-Windows, or Macintosh), and provide to the user a familiar interface, much like a graphical word-processor. That is to say such a workstation can be configured to display chapter titles in a larger, underlined font, and paragraph text indented in a smaller point size.

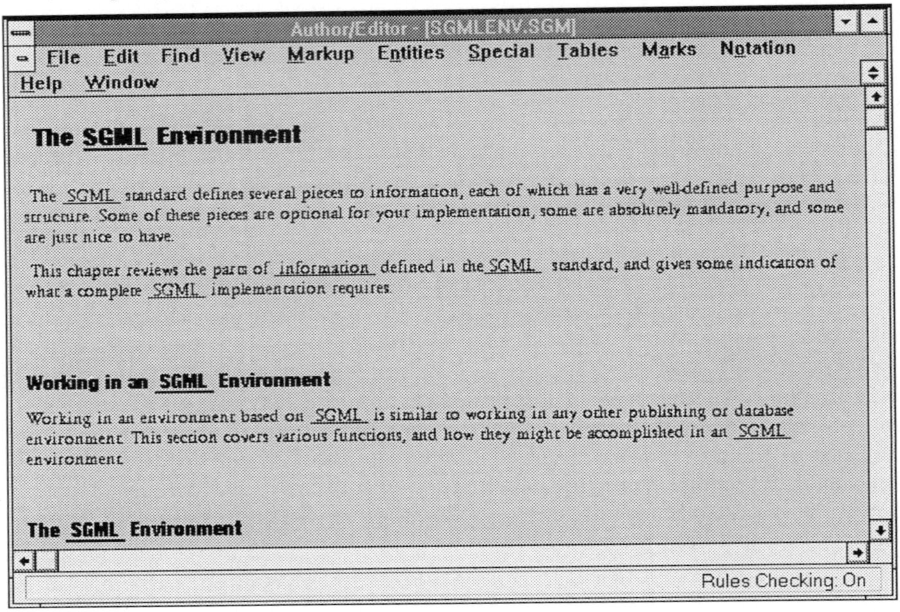

Figure 15. *Author/Editor SGML Editor (WYSIWYG Mode)*

The view indicated here is not quite the so-called "What-you-see-is-what-you-get" or WYSIWYG view. A WYSIWYG view attempts to match the exact rendering of the information that will appear in final delivered form, such as printed pages complete with running heads and folios. Since SGML data will most likely be used in more than one delivery format, developers of SGML formatting editor applications try to emulate the appearance of the text in its deliverable form but leave the delivery-format-specific information out of the screen format. This near-WYSIWYG is sometimes referred to as "QUASIWYG". Most formatting editors can also show or hide the tags so the user can see what the structure is.

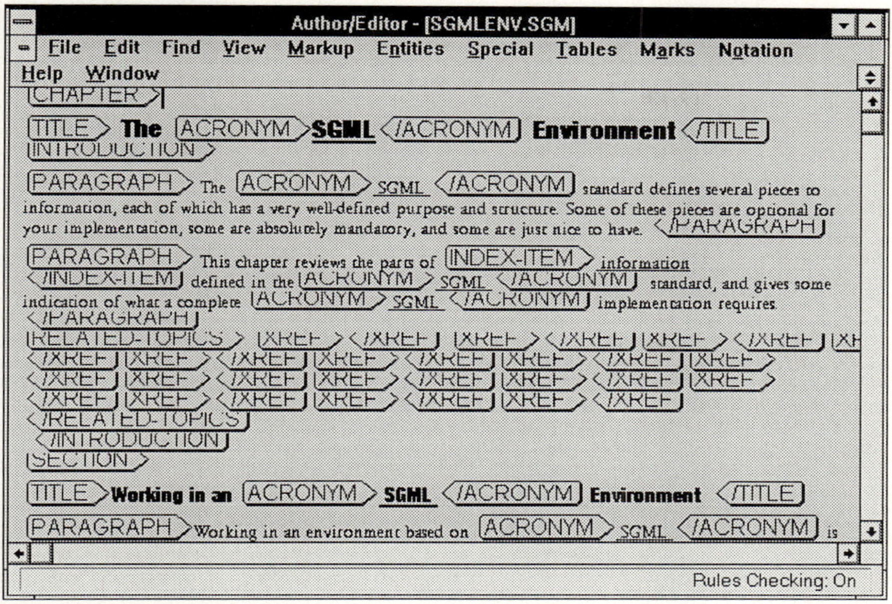

Figure 16. *Author/Editor SGML Editor (View Tags Mode)*

These workstations are the SGML industry's answer to the popularity of unstructured word processors; they provide a familiar face into the SGML database, and so are popular with authors and editors who need to create and maintain their documents. Because they know the structure of the SGMLinstance, the SGML editorial workstation can assure that the user does not create a structure that is not supported by the SGML processing system.

Another type of SGML editorial workstation shows structure and content side-by-side. Author/Editor has a mode where the element hierarchy is shown, and a product called InContext provides a structural view as its default.

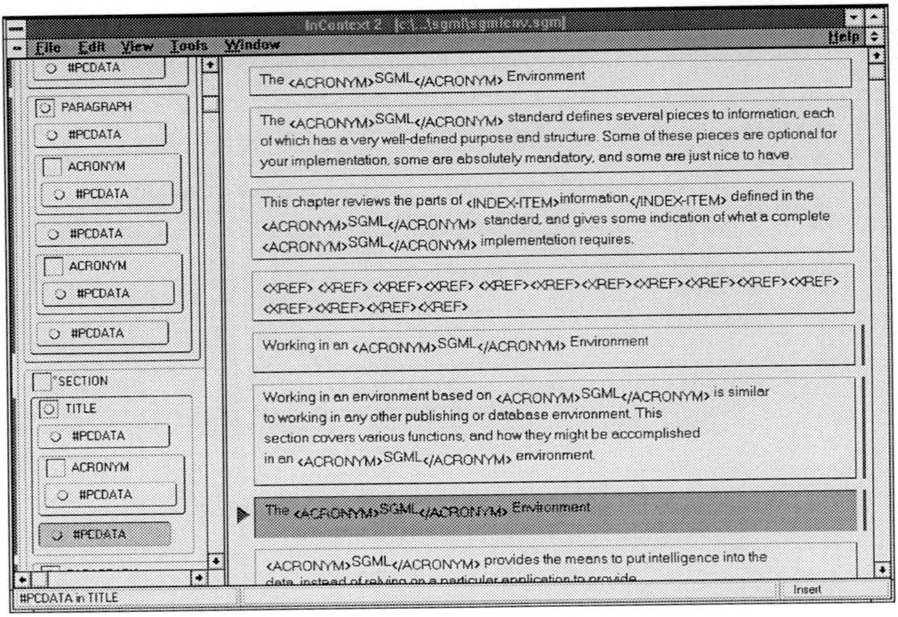

Figure 17. *InContext SGML Editor*

Notice that the structure is indicated by a "topographical map" indicating structural hierarchy. Notice, also, that there is no formatting on the content side of the screen. We have found that this type of editing environment allows authors to concentrate on the content (which is their job) and not worry about some eventual rendering of the data (which is most likely someone else's job).

Although both of these visual approaches to editing are good for authors and other creative people, it tends to be cumbersome for bulk input operators or other production personnel. For example, in order to insert an element in Author/Editor, the user must remove his hands from the keyboard, reach for the mouse, pull down a menu and select an element. This process could be partially automated by the use of macros or other programming functions, but the paradigm is still one of friendliness and ease-of-use over input speed. This is a very satisfactory trade-off for the occasional user or the user who is more concerned with writing thoughts down, but tends to get cumbersome for the production keyboarder.

Production keying facilities can use their text editor with pre-defined macros for fast tag insertion, or create pseudo-marked up files in an unstructured environment for later programmatic conversion. The important thing to note is that if a non-SGML-smart application is used to create the SGML instance files, they should be parsed with a validating SGML parser before loading into the database (See *Conversion Through Attrition* on page 165).

SGML ADD-INS

Some vendors of word processing and page makeup software market add-ins for their product that adds the capabilities of structured editors to their products. As of this writing, Frame Technology Corp., Microsoft, and WordPerfect offer these.

See *The Holy Grail* on page 108 and *SGML-Smart Enhancements* on page 109 for implementation issues with these products.

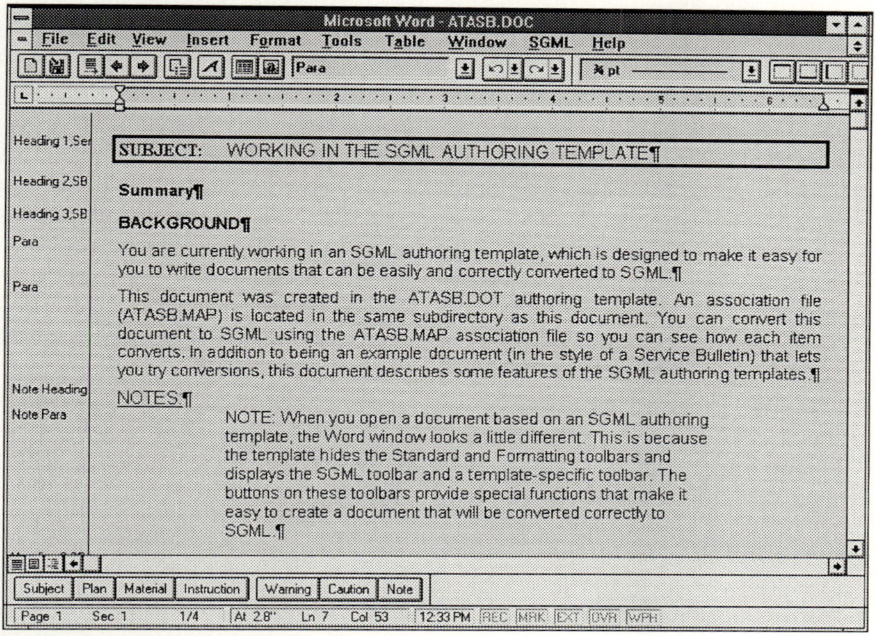

Figure 18. *Microsoft Author for Word*

DELIVERY VEHICLES

Composing your SGML information for delivery is probably the most important consideration when designing a system. The fact is, that most SGML systems start out as a replacement for an existing paper-based publishing/typesetting system. This capability must be addressed before even the simplest system is installed.

There are two basic classes of delivery: hard-copy delivery (paper) and electronic delivery (CD-ROM, commercial on-line services. Internet, etc.).

Hard-copy Composers

Getting "type on paper" from SGML can be as easy as writing translators to convert the SGML into typesetting codes, or it can be as complicated as integrating the composition function directly into an SGML-enabled database.

In this section, we will refer to the tool that achieves the composition process as a "composition engine" This word is used because it implies that the tool is part of an overall system, which might do more than a simple typesetter. It implies, in fact, a database approach to getting type on paper.

Typesetting systems costs range from nothing to hundreds of thousands of dollars. Most modern word processors can be used as composition engines. In fact, this book was composed from SGML using a translator that created text files with style and formatting information, which was poured into Corel Ventura Publisher and printed (See Appendix 4, *Colophon: How this Book was Produced* on page 401).

There are few composition engines designed for direct typesetting from SGML files. In fact, at the time of this writing, only Frame Technology Corp.' DL Pager and DL Composer and ArborText's Adept•Publisher are capable of reading SGML files directly. DL Composer and ArborText Adept•Publisher use FOSI (format output specification instance) files to drive the typesetting process. We expect to see more composition tools in this segment as the Document Style Semantic Specification Language (DSSSL), and its subset, DSSSL-Lite, are implemented by vendors.

The most common way to integrate type-on-paper processing is to use a composition engine that provides the functionality for the type of work you are doing, and translate your SGML into the native codes used by that typesetter. Often, a company will use the composition engine they currently have, if it has the functionality required to meet their composition needs so far. It is usually a manageable task to convert from SGML to typesetting codes.

Electronic Delivery

In order to provide to users electronic delivery of information contained in an SGML database, some application must be used to convert the data into a usable form.

SGML BROWSER. For electronic delivery of SGML-tagged information, there is a class of applications called "SGML browsers". Each vendor approaches the problem of getting structured information into an electronically browseable format, but all vendors who support SGML seem to be committed to delivering intelligent documents, complete with the appropriate structure, hypertext links, and access to external information.

Most of these tools run under a graphical environment, providing similar visual clues to element hierarchy as SGML editorial workstations do. Most allow the inclusion of non-SGML data like vectored and bit-mapped graphics, sounds, movies, and whatever else might come in the future.

SGML browsers offer context-sensitive searching capabilities so that the user can quickly access the required information. This is an important feature that cannot be provided with tools that do not track information in a hierarchical manner. For example, a search can be defined to allow a user to search for a part number, but only if it is contained in a chapter that was updated after a certain date. Or, a user can have the browser return a list of all sections containing a particular phrase, but only if the phrase is contained in a note. These are examples of context-sensitive searches.

A typical SGML browser is Electronic Book Technologies, Inc. DynaText, which is shown below:

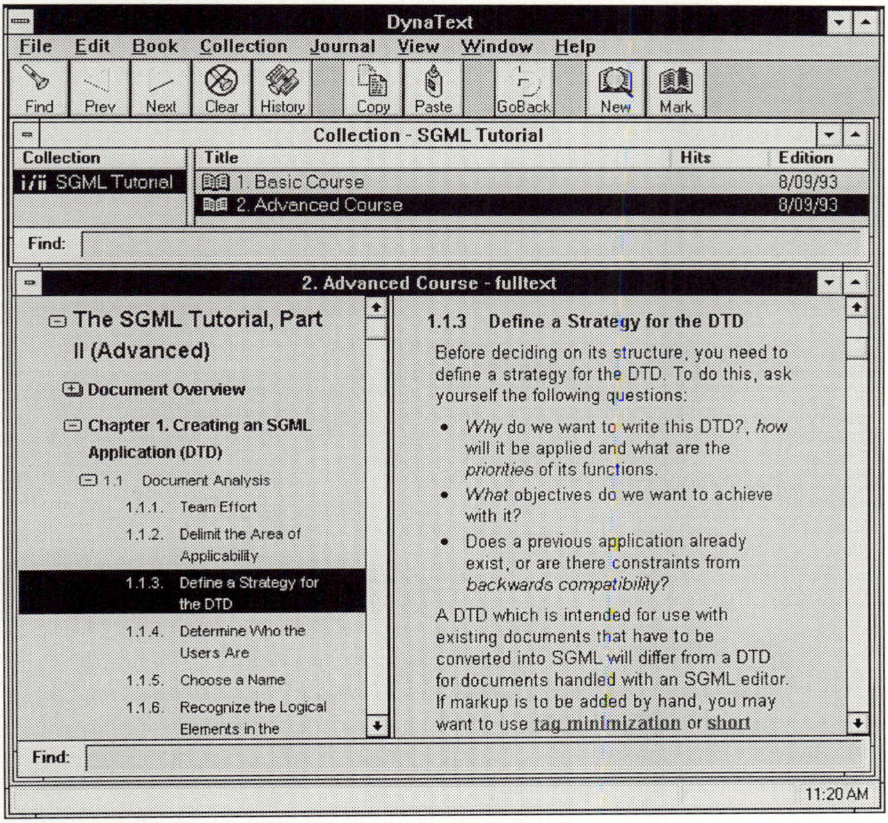

Figure 19. *DynaText from Electronic Book Technologies, Inc.*

DynaText accepts SGML files directly, allowing the user to export files from a database and build an electronic book. The product also has a rich application programming interface (API), allowing for the integration of the product into a new or existing system.

With the popularity of the CD-ROM, there are many companies that offer tools that can be used to deliver non-SGML data electronically. In order to reach a larger market, most of these tools do not accept SGML directly, but offer a means to get SGML into their proprietary format that works with their indexing, rendering, and browsing tools.

One such tool is Folio Views. Views provides a hierarchical view of data that is similar to the way SGML defines data structures. This product requires an external transformation step to translate the SGML data into its input form. Many companies are using Folio because of its affordability and flexibility.

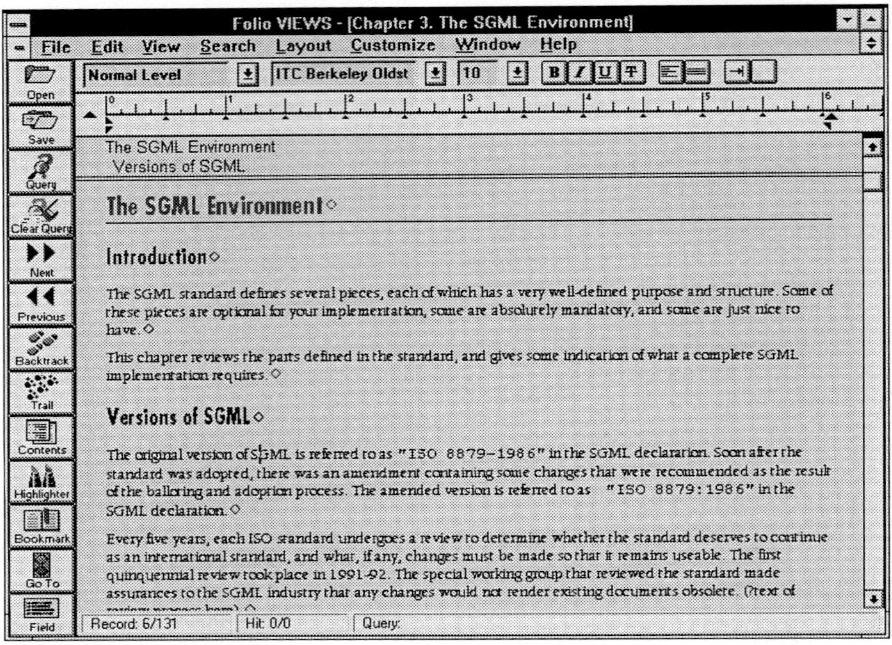

Figure 20. *Browsing SGML Documents with Folio Views 3.1*

Even though the view provided by Folio Views is hierarchical, like others in this category, it attempts to create a hierarchical version from flat word processors and desktop publishing systems. Folio relies on the intelligent application of styles to make this happen, much like a technique often applied to the conversion of word processing files into SGML.

It is important to note that there is a translation step required to convert the hierarchical structure of your SGML document into the flat model required by these products. Folio offers an "SGML Toolkit" containing Exoterica Corporation's OmniMark SGML programming language, and some add-ins to associate a customer-written OmniMark source file with an SGML document instance. In this way, SGML becomes another file type that is imported into Folio Views, just like WordPerfect or RTF.

Other manufacturers offer similar approaches to providing SGML support.

It is important to note that there is no such thing as an "SGML to X" converter, where X is some existing or future word-processing, desktop publishing, typesetting language, or electronic delivery tool. SGML is a tool used to create your own language. Once your custom language (in the form of a DTD) is created, it is possible to create a series of "Your-SGML-Language to X" converters for each X in the set.

The approach of Folio and others in the same market segment, is to allow you to associate "Your-SGML-Language-to-X" converters into their system. This provides a powerful way to ease SGML into an existing publishing system, because it appears to the users to be just another file format.

ON-LINE DELIVERY. On-line database services such as Compuserve and LEXIS/NEXIS from Mead Data Central have been around for many years. Their high usage costs led to the popularity of the CD-ROM for data distribution in volumes that exceeded magnetic floppy disc capacity. For a brief time, the high capacity of a CD-ROM was seen as a panacea for delivering massive amounts of information to end-users. Over 600 megabytes of data can be squeezed onto a little silver platter. The price of CD-ROM drives dropped precipitously in a short time, and it became feasible for commercial publishers to convert their printed documents to CD-ROM and delivering them for about a dollar apiece.

The party was short-lived, however, as publishers found out just how little 600 megabytes was. One medium-sized legal publisher is planning to distribute 4,000 megabytes of data as their complete collection. Multi-gigabyte CD-ROM drives are on the way, but it will be a while until it will be cost-effective for commercial publishers to deliver using this medium.

At the same time as the realization that the CD-ROM was limited in capacity, interest increased once again in direct on-line delivery, where the end-user is connected directly to some central data server. There are several advantages (and some disadvantages) to this model. Much more data can be served from a central source than can be provided, even from a rack of CD-ROM drives. If a publisher has more data than will fit, they install another shared data source and users have instant access to it. Another advantage is the immediacy of the data; theoretically the user can always get up-to-date information since the publisher has access to the entire distribution channel.

The main disadvantage of an on-line server is the speed and cost of access. For about a dollar plus shipping, a publisher can deliver a CD-ROM to a user, who can have unlimited access. Typically, an on-line service costs money every time a user accesses the network.

Even this is quickly changing. For a fixed fee, there are several companies that provide access, via a local telephone number, to large networks, most notably the Internet. Another factor that makes on-line distribution attractive is the advent of the World Wide Web, a protocol designed to make Internet access easy and non-confusing for normal people. The World Wide Web (WWW) is based on an SGML-like language called HTML (hypertext markup language). Documents are tagged using the HTML tag set and placed at a site accessible by users of the Internet's World Wide Web.

HTML provides a simple means to place hypertext links in your document. These links can point to locations in your own document, to other documents at your site, or even to documents at other sites around the world. Because of its ability to link between documents in a standard, common way, it is not an exaggeration to say that the World Wide Web constitutes a huge, single document. Several HTML browsers are available.

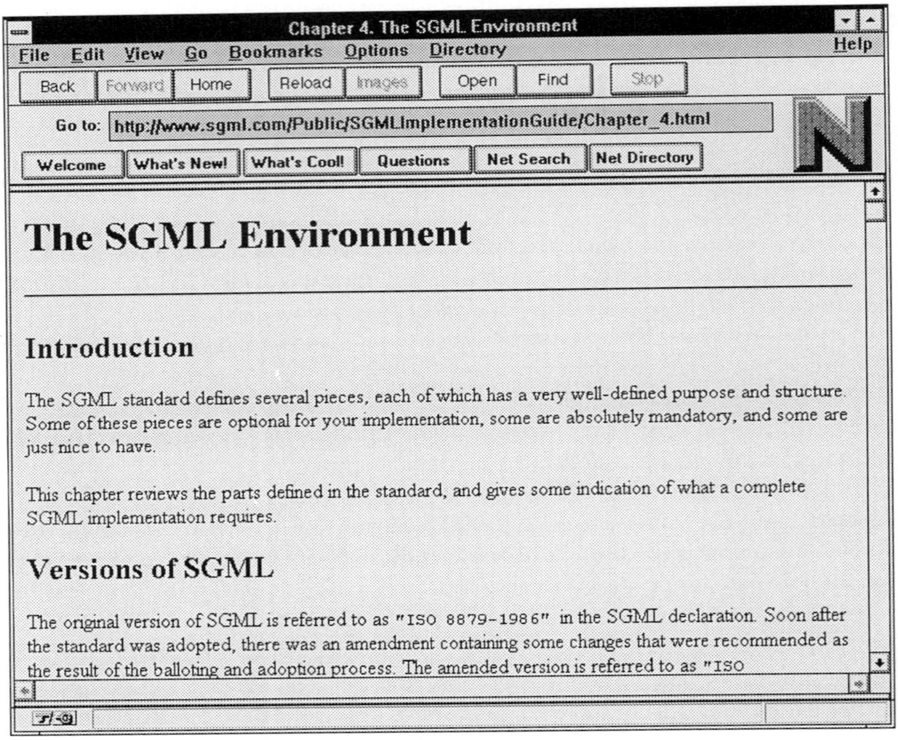

Figure 21. *Netscape from Netscape Communications Corporation*

HTML is not really SGML. Since the release of Mosaic, groups have taken two steps to put SGML into the World Wide Web. First, there is now a DTD that describes HTML. This is called HTML 2.0. Now, an author can create HTML documents and can use an SGML parser to validate the structure before publishing it on the network.

Even with a DTD, HTML has a flat model, optimized for fast delivery and display on a screen. For publishers who want to distribute their information on the World Wide Web, they must translate their documents into HTML. SoftQuad, publisher of several SGML editorial and browsing tools, offers a product called Panorama, which allows for the viewing of any SGML file, as long as the author has included a separate style-mapping file. This file uses the output specification language.

Panorama incorporates many of the concepts of HyTime to make a very interesting and useful product. Panorama uses the HyTime `treeloc` and `dataloc` architectural forms, among other things, to identify links without the need to put anchors in the target files. This is particularly effective when the author wants to link to a section of someone else's document that does not have an anchor `treeloc` and `dataloc` provide a way to access these documents.

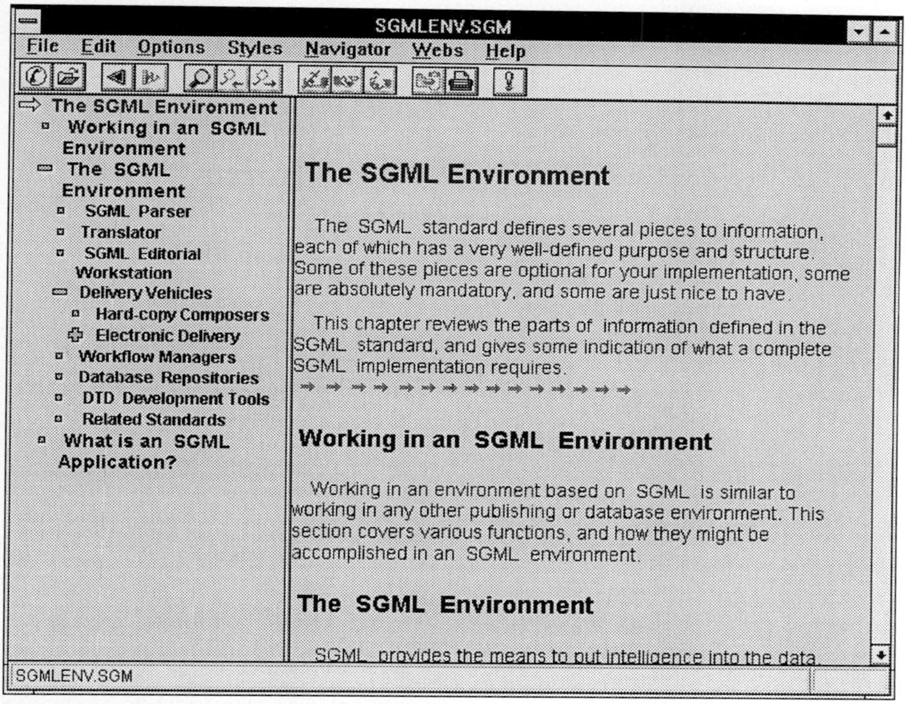

Figure 22. *Panorama Pro from SoftQuad*

It is certainly possible that documents tagged to a given DTD cannot be delivered using these tools. This is because a DTD can describe the structure of a document, not necessarily its display characteristics. Such a structural approach to document database design will require some kind of translation into a flat display model for publishing. This is not really a problem, since, after all, it is what is required when publishing to paper.

WORKFLOW MANAGERS

Workflow management tools are becoming available as a part of a whole-system approach to document databases.

Every company now has a workflow manager. Without one, nothing would ever get done (it may actually be more than one person, or different people for different workflows). For example, when a person applies for a job, he completes an application. This application is reviewed by a clerk or analyst in the personnel department, who makes a determination to pass it on up the line. The event of a person applying for work sparks a workflow, which, in turn, can start other work-flows until the person is hired or is given a rejection letter.

Automated workflow tools attempt to mimic the processes that people have been using for millennia, and to improve on them by adding the processing power of the computer and communications facilities of modern networks.

See *Workflow* on page 205 for more information on workflow managers and implementation.

DATABASE REPOSITORIES

SGML-enabled databases make use of SGML's features to provide to store and track the data more effectively and accurately. There are some tools available that put a layer of SGML-smart software atop a commercial object-oriented database engine.

One example of a product using this approach is Astoria from XSoft, a division of Xerox. Astoria provides a view into an SGML database with a graphical front-end. Under the covers, Astoria (like most similar products) provides a rich array of data storage, retrieval, and query capabilities. See Chapter 9, *SGML Data Management and Workflow* on page 183 for how these work.

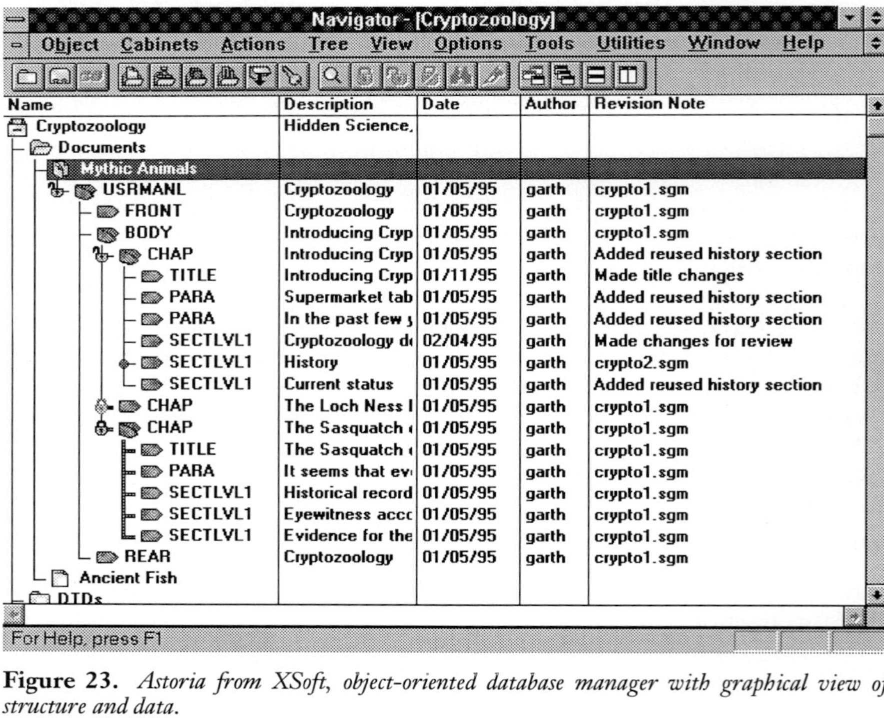

Figure 23. *Astoria from XSoft, object-oriented database manager with graphical view of structure and data.*

DTD DEVELOPMENT TOOLS

With the popularity of SGML, it was inevitable that tools would be developed that eased the drudgery of DTD development. One such tool, Near&Far, by Microstar Software Ltd., is a graphical tool used to develop DTDs. It provides a colorful, graphical view of an existing DTD, or allows the user to create a new one from scratch by dragging tools around the work area.

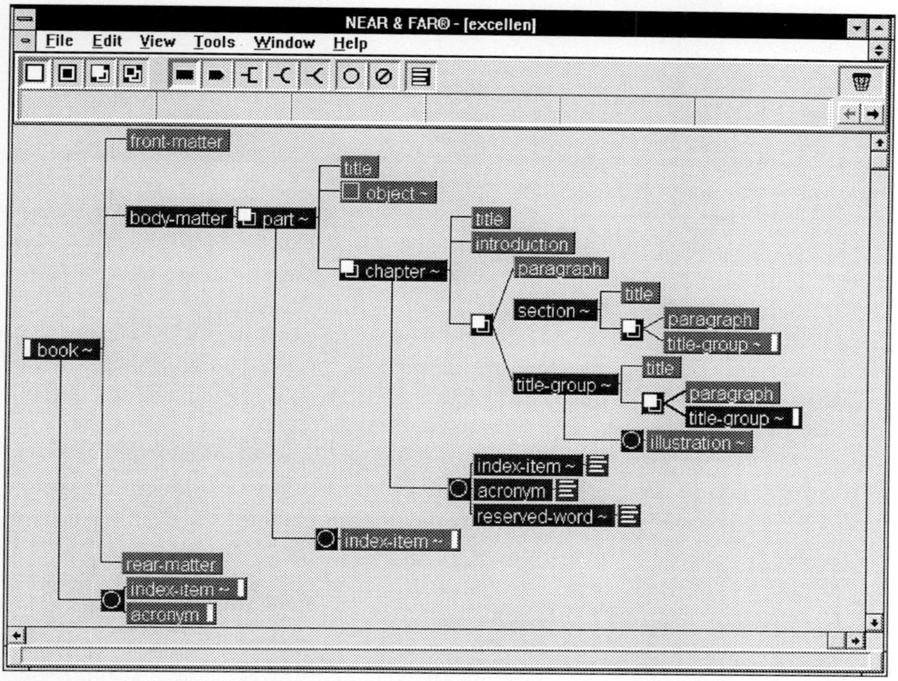

Figure 24. *Near&;Far by Microstar Software Ltd.*

Microstar Software Ltd. also sells a template that allows workgroups to collaborate on the development of a DTD by using Lotus Notes workgroup software.

RELATED STANDARDS

The following diagram[1] illustrates the document processing concept using ISO standards:

1 Adapted from SGML and Related Standards, by Joan M. Smith

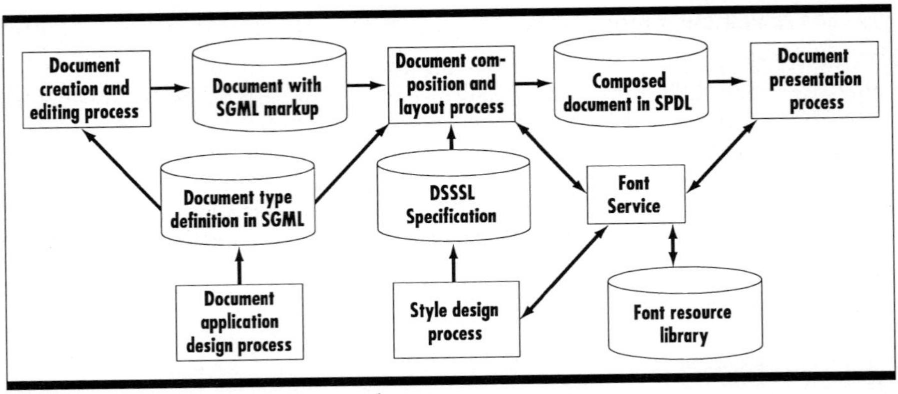

Figure 25. *The ISO Standards Model*[1]

First, a DTD is created using tools for such a purpose and assuring that it is valid before putting it in the database. Next, an SGML document instance is created and edited using the guidance of the DTD.

As a separate task, a style design process has produced a DSSSL specification, mapping the element structure defined in the DTD to codes suitable for creating some sort of output. The DSSSL specification is loaded into the composition process, along with document instance and DTD.

Another input to the composition process is provided by font services, which calls upon a library of font resources. The composed document is sent, along with all of the appropriate font information, to the presentation process, which actually renders the document for delivery.

What is an SGML Application?

There is common confusion concerning what constitutes an "SGML Application". The standard defines "application" as "text processing application[2]", and "text processing application" as "A related set of processes performed on documents of related types[3]".

This definition can be interpreted in many ways, often conflicting. Some say that a document type definition is an application. Some say a parser is an application, and some say an entire SGML implementation is a single application.

1 Adapted from "SGML and Related Standards", by Joan M. Smith

2 ISO 8879:1986 4.5

3 ISO 8879:1986 4.318

All of these interpretations are correct, in accordance with the definition in the standard, but are confusing. Because of the looseness of the standard's definition, in this book we will consider an application something that has SGML functionality, but we will be more specific when talking about all the various things that could fall into this category.

For example, an SGML-smart editorial workstation is an application by the definition in the standard, but we prefer to call it a tool. We generally refer to a conversion program that has an SGML parser as a utility or conversion program. A DTD can also be called an SGML application, but we will call it a DTD. We call something that consists of tools, DTDs, and other pieces a "system".

PART • II

Part II / The Project

CHAPTER • FIVE

Document Analysis

Introduction

Exactly what constitutes a document has been blurred with the introduction of databases and electronic products. For SGML implementors, all the uses of the information contained in documents must be discovered, understood and defined. This process is called document analysis. The methodology for performing document analysis is described with particular attention to the document analysis team, skills, and design and system-related issues. An example of how document analysis can be done with different goals in mind is provided at the end of this chapter.

Related Topics

- Chapter 2, *Evolution of Publishing Systems* on page 23
- Chapter 6, *The SGML Application* on page 101
- *Using SGML to Restructure Processes and Information* on page 124
- Chapter 8, *Information Conversion* on page 151
- *Planning* on page 160
- Chapter 9, *SGML Data Management and Workflow* on page 183
- *Markup* on page 219
- *Declarations* on page 223
- Chapter 11, *Building the DTD* on page 275
- *Common Elements* on page 288
- Chapter 12, *Tipniques and Pratfalls* on page 301
- *Elements vs. attributes* on page 304

Documents and Document Models

Document analysis is the process of identifying all of the components of information needed to support an organization in order for it to complete its mission successfully. The document analyst must consider all of the uses for the information and the level of detail needed in that information to support all of the processes and uses.

Document analysis is the term used in the industry to describe the process of identifying, analyzing, and addressing the issues involved with document design. The concepts behind document analysis are similar to the concepts behind traditional systems analysis. That is, all people, processes, equipment, and services must be considered when performing a comprehensive analysis. Document analysis covers one more important piece: the information in the document.

As we move from book-based publishing to information distribution, we also change the meaning of the word "document". A document becomes not a collection of words printed on paper, but a collection of information for the purpose of communicating an idea or concept. Publishing becomes, not the process of putting ink on paper and getting it to the reader, but the process of collecting information from its source and presenting it in a manner to achieve the goal of communication. A document is a subset of a larger information base. A document consists of that subset of the larger base designed to convey a particular concept for a particular audience.

In light of this definition, then, the document analysis process should be called the information analysis process because it involves more than just analyzing a particular document instantiation; the process is concerned with analyzing the information base used to create one or more document instantiations. But, in the industry, the process of defining the information and its uses has come to be known as document analysis, and is the term most widely in use today.

A document is only one occurrence or instance of what all similar documents of the same type might be like. A document model is the cumulative whole of all the structures and content of all documents of a single class. You might have two text books, one containing topics and quizzes, the other containing topics and graphics. Each is a different document instance of the document model that allows for topics, quizzes and/or graphics. Defining the document model is the goal of the document analysis team. This is done by looking at all of the instances available to you that belong to a single class, or adhere to a single model.

The Document Analysis Team

It is essential that all parties who have a stake in the information be represented or be present on a team that performs the document analysis, or the specific requirements of their processes and uses may be missed. Inadequate definition will require at least re-definition, maybe hastily during critical stages of implementation, and at most will lead to failure of the implementation overall. Broad representation will improve the analysis and hopefully hone the definition of elements to the specific few needed to meet the objectives of the entire system.

Functions performed by members of the document analysis team, as defined by common practice, are described below.

THE EVANGELIST

There is usually in an organization a person who can see the benefit of using SGML. We call this person the SGML evangelist, because he feels inclined to bring the religion to the rest of the company. The SGML Evangelist isn't always someone in the documentation department. Sometimes it is a writer or editor, or even a systems person. This is usually a self-starter who does the work and doesn't have any budget authority. This person provides vision and communicates the benefits to all levels, from top management on down.

The SGML evangelist must build a case for the organization in order to convince management to fund a project to research the implementation of SGML. The evangelist can write reports and give presentations that describe the benefits of SGML-based systems, or can quickly implement a small prototype to demonstrate the approach and potential benefits.

The evangelist may participate on the subsequent design and development activities after the interest has been established in pursuing SGML. Some evangelists are in the management ranks and will not be intricately involved in the process of implementing SGML.

THE DOCUMENT ANALYST

There is a need for someone to play the role as the lead document analyst during the development of your design effort and subsequent DTD development. This process does not stop after the first draft of the DTD is complete. A DTD is like a living thing; during development it needs constant attention and care. The document analyst will need to maintain a DTD even after all the development work is completed and the system is in production.

The document analyst can come from an existing department or, initially, be an outside consultant hired to facilitate the design process. Using members of your staff will improve the skill set of the people who work for your company, making them more valuable and better able to lead future projects of the same type. Inside people also have institutional knowledge about the information, the creating/using organizations, and the subtleties of what is important about the information that may make it valuable to the end-user customer.

On the other hand, an outside contractor may provide the experience needed to expedite the document analysis sessions, keep them on track, write a DTD that is functional, and avoid design problems that come back to haunt an inexperienced designer later at a more critical stage of the project.

Many people have found it useful to hire outside help for the first SGML project or two. But, it is extremely useful to develop good SGML-oriented design and DTD development skills in your own people since it is they who will have to sell the ideas to others, develop related tools to process the data, and maintain the tools and DTD after implementation.

The document analyst role varies from company to company, or even from project to project within a company. Document analyst is really a misnomer (one of many in the SGML world). Generally speaking, a document analyst should be logical and have a good understanding of the entire process of capturing, enhancing, delivering, and using the information. The term "document analyst" may sound like someone who simply looks at the pages of a document and notes what is found there. This approach is inadequate since much of the information to be managed never appears in print on the page. Additional information might include information about the text such as owner, creator, reviser, security classification, as well as other elements that are used for organization and information management. The arrangement of text on a page may be a suitable way to organize information for delivery in print, but it may not be the best way to organize information being managed in a database, accessed by multiple users at the same time, extracted, generated, and otherwise processed. The document analyst is ultimately responsible for identifying the uses and processes that affect the definition of the information. To do this, the document analyst will most likely require the help of a team of representatives from different parts of the organization.

This person must be able to work well with others on a team since it is likely that others will be needed to contribute to the design process. A document analyst may not need to be a diplomat, but a dictator will be less likely to encourage the level of participation and input needed to lead a team to a design that best reflects the needs of the entire process flow.

THE DOCUMENT ANALYSIS TEAM

As stated earlier, participation in the process of information or document analysis is required, in person or by proxy, from all authors, processors, and users of the information representing the entire life of the information. That is, there should be a representative for every function that has a stake in the data being defined. This includes not only the data in the document, but also computer development and operational processes as well. The following list of roles, albeit not comprehensive, may be a good place to start:

- authoring,
- editing,
- editorial management,
- DTD development,
- data conversion programming,
- composition format development,
- workstation screen formatting development,
- electronic delivery product development,
- marketing (to provide focus on business and product goals),
- database management, and
- end users.

Participation on a regular basis from members from each of these areas could prove to be overkill, or even bureaucratic: we have heard the cliche gripe about the amount of work a committee can get done—the bigger the committee, the less work that gets done. But a small core team of people should be expected to be closely involved in the design process even on the smallest project.

Document analysis is a great example of how true teamwork can provide better results than a group of people working individually. Each session will be an education for each team member, learning about how the other department works, how their tools and processes function, and what is important about the information from another perspective.

The team must dedicate the time required to complete the design in sufficient detail and with the accuracy that will support the degree of automation required (per the goals of the system as defined in Chapter 7, *Implementation Planning* on page 121). For some this participation may only be in the form of an occasional review meeting, for others it may require full-time attention for several weeks or more depending on the complexity of the design. In consulting, speaking, and teaching activities we are often asked, "How long does it take to write a DTD?" To which we sometimes reply, "Six. We just aren't sure what unit of time we are using." It depends. The complexity of the information and the systems and processes to be used, the ability to get the group to meet, the level of experience of members of the team, the goals of the project, all affect the process of document analysis. In general, though, a simple DTD can be done in minutes, and it is reasonable for large multi-organizational DTDs to take months, or even years, to complete. Remember that taking the time to conduct a thorough analysis up-front will lead to a good design and improve the chances of successes for the project.

The document analysis team will need to be educated from the onset in the specific goals of the implementation project. These goals may even need to be posted prominently in the room where the meetings are held to serve as a constant reminder as to why the team is gathered. For example, a reminder that certain aspects of the publishing process will be automated may come in handy when trying to decide whether to identify the sub-elements in a part number (each of which may have a specific nomenclature that requires validation in order to automate their processing).

Significant change, either cost savings or increased data value and reusability will require significant effort up front. Document analysis is the homework that needs to be done thoroughly in order that the goals of the implementation are met. A solid understanding of the concepts of SGML will most likely expedite the document analysis process. It is time-consuming to translate fairly complex or unusual ideas into lay terms or plain language for end users when the syntax and constructs of SGML may express these ideas more precisely and succinctly. That is not to say that all members of the team must be able to write a DTD. The ability to understand content models and attributes will suffice for the average end user on the team. Train the team early in SGML concepts.

The Document Analysis Methodology

Most shampoo bottles in the US have the instructions:

- lather,
- rinse,
- repeat.

It is hard to tell when to stop repeating these steps given this limited set of instructions (except, perhaps, when the bottle is empty). The process of analyzing a document type is similar in that it requires the process to be repeated, and sometimes it will take many cycles until it is sufficiently complete to go on to the next steps. The document analysis process is iterative and requires the analysts to learn from each previous step in order that the document model grows until a sufficiently rich design is achieved.

Every environment and document class will have its own peculiarities, but the basic design process flow should include the following steps:

1. Preliminary analysis,
2. Expanded group analysis,
3. DTD development,
4. Testing and implementation, and
5. Repeat until done.

The Document Analysis Report

A typical deliverable from the document analysis process is a document called the Document Analysis Report. This document will list all documents and elements that have been classified, their relation to each other, process-specific information, a description of the element, and any other information about the element required to build the system.

Some sample pages from a Document Analysis Report are shown here.

```
                    Document Analysis Report
                    ------------------------


Object: part number

Description:
    The number of a part referencing a part number in a
    product-specific parts database.

Contents:
    The number of the part, and the appropriate database where
    it is found.

Process-specific information:
    Part numbers are rendered in an italic font when printed,
    and in a green, underlined font when rendered on the
    CD-ROM product.

    When delivered in an electronic form, the user will click
    on the part number, which will generate a query to the
    appropriate parts database and return whatever information
    is necessary to the particular application. Possible data
    includes:
        .  a description of the part
        .  a picture of the part
        .  supply and warehousing information
        .  price and cost information
```

```
                    Document Analysis Report
                    ------------------------

Object: structural paragraph

Description:
    The structural paragraph is the structural foundation of a
    set of similar ideas. It contains a descriptive title and
    grammatical paragraphs.

Contents:
    title, grammatical paragraphs. Contains a label indicating
    its location and sequence in the hierarchy.

Process-specific information:
    The label and title should be rendered in a bold or
    colored typeface and run-in with the text.
```

```
                    Document Analysis Report
                    ------------------------

Object: grammatical paragraph

Description:
    The basic component of textual information.

Contents:
    Words, cross-references, part numbers, footnotes, warnings,
    highlighted phrases, illustrations, tables.

Process-specific information:
    The label and title should be rendered in a bold or
    colored typeface and run-in with the text.
```

This report forms the basis of the DTD design and subsequent application development and maintenance. In fact, the document analysis report forms the informal portion of the DTD. See *The Prologue* on page 217 for more information about the formal and informal portions of the DTD.

PRELIMINARY ANALYSIS

An initial design can be accomplished by an individual document analyst with familiarity with the document type and the overall system objectives and configuration. Most likely, this will be a person with experience in document analysis and DTD development. This may be an outside contractor if nobody on your staff possesses these skills.

The initial design process should include analysis of a representative sampling of the document information. This will most likely include scanning many printed pages, but could also include reviewing composition and processing documentation, editorial style manuals, database definition documentation, internal and external standards manuals, and perhaps interviews with knowledgeable authors, editors, and technical development staff from the database and composition departments.

A very thorough analysis will inevitably lead to a conversion plan. Therefore, it is extremely useful to conduct a code analysis if the legacy data is available in electronic form in which all typesetting codes and/or database fields are identified. A determination must made on what the information is, how it will be converted, and whether it will be combined with other information, enhanced, or even split into sub-elements. A thorough code analysis is a valuable means for specifying the conversion of the information, especially if an outside conversion service bureau is utilized (See Chapter 8, *Information Conversion* on page 151).

The resulting documentation of the preliminary analysis can be any combination of a first draft DTD, textual descriptions of the structure of the document and each element, graphic diagrams illustrating structure and element relationships (see below), sample marked-up pages, or sample SGML tagged data.

EXPANDED GROUP ANALYSIS

Once an initial analysis has been performed, the document analysis team will begin its work in earnest. The preliminary design will need to be scrutinized and reviewed from all angles. The person representing each area must test the design and express all concerns, issues, and suggested changes in order that the design will better fit the needs of their respective areas. The following chart illustrates a flow where a preliminary design is analyzed by several groups within the organization:

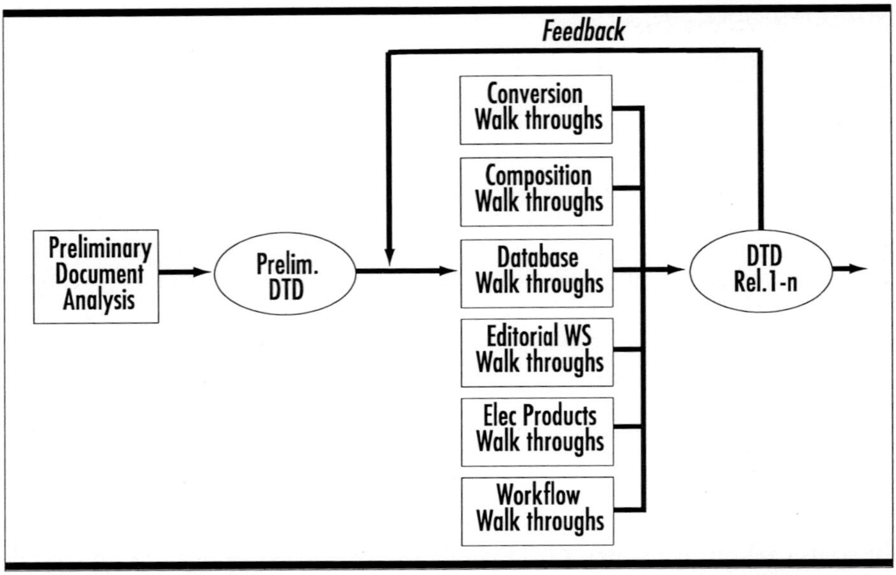

Figure 26. *Document analysis flow*

During the document analysis sessions the following questions should be considered to ensure a thorough analysis is made. Your organization may need to add other ideas to this list. You may choose to enlarge this chart and post it in the room in which the analysis is being conducted to remind participants to try to maintain the macro view and not create elements that merely expedite a single process at the expense of other processing. For example, try not to create a bunch of composition-oriented codes to simplify the composition processing if it means that the editors will then have to add and maintain the additional coding.

Design Questions

- What are the essential information elements for your business?
- What are these things called?
- What are the relationships between elements?
- What information needs to be identified, extracted, verified, processed, etc.?
- Who will know what and when?
- How will information be managed?
- What information about the information would be useful?

Design Issues

- Focus on ideal design goals, not existing data
- Focus on intellectual elements first, pragmatic considerations later
- Assign unique names
- Resolve subtle name and element similarities and differences
- Develop a working vocabulary
- Identify control information to aid processing
- Allow ambiguity at first, refine later
- Similar things may be different
- Different things may be the same
- Documents can be grouped into classes
- Different models can share elements
- Identify boilerplate text
- Identify presentation-specific things
- Granularity is based on need

Work Flow Issues

- Identify timing and security issues
- Determine efficient handling and storage techniques
- Recognize that existing organization may need to change
- Identify what processes/tools will be used to apply markup

The Document Model

A document, as described above, is a collection of information used to convey an idea or concept. Books, articles, and manuals are documents, but so are database reports and sheet music. Even a movie is a document.

For the scope of this chapter, we will consider the whole of the information for analysis. For example, a company that makes brakes for land vehicles might produce a technical repair manual for each version of the product, a training manual for maintenance personnel, a set of descriptive documents for different markets, and an interactive field repair manual on CD-ROM. Each of these is a document, but all of them together comprise a set of information that is highly cross-linked.

The document analysis process should consider each of these independent output forms when designing a system to produce them all. In addition, there are factors outside of the scope of any single document that must be considered when producing the information analysis report.

DISCOVERING THE INFORMATION IN DOCUMENTS

Once you have set your scope on what your database of SGML information will contain, you will need to analyze the potential contents of each document to determine what its structure will be. This structure will eventually be defined in the document type definition. Since SGML allows you to define a totally customized structure, you may find the process overwhelming, sort of like a writer faced with a blank sheet of paper and a case of writer's block. What is the structure that you should define?

Fortunately, there is a logical way to approach document analysis, just as there is for all design. Start by asking yourself, "What is the purpose of your design, and therefore, what are the things necessary to satisfy this purpose?" In other words, what are we creating? A single typeset book view? Or a database that supports many alternative views? SGML can define either, or a combination of the two that balances future goals and existing technology.

Focus on intellectual concepts first. Start very specific and rigorous and give up the purist view only as you find it necessary to do so due to realistic constraints, limitations, and revelations about what is really needed and what is expendable.

Remember that the goal of document analysis is to define what information is essential for the survival of the business and for the business to meet it objectives. Define names, use, similarities and differences between related information, relationships to parent, peer, and subordinate information, rigor, availability, class of creator/user, sources, and anything else that you feel is pertinent to creation, maintenance and use of the information.

Defining Information Elements

Documents contain information. Information can be broken down into elements, which can be broken down further into other elements. The process continues until the information is defined in sufficient detail to allow effective management and processing of the information. The granularity of the design depends on the requirements of the business.

Develop a working vocabulary to eliminate confusion where we say the same word, but have slightly different meanings in mind (*e.g.* `<p>`, `<par>`, `<para>`)

Educate participants to think in terms of structure and content identification first, pragmatic consideration later. Focus on objectives such as automation, validation, identification. Hands-on experience will improve buy-in and will make ambassadors of SGML out of the entire team. Get them used to the idea that the details of the design will change constantly. Get the team comfortable with the necessary level of ambiguity during the design phase during the process of refining the design.

A business should spend no time and money defining and managing information in smaller chunks than they need to. That is, unless they anticipate a realistic need beyond what is possible with the current technology.

If a document managed as chapters and paragraphs satisfies all the processing and management requirements, there is probably no reason to define additional levels of hierarchy or detail information elements such as cross-references and part numbers. A simple design such as the one just described would most likely yield only basic benefits along the line of basic typography and flat file data management. If the organization implementing SGML is striving for a more sophisticated publishing solution, more detail will be needed. For instance, if all cross-references are to be verified automatically and all part numbers are to adhere strictly to a rigorous nomenclature to allow them to be validated against a product database, then more care and detail should be provided in resulting data design than simple generic hierarchy elements such as heads and paragraphs.

Develop a database schema for managing information and tasks within a process based upon the workflow. Think of the data model, not an instance of the data when making design decisions. Determine an efficient form for storage, access, management, creation, conceptualizing (after all, humans will have to work with the model), and delivery and transformation. Get the team to think of the document concept as ephemeral instances of the overall data model. Consider relationships of data within the model, not just links and hierarchies in the document instance.

Recognize that existing organizations may need modification to allow an optimum solution to issues related to data capture, management, use, and delivery. Identify who owns the data and what groups merely support its processing for development and management. The workflow or process used to create and publish the information needs to be understood if not fully fleshed out in minute detail, the process is the glue that holds the information together. It is like the chicken and egg dilemma—the information needed defines the process to be used and the process in use defines what information is available and when.

Identify control information that would enhance data or allow better management, automated processing, or identification of elements. Identify how markup will be added and who will be doing it, what skills and tools will be involved, how much will be known and when it will be know, what can be resolved at input time and what must be added later.

This discussion is intended to reinforce the need to focus on the business objectives when deciding on how to proceed when analyzing your documents, deciding what information is necessary and will need defining, and creating the subsequent document model. The level of sophistication required to provide very specific access via the database front end will be important during the document analysis process, as will the complexity needed to support professional typography, flexible data manipulation and reorganization, and quality assurance processes.

Using Clues Found in Type

You may have a large collection of information in printed form that can provide visual clues to the various elements of information in use. Differences in typographic representation usually provide good clues to determining the different pieces of information. But typographic clues can be misleading and are, at most, always incomplete. Most existing legacy datalegacy data has been prepared inconsistently, especially if the information spans many years, and, perhaps, many different publishing systems. There may also be a lot of important information that either does not appear in the printed volumes, or does not appear in a different typographic style than other elements, but still will need to be identified.

For instance, cross-references and proper names may need to be explicitly identified (for automation or verification purposes) even if they do not appear in a different type face than surrounding text. Information about the document itself, its authors, revision dates, security classification, etc., may not appear on the printed page, but may be essential in order to control access to the information using a database management system.

Things that appear identical from a typographical perspective may be vastly different from a logical or intellectual perspective. The same typography may be applied to both a figure caption and a third-level heading. But we would hope that the appropriate information could be identified when creating a table of contents and a separate table of figures. If the document analyst relies too heavily on the physical representation of the information, subtleties may be missed, automation opportunities may be missed, and projected costs savings or increased revenues may be missed.

Defining the Document

Documents have structure, content, and order. These things must be recognized and recorded by the document analysis team. In addition, some formatting information and information relative to desired versions, revisions, and by-products should be recorded and utilized in development tasks if not in the DTD design itself.

ILLUSTRATING INFORMATION STRUCTURE

In order to communicate document structure, it is sometimes helpful to come up with a methodology that seems comfortable for the team members.

Tree Diagrams

Tree diagrams provide an easy way to describe document hierarchy. A tree diagram is like an organizational chart or a family tree. Each box has a name, and it may or may not have descendants.

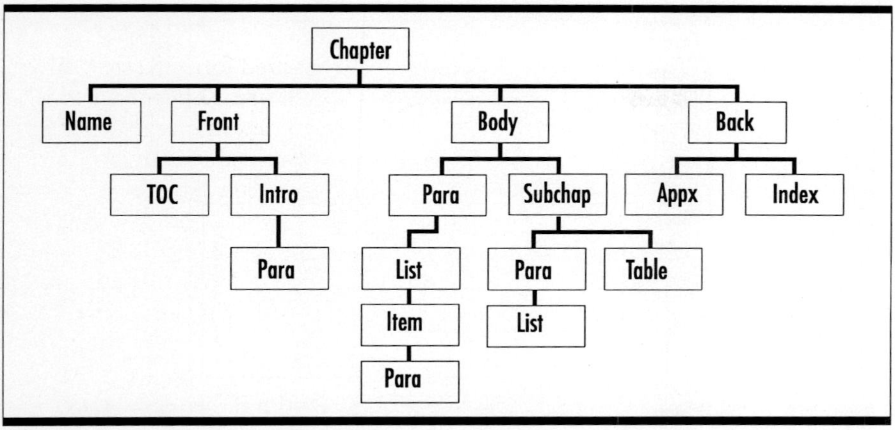

Figure 27. *Tree diagram showing document instance structure*

While a tree diagram is useful to communicate graphically the structure of a hierarchical document, it alone does not give the SGML designer (or the computers that will eventually process the data) enough information to create the DTD. However, it is an intuitive way to communicate structure to casual members of the team or those not willing to learn the more powerful grammar of SGML (See Chapter 10, *Understanding SGML* on page 215).

Box Diagrams

Like tree diagrams, box diagrams provide another way to describe document structure. In a box diagram, each element contains other elements, and is contained by other elements. This approach, while more accurately describing document structure than a tree diagram, is harder to visualize.

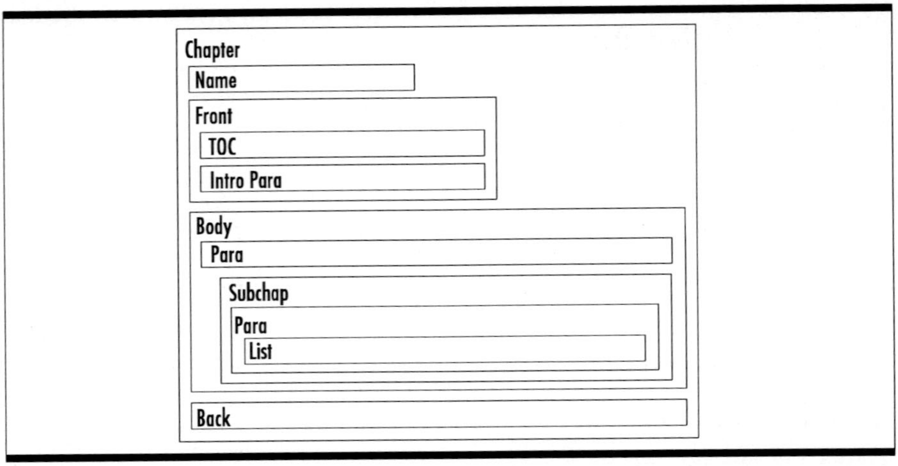

Figure 28. *Box diagram showing document instance structure and containment*

Like a tree diagram, a box diagram does not provide the SGML designer with enough information to create the DTD or accurately record decisions regarding the information model being built. Even so, box diagrams are useful when trying to explain the concept of element containment, elements containing other elements within their own structure, to others who are more familiar with processes that do not support containment and rely on state changes in flat files.

Sample Marked-up Pages

Sample pages probably provide the most familiar view of the document. By taking photocopied sample pages from the documents being analyzed and applying tags to every element you see, you are beginning the process of defining a language to describe your elements.

When creating sample marked-up pages, look for visual clues and determine why the typography has changed, what the underlying purpose the clue was designed to point out. Apply tags freely until you see patterns emerge. Then try to normalize things that might be the same by using the same markup for each. Also, begin to differentiate things that might in fact be different elements even though they have the same physical appearance.

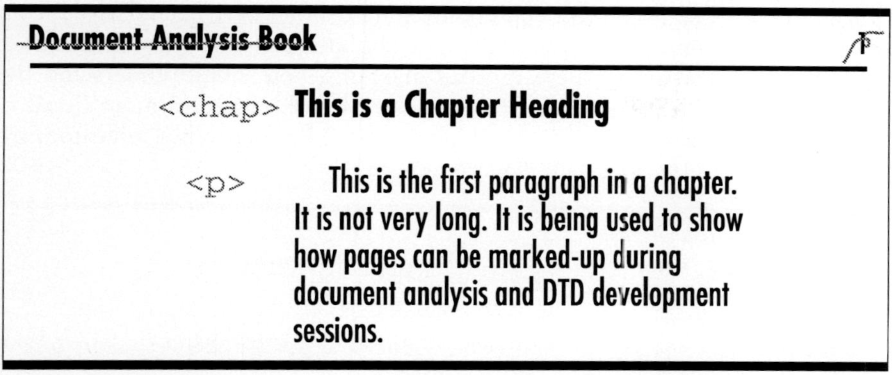

~~Document Analysis Book~~

<chap> **This is a Chapter Heading**

<p> **This is the first paragraph in a chapter. It is not very long. It is being used to show how pages can be marked-up during document analysis and DTD development sessions.**

Figure 29. *Sample marked-up page example*

In this very simple diagram, the typeset page has been annotated (in gray) to begin the process of assigning names to elements found in the document analysis and to record these decisions. Material that will be generated or supplied by the application has been crossed out. Tagging has been applied to the content that will remain in the database.

The best pages to start with during the analysis are the reference pages: table of contents, list of figures, list of tables, index, glossary, as these pages usually show the document hierarchy, alternative views of the information, and the various non-textual information required. Eventually a representative sample should be analyzed and marked up to serve as a test of the markup language and the model being developed.

The danger of using sample pages is that they tend to cause the team to focus on a particular document, instead of the underlying information that makes up the printed document and will be the basis for your information model. Sample marked up pages do not express the rules behind the markup that can only be captured in a DTD. The example above is an extremely simple one. Typical publication pages can be very densely populated with typeset text and can be much more difficult to annotate in this way. Also, preparing sample documents for a good cross section of pages and instances of information elements can be very time consuming.

With this in mind, however, sample pages are a valuable resource to the document analysis team. Marked-up pages are only a tool to be used for analysis of your documents. Marked-up sample pages can also be very useful when describing the resulting DTD to users and developers as well.

Railroad Model Diagrams

Tree structures, box diagrams, and sample marked-up pages are ways of representing instances of a model, not the model itself to which the instance belongs.

There are ways to graphically represent the model that have been derived from database and computer science modeling techniques called railroad diagrams.

Before discussing these railroad diagrams, you should understand the SGML syntax for expressing occurrence and order (discussed in more detail in Chapter 10, *Understanding SGML* on page 215). The occurrence indicators are shown in *Table 1, Occurrence Indicators* on page 82.

Indicator Following an Element Type Name in a Content Model	***Meaning***
`(nothing)`	sequence, required, one must occur
`?`	optional, zero or one can occur
`+`	required & repeatable, one or more must occur
`*`	optional & repeatable, zero or more may occur

Table 1. *Occurrence Indicators The connectors indicating ordering rules are:*

Connector between Element Type Names in a Content Model	***Meaning***
`,`	is followed by
`( )`	grouping
`|`	or, one of the elements in the group may occur
`&`	and, all must occur in any order

Table 2. *Connectors*

Occurrence indicators and connectors can be used in combination. For instance, the element chapter may be defined as containing a name followed by either one or more paragraphs (para) or graphics using these indicators as a form of shorthand notation for expressing document rules. The following describes the rule for chapters that contain a required name followed by one or more paragraphs or graphics in any order:

```
chapter = (name, (para | graphic?)+)
```

A similar rule that a required name is followed by a required paragraph and may be followed by an optional graphic would be written thusly:

```
chapter =  (name, para, graphic?)
```

The end goal of this whole process is to use the SGML syntax to describe the structure in what is called a "content model". A content model is a rigorous description of what other elements are allowed in an element, in what order, and whether they are required or not. (Content models and the SGML language are described in *Content Model* on page 231). Having someone on the team who can teach team members how to create a content model will certainly be helpful, and in the long run, will allow a more accurate description of the document model. Even so, during document analysis you may want to quickly jot down rules to make a point to other members on the team. Sometimes it is useful to use a simple pseudo-SGML syntax to keep the discussion simple. You could, of course, use the complete declarations and syntax of SGML, but that might be intimidating to the less technical people on your document analysis team.

Railroad diagrams are useful at depicting these model rules graphically to increase understanding. For instance, moving left to right, the rule that a chapter must contain one required name followed by one required paragraph (para) is expressed as follows:

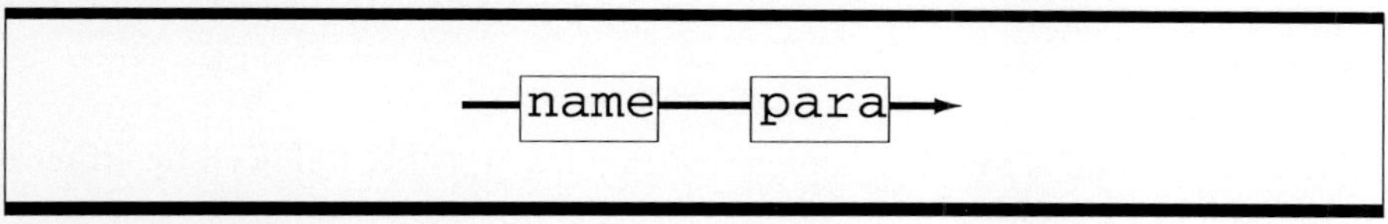

Figure 30. `chap = (name, para)`

The rule that a chapter must contain a name followed by one or more paragraphs can be depicted graphically thusly:

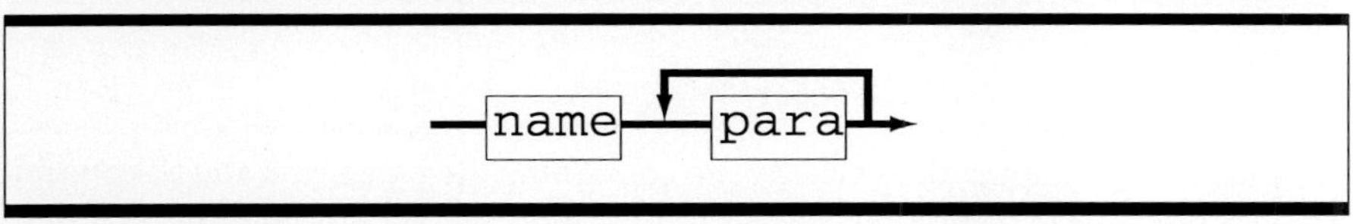

Figure 31. `chap = (name, para+)`

The arrow moving from left to right indicates the flow of the order of the elements in the model for the chapter. The fact that name has no other arrow means to get past it, you must first have a name, or satisfy the model for chapter with a name followed by one or more paragraphs (para). The arrow that goes back around the para indicates that after you have the first para you can either go back and allow one or more additional ones or finish the model for chapter after only one.

The following graphic shows a similar model for chapter except that the paragraph is optional:

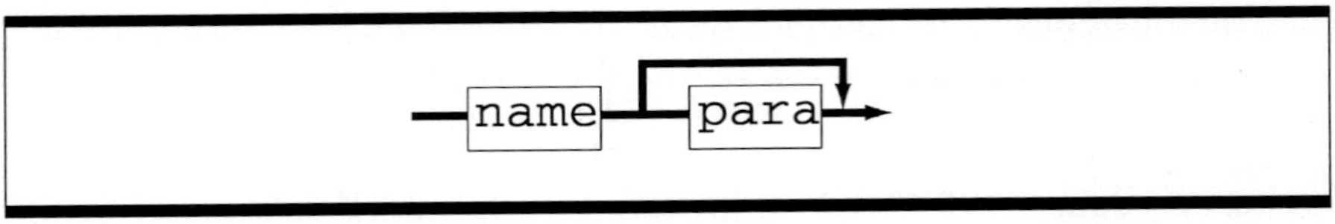

Figure 32. `chap = (name, para?)`

The next graphic is again for a chapter, but this time it is both optional and repeatable:

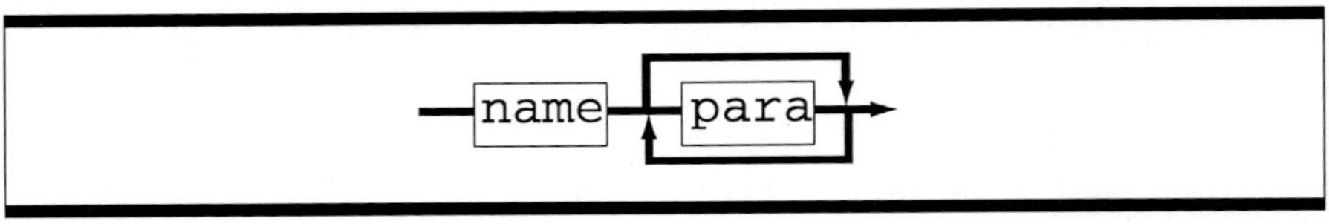

Figure 33. `chap = (name, para*)`

The next graphic is for the chapter that requires a name, followed by either a paragraph or a graphic:

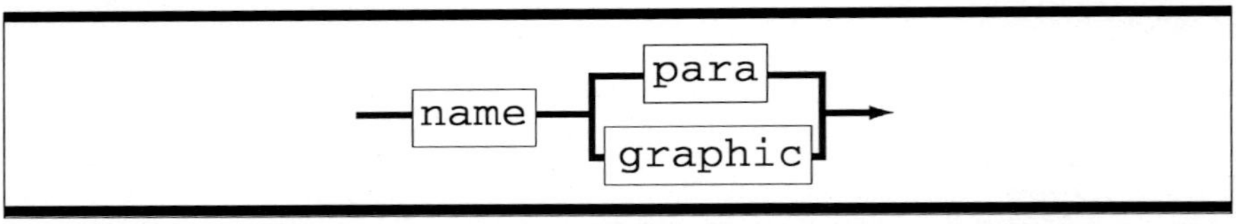

Figure 34. `chap = (name, (para | graphic))`

The following chapter allows the group containing the paragraph and the graphic to be repeatable (through the use of the `OR` connector in combination with the + occurrence indicator applied to the group). In other words, either one can occur as many times as needed, but at least one or the other must occur at least once.

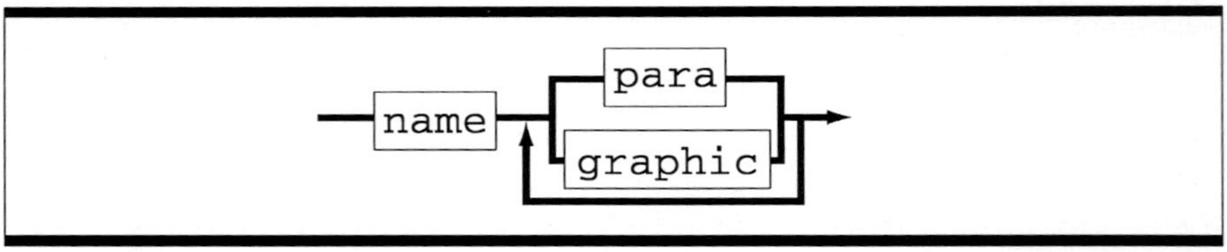

Figure 35. `chap = (name, (para | graphic)+)`

The following chapter requires that both the paragraph and the graphic occur once each, but in any order (note the use of the `&` connector):

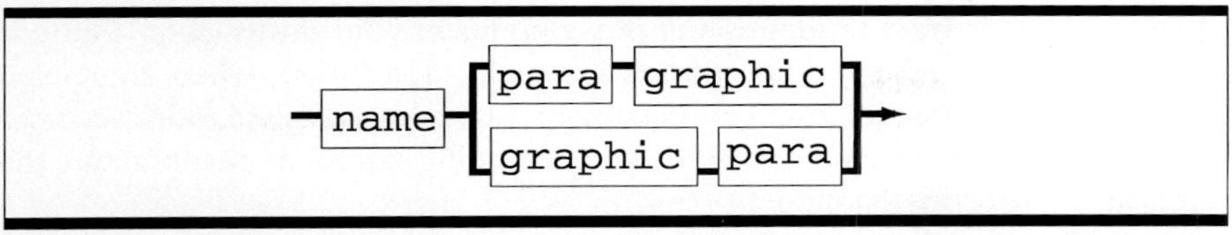

Figure 36. `chap = (name, (para & graphic))`

Note: the use of the AND connector is often confusing to new users and hard to depict graphically. The graphical syntax used above is not as intuitively obvious as the rest of the syntax (this graphical syntax cannot represent everything you can potentially do in SGML). The AND rule is equivalent to the following rule where two groups have been used, one for each possible combination of para and graphic defined in the above rule where the & was used. Instead, the rule is expressed using the OR connector between the two possible groups allowing only one or the other to occur. The railroad diagram would be as follows:

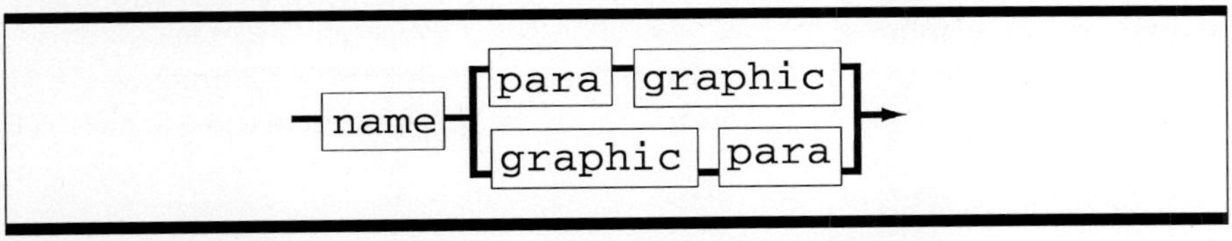

Figure 37. `chap = (name, ((para, graphic) | (graphic, para)))`

Railroad diagrams are not necessarily a useful way of depicting an entire document model. Some elements in a document can contain many other elements, in several groups with optionality and repeatability, thus making the railroad diagram for that model very complex and detailed. On the other hand, when trying to describe the rules as you find them and isolate a small portion of the model to use as a point of discussion, railroad diagrams can be effective communication tools.

SGML is a very rich language that can be used to express many things about the information being modeled with it. Many of the features of SGML would be difficult to express in railroad diagrams or other graphical techniques. It is better to have the team learn SGML and to use it to depict this type of complexity. Some SGML developers have striven to express some of the features of SGML (not shown here) and have created their own flavor of railroad diagramming. These are sometimes discussed at SGML conferences.

Other Techniques

There are other ways of identifying the contents of your documents. There is even a product available that consists of "paper dolls" that, when connected properly, forms the structure of a document. Some methods are more accurate than others for performing analysis and recording decisions made about the underlying information model.

There are even products that allow a user to develop a DTD using a graphic modeling interface and then produce a report of the resulting model in the SGML syntax (Near&Far is described briefly in *DTD Development Tools* on page 58).

Use of graphical models may help illustrate design structure during conceptualizing stages. Inevitably you will find yourself writing the DTD to express design since SGML provides a rich language to express these types of ideas. Using a DTD too early tends to confuse the uninitiated and to prematurely give a sense completion. We too often focus on the construction of the DTD before the analysis and brainstorming process is complete. At some point it will be difficult to track the design without resorting to the SGML syntax. Start by first creating element lists or other tools to help track your design, then add rules using the pseudo-SGML notation used above, add a few more syntactical things and, suddenly, you have a very basic DTD. It may not be the finished product yet, but you are now doing SGML.

It is important to note that, however helpful these techniques are to describing the structure of the information, the best representation of the DTD is the DTD itself.

Documents and Databases

There are relationships between parts of some books and others. A repair manual will have many of the same information elements in it that its corresponding parts catalog does. A single database could be designed to contain all of the information of both books, both views of the same collection of information, and be used to extract each view. An advantage of using database techniques for managing text is that the information that is the same in each book view only has to be maintained once even though it is reused two (or more) times. Also, the links between books can be better maintained and content of each book can be kept up to date with the other.

Since we have a long history of writing information in the form of a book, it is difficult to think of information in any other way. This is especially true for textual information since it tends to be less consistent and rigorous than the types of information that we have successfully built into databases. But as our understanding of SGML combined with database techniques increases we are seeing more applications that manage text more as information than a printed page. Even the names of the information elements have changed to reflect more of what the information is rather than what it looks like.

Often, textual information has language at the end of each division that serves as a segue to the next division making it difficult to break a "book" into independent information objects. Also, many text passages make sense only when in the context of other sections at the same level or higher levels in the document hierarchy and are not written in a form complete enough to allow the individual passages to be used as independent information objects. As we learn more what information databases can do for us, we will need to adjust the way we prepare out textual information and even go back and rewrite portions of existing text to allow it to be used to its fullest potential. (A more thorough discussion on textual databases appears in Chapter 9, *SGML Data Management and Workflow* on page 183.

Formatting and Structure

There are three basic approaches to defining a document:

1. Format
2. Structure
3. Content

A successful structural definition will be a balance of these three approaches. Using any one to the exception of the others may or may not work, but the document analyst should be aware of the various tools before embarking on the document definition.

FORMAT TAGGING

Format tagging is the process of creating markup that is based on the style or appearance of an element. This is necessary to describe some elements, because of their inherent link to format. Highlighted text is an example of format tagging. An author might want to make a word bold in order to make a point in the text.

Another format-oriented element is the page-break tag. This element may be necessary in loose-leaf publishing systems where page boundaries are required in order to print just the pages that have changed.

Tables are, by their nature, very format-intensive. Tables provide an efficient means to display certain types of information, but the representation is largely format-driven. It is also possible to define the data in a table using a content-oriented approach, but more analysis is needed to define each table. Almost every DTD we have seen contains a general-purpose format-oriented table structure.

Examples of format tags:

```
<head1 q='left' w='bold'>This is a heading that is quad left and
bold
<p in='1em' type='bold'>This is an indented paragraph
The author wants to <emphasis/emphasize/ this word.
```

The danger of relying too heavily on a format tagging approach is that the tagged data is less usable for alternative products. Format tagging indicates the element's look, not its identity or function. It relies on verbs describing the processes to be performed, not nouns naming the information object itself. By not separating the appearance of the element from its purpose, it may be more difficult to use the information for purposes that do not rely on format such as search and retrieval applications that use context. For example, if both a heading and a figure caption use the same format tagging element, then a query could not be made that searches for a value only in headings and not figure captions.

STRUCTURE TAGGING

Structure tagging is based on generic hierarchy. Elements are defined by their hierarchical name, rather than relying on the hierarchical nature of the SGML model to determine the structure.

Structure tagging is useful when handling many different types of hierarchical data. By defining elements in terms of their structural positions, fewer tags are required than by explicitly identifying them by their content.

Examples of structure tags:

```
<head1>This is a First Level Head
<head2>This is a Second Level Head
<para0>This is a high-level paragraph
<list1>This is a first-level indented list item
<list2>This is a second-level indented list item
```

Structure tagging tends to be too generalized to support some content-specific processes. Many things that occur at the same level and have the same appearance may, if identified with only one tag, not be differentiated. If they cannot be differentiated, different processes cannot be applied to the two different elements as needed.

For instance, if you produce training manuals and you require each to have a statement of objectives at the beginning of each lesson, you would be limited in a structural tagging approach. The division of the lesson labeled "Statement of Objectives" would most likely have the <head2> tag, as would other elements at that level of the hierarchy. When trying to enforce rules about what the lesson needed, the only way you could differentiate these headings is to interrogate their contents to see if they contain the phrase "Statement of Objectives". If your authors are inconsistent in their wording, you may have difficulty performing this validation.

CONTENT TAGGING

Content tagging is at the heart of generalized markup. By identifying elements according their content and purpose, rather than their looks or their hierarchical position, maximum flexibility can be achieved in an application.

When defining content tagging coding, you will give different names and rules to elements that typographically look identical.

Examples of content tags:

```
<lesson>How to peel an egg
<intro>In this lesson, we will present the best ways to peel
two kinds of eggs.
<intro>
<obj>Successfully peel a hard-boiled egg</obj>
<obj>Successfully peel a raw egg</obj>
```

It is easy to get carried away with content tagging, however, since there are many elements that could be found to be unique, even though a process might never need to differentiate. Some information models that were excessive in the use of content tagging techniques proved to be unmanageable and expensive to support in developing the programs that will eventually process the data.

Even so, an argument can be made for applying some content tagging to a document model designed for a specific class of documents. We offer the following examples of content tagging that might prove useful for the specific classes under which they are grouped.

Technical Manual:		**Training Manual:**		**Periodicals:**	
<part>	**Part Number**	<les>	**Lesson**	<au>	**Author**
<mod>	**Model**	<obj>	**Objectives**	<hl>	**Headline**
<chkl>	**Checklist**	<ex>	**Exercise**	<en>	**End Note**
<cau>	**Caution**	<def>	**Definition**	<blurb>	**Blurb**
Computer Manuals:		**General**		**Legal:**	
<command>	**Command**	<fw>	**Foreign Word**	<case>	**Case Cite**
<opt>	**Option**	<name>	**Name**	<reg>	**Reg Cite**
<parm>	**Parameter**	<gl>	**Glossary Word**	<code>	**Code Cite**
<key>	**Keystroke**	<xref>	**Cross Reference**	<squib>	**Squib**

Figure 38. *Content tagging examples*

SGML allows you to develop your own tag names. The ones listed above only serve to show the flexible naming approach provided by content tagging.

BALANCED APPROACH

It is usually easy to identify the first DTD someone has written, and what their background is. People who come from a typesetting background tend to create format-oriented DTDs because of their familiarity with type on paper. People with an editorial background tend to think in terms of structure: chapters contain sub-chapters, which contain sections and sub-sections. Systems people tend to think in terms of content, since they look at the documents as a collection of named objects that are put together and processed, similar to database fields.

We have seen extreme examples of each type of tagging approach. One case of "content-overdose" was a DTD delivered to a government contractor. First some background. A DTD can vary greatly in the number of elements it contains. If we were to pick a typical DTD it would probably contain between 50 and 200 elements, in our experience. This is not to say that there cannot be excellent DTDs that have more than that number, or that any DTD that contains less than that number can solve a particular problem. It is just rare to see a DTD with more than 200 elements (with the exception of industry initiative DTDs).

The DTD in this case was a combination of content tagging and format-tagging. Every element was given its own name, even though it would probably never be necessary to differentiate them in processing. There were a dozen elements for paragraphs, that were named according to their formatting (flush paragraph, indented paragraph, flush paragraph with 1 em top spacing, indented paragraph with 2em top spacing, etc.). The result of this combination of tagging approaches was a DTD with over 700 elements. This kind of DTD, while perfectly valid, may cause processing problems, and will certainly cost more to develop applications. An experienced analyst spent an hour with the DTD and reduced it to less than 300 elements without adversely affecting the structure.

There is usually more than one way to achieve a certain goal. Deciding which approach to take when defining a structural element depends upon several factors:

1. System performance
2. System limitations
3. Degree of automation to be achieved
4. Usability and understandability for the user
5. Reusability of text in alternative versions and by-products
6. Longevity of the data

These are described in more detail in the following section.

Usability and Understandability

A content-oriented approach to tagging might confuse the user, especially in the case where two elements have similar names. For example, a user might not be able to differentiate between a part number and a model number. In this case, training and computer-assisted help can make the job easier for the user.

REUSABILITY AND BY-PRODUCTS

The more intelligent the data is, the more re-usable it is. If a document is defined as consisting of just titles and paragraphs, it has enough information to create a simple hard-copy document or HTML, it is difficult to create, say, a book containing abstracts of articles in all books, or an index of all legal citations used within a book unless they have been explicitly tagged using a content-oriented tagging approach.

LONGEVITY OF DATA

If the data is expected to outlast the processing system, care must be taken to capture information that might be required by its successor. For example, if a book is printed now, there might not be any need to create links from the book into external books. But if an electronic version is desired, those links will certainly be helpful. When you spend time adding the extra detail is dictated by your business objectives and the schedule for implementing the electronic product.

Each of these factors represents a trade-off. Limiting the number of elements might improve system response time at the expense of maintaining a rich information set, which will lead to limited by-product possibilities, and vice versa.

COMMON ELEMENTS

There are certain "basic document elements [1]" that most documents share. Our experience has lead us to develop certain methodologies for dealing with common constructs. Techniques used in modular programming for separating common modules and specific modules can be used in DTD development (See *Common Elements* on page 288 for more information).

A discussion on some of these elements (tables, equations, quotes, footnotes, graphics, and indexing) can be found in *Common Elements* on page 288.

System Issues

PERFORMANCE

If there are a large number of elements in a DTDat a particular level, a system can experience sluggish performance while it loads everything into memory. Fewer tags might help, but at a loss of detailed definition.

1 Bill Davis, the chairman of the X3V1 committee that developed SGML, has a theory that there are a finite number of "basic document elements" that all documents consist of. Different people may call them different things, but they are basically similar and could be managed using the concept of architectural forms defined in HyTime (ISO 10744).

SYSTEM LIMITATIONS

Some systems have a limit to the number of elements that can be open at any time. With these systems, a structured approach generally works better than a content approach, because there are fewer elements and the model is flatter. For example, when considering which editorial software and DBMS application to use, you should determine how many levels of structure can be opened and managed at once without adverse affects on performance or reaching system limitations. Your DTD should not contain more levels of structure than needed.

DEGREE OF AUTOMATION

A flat data model more closely mimics the word-processor or typesetter paradigm than a hierarchical model. If the SGML data is being used to create typesetter output in an automated production situation, or if a word processor is being used as an editor and an automated translation into SGML is required, a flat, format-oriented data model is easier to map to these forms. However, the value of the data is diminished compared to text prepared in an environment that can handle structure. For example, some composition systems use the concept of inheritance when determining formatting attributes for text such as indents, leading, keeps, and automatic numbering. You may be able to avoid making the user enter values or tags to accomplish what the composition system is able to determine from context. In this situation your DTD can be made simpler in some respects and also utilize hierarchical structure.

Defining a Markup Language — The Recipe

In real life it is hard to separate document analysis and DTD writing since it is an iterative process. It is a bit like the chicken and egg dilemma you need to know a little about one to do the other. It quickly became clear when designing this exercise that in order to make a useful exercise, at least some knowledge of DTDs would be useful to the reader. We hope you will read this exercise now, and return to it later when you complete Chapter 10, *Understanding SGML* on page 215.

Below is a sample recipe taken from a major cookbook. It is a real example of information we use everyday. If you have ever tried to cook from a book before you should be able to identify some of the information elements that make up a recipe.

CREAM OF CHICKEN SOUP

About 4 1/2 Cups
4 servings: approximately 300 calories each

Simmer:
3 cups *Poultry Stock*, 523
1/2 cup finely chopped celery
When the celery is tender, add and cook 5 minutes:
1/2 cup boiled rice, 206
Add:
1/2 cup hot cream
1 tablespoon chopped parsley
salt and paprika
→ Do not boil the soup after adding the cream. For a fresh approach, see *Cream of Watercress Soup II*, 186.

Figure 39. *Recipe example as it appears in the printed book*

By suggesting that we use only one recipe in our attempt to create a set of rules for all recipes, we are breaking the first rule of document analysis. You will obviously need to gather as many samples of documents as you can from the class of documents your are analyzing in order to create an effective model.

Without looking ahead, try to identify as many information elements in this recipe as you can. Think of what it will take to write and compose the information, store it in a database, gather and collect many recipes and create a cookbook. You might even want to photocopy this recipe and write sample tags on the copy to keep track of what you find. When you are finished please continue reading.

ELEMENTS IN A RECIPE

At first glance it is easy to find the recipe name, some flush right paragraphs that describe serving information, some flush left paragraphs that contain instructions, lists of ingredients, and even some cross-references and a note paragraph that has a little arrow in front of it. Also, note the alignment of the ingredients and the measure of each.

A format tagging approach to creating this model we might have identified the following elements:

Element	*Description*
<head1>	for the bold head
<p1>	for the flush right paragraphs
<p2>	for the flush left, indented paragraphs
<p3>	for the list items
<p4>	for the flush left block paragraph (using arrow character)
<pr>	for the number in the <p3> which is aligned flush right
<pl>	for the rest of the list item that is aligned flush left
<it>	italicized phrases

Table 3. *Elements in a recipe — Format-tagging*

These tags would suffice if all you wanted to do was typeset a book if provisions were made for some of the special characters appearing in the text (the fractions, the arrow). But they do not provide any information if you need to enforce rules about the serving information being required, or if you want to create a CD-ROM product that is searchable on titles of recipes, but not on other titles that occur in text.

A structured tagging approach might utilize the following tags:

Element	*Description*
<rechead>	for the recipe name (bold head)
<subhead>	for the serving information (flush right)
<para>	for the instruction paragraphs (flush left, indented)
<list>	to indicate the start of a list (start indent)
<item>	for the ingredients list items (indented paragraphs)
<itemnum>	for the measurement (flushed right)
<itemterm>	for the rest of the item (flushed left)
</list>	to end the list (end indent)
<notepara>	to have system always add arrow
<emphasis>	for emphasized phrases (italic)

Table 4. *Elements in a recipe — Structure tagging*

This combination of structure and content tagging indicates that there is a hierarchy here. You can build rules into the model to enforce this hierarchy and make certain information required, such as the <rechead>. The rule might be stated in plain language as:

"A recipe consists of a required recipe heading, followed by one or more required subheads, followed by one or more textual paragraphs or note paragraphs. Paragraphs may contain characters or lists. Lists must contain one or more list items. Headings, subheadings, and list items may contain characters or emphasis. Emphasis may contain characters."

Or, you could use the shorthand notation described earlier to express these rules:

```
recipe = (rechead, subhead+, (para |notepara)+)
para = (characters | list)+
list = (item+)
rechead | subhead | item = (characters | emphasis)
emphasis = (characters)
```

An approach that utilizes content tagging to a greater degree might consist of the following tags:

Element	*Description*
<recipe>	to contain entire recipe (set context)
<name>	for bold name
<about>	for estimated quantity produced by recipe
<servings>	for estimated servings/calories
<instruct>	for paragraphs that give instructions
<ingred>	for ingredients listing (containing element)
<qty>	for quantity of ingredient (*e.g.*, "3")
<m>	for measure of ingredient (*e.g.*, "cups")
<i>	for ingredient name (*e.g.*, "Poultry Stock")
<crossref>	for cross-references to other recipes, pages etc.
<note>	for paragraphs with arrow generated

Table 5. *Elements in a recipe — Content tagging*

Now, with these content tags you could build an application that allows a user to search for recipes that contain the ingredient "poultry stock" and make at least four servings. The application might also take over generating the page numbers by using the cross reference to find out what page the referenced information is on. In order to make it easy for a cross reference program to automatically track to where the-references are made you might need to trap the name of the referenced recipe in an attribute as follows:

```
<crossref recipe='pltrystk'>
```

or using some other unambiguous naming convention.

You can see how much more powerful information capture in a content tagging approach can be, and how much more overhead there is. Even in this simple example there are far more tags.

Using these content tags, a sample marked-up page might look like this:

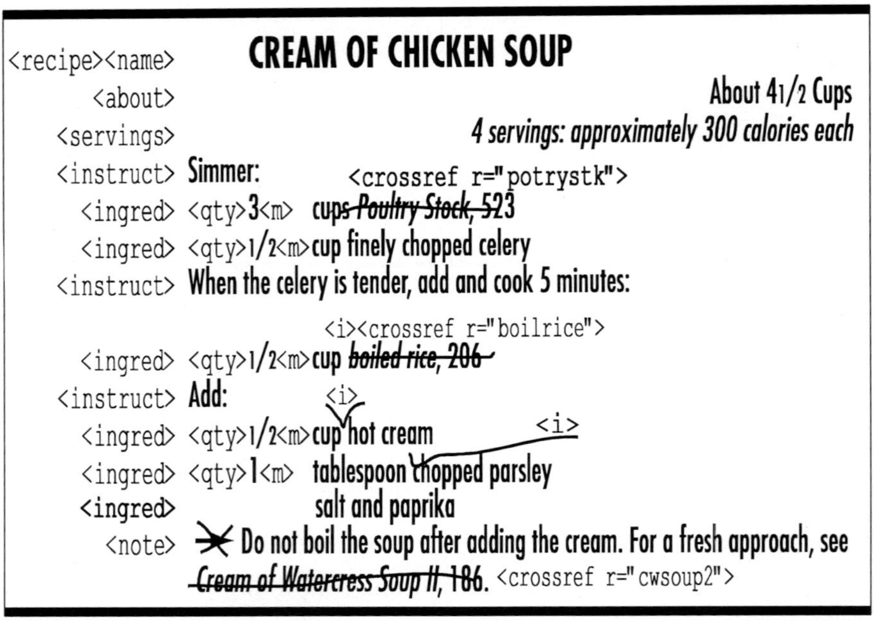
<recipe><name> CREAM OF CHICKEN SOUP
<about> About 41/2 Cups
<servings> 4 servings: approximately 300 calories each
<instruct> Simmer: <crossref r="potrystk">
<ingred> <qty>3<m> cups ~~Poultry Stock, 523~~
<ingred> <qty>1/2<m>cup finely chopped celery
<instruct> When the celery is tender, add and cook 5 minutes:
<i><crossref r="boilrice">
<ingred> <qty>1/2<m>cup ~~boiled rice, 206~~
<instruct> Add: <i>
<ingred> <qty>1/2<m>cup hot cream <i>
<ingred> <qty>1<m> tablespoon chopped parsley
<ingred> salt and paprika
<note> Do not boil the soup after adding the cream. For a fresh approach, see ~~Cream of Watercress Soup II, 186~~. <crossref r="cwsoup2">

Figure 40. *Recipe sample, marked-up using content-oriented tagging*

In the sample marked-up page above, bold lines represent someone having crossed out material that will not be characters in the text file, but rather will be generated by the application. Also, bold lines represent pointers to where some tags should be inserted to create the file below. A final unformatted, tagged document instance might look like this (The DTD atop will make more sense after you have completed Chapter 10, *Understanding SGML* on page 215. We show it here for your reference.):

```
<!DOCTYPE cookbook [
<!ENTITY    onehalf     '1/2'                        >
<!ELEMENT cookbook    O O          (recipe+)         >
```

```
<!ELEMENT recipe      - O        (name, about, servings,
                                 (instruct | note)+)
                                          +(crossref) >
<!ATTLIST recipe      id         ID              #REQUIRED>
<!ELEMENT name        O O        (#PCDATA)                >
<!ELEMENT about       - O        (#PCDATA)                >
<!ELEMENT servings    - O        (#PCDATA)                >
<!ELEMENT instruct    - O        (#PCDATA | ingred)+      >
<!ELEMENT ingred      - O        (qty?, m?, i)            >
<!ELEMENT note        - O        (#PCDATA)                >
<!ELEMENT (m | i | qty)
                      - O        (#PCDATA)                >
<!ELEMENT crossref    - O        EMPTY                    >
<!ATTLIST crossref    r          NAME            #REQUIRED>
]>
<recipe id='ccsoup'>Cream of Chicken Soup
<about>About 4 Cups
<servings>4 servings: approximately 300 calories each
<instruct>Simmer:
<ingred>
<qty>3
<m>cups
<i>
<crossref r='pltrystk'>
<ingred>
<qty>&onehalf;
<m>cup
<i>finely chopped celery
<instruct>When the celery is tender, add and cook 5 minutes:
<ingred>
<qty>&onehalf;
<m>cup
<i>
<crossref r='boilrice'>
<instruct>Add:
<ingred>
<qty>&onehalf;
<m>cup
<i>hot cream
<ingred>
<qty>1
<m>cup
<i>salt and paprika
```

```
<note>Do not boil the soup after adding the cream. For a fresh
approach, see
<crossref r='cwsoup2'>.
</recipe>
```

There are several things you might notice in the sample SGML marked-up file above. If you haven't read Chapter 10, *Understanding SGML* on page 215, you might not know what some of the markup used in this example means. For instance, the "one-half" symbol as shown does not appear on a regular ASCII keyboard. A way of defining special characters exists in SGML called General Entity References (See *General Entities* on page 250). A General Entity Reference, such as the `&onehalf;`, can be keyed in by the user or entered by the editing software to generate the one-half symbol when rendered by the typesetter.

This example contains SGML data that is much more versatile than simply being usable for typesetting. You could build an application that looked up the page number of the cross-references and inserted it an the recipe name in the output stream. You could, in an electronic version of this cookbook, allow users to increase the number of servings desired and have the quantities of ingredients automatically calculated. You could even have a nutrition database integrated into your electronic product, and if milk was substituted for the cream, have the calories automatically calculated.

```
<!DOCTYPE recipes [
<!ENTITY     onehalf      '1/2'                                     >
<!ELEMENT recipes      O O          (recipe+)                       >
<!ELEMENT recipe       - O          (name, about,
                                    (instruct | note)+)
                                                        +(crossref) >
<!ATTLIST recipe       id           ID                  #REQUIRED>
<!ELEMENT name         O O          (#PCDATA)                       >
<!ELEMENT about        - O          EMPTY                           >
<!ATTLIST about        serv         NUMBER              #REQUIRED
                       number       NUMBER              #REQUIRED
                       m            CDATA               #IMPLIED
                       calsper      NUMBER              #REQUIRED>
<!ELEMENT instruct     - O          (#PCDATA | ingred)+             >
<!ELEMENT ingred       - O          (#PCDATA)                       >
<!ATTLIST ingred       qty          CDATA               #IMPLIED
                       m            CDATA               #IMPLIED
                       i            NAME                #REQUIRED>
<!ELEMENT note         - O          (#PCDATA)                       >
<!ELEMENT crossref     - O          EMPTY                           >
<!ATTLIST crossref     r            NAME                #REQUIRED>
]>
```

```
<recipe id='ccsoup'>Cream of Chicken Soup
<about serv='4' m='c' number='4' calsper='75'>
<instruct>Simmer:
<ingred qty='3' m='c' i='pltrystk'>
<crossref r='pltrystk'>
<ingred qty='.5' m='c' i='chpcel'>finely chopped celery
<instruct>When the celery is tender, add and cook 5 minutes:
<ingred qty='.5' m='c' i='boilrice'>
<crossref r='boilrice'>
<instruct>Add:
<ingred qty='.5' m='c' i='cream'>hot cream
<ingred i='spice'>salt and paprika
<note>Do not boil the soup after adding the cream. For a fresh
approach, see
<crossref r='cwsoup2'>.
</recipe>
```

This example serves to show how detail may enhance the value of the data and improve the flexibility of data in order that it may be designed to be used in applications not limited to rendering for print.

CHAPTER • SIX

The SGML Application

Introduction

An SGML application is where the real work gets done in an SGML system. In order to build an application, your organization must be willing to support the development, implementation, and delivery of the application and the tools that comprise it.

In this chapter we will discuss the application itself, and give some idea of what it takes for an organization to build, implement, and maintain an SGML application.

Related Topics

- *The Problem with Unstructured Information* on page 4

- *The Power of SGML Databases* on page 11
- Chapter 2, *Evolution of Publishing Systems* on page 23
- *Integrated Publishing Systems* on page 33
- *Federated Publishing Systems* on page 34
- Chapter 3, *Desktop Publishing and Professional Publishing Systems* on page 37
- Chapter 4, *The SGML Environment* on page 43
- *System Issues* on page 91
- *System Evaluation and Design* on page 122
- *System Development* on page 139
- Chapter 9, *SGML Data Management and Workflow* on page 183
- *Ongoing Production Feeds* on page 172
- *Generation/Extraction* on page 174
- *Workflow* on page 205
- Appendix 8, *SGML Resources* on page 445

The Application Defined

The standard defines "application" as "text processing application[1]", and "text processing application" as "A related set of processes performed on documents of related types[2]".

So, an application is something that processes SGML documents. In order to process an SGML document, the application must have a parser. We have been saying throughout this book that SGML is a way of storing information, not necessarily just documents, which are merely an instantiation of a particular set of information. We have also been talking about more than just text; we have shown techniques for accessing non-character data and including graphics, sounds, and information from external data sources. Now, the standard tells us that an application deals with text, performing processes on documents. What gives?

Text in this case is not necessarily words that an author writes, and documents are not necessarily paper products that are bound along a spine. Instead, a document is any object that has a purpose to communicate information between people, and text is the medium—be it words, pictures, sounds, or smells—that make up the document. Using these definitions, the standard's definition of text and document are consistent with what we have been saying in this book.

1 ISO 8879:1986 4.5

2 ISO 8879:1986 4.318

This chapter is designed to provide an overview of what an SGML application is, and some guidelines for developing, purchasing, installing, and using such applications.

SGML applications fall into four general categories:

1. Capture,
2. Creation,
3. Output, and
4. Database

An SGML system will probably have at least one application for each of these functions, and probably several for each one. In addition to the applications, a certain amount of system-integration "glue" must be created in order to create a workable system.

The Application Development Team

Like any system-development project, an SGML application requires a team consisting of people who specialize in certain areas. Each person has a particular role in the analysis and planning phases.

OWNER

There is usually an owner of the SGML system. That owner might be an officer, a committee, or one of the workers in a department. The owner is usually someone who has a good overview of the entire system, and can see what is necessary at each step in the process. This person might not be a team leader, but could be the "SGML Evangelist" described in *The Evangelist* on page 67, or the manager of the user organization. The owner acts as the customer and must be satisfied ultimately that the system meets performance requirements.

MANAGERS

Managers are responsible for maintaining control of the project and assuring success. The best use we have found for managers is to provide support for the analysts and programmers and protect them from the rest of the organization. That might mean making sure there is enough money in the budget to do what is necessary.

The manager should make available resources necessary to complete each task. Resources are people, systems, and money. Without commitment from each one of these, the project is doomed from the start.

This is not to say that managers should give the development people *carte blanche* to do whatever they want. The project should be defined well enough to give the people who are responsible for supporting the funding and resources a feeling that the project is worthwhile. The manager must direct the team to keep them focused on the objectives of the project. By protecting the development staff from the organization, we mean that there is a tendency to dwell on daily and weekly achievements and change the scope of the project before real progress is made. It is the manager's responsibility to "sell" the project in the organization, and to manage expectations of the directors, leaving the development people to develop.

ANALYSTS

The application development process begins with a commitment to evaluate SGML in the organization. This is mostly the job of the analyst, who might draw upon the collective knowledge and requirements of the rest of the organization that is affected.

An analyst is usually assigned to each project. There may be several analysts involved in the project at-large, all reporting to a manager in charge of the system. An analyst's necessary skill set is dependent upon the area of the project that is managed. The analyst is the technical head of the project. The analyst may or may not have supervisory responsibilities, but should be given access to programmers, users, other analysts, and who ever else might be helpful in the systems analysis.

The implementation task revolves around the analyst, who provides the vision of what needs to be done. Usually, the analyst is given the task to evaluate whether the organization can benefit from SGML. See Chapter 7, *Implementation Planning* on page 121 for more information about planning the implementation and performing analysis.

There are two basic kinds of analysts in an SGML implementation: Documentation Analysts and Systems Analysts. The documentation analyst should understand the concepts of SGML detailed in this book, as well as the current documentation systems. The Systems Analyst should have a strong knowledge of the corporate computer systems, and have some idea about the documentation process.

They should also understand their corporate structure, both from an organizational standpoint as well as a technical standpoint. They should know the computer systems, networking, workstations, software, training resources, organizational structure (both formal and informal), and any other information that might help them recommend and install a system.

The Document Analyst and Systems Analyst could be the same person.

PROGRAMMERS

Programmers should have an understanding of basic system processes, especially the ones that are unique to the in-house systems. There are some special languages that make SGML programming easier. There are parsers that contain hooks (APIs) so external systems can control the operation of the parser for the purpose of customization and integration into the corporate systems environment.

Programmers should be comfortable with the technical concepts of SGML, since the tools they will be using will employ SGML concepts. Programmers should also be comfortable with integration with external and internal systems, since a typical SGML implementation relies heavily on existing data and systems.

Programmers should be involved in the technical design phase of the implementation. It is conceivable that a system could be designed that is not possible to implement, because of existing system constraints like speed, storage, or access, or because of a lack of expertise required to carry out the plan. Involving programmers is important in order to assure a system that is implementable.

USERS

Users should be involved at all phases: design, development, testing, implementation, and, of course, training. Users who are involved have ownership in the process, and are much more likely to identify issues and work with the development team to solve problems before they get out of hand.

Don't discount the role of users when installing an SGML system. User involvement is necessary, as in any system installation, because of their proximity to the final product. If the users don't have strong buy-in, the project could be doomed to failure. This is particularly true in an SGML environment because of the competition of unstructured "documentation solutions" like word processors and page-makeup programs. SGML is sometimes a hard sell if it means competing with the ease-of-use and freedom from structure that these products promote. Users must be able to see the benefits of SGML from their standpoint, because their jobs will change and there is a natural human aversion to change.

Application Considerations

The SGML application can take many forms, from a simple validating parser executed from the command-line, to a full-blown menu-driven desktop that allows workflow and automated data flow throughout the system. We have seen these extreme applications, as well as everything in-between. One result of the analysis process will be to determine where on the continuum your SGML project will be.

For the rest of this chapter, we will discuss various applications, and the implementation factors involved with each type. All products mentioned can be found in Appendix 8, *SGML Resources* on page 445.

CAPTURE

Capture is the process of getting your data from some other form into SGML. You probably have mounds of data in some other form that you need to get tagged and loaded into the SGML database. If you decide to create the applications yourself instead of hiring a conversion service, there are some things to consider.

Conversion

Getting data into SGML is usually called conversion or auto-tagging. Conversion is the process of reading sequential files and creating SGML input. Auto-tagging, in particular, is the process of "viewing" a page of data and recognizing the elements thereon. There is not a clear consensus about the differentiation between these words, but we will use the term "conversion" to mean the broader category that includes auto-tagging.

Although the resulting file must be parsed with a validating parser, any non-SGML text conversion utility can be used to write applications to convert the data. These include AWK, lex/flex, SNOBOL, perl, and even grep for rudimentary conversions.

When dealing with these conversion utilities, it is important to maintain SGML compliance by parsing with a validating parser after each step. Some of these products have an SGML parser included, and so can provide the necessary parsing capabilities as part of the process. Most sites that have made a commitment to SGML will spend the money to purchase a supported product that has the SGML capabilities that are needed to perform the conversion function.

Our favorites are OmniMark and Balise, because they ARE both general-purpose programming languages that are SGML-aware and can be used in both the conversion environment and the output environment, where the SGML files are used to create formatted output. See Chapter 8, *Information Conversion* on page 151 for more information on conversion tools and strategies.

EDITORIAL WORKSTATIONS

Most SGML implementation will employ some sort of SGML editorial workstation for the authors or editors of the documents in the SGML database. In keeping with the "building-block" approach to creating an SGML environment, most of these tools have a high degree of customization capability. This is good from the system standpoint, because they can be integrated into most any environment.

Like any other product, there is no perfect editorial workstation. Each type of tool has its benefits and liabilities. The requirements for a technical writer are different than those of a production keying clerk. We have identified three basic categories of Editorial Workstations. These categories are not exact, as there are some products share have properties of more than one category. The categories are:

1. SGML-Smart Editors,
2. Non-SGML Structured Editors, and
3. SGML-Smart Extensions.

Because of the open nature of SGML, products that fall into these categories can be integrated into a single SGML implementation. There are some things to be considered when implementing each particular type of editorial workstation. Refer to Appendix 8, *SGML Resources* on page 445 for particular products that are available in each category.

SGML-Smart Editors

SGML-smart formatting editors provide assistance to the user during editing. These are popular because they provide certain benefits to the implementing organization:

1. provide a pleasing interface that shields the user from the markup
2. enforce the rules of structure
3. require minimial training to implement
4. provide a launching point for the entire editorial process.

In addition, SGML-smart editors provide integration to workflow and database tools. These tools have the ability to validate a document instance against arbitrary DTDs.

Usually an organization will put SGML-smart editors workstations on the desks of authors and editors, but will not provide clerical production personnel with such products. There are several reasons for this:

1. they are expensive compared to non-SGML text editors,
2. they are usually graphical in nature and require much interaction with a mouse, which can lead to a lack of productivity in a production environment,
3. production people usually process large quantities of similar material, while authors and editors need to concentrate on the creation process and can be helped by the intelligent workstation tools.

Since this is where most of the people in the organization interact with SGML, it is important to commit the resources required to implement this piece of the system. Pay close attention to the implementation pointers listed in *Vendor-Supplied Applications* on page 117.

Non-SGML Structured Editors

Structured editors are tools that are used to create documents that have structure, but do not enforce SGML rules. A word processor, while capable of creating a document with styles, does not enforce rules concerning structure, so is not considered a structured editor. Using structured editors (like FrameMaker+SGML or Interleaf) or unstructured word processors (like Microsoft Word or WordPerfect) in an SGML environment raises some issues of integration and the ability to ensure adherence to the structure enforced by an SGML DTD. To assure adherence to the DTDs, a post-editing validation step should be performed after editing. In this process, the data is checked and perhaps manually cleansed before it can pass to the next process, such as a database load. This delay is avoidable if SGML-smart structured editors are used.

THE HOLY GRAIL. There is a strong desire to get the benefits of SGML without sacrificing the ease-of-use and comfort level users have with graphical word processors. We have been asked many times for a system that would allow users to keep using their word processors and page-makeup programs, but be able to load the files into an SGML database for the purpose of creating by-product applications and generally getting control of their data. In short, they want a two-way, production-oriented conversion facility. We call this the Holy Gail because, if it does exist, no mortal has yet seen it.

The problem is impedance mismatch. This is a term used in the electronics industry to indicate that two components have dissimilar properties, and that it is necessary to provide some kind of bridge between them. In electronics, like in conversion, this bridge makes the connection, but for a price.

A word processor file is flat in structure. Even if it contains style sheets, and if each element is assigned a style according to its name, it is still a flat object. SGML files, in the other hand, have the ability to define a document in terms of its hierarchical structure. It is easy to "flatten" a hierarchical structure, like is easy to photograph a building, because the process strips information on its way down.

On the other hand, creating structure where it does not exist is more difficult. While it is possible to build a building based on a photograph, there is much information that must be inferred to do so. You must interrogate the picture, determine how the original building was constructed, and make assumptions about those things you can't see. This is the process of inferring new information by querying the existing information. However, it might be impossible to put the whole building together because some information might have been irretrievably lost.

Conversion between a flat information structure and a hierarchical one is similar. Take the case of a part number and a department code. These two numbers look similar in our organization. In the word processor, both should be set in an italic font. It is easy to take a part number element and generate the word-processor code to render it in italic. It is just as easy to render the department code in italic. However, when the document is translated back to SGML, the word-processor conversion tool will find a block of text that is italicized and not know whether it is a part number or a department code. Word processor style sheets could be used to give the conversion program some hints as to what each structural piece is. This is a popular way of doing conversion, but it is not foolproof, since style sheets cannot capture all of the attribute information usually necessary by the application.

Another problem with converting from a word-processor format to an SGML-tagged form is the absence of validation in the word processor. Let's say that a chapter consists of a mandatory title, followed by a mandatory abstract, followed by one or more paragraphs. An SGML editorial workstation, through the use of an internal SGML parser, will assure that the required elements are entered by the user, and will not allow a document to be created that violates the rules. If the user is writing this document on a word processor for automatic conversion to an SGML database, the user could create ten chapters that do not have an abstract, or have it in the wrong place. The conversion utility that reads that file will not find the required elements and issue an error. The problem is that the author is no where to be found; he finished his work and handed it to the conversion person or process weeks ago. The problem needs to be corrected, and the author will probably need to get involved again, an expansive and time-consuming task.

If a program could validate the information as the author wrote, it could have indicated the error at authoring time, when the author could have corrected it easily.

It is possible to create an SGML structure that is flat, mimicking the word-processor format. This would allow for machine conversions back and forth. There is, in fact a DTD written for such a situation. It is called Rainbow, and is available in the public domain. There are programs, also in the public domain, that convert word-processor input into the Rainbow structure. These are called Rainbow Makers and are available for most word processor and page-makeup programs (Microsoft Word, WordPerfect, Frame Technology Corp. FrameMaker, Interleaf, etc.).

The problem with this approach is that you do not have any more intelligence in the SGML file than you had in the word-processor file. If this is the only motivation, SGML is not the answer. The developers of Rainbow acknowledge the fact that their format is flat, and that it is not "real" SGML, but they see a situation where Rainbow becomes a common, intermediate, form for conversion from word-processing format to a more intelligent SGML structure. In fact, there are products available that will aid in the conversion from Rainbow form to your SGML DTD. See Appendix 8, *SGML Resources* on page 445 and *Conversions Using the Rainbow DTD* on page 167 for more information on the Rainbow DTD.

SGML-Smart Enhancements

Several companies have introduced products that are designed to allow an implementing organization to keep their beloved non-SGML editorial workstations, while giving the benefit of SGML. These products attempt to "find the holy grail" by adding structure to a flat-data product.

There are at least three products that use Microsoft Word as an editorial platform, and two that use WordPerfect. Other word processor and page-makeup vendors are working on products, as well.

Implementation Factors

The main implementation factor with these tools is their applicability to the task of creating and maintaining SGML documents. All tools should have the features required to validate documents to your DTDs. A product that does not deal with attributes, for example, might require re-writing of your DTDs.

For non-SGML-smart structured editors, you will need to assure that files created or edited are parsed with a validating parser before they go into your data repository. This is easily done using shell scripts or batch programs. After editing, the script should parse the document and report errors back to the user. By keeping validation close to the author, changes can be made quickly and efficiently.

Such validation is not usually necessary with an SGML-smart editorial workstation or SGML-smart enhancement. However, it is always a good idea to make sure the document is valid. Most SGML-smart editorial tools have the ability to parse the document before saving. One calls this function "Validate Document", another calls it "Check Completeness".

Some SGML-smart editorial workstations save documents in a binary form for fast saving and loading. This binary form is not SGML, and, as such, is useable only by the owning tool. To get SGML data into such a tool, there is usually an "import" function. Likewise, to create an SGML file useable by other tools, an "export" function is usually provided. This trade-off between efficiency and open standards is a difficult one to make for a tool vendor. Fortunately, most vendors of editorial workstation products make available toolkits that provide a way to customize the application to suit your needs.

These toolkits, also called an application program interface (API), allow the implementor to integrate the functionality of other tools into the editor. For example, when the user selects Print from the File menu, the editor could be directed to validate the file to the DTD, translate it from the proprietary format to SGML, then pass the valid SGML to a typesetting program to get fully composed proof pages. Another common function is to disable the Save function, and have the file be exported to SGML each time it is saved.

These API toolkits are quite versatile, and can ease the burden of implementing different types of editorial workstations into a cohesive system.

SGML Browsers

In order to deliver SGML information, some kind of electronic delivery mechanism is needed. This can be a simple as a file browser, or as highly evolved as an SGML document browser. SGML browsers have been around almost as long as SGML has been, since the need to deliver in electronic form is one of the reasons companies move to SGML. SoftQuad's Explorer and Electronic Book Technologies, Inc.' DynaText are examples of products in this category.

In considering these products, you should be aware of their ability to be integrated into the environment of the user, which is not necessarily the environment where the SGML data resides.

Databases

In implementing an SGML database, the most important factor is to determine the level of granularity. That is, which objects should be tracked and managed as a single piece. Sometimes this is a chapter or section, but it could be as large as the entire book or as small as every element or word.

Granularity and other database implementation factors are discussed in detail in *Database Implementation Factors* on page 202.

COMPOSITION ENGINES

Some composition engines can read an SGML file directly and create quality output. In considering these products, you should find out how much work it is to create applications that can read a particular DTD, and what limitations there are on what the formatter can render. Frame Technology Corp. DL Composer and ArborText Adept•Publisher both contain SGML-smart composition engines that are controlled by a FOSI[1] and read native SGML-encoded data (See *FOSIs* on page 141 and *FOSI hints* on page 350 for more information on FOSIs).

TRANSLATION TO NON-SGML APPLICATIONS

In addition to the products that support SGML natively, there are many good products that can be used in an SGML environment by using the appropriate tools. Products in this latter category require the use of some kind of SGML front-end to create the structure they need.

This book for example, was authored as SGML files. An SGML-smart conversion program, OmniMark, created Ventura tagged-text files, which were imported into Corel Ventura Publisher for printing. See the world's longest colophon, Appendix 4, *Colophon: How this Book was Produced* on page 401, for more details.

PUBLICATION-SPECIFIC DEVELOPMENT

There are many reasons a company implements SGML. Probably the most important reason is that an SGML system provides the ability to create more than one output form from the SGML database. Things like printed products, CD-ROM, on-line service inputs, and others can be created from the same base of data just by developing applications that read the SGML source data.

1 Format Output Specification Instance.

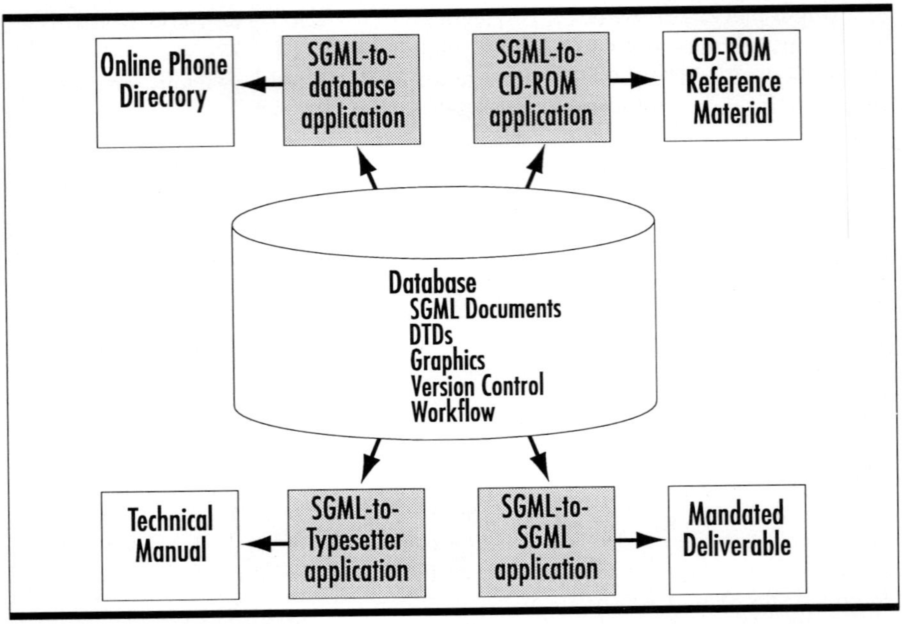

Figure 41. *Reuse of SGML data*

Figure 41, Reuse of SGML data on page 112 shows how a single SGML database of corporate information can be used to create different outputs, just by developing different SGML applications (shown here shaded) for each one. These applications fall into the broad category of SGML translation. Our definition of translation is the process that converts from SGML to something else (including SGML). This differs from our definition of conversion, which is to convert some non-SGML source into SGML. The following are examples of SGML translations:

Paper product

Since most SGML files are still rendered for printing, this is probably the most common application. The main problem for the application designer is in creating the appropriate output for the chosen typesetting environment. This requires a knowledge of the codes needed to run the typesetter, as well as a knowledge of what the customer wants.

We have found it useful to get a sample of the same product while it was still in typesetting form. These samples are usually available, since most applications came from typesetting anyway. By seeing what the typesetting codes look like, along with the new SGML source, the application designer can make the appropriate mapping. If it is a new product, or extensive changes are desired for an existing one, the format developer and product owner will need to meet several times to review the formats until they are correct. This is similar to type style development in any system.

One area of potential problem is in creating different output depending upon whether the element is the first, middle, or last one in a series. Some applications require more leading before the first list item, for example, then the ones in the middle. Some books are printed such that, if there is a single paragraph at a particular level, it is not given a number, but when there are two or more, they are both numbered. This can cause a problem, because when the first paragraph is encountered, there is no indication about its younger siblings. See *SGML Data Pre-processor* on page 334 for an approach to this problem. Some of these issues can be dealt with by the SGML application, others may be dealt with by the downstream formatter.

CD-ROM

In evaluating a CD-ROM output, you are essentially creating a typesetter input file. The application, instead of sending codes instructing the typesetter how to create a page, sends codes instructing the CD-ROM processing program to render the data in its specific form.

With the advent of graphical interfaces for CD-ROM delivery tools, like Folio Views, the similarity to typesetting is even more appropriate. These products have fonts, colors, and graphics, like typesetters, but also have the ability to link to internal and external references, and to execute programs to display movies or create sounds. The SGML file must contain enough information to be able to drive the process.

On-line services

On-line services, such as LEXIS, CompuServe, and sites supporting the World-Wide Web protocols, require the same sort of input files as CD-ROM deliverables. These services are increasingly adding the capabilities to add rich text (proportional fonts, formatting information, color, etc.) to their information base. Each service has its own requirements, so the specifications should be available before starting development. Also, like any translation, sample document are very helpful.

Mandated Deliverable

Some industries have developed common DTDs so that members can interchange information to their mutual benefit. Besides industry, some government agencies require that contractors deliver their information in certain forms. The concept behind this is that shared information becomes a valuable commodity when communicating with suppliers and distributors in an industry.

However, for a company that delivers the same part to two different industries, it might be necessary to adhere to two different structures. Add to that the fact that this company might already have its data in its own SGML database, it becomes necessary to create an application to convert between different SGML structures.

This can be done fairly easily with an SGML translation application. The most important factor is to be sure there is enough information in your corporate database to create all of the necessary outputs. This determination is done at document analysis time, as the SGML deliverable becomes another output type.

When creating an SGML file from another SGML file (also called tree-transformation). See *Tree-to-Tree Translation (Transformation)* on page 180 for more information. It is important to assure that the resulting SGML file is parsed with a validating parser to assure that it has been tagged according to the deliverable DTD.

FOSIs

A format output specification instance (FOSI) is actually an SGML file that contains information about how another SGML file is to be formatted in certain contexts. FOSIs provide a standard way to add semantic information to the SGML data file.

FOSIs use the concept of specifying an element by its hierarchical context. The main element in a FOSI is the "element-in-context" tag. The following illustrates the use of the e-i-c tag and the kinds of information can be conveyed:

```
<e-i-c gi="title" context="cover">
<charlist>
 <font style="sanserif" famname="helvetica" size="18pt"
posture="upright"
       weight="medium" width="regular">
 <leading lead="20pt">
 <hyphen hyph="0">
 <quadding quad="center" lastquad="lcenter">
 <highlt allcap="1">
 <postsp nominal="13pt">
 <textbrk startln="1" endln="1">
 <savetext textid="title" conrule="#CONTENT" placemnt="after">
</charlist>
```

This set of typesetting commands will be passed to the application when a "title" that is a child of "cover" is encountered. The FOSI specifies the font name, style, size, and other formatting information. There might be another e-i-c element that specifies how titles are to be formatted when found inside an appendix, and another specifying the formatting for a chapter title.

FOSIs provide a device-independent way to specify semantic information. The FOSI shown above could be read by a typesetter creating paper or a browser rendering characters on a graphical display device. It is up to the application to provide the system-specific information required to render the font information.

The FOSI, even though it provides an important service in separating formatting information from a specific output device, is limited in its functionality. The standard was created quickly to serve a specific purpose, and was not given the power to do more broad specifications.

Because of these limitations, it is sometimes necessary to put some kind of pre-processing step in front of the SGML data file that utilizes the FOSI. For example, a FOSI processor cannot add two numbers. If the rendering depends upon the use of such a feature, a pre-processor can provide to the FOSI an intermediate file that can do the necessary processing.

DSSSL

The problems that the creators of FOSIs had in implementing their language was felt by the committee that developed the document style semantics and specification language (DSSSL) standard (ISO 10179). DSSSL has the same context-sensitive specification as FOSIs, but has much more processing power, including the ability to query the contents of the input file.

The model of DSSSL is much more complex than FOSI. While FOSI is basically an element-to-output model, a DSSSL processor can do very sophisticated transformation of the source document. The basic pieces of a DSSSL processor are the general language transformation process (GLTP), which performs the contextual element transformation of the input files and creates the proper model for the next process, the semantic-specific process (SSP), which does the actual output processing.

Below is a fragment DSSSL specification. The comments (all text following a semicolon (;) are comments) indicate what is happening.

```
(define default-font-family
  "UNREGISTERED::Adobe//Font Family::Times")

(define-unit cm .01m)                 ; centimeter
(define-unit in 2.54cm)               ; inch
(define-unit pt (/ 1in 72))           ; point
(define-unit pi 12pt)                 ; pica
(define e 10)                         ; 1e1 = 10

(sd (root
     writing-mode: 'left-to-right
     font-size: 10pt
     font-family: default-font-family
     font-posture: 'roman
     font-weight: 'medium
     ;; The next line would be implied if not explicitly
specified.
     content: (process-children)))

(element doc
```

```
         (page-sequence
          initial-page-model: (list section-first-page)
          repeat-page-model: (list section-other-page)
          page-order: 'left-to-right
          content: (column-set-sequence
                    column-set-model: outer-column-set
                    content: (column-set-sequence
                              column-set-model: inner-column-set
                              label: 'text))))

;;; Page formats

(define-page-model section-first-page
  (region
   (x-origin .75in)
   (y-origin 1in)
   (width 42pi)
   (height 5in)
   (flow columns))
  (filling-direction 'top-to-bottom))

(element p
         (paragraph
          first-line-start-indent: (if (am-first?)
                                       0pt
                                       10pt)))

;;; Footnotes will be numbered, same number on reference and
;;; footnote.  Footnotes will be on the same page as the
;;; reference.

(element footnote
         (let ((n (number->string (linear-number))))
           (sequence
             (sequence
               font-size: 8pt
               placement-offset: 6pt
               content: (literal n))
             (sync
              (anchor)
              (paragraph
               label: 'footnote
               content: (sequence
                          (literal n)
```

```
                (process-children)))
        type: 'page))))
```

The DSSSL standard itself is an SGML document instance.

HyTime

HyTime (ISO 10744:1992) was designed to allow for the inclusion of hypertext and time-sensitive information to be conveyed in an SGML database. It had its start as a way of defining music, and grew into an international standard.

HyTime uses, among other things, the concept of "architectural forms", which identify what an element should do without actually naming the element. Any SGML document can use the HyTime features, assuming the application has a HyTime capability, commonly referred to as a HyTime engine. The communication between your document and the HyTime engine is accomplished through a HyTime attribute on any element. This attribute points to an architectural form, for which the HyTime engine has been given semantic instructions. Using architectural forms is like saying that differently named elements are really members of the same class of elements and should be processed accordingly.

Like FOSI and DSSSL, HyTime is an SGML DTD.

Vendor-Supplied Applications

There are many applications available as shrink-wrapped and customizable tools that can be integrated into an SGML environment. In virtually every category, there is more than one competing product. Appendix 8, *SGML Resources* on page 445 has a comprehensive listing of SGML resources available, along with some descriptive information. This information changes quickly, however, as new versions are introduced and more players enter the marketplace.

The most important thing to look for in a vendor-supplied application is its suitability to your environment. Consider the following factors:

CUSTOMIZABILITY

Can you change the operation of the program to fit into your environment? Is there an application program interface (API) available to the system developers? If so, is there an interface using the programming language familiar to your programmers?

Does the product allow access to the parser? This might be necessary if you want to do specialized processing based on certain parsing events like notation processing. Can you access the screen? You might want to change the colors and fonts on the screen to fit your corporate design standards.

SGML Features Supported

Does the product support variant concrete syntaxes? If not, you might be stuck with 8-character tag names and only certain features. Has the parser passed an industry standard conformance testing process? How does the application deal with non-conformant document instances.

Does the application allow for different character sets? What content notations are supported, if any? Are any public entity sets supported? Can a user declare entities in the declaration subset prior to the document instance? Is APPINFO supported?

Integratability

If an API is available, does it have the necessary "hooks" to be integrated into your environment? If you are running in an OS/2 environment and need to make client request to a TCP/IP server, you might need to assure the API can pull this off.

Does the programming language for which your developers are trained work with the API? If not, does the vendor provide development support?

System Compatibility and Resources

Does the product run on your operating system? This seems like a basic requirement, but in a multi-operating system client-server environment, it gets complicated quickly. Can your hardware handle the increased load these products will impart?

Are there any database issues to consider? Can your database access the application's structure, and can the application access your database's structure?

Support

Does the vendor provide training for the application? Does the vendor provide technical support for your developers? Can the vendor provide custom consulting and assist in the integration process?

How often are new versions released? What is the procedure for reporting bugs and getting updated versions?

Price

What are the fixed costs? What are the costs per workstation for the application the vendor is providing? How much extra does training add? Is there a charge for the API? What is the development consulting time cost? What are the maintenance costs?

SGML Application Integration Issues

Developing in-house SGML application is as difficult or as simple as any other system development. In-house-developed applications usually consist of separate application modules and the code necessary to "glue" all of the vendor-supplied applications together. This process is usually called "system integration" and is required to make general-purpose applications work in a specific environment.

GLUE

The key to creating a successful SGML system is in the ability to integrate the various pieces to achieve a whole system. An SGML system exists as a collection of individual pieces that perform a particular function. The power of SGML is that these pieces are able to communicate between themselves with a common data structure, but there are still some incompatibilities in the way each vendor approaches the task.

For example, some vendors require that an SGML instance be normalized[1] while others can take any valid instance, minimal or not. Some require that the doctype declaration exist at the top of the file, while others expect the first character to be the start of the first tag. Another area of incompatibility is in the mapping of `PUBLIC` identifiers to system names (See See *Generate Public Identifier Mapping Files* on page 327).

The SGML Open vendor consortium has developed a standard way of dealing with these integration issues. Until all vendors support this standard, an SGML system needs to have code that sits between these application to perform the appropriate data manipulation to make SGML files compatible across vendors' applications. We call this "glue". Glue is usually performed at the operating-system level. See *Using Glue to Hold an SGML System Together.* on page 316 for examples where glue required.

CROSS-PLATFORM COMPATIBILITY

When developing applications for use across operating-system platforms, or across systems with different character sets, certain the appropriate steps must be taken to assure that the documents flow properly between the systems.

The main problem with translation between ASCII systems is in the way line ends are handled. Programs that move data between systems usually take care of translating line ends appropriately. If this is not done, however, the programs that manipulate the data must be aware that there might be a difference in line ends.

When dealing with operating systems that have different character sets, some changes to the SGML declaration need to be made. This happens regardless of whether the difference is between similar character architectures (ASCII vs.

1 No minimization features. That is, all attribute names and start- and end-tags must be specified. This is also called a "minimal" document.

EBCDIC) or different natural languages (single-byte character sets vs. multi-byte character sets—MBCS)

See *The SGML Declaration* on page 225 and Appendix 6, *Fully Commented SGML Declaration* on page 425 for information on changing the SGML declaration.

CHAPTER • SEVEN

Implementation Planning

Introduction

The process of implementing SGML is like any other information technology development project in many ways. The development life-cycle approach used in large organizations is a suitable framework for organizing your SGML implementation project. Smaller projects may need fewer tasks, but should follow the same approach. The ISO 9000 standard on quality includes a development methodology (not formally observed in this book, but worth considering).

An SGML implementation project can be broken logically into the following phases:

1. Requirements evaluation and system selection
2. Design, development and testing
3. Implementation
4. Production

Following implementation you should also review how well the resulting system provides the benefits stated as your goals.

The key to a successful implementation project is doing your homework. Inadequate analysis and design could have serious consequences once you begin to implement your system. Don't rush through the first phases. You may think you are doing a good thing by implementing quickly, but if you implement the wrong system, you may have to start over, resulting in a longer implementation schedule than you had expected, or ongoing corrections that result in a horrendous DTD or higher overall costs.

In keeping with the nature of this book, this chapter is intentionally brief and generalized. We have, however, striven to illustrate issues specific to an SGML implementation project. As always, the size of the project dictates how much detail will be needed during the planning and design phases. There are other sources dedicated to the topics discussed briefly in this chapter, such as project management, system evaluation, and financial analysis of a system's value and potential benefit. These sources are too numerous to mention, but they include many books, college courses, and trade seminars.

Related Topics

- *The Power of SGML Databases* on page 11
- Chapter 2, *Evolution of Publishing Systems* on page 23
- Chapter 4, *The SGML Environment* on page 43
- *Working in an SGML Environment* on page 44
- Chapter 5, *Document Analysis* on page 65
- Chapter 6, *The SGML Application* on page 101
- *Data Conversion Planning and Implementation* on page 160
- *Workflow* on page 205
- Chapter 11, *Building the DTD* on page 275
- Appendix 8, *SGML Resources* on page 445

System Evaluation and Design

In this section we will discuss the first stages of the SGML implementation project, define requirements of a system, describe methods for evaluating applicability and performance of potential solutions, and finalize the selection based on technical and financial analysis.

The early stages of a technical development project are usually hurried or even completely bypassed due to the participant's lack of understanding of the importance of these tasks. The requirements development task is probably the most critical task in the entire project. Inadequately defined system requirements and objectives may lead to selecting inadequate tools or system components, a mistake that may not be a problem until you are in the midst of implementation.

How much effort should be applied to defining your requirements before you start implementing depends on several factors: the scope of the project, the complexity of the data and the processes applied to it, the sophistication of the users and developers, and the amount of available time to complete the project. For a simple project, the requirements analysis effort may be simplified greatly, perhaps a quickly prepared list of desired functionality, but it should be done in one way or another. If you do not state your target destination, how will you know if you get there after implementation?

PROJECT SCOPE

Understanding the scope of the project involves determining what publications, databases, users, organizations, and business objectives need to be considered in designing a new system. The scope of the system defines the conceptual boundaries of the system itself. It is important to have a clear idea as to where these boundaries lie when defining what features will be needed, what level of sophistication is required, and how much cost can be justified.

To determine the scope of your project, start with a series of lists. Make a list of all organizations that will be affected by the new system, either as hands-on users of the system tools, or as providers or recipients of the information being managed and processed. Make another list of all the publications and information products (databases, CD-ROM and on-line files, etc.). You must remember to focus on the business reasons why you are about to embark on a potentially expensive and disruptive system development project to help you narrow down your lists. You will most likely find that in the first draft of your lists you included tasks that are not essential but could disrupt the process or the success of the entire project. These tasks should be avoided or put off.

Defining your scope should be an iterative process where you make changes with each list as the result of ideas from other lists. For instance, you may find that a new organization, perhaps marketing, should be added because of the need to include the business objective of facilitating cheap and fast product prototyping in the overall scope.

You may feel as though you are stating the obvious in actually writing these lists, but if your scope is documented and available in written form, it will be easier to focus on it as you perform subsequent tasks in the migration process such as evaluating how well potential tools meet these requirements. If you find that you have written an extensive set of lists or statements, prioritize them, and perhaps reduce the scope to a more manageable size.

Use business terms for clarity, not technical jargon. Not everyone involved in the project will have a technical background. If you can't come up with a clear statement of scope stated in simple business terms, you probably don't have a clear idea of what benefits this project is supposed to bring.

STATING BUSINESS OBJECTIVES

Unless you are in an academic institution or are doing pure research, you probably have business objectives driving the project. In the public sector, government and defense organizations, objectives may be different than in a private sector organization with profit motivation. But, either way, there are certain performance-, cost-, or quality-related objectives for doing a project. Typically, an SGML system implementation has one or more of the following objectives:

1. Automate processes to reduce production costs and/or time frames.
2. Add structure and detail to reduce costs to producing new products or changing existing products in order to meet business needs.
3. Reduce cost and time associated with moving information between systems and/or processes.
4. Provide validation and quality assurance processes designed to improve quality and completeness of data.

The fact that you are reading this book suggests that you have identified that you are faced with at least one of the problems that could be alleviated by meeting any of the above business objectives. Most likely, you are also faced with growth in either the number or size of your products, increased demand in quality, timeliness, or cost reduction, which will exacerbate the difficulties you already face.

Obviously SGML can assist in solving these problems. But SGML can also do things that may be irrelevant to the problems faced by your company. Pursuing solutions to problems you don't have is a waste of money and time. Fitting your requirements to solving your business objectives is very important.

USING SGML TO RESTRUCTURE PROCESSES AND INFORMATION

Before you write the requirements for your new system, you should develop an idea of what type of processing is possible given today's technology. SGML is an example of looking for a technology that will allow radical changes, and therefore radical improvements, to existing systems. Try to visualize what is possible when defining your requirements. Otherwise you will end up recreating a slightly faster electronic version of the existing process. Gains, if any, will be modest. This is called "paving over the cow path".

There are two very important bits of homework that should be done which will facilitate visualizing a re-engineered system with significant improvements. First, become acquainted with all the potential systems and tools that might vaguely be of some use to your organization. Go to the conferences (See Appendix 8, *SGML Resources* on page 445) and get the marketing literature, and read the reviews in technical magazines. Brush up on what is (or soon will be) possible.

Second, spend some time on an exercise designed to break you out of a rut in your current thinking. Process re-engineering[1], describes the process of identifying the important aspects of a process and organizing your process into the most effective form. Many of the tasks we perform in producing our publications, or manufacturing our widgets, are either cultural baggage that no one has the nerve to discard, or are non-value-adding activities that can be eliminated or reduced through the use of smarter tools or organizations.

An example of an exercise that breaks stale thinking is to consider the threat a real or hypothetical "start-up" company could have on your organization. A start-up does not have the legacy systems, data, bureaucracies, and personnel skills that an existing company must deal with. This allows a start-up to "leap-frog" to the newest approaches and tools without a legacy migration plan and effort. (This leap-frogging is common in developing countries adopting technology for the first time, such as the rapid progress made in Singapore in implementing computer technology.) Your implementation team should go through the exercise of thinking like a startup and determining what kind of system you would build if you were working from scratch in order to come up with an ideal plan rather than one that attempts to use new approaches to patch legacy systems. After you identify what is probably the best system for meeting your goals, you will have to make a plan to migrate to that system from the legacy environment.

Tools such as SGML allow us to break the mold and redefine our organization around business needs. Not all SGML implementation, however, will require the effort of a re-engineering project, and significant changes cause conflict and upheaval which will need to be managed. But, if you do your homework well, document realistic yet dramatic benefits, and sell them to the powers that be, you can succeed in dramatically improving your business.

Changing Roles

It may be possible to move certain tasks from one part of the organization to another through automation and SGML encoding. For example, SGML coding greatly enhances the ability to produce automatically tables of contents, indexes, cross reference tables and other "finding aids". In many cases, these finding aids can be totally automated and even executed by non-technical clerical staff. Automating the creation of finding aids could reduce production costs and time frames as well as eliminate many errors introduced by creating this information by manually authoring it.

Composition processing may also be executed by non-technical staff, therefore allowing proof pages, and even final hard copy to be generated in the

1 "Re-engineering the corporation", Michael Hammer and James Champy, Harper Collins, 1993, ISBN 0-88730-640-3.

authoring or editing department. Traditional composition departments will most likely continue to be affected by automation, resulting in reduction of some staff. New, more technical programming roles may be created in composition departments, but each of these people will now be doing work that previously required many manual laborers. They may be using sophisticated composition workstations to clean up composed pages, or they may be writing batch programs that approach 100-percent composition without interactive clean up required. Newer composition tools provide capabilities that make it very easy for non-technical personnel to develop composition routines. These tools may be interactive graphical interfaces that assist in developing the composition routines, similar to creating style sheets in word processors.

Some staff will be needed to create material that is either ambiguous and cannot be handled in a structural coding scheme or is unique and not worth spending time developing programs to handle it. It is possible that these people could work in the editorial department right next to the people who write the content and do the spell-checking. The chart below illustrates some of the more common roles in the publication process and how they may shift using new approaches.

	Editorial Roles	Production Roles
OLD	Content Simple Coding Review	Structure Complex Coding Proof Generation Composition Page Inspection/Correction Data Management Typesetting/Imaging Electronic Delivery Prep System Management
NEW	Content & Structure Proof Generation Simple & Complex Coding Review Page Inspection/Correction Data Management Composition	Typesetting/Imaging Electronic Delivery Prep System Management

Figure 42. *Changing roles as the result of SGML systems implementation*

New roles have emerged in the process of adopting structured approaches to publishing, such as the need to have someone develop and maintain DTDs similar to the way editorial styles have been created and maintained.

Some implementations have failed due to lack of user acceptance even though they were technically and financially sound. Many project leaders underestimate the importance of managing cultural issues and focus only on technical development and financial analysis. There is an increasing awareness among SGML implementors that "people" issues are just as important to the success of a system. We are, after all, changing the way we do business when we implement SGML.

Effective and persistent communication will improve use understanding and acceptance, and may avoid misunderstandings. For instance, we have found that some less-technical users interpret the stated benefit of automating processes as a process of de-professionalization and even job elimination. Benefits need to be described sufficiently so that users can see how automating some processes allows them to focus on what they do best, creating information, not formatting and accessing it. Successes need to be stated and understood in terms other than merely their effect on "the bottom line".

Some systems are implemented as a matter of survival for the organization as a while which may mean some job elimination. Departments that perceive their role as being threatened by the new system, such as production areas, will be particularly resistant to change. Their obstructionist complaints may spill over to the areas not usually eliminated—such as authoring groups—and foment resistance throughout the company. Strong leadership and effective communication of the benefits to the organization as a while are needed to win-over those who will have to adjust to and live with the change.

FUNCTIONAL EVALUATION

There are several aspects of each system you are considering that need to be evaluated. The first aspect is how well does each potential system perform the tasks needed. This is called a functional evaluation. Other aspects of a proposed system that need to be evaluated and will be discussed later are costs, benefits, and risks.

Before you go kick the tires on a new car, you probably give some thought to the type of car you want. You consider your requirements concerning function, how often you will drive, and what performance expectations you have.

It is no different when buying computer equipment, software, or any other significant investment. Since the task of evaluating an SGML-based publishing system can be fairly complex, you should use the practices of functional requirements evaluation used in large system development projects. If your project is more modest, you can be selective in the amount of detail or number of actual steps you take. You may just want to read up on the latest tools in a trade magazine and make a quick list before you buy. If the stakes are higher, you will want to perform a more thorough analysis before you commit to a solution.

Functional requirements are really just a list of things you expect your system to be able to perform. You must define them in unambiguous terms. Don't say, for instance, that you want a parser. Be more specific. Do you need to report SGML errors in the text instance? If yes, say so. State whether it is required, or if an alternative could be substituted. Prioritize functional requirements as required or merely desired and optional. Consider the value of the requirement. Would it still be required if it was very expensive? Be specific. Do you want to utilize some of the optional features of SGML such as tag minimization or Short References? If yes, then list them. What features does your SGML-smart editor require? Can you work in complete document chunks with both start- and end-tags required, or do you want to support minimization in the editing session? What type of tagging assistance is required? Describe it. It can simply be context-sensitive tagging, or the editor can give you visual clues and other support that will make a structured editing easier for the user.

Gather representatives from key areas who will either develop or utilize the system once installed. Conduct several brainstorming sessions where everyone simply states functions that they believe are necessary. Compile a complete list, even if some of them are slightly redundant. Have the group work together to make the items as clear as possible and to combine redundant items.

Some items on your requirements list may need to be broken into two or more separate items because they try to cover too many points in one item. For instance, in being specific you might want to list as separate items the requirement for a software editor, and the requirement for a spell-checker even though it is likely that the editor will have an integrated spell checker. This allows you flexibility in evaluating systems. The degree of granularity in your requirements is up to you, and it may take you several editing passes before you feel comfortable that you are not being too granular or not specific enough.

Simplify the language in each item in order to avoid confusion or inconsistent interpretations by vendors or members of the evaluation team. Expect constant updating of the language used in the items, even as you conduct your evaluations.

Conduct system surveys to determine if your requirements are reasonable given the state of the current technology. Also, you may find that you overlooked functionality when assembling your list. Go to vendor demonstrations and trade shows to see what systems can do today and what is promised in the near future.

You will need to organize your list into categories. Categories are useful to organize them by sub-processes. You may find that a particular sub-process is not offered by a vendor and you might have to integrate a third-party tool. Categories could include the following and other logical divisions:

1. SGML editing
2. Data management
3. Data transformation
4. Composition
5. System hardware and software

Be specific in terms of quantities where possible. If your publications include thousands of cross-references and footnotes, make sure your requirements list the need to support that many. Recognize the value of existing systems (sunk costs) which you expect could play a role in the final system. If you have a large installed base of PCs on your users' desktops and would like to utilize these existing resources, make sure you mention that the editorial software should run in Windows, DOS, or OS/2 to avoid the need to purchase and install new workstations. If your publications have complex requirements for running heads, such as variable information based upon content of the text, then list them under composition. If your publications contain graphics, be specific in describing them; their quantity, formats, frequency of update, and complexity. By not being specific, many implementors have bought systems only to find that they cannot be used to produce their publications and were faced with the embarrassing situation of buying more equipment or even the complete failure of the project.

You might want to share your requirements list with the vendors you think are likely candidates for selection to get their opinions on what is being asked for and to determine if your are stating your requirements clearly. In a formal government procurement process, this review would be handled through a series of question-and-answer sessions where, for fairness, all potential vendors are invited to participate and listen. In the less formal commercial world, you can manage this any way you feel meets the needs of your company. Casual one-on-one meetings with several vendors might suffice.

Develop evaluation criteria that will be used to determine how well a system meets the requirements. This is not simply a yes or no question. You may require, for instance, context-sensitive tagging support and find that the various editorial software products you are evaluating take very different approaches to meeting this requirement. Some may be more intuitive, others faster to use. You will need to determine the criteria for each item.

Criteria to Evaluate Each Requirement

Evaluating a system's ability to meet functional requirements is not always as simple as answering a yes or no question. You need to consider defining evaluation criteria such as the following:

1. **Correctness**. How closely does the feature meet the requirement as it was intended?
2. **Reliability**. Does it perform consistently with the appropriate results every time?
3. **Efficiency**. Does it perform efficiently and not cause excessive delays or waiting?
4. **Integrity**. Does it perform according to expectations or stringent requirements (such as compliance to ISO 8879)?
5. **Usability**. Is it logically designed and easy to use or is it cumbersome and/or inconsistent with the environment in which it will be used?

You may also develop your own criteria or better definitions of these criteria. There may be other criteria you are interested in listing for each requirement. You may also combine some of these to simplify the evaluation (perhaps reliability and integrity).

Ranking for Need

You will also need to determine if your requirements are absolutely required or not. We suggest the following distinctions be considered:

1. **Mandatory—day one**. Must exist on day one of the implementation.
2. **Mandatory—can wait**. Must exist very soon after implementation.
3. **Optional but Valuable—day one**. Desired but not essential, can provide benefit if provided, but must exist the first day.
4. **Optional but Valuable—can wait**. Desired but not essential, can provide benefit if provided, must exist very soon after implementation.
5. **Optional**. Desired but not essential, useful but no benefit can be attributed directly to this requirement.

This list is designed to help you sort your requirements into two distinct groupings; mandatory and optional. This list also tries to take into account that some features may need to be customized or newly developed for your implementation. You need to determine if you can wait a few months and provide an interim process or procedure until the requirement is met. How many months is up to you, but the longer the waiting period, the higher the risk that the feature will not be delivered as planned.

Weighting Criteria and Requirements

The lists for evaluation criteria and mandatory versus optional are also designed to allow numerical weighting to further hone the evaluation. Before you automatically assume that weighting each criteria and the requirements themselves is a good thing, be aware that the results of the evaluation will be only as good as the weighting you assign. You need to be very scientific when assigning weights or you can erroneously skew the evaluation and potentially wind up choosing a system that is less valuable to you than the other options.

You may want to consider not using a numerical weighting system. The danger of numerical weightings is that they seem so definitive, so exact, and they are really only as exact as you are in assigning weights. You may, for example, assign equal weight to each criterion, or higher weight for mandatory requirements and lesser weight for optional ones. Then, performing your evaluation and filling-in the results, you may find that one system scored an 85 and the other an 82. This may not mean that the one that scored higher is a better system. Your numbers may be skewed, albeit unintentionally. You have not created an evaluation model that is precise enough to differentiate between close scores. If your numbers were more along the lines of 85 and 50, you may have found some differences that you can rely upon.

The following grid shows a slightly simplified evaluation model using graphic symbols instead of numerical scores. All criteria are considered to be equal, including mandatory and optional requirements. The symbols indicate, more or less, how well each criterion was met; the solid circle is the equivalent of a high score, the half circle is less, the outlined circle is the lowest, and an empty cell means the feature does not exist or does not satisfy the requirement at all. This example shows only the first few requirements in an actual evaluation, which contained grids for over 130 requirements in seven categories.

No.	Rank	Requirement Name	System X				
			Correct	Reliability	Efficiency	Integrity	Usability
Editorial Workstation							
1	M	Full Screen Edit	●	●	●	●	●
2	M	Programmable Keys	◗	●	●	○	○
3	M	Cut, Copy, Paste	◗	◗	◗	◗	●
4	M	Search/Replace	●	●	●	●	●
5	M	Simultaneous Multiple File Access	○	●	●	○	●
6	M	Spell Checking	◗	●	●	●	●
7	M	Extensible Spelling Libraries	○	○	○	○	
8	M	On-line Access	●	●	●	●	●
9	M	Autocite Access	○	●	●	○	●
10	M	Changebar/Redlining	●	●	●	●	●

Figure 43. *Requirements evaluation grid*

This grid only represents the first 10 requirements under the category Editorial Workstation. When the grid for this system was compared to others, it was easy to see which had the most dark spots. This type of graphical system is commonly used in commercial magazines when evaluating consumer products and computer equipment, probably for the same reasons of needing to be clear but to avoid the risk of looking more scientific than the evaluation really is.

Vendor Demonstrations and Prototypes

It is useful to have the vendor prepare a presentation showing how the system meets the specific functionality you have listed.

You have to be careful to stick to the original intention of the requirements and not let vendors convince you that you don't need some of the items on your requirements list. That type of discussion usually only happens when a vendor's system cannot meet a particular requirement and they do not have a plan on how to add the required functionality.

Be wary of promises that vendors make on developing functionality to meet your requirements. Software development can be complex and time consuming, and even honest developers may be too optimistic in their estimated schedules. Anything being promised later than three to six months can be considered too risky to count on. It is very difficult to anticipate what changes a developer may need to make in priorities in that time frame. You should look at the vendor's track record for delivering promised functionality.

You may ask each vendor to develop a prototype of their system using your data and DTDs. A prototype is useful in that it gives you and your evaluation team a chance to see how the system would work in practice. You may have to compensate the participating vendors since they will encounter costs to prepare a prototype.

A prototype test can be used as a tie-breaker in the event that you've narrowed it down to two systems and cannot commit to either over the other, even after considering the costs, benefits, and risks. A prototype may also be the best way to really familiarize you, your development team, and your users to the type of system and tools you are about to implement.

If you choose to require prototype demonstrations you will need to prepare a DTD and a test document or two for each vendor to work with. Have the vendor describe any changes to your design and test document they needed to make the prototype work.

Demonstrations and prototype testing provide you with the ability to observe details that will improve your evaluation, especially when considering the detailed criteria listed above. You need to observe the timing and complexity of tasks. Do they work well? Are the procedures clear and manageable by the users who will need to execute them? Write down your observations during the demonstrations so you do not forget them by the time you meet to compile your evaluations. Later when you do meet, discuss your observations as a group.

Each person participating in the evaluation will have made different observations. The editorial people in the evaluation will notice different things about how the system will be to work with. The technical people may observe issues related to the system or the tools that may have been missed by the editors. The evaluation is a good example of how teamwork can improve the results by getting several different points of view.

You can easily over-complicate the evaluation process. Remember, the purpose of a functional evaluation is to narrow down your choices of systems to the two or three most likely candidates. Once you think you know which systems can do the job, you must then evaluate each system for costs, benefits, and risks. You probably cannot afford the time it would take to collect and digest cost and benefit information for more than a small number of potential systems. The functional evaluation will allow you to identify which systems are worth evaluating in more detail, and perhaps worth embarking on prototype implementations.

CONCEPTUAL DESIGN

You may need to develop a conceptual design of what your resulting system might look like in order to continue your evaluation. A conceptual design, as opposed to a detailed design, is useful to illustrate your vision on how the system might work and to make ball-park estimates on what it might cost. You most likely will need to prepare a conceptual design to conduct the cost evaluation and convince management to let you proceed with the project.

The conceptual design should be a high-level design based upon each of the systems you have narrowed your evaluation down to during the functional evaluation process. Don't get too detailed when creating a design at this early stage of the project. You might constrain yourself by making assumptions that do not match potential solutions available to you. Also, too much detail might require that you create a slightly different design for each potential system.

The conceptual design should take into account the number of workstations and servers that will be needed, networking and output requirements, and system software required for the type of system you are planning on implementing. A conceptual design could be a network diagram or a simple list of system components. Remember that the purpose is to be able to estimate overall costs, not to use as a blueprint for installation. You may need to include costs for space preparation (remodeling), air-conditioning, and improvements to electrical services, etc., in the system costs.

COST AND BENEFIT EVALUATION

The cost evaluation of a system is widely understood as a key determining factor in selection. Even so, it is easy to overlook some costs, especially those that are either incurred or avoided by adopting SGML instead of an unstructured approach.

At first glance SGML systems seem to be more expensive to implement, and in some ways they are, but it is not always true that SGML costs more. It may be more difficult to convert unstructured data to a detailed structured form than to change one vendor's unstructured coding to another's with roughly equivalent functionality, but this statement is isolated and does not consider other requirements that are cheaper to meet in an SGML system. These include transforming data into multiple forms for various types of delivery (print, electronic, etc.) which is always easier and cheaper when the information starts in a device-independent, structured form. Another area where SGML systems are superior is in reorganizing and reusing data. It is in the overall return on investment that SGML systems shine. The difficulties associated with managing and reusing unstructured information can be greatly reduced or eliminated when using SGML. These benefits translate into cost savings or avoidance and can mean that an SGML system can be significantly more valuable.

You should not simply rely on the purchase price alone for your cost evaluation. Costs associated with running the system, maintaining it, user productivity, imaging, and the impact to the organization must be included in your cost evaluation. If user productivity goes up, costs of producing each product are reduced. If steps can be automated or eliminated, the overall operating costs can be significantly reduced. If the data is easily reusable new revenue producing products, or the elimination of expensive ones may be possible, translating into significant revenue increases or cost avoidances. These are the true measure of a system's worth.

For example, if a computer manufacturer produced paper documentation for a line of personal computers, the documentation costs may easily be US$100-200 in a print-oriented unstructured publishing system. But if the documentation can be easily produced in electronic or print forms, customers can opt to receive their documentation in the cheaper electronic form. A single CD-ROM can easily hold all of the documentation of a small computer system and is dramatically cheaper to produce. The production costs for a book are somewhere between US$5 to US$15 (or more) and there may be several books in a documentation set. Meanwhile, the production costs of a CD-ROM are well below US$2 if the publishing system can produce either format. You do not necessarily need SGML to produce CD-ROMs, but if you need to produce both print and electronic products, device- and delivery- independent structured information will allow you to do so more cheaply than a system dedicated to producing either form without considering the needs of the other.

Costs, savings and revenue increases associated with production, maintenance, and new products, as well as purchases must be considered in the cost/benefit evaluation to get an accurate picture of the worth of each system being evaluated.

QUANTIFYING BENEFITS

The flip side of costs is benefits. Benefits can be described as the savings and revenue opportunities inherent with each system. A reduction in composition costs due to cheaper materials and equipment and increased productivity is a good example of a benefit. The ability to produce a new spin-off publication from existing data for resale is another. Improvements in the quality of your data reducing dependence on the telephone support service you offer is yet another. Identifying benefits can be easy. Quantifying them may prove to be much more difficult.

SGML is not like other approaches that have been traditionally taken in publishing systems development. You may have to look at your system in a new way to find opportunities and savings that could be made available and be included in your evaluation. A more comprehensive discussion of potential benefits from adopting SGML are listed in Chapter 1, *Your Publishing System is Broken!* on page 3.

Tangible and Intangible Benefits

Benefits can be grouped into two categories; the ones that are easy to quantify are called tangible, or quantitative, benefits, and the ones that may be more difficult to quantify are called intangible, or qualitative, benefits. Qualitative benefits cannot be reliably assigned a value (dollars, time, etc.) and plugged reliably into an economic model measuring the cost and benefit of a system being evaluated. They tend to be arbitrarily quantified at best. When selling your cost/benefit analysis to management, they may be easy to challenge resulting in reduced confidence in your evaluation.

An example of a tangible benefit from an SGML implementation would be the immediate reduction in production costs associated with producing a CD-ROM version of a print product where the CD-ROM has been previously produced as an add-on system to a print process. All of the costs associated with manual conversion of print-oriented markup to a format suitable for inclusion on a CD-ROM disc can be eliminated if the information is produced in a form that allows automated production of both delivery formats. The difference between these two approaches is the tangible benefit.

An example of an intangible benefit from SGML implementation would be the claim that the productivity of authors will go up. The first question you will be asked after making this claim is, "By how much?". Don't be tempted to try to quantify it if you do not have confidence in a tangible value. It is better to just list qualitative intangible benefits as additional benefits to be considered in addition to the quantitative tangible benefits than be pinned down to a specific number.

If the tangible benefits are not sufficient to justify a system, or to differentiate between potential systems, you may want to rely on intangible benefits. One way to express intangible benefits in tangible terms without creating issues regarding the reliability of your numbers is to use ranges of possible tangible benefits. For instance, the productivity increase of the authoring process could be expressed as 10- to 20-percent and then multiplied against authoring costs.

You may want to show intangible benefits in another way. As the saying goes, a picture may be worth a thousand words. The following diagram may be a better way to include the intangible benefit of increased productivity in a presentation to management.

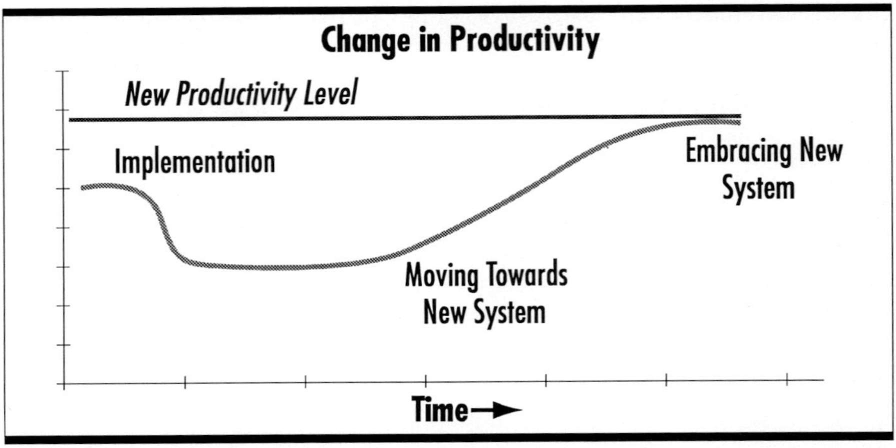

Figure 44. *Showing the intangible benefit of increased productivity*

A nice feature of this diagram is that it not only illustrates that you believe productivity will increase, but that it also shows you recognize that initially productivity may drop while the bugs are worked out and the users learn how to use it.

In the process of implementing a system you will be faced with the need to sell its benefits to users, managers, and even technical implementors. You will need to include tangible and intangible benefits in your arguments.

Gathering Evaluation Data

Gathering the evaluation data for each potential system can be done in a number of ways. The US Federal government requires a formal process for requesting bids and evaluating them for system acquisitions. Other organizations may use less structured or formalized approaches. Common activities and terminology in this area include Requests for Quotations (RFQ) and Requests for Information (RFI). A Request for Quotation would be solicited where potential vendors are requested to submit binding quotations for service, systems or system components to be considered during system evaluation and selection. A Request for Information would be solicited where potential vendors are requested to submit information on providing services, systems or system components to be used in the design and evaluation of systems. Other less formal mechanisms can be used to gather information, but eventually you will need to get binding quotes from each potential vendor to prepare cost information during the evaluation. You will find that for larger or complex purchases, several rounds of negotiations will be needed to determine exact licensing terms, unit pricing and volume discounts, support and maintenance terms, and other contractual issues.

THE COST/BENEFIT ANALYSIS CALCULATION. You will need to prepare a final cost/benefit analysis for the finalist systems you are evaluating. Financial analysis of information technology is the subject of much debate, especially around systems that are considered "strategic" and where it is hard to quantify their value. SGML implementations often fall into this category.

The following discussion presents an oversimplified method to determine the "value" of a system. You may need to spend time with the Controller or Chief Financial Officer of your organization to develop a more sophisticated model for determining the value of information technology. But, this discussion is presented to set the framework for thinking of SGML development as an investment with costs and a benefit or return on investment.

First, list each cost and benefit category and enter the numbers associated with each system. Add them up and the system with the right balance of cost savings and benefits can be determined. Remember that the costs and benefits must be considered for the entire life of the system. These analyses usually are prepared for a three to seven year period or system life, with five years being the most common. Below is a cost/benefit analysis (expressed in thousands of dollars) for a fairly large implementation with a five year system life.

Costs (in 000's)	1995	1996	1997	1998	1999	Totals
Hardware/Software	250	40	40	40	40	410
Training	150	20	21	22	24	237
Conversion	400	100	0	0	0	500
System Development	350	100	50	50	50	600
Total Annual Costs	1,150	260	111	112	114	1,747
Accummulated Costs	1,150	1,410	1,521	1,633	1,747	
Benefits (in 000's)						
Composition Savings	300	420	441	463	486	2,110
Electronic Production Savings	80	150	158	165	174	727
Total Annual Benefits	380	570	599	628	660	2,837
Accummulated Benefits	380	950	1,549	2,177	2,837	
Annual Costs/Benefits	(770)	310	488	516	546	
Accummulated Costs/Benefits	(770)	(460)	28	544	1,090	

Figure 45. *Cost/benefit analysis of an SGML system implementation*

In this analysis model costs are totaled each year and compared total benefit for that year. But, these numbers can be misleading, since the first two years represent a loss that has to be carried over to the next year. Accumulated costs and benefits are calculated to account for costs and benefits for the entire life of the system. The accumulated costs will be higher than the accumulated benefits for the first two years (as indicated by negative numbers in parenthesis at the bottom of the 1995 and 1996 columns). But some time into the third year the system starts making money for the implementing organization. This is called the payback period. In this case the payback period is about 3.2 years, or it will take about 3.2 years before the system is profitable. The total accumulated benefit less costs for the entire five-year life of the system is US$1,090,000 in today's dollars.

Note that although some figures show adjustments for anticipated inflation (training for example) these figures do not take into account the value of the dollars as affected by inflation. Also, there are maintenance costs and ongoing training costs shown in this example. Also note that the benefits will not be fully realized in the first year since you have to allow for time for developing the system and that the benefits will start to accrue some time later in the year.

The total worth of the system, the Total Accumulated Cost/Benefit across five years, is a positive number. The system is worth implementing since it will save money in the long run; in this case more than a million dollars.

If your payback period is too long, your management may feel that investment in that system cannot be justified. Conversely, if your payback period is too short, it may seem unrealistic, or that you might be missing a cost somewhere. Rethink and adjust your numbers until they seem realistic. Generally speaking, a realistic payback period is more than one year for larger system, but may be only a few months for smaller implementations. Payback periods of less than a year are not uncommon for SGML implementations.

If you prepare an analysis such as this for each of your final potential solutions you are evaluating, you can see which will have the greatest accumulated cost/benefit or value. Again, cost is not the only issue. You need to have considered the functionality of each system before you prepare a cost/benefit analysis. If, for instance, one system reduces composition costs more than another for some reason, you will find that out during the functional evaluation. Then you must quantify it to include it in your cost/benefit analysis.

If another system did not eliminate the CD-ROM conversion costs due to functional requirements not being met adequately, you would not be able to include any savings in the cost/benefit analysis for that system. It might prove to be that requirement not being met would not make the system feasible. If none of the potential solutions satisfy all of your functional requirements, you need to incorporate the costs of developing that functionality.

If your payback period is too short (whatever that means to you) it may be suspect or considered unreliable. If you feel your payback period is too short, re-examine your costs and projected savings. Look for things you might have overlooked, such as maintenance costs, or underestimated, such as training or conversion costs. Look for things you may have been too optimistic on, such as savings or the speed of implementation. After re-examining your values, recalculate your analysis.

There is a very real issue that is not entirely obvious in this type of analysis, but which needs to be considered. An analysis for a system may show that it has very dramatic value. The cumulative cost/benefit could be negative and too high in the first year or two for a company to manage. Not many small companies could afford the investment in the analysis above. They would go out of business before the payback period is reached. If this proves to be the case, perhaps a smaller implementation would be better. You need to have realistic expectations on how much investment your organization can afford to make.

Risk Evaluation

Every system has inherent risk associated with it. You need to determine what risks exist and try to express them as tangible costs or in intangible terms.

For instance, you need to consider the economic health of the vendors you are considering to determine if they will be around to support your system once installed. If there is a chance that they may not, perhaps they are in financial difficulty, you may want to consider negotiating to purchase the source code for the system or have it placed in a software escrow. These costs would need to be included in your analysis.

Another example of risk might be that the tools being evaluated and promised are still in development. If there is no clear indication that the tools will be successfully developed by the vendor, prior history is a good indication, then you need to consider the effectiveness of the system without these features. It may mean that you have to develop them yourself, or that your cost savings might be affected. You would, in this situation, need to reflect the additional costs to develop, or the reduction in savings in your cost/benefit analysis.

The types of risks a system might entail are too numerous too mention. But it behooves you to try to identify and evaluate the impact of risks inherent in the systems you are evaluating. You may find enough risk to justify eliminating a potential solution on risk alone, even if it seems to offer the most functionality and total accumulated cost/benefit without considering that risk.

You will need to determine for yourself what risks are reasonable to assume. And, whenever possible, include risk in your evaluation in the form of a quantitative cost.

System Development

Once you have completed your evaluation and made your system selection you will need to plan the implementation of the system. Some preliminary planning may have been needed to convince management to approve your proposed system, but now that your are ready to implement you will need to create a detailed plan.

An implementation plan is very useful for several reasons. Planning makes you think of everything that needs to be done, in what order, by whom, and according to what schedule. Without a plan you may not anticipate the proper order dependent implementation tasks need to occur, what resources will be assigned and/or are available, and when to anticipate certain events such as product migration and user training.

IMPLEMENTATION TASKS

There are several areas where you will need to develop plans for addressing specific tasks. Not all implementations will require tasks from all of these, but a large implementation might need to be broken into the following areas:

1. Data design and DTD development
2. Legacy information conversion
3. Formatting development
4. System tools development
5. Training development and implementation

The plan you develop to implement the entire system must take into account dependencies between these separate areas of development activity. A master plan should track the entire project, and leaders of each task in these areas must be familiar with the relationship of their work to other areas. The plan must also consider the role of the vendor(s) you are working with in performing and/or leading various tasks in the project. Strong project leadership will be essential, especially for larger implementation projects.

Data Design and DTD Development

Data design and DTD development is covered in greater detail in *Data Design and DTD Development* on page 140 and Chapter 11, *Building the DTD* on page 275. But it is worth noting in this context that it is the design and subsequent DTD that will affect nearly every other functional design in each of the other development areas. The functionality of the systems being built implicitly dictates the level of detail needed for the DTD and vice-versa. All processes employed in the system must have information with the appropriate level of coding detail, albeit generically and logically implemented, in order to function effectively.

Planning for the DTD development must be carefully timed with all other tasks. As plans for information conversion and format development and other task areas are finalized, additional tasks will most likely be necessary to review the impact of the tools being developed on the DTD and time allowed for the DTD to be updated and tested as needed.

Legacy Information Conversion

Legacy information conversion is covered more comprehensively in Chapter 8, *Information Conversion* on page 151. But just as the DTD development is affected by nearly all other development areas, so is information conversion. The converted information is the realization of the design specified in the DTD. It must contain the appropriate coding and detail described in the DTD and needed for the system to function. As with DTD development, significant changes to format and system development might require changes to tasks associated with information conversion.

During the implementation regular walk-through meetings may be needed to allow developers from all of the implementation areas to raise design issues and to come up with mutually compatible solutions.

FOSIs

The SGML world has recognized the need to supplement the intellectual information captured in SGML data with formatting semantics. The semantics of formatting will eventually be handled by DSSSL, but until vendors support the international standard, alternative means of capturing formatting information have been developed. Most significantly is the use of a Formatting Output Specification Instance (FOSI). See Chapter 4, *The SGML Environment* on page 43 for more information on DSSSL and FOSI.

A FOSI is actually an SGML document that captures formatting-specific information about the appearance of SGML elements. FOSIs can be used to drive formatting applications such as formatting SGML-smart editors and composition systems. FOSI-smart applications do not require the SGML data to be down-translated into a proprietary format. Instead, raw SGML data can be read and associated with formatting specification contained in the FOSI and process for viewing or composition.

Formatting Development

When we think of formatting development, we typically think of typesetting. But with electronic products and SGML systems, we must add electronic delivery formatting requirements and SGML-smart formatting editor development to the list of tasks associated with formatting our information. The following formatting application and tasks may be needed:

1. Data transformation routines (down-translates) for print and electronic processing (This is also covered in Chapter 8, *Information Conversion* on page 151).
2. Composition format application development.
3. SGML editor screen format application development.
4. Specialized data extraction and manipulation routines for:

    a. content generation,
    b. product information reuse, and
    c. product reorganization and cleansing.

5. Database loading and unloading applications.

The DTD development process must begin before the formatting tasks can start since the DTD dictates the coding and structures that will be the basis for the down-translation, composition, extraction and sorting, and management that is accomplished by the formatting applications.

Formatting application developers must take into consideration performance issues and application development difficulty. If there are issues related to the way a DTD is designed that affect the format developer's ability to develop an efficient and reliable application, the developer must raise these issues in the DTD design and walk-through meetings. There may be realistic issues that could affect the DTD design. This is not to say that the DTD should be format driven to accommodate an efficient formatting applications. DTDs must be logical and device-independent, but when faced with a DTD that may create processing inefficiencies, the solution may be as simple as requiring end tags, or breaking an attribute into several attributes to improve the performance of formatting applications. The DTD must remain free of processing specific semantics, but must provide the appropriate detail needed to drive the formatting applications.

Formatting development for SGML editor screen formats usually involves either a unique language or development environment that must be learned by the people performing the application development. Plan for training personnel in the use of these tools and provide some time for learning the ins and outs of the tools when committing to schedules.

FORMAT DEVELOPMENT CHECKLIST. Following is a checklist of tasks that may need to be addressed by the formatting development team (and to get approval for what may be a new document "look"):

1. SGML-smart Editorial Workstation:
    a. Screen formatting application(s)
    b. DTD-specific application configuration
    c. Integration of the SGML editor with other tools
    d. Specialized functions such as data/DTD fragment handling for granular updates and loose-leaf production
2. Composition for Print:
    a. Translation applications to composition coding.
    b. Main text formatting applications.
    c. Front and rear matter, cover pages, and miscellaneous material formatting (such as indexes and tables of contents).
    d. Manipulation and re-organization routines for product management.
3. Formatting for Electronic Products:
    a. Translation applications for electronic delivery formats.
    b. Electronic delivery "composition" applications.
    c. Specialized electronic format processing applications.
4. Specialized Applications:
    a. Content extraction and generation applications to create indexes, tables of contents, cross reference tables, etc.
    b. Database loading, unloading, and management applications.

System Tools Development

The system tools involved in an SGML implementation span a broad range of disciplines including database management, system software and hardware, networking software and hardware, and system and user software configuration, integration and development.

Much of the activity of the system developers will center around installation and configuration of the software and hardware. Integration may be needed of the SGML-smart editor into the database management environment, as well as configuration of the database management tools to accommodate the workflow, security, user management, and system resources required to support the desired workflow.

System Development Checklist

Following is a list of task areas that may need to be addressed by the system development team (ISO 9000 and industry organizations may have additional requirements):

1. Database
    a. Installation and configuration
    b. User management and security
    c. Tasks management and initiation
    d. Product-specific setup and definition
    e. Database loading and indexing
2. System Resources
    a. Workstation installation and configuration
    b. User software installation and set up (including development of specialized FOSI or environments under this software)
    c. Servers and centralized resource installation and setup
    d. Composition system setup
3. Networking
    a. Physical network design and installation
    b. Network operating system and hardware installation and setup
    c. Network resources (*e.g.*, printers) installation and setup

Training Development and Implementation

Training can easily be underestimated and poorly implemented. In fact, proper training can become very expensive and time-consuming. Someone once said that if you think training is expensive, consider the cost of ignorance. Effective training must have pre-established goals for what the participants are expected to learn and include follow-up evaluation to determine the success of the training.

When we first think of training requirements, usually we think of end-user training. Other areas of training that need to be considered, and implemented before end-user training, are:

1. Developing and conducting training in SGML concepts for development personnel
2. Developing and conducting training in the new system tools for development personnel
3. Developing end user training in end-user and system administration tools

Once everything has been developed and installed and you finally get around to end-user training, you will probably need to cover the following training topics:

1. SGML concepts (how much SGML knowledge end users must have is often debated, but we suggest a basic understanding of the value of structure to the organization and the basics of SGML markup is useful if not essential)
2. Editorial tools
3. Custom-developed applications and utilities
4. Database access environment
5. Operation system environment(s)
6. Workflow and processes

Implementation Resources

You will need an overall schedule for implementation and migration of products to the new system. In Chapter 8, *Information Conversion* on page 151 we discuss a product migration strategy that involves three phases; prototype, critical-mass, and follow up. This phased approach can be reflected in the overall plan. You need to identify what tasks need to be accomplished in order to achieve each phase. Most of the system development and installation will be needed before the first publication can be loaded to the database. The following chart shows the first few tasks in the migration of a large collection of publications to a new SGML publishing system.

				1994		
Phase 1:	**Pages**	**Convert**	**Develop**	**Verify**	**Support**	**Total**
System Hardware and Software						$297,450
New User Training						$34,572
Titles						
Pub A	3,200	$11,200	$7,120	$3,840	$6,771	$28,931
Pub B	624	$2,184	$7,120		$1,320	$10,624
Pub C	10,000	$35,000	$7,120	$12,000	$21,159	$75,279
Phase Totals:	13,824	$48,384	$21,360	$15,840	$29,250	$446,856

				1994		
Phase 2:	**Pages**	**Convert**	**Develop**	**Verify**	**Support**	**Total**
System Hardware and Software						$577,080
New User Training						$224,718
Titles						
Pub X	36,000	$126,000	$39,160	$43,200	$14,464	$222,824
Pub Y	21,000	$73,500	$3,560	$25,200	$8,438	$110,698
Pub Z	2,400	$8,400	$3,560	$2,880	$964	$15,804

Figure 46. *Phased implementation schedule*

In this schedule, the costs associated with each phase are subtotaled at the completion of the phase. The costs include information conversion, system hardware and software acquisition, setup and installation, and training costs. The system hardware and software costs and training costs increase in the second phase since the prototype phase was a limited implementation of only a few of the workstations. Most of the core system functionality is installed in the first phase though, including the database server and software, and the network.

Following the prototype phase is the critical-mass phase. During the first phase many problems were found and resolved with the system, editing applications, composition routines, and even the DTD and converted data. These problems need to be resolved before starting additional phases or the problems will be exacerbated. If resolving a problem requires cleaning up converted data due to a DTD change needed to solve the problem, you will want to clean up all the data and modify the DTD and system programs before converting any additional data.

This schedule shows the costs associated with each product as it is migrated into the new system. The product migration costs are broken into four categories: convert, develop, verify, support. The conversion costs are described in more detail in Chapter 8, *Information Conversion* on page 151. The development costs are associated with product-specific applications such as screen and composition formatting as described above. The verification costs were associated with verifying that all the data was converted correctly and remained intact with no pieces missing or duplicated. The support costs include any other costs such as miscellaneous processes and photocopying needed to implement each product. The training and system costs are tracked by phase not publications. Each phase can then be totaled and the true costs analyzed across the duration of each phase.

Notice that the conversion costs increase proportionately with the volume of pages being converted and verified, but the format development costs do not. This is because if all the pages in a publication are basically the same format, only one format is needed regardless of the number of pages involved. Some products may include a variety of data types and involve complexity that will require a larger amount of application development work and conversion effort.

One of the hardest technical resources to find is someone already trained and skilled in the implementation of SGML tools. That is why there are so few SGML consultants offering their services these days. If you don't have existing SGML-related skills in house you have three choices:

1. Training existing personnel in the use of the tools and in SGML concepts,
2. Hiring contractors to do your development work
3. Stealing people with existing SGML expertise from other companies.

Training Existing Personnel

If you already have a staff of technical developers you can train them in the concepts of SGML and the specifics of the tools you have chosen to implement an SGML-based system. Training existing personnel is usually the best solution because it solves several problems simultaneously.

First, you have a staff available that already understands the products, culture, and environment in which they will be working and for which the tools will be needed. Second, it would be nice to keep your current employees employed, so teaching them to develop with the new tools gives them a career path to work on the new system. People who do not keep their skills current with the needs of the company will eventually become liabilities. Lastly, there are probably already team dynamics in place that make for more effective teams and a more rapid development schedule. New people will have to learn the ropes and personalities, and some may simply not work out.

There are difficulties in using existing personnel to develop the new system tools. First, you will most likely still need your existing people to continue to support the old system, so some of their time will not be available to work on developing the new system. Secondly, they do not bring experience in using the new tools to the project. Their inexperience may be a hindrance.

Lastly, it may be hard to "teach old dogs new tricks". Many technical people gravitate to tools and techniques that they have already mastered. Some of the existing tools and techniques in use may not be suitable for the new environment. For instance, someone accustomed to writing code that interrogates content to find elements might not be inclined to create an element that unambiguously identifies the same information with markup. People with composition experience tend to think in terms of format and may have difficulty in learning how to think of text as information with a logical structure. Similarly, computer science people may not know enough about the intricacies of composition and textual information to cope well with the requirements of an SGML publishing system without some training.

Using Contractors to Develop Tools

Contractors provide an attractive means to acquire expertise quickly in order to develop new technologies such as SGML. Contractors, well chosen, can bring a significant amount of experience to the project and may be able to solve problems quickly that they have encountered in prior implementations. Usually vendors can offer consulting service to assist you in implementing their systems. They might even have good relationships with other consulting companies and can recommend the services of others.

Contractors are not cheap. You pay a premium for this expertise. Also, contractors with SGML experience are in high demand due to the rapid increase in interest and implementation of SGML. There are no certification boards or tests for SGML consultants. It is, therefore, important to ask for recommendations from past clients before trusting your project to an outside consultant.

A significant drawback to relying on contractors is that you may never develop the expertise in your own staff. A balance of training your own people and using experienced contractors to help trainers and solve the really tricky problems is a good strategy for choosing implementation resources.

Choosing a contractor to perform training is not as simple as selecting a low cost source or using the most popular source. Implementing an SGML project is not the same as implementing, for example, an accounting system. The concepts are not as well-developed as accounting principles nor as widely understood. Training developers in SGML requires knowledge of your products, customers and processes. You cannot abdicate your responsibilities to someone else — someone who will be gone when the work is done. You must be intimately involved in the development of your resources. Many implementors choose to have contractors develop customized training programs and to train their own personnel in conducting them.

Stealing Resources from other Companies

The third option, that usually remains understood but unspoken, is to steal expertise from other companies where it is already well developed. This is a quick way to ramp up these skills. Even though movement of personnel between companies is a normal process, you will have to consider how stealing resources from other companies is perceived. These resources may bring valuable knowledge about implementing SGML, but they may also bring biases and habits they obtained at the other company that do not fit in your environment.

Project Progress

The first phase of implementation involves a small team performing the requirements and evaluation steps. Once development begins, costs begin to rise dramatically. Productivity drops slightly during the early days of use of the new system in the pilot and prototype phases. After a while, productivity begins to increase and costs related to development diminishes. Eventually the benefits become greater than the costs. Eventually, the total costs represented by the area labeled "a" in the chart below will be much less than the economic benefits represented by the area labeled "b", especially when the full life cycle has been completed.

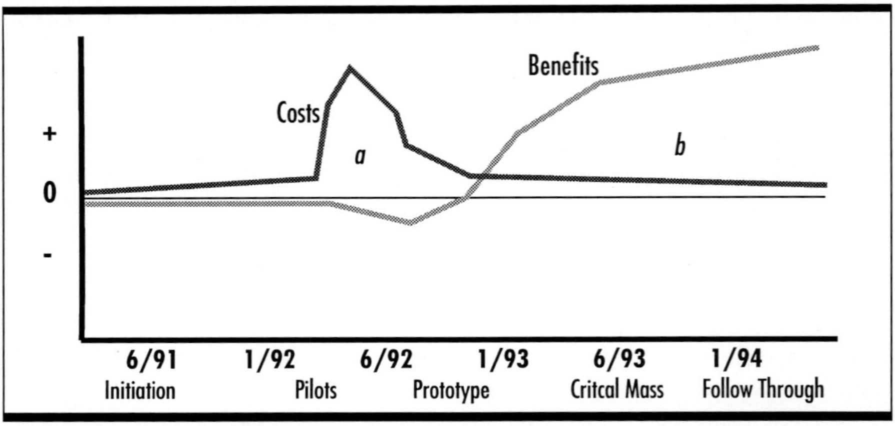

Figure 47. *Cost/Benefit Chart of Implementation*

The chart below shows user and developer confidence during the implementation process.

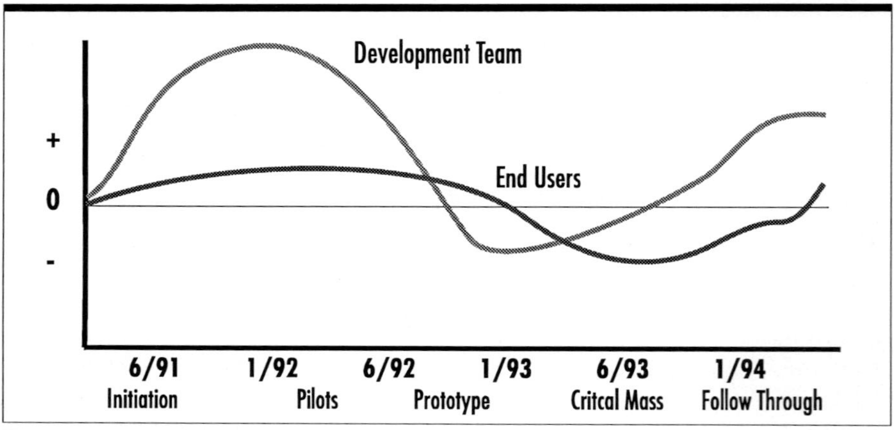

Figure 48. *Implementation Enthusiometer*

As typical with most computer development projects, the development team's enthusiasm is a little ahead of the end user's. The development team also goes through a brief spell of depression when the pressure is on to show results and there is still a lot of work to be done. This is where it is critical to have strong leadership on the project to both manage the expectations of the users and motivate the development team. Eventually, as the bugs are worked out of the system, enthusiasm and optimism will return, first to developers as they deliver technical solutions, then to users as they begin to use and learn the new tools and the benefits are realized.

CHAPTER • EIGHT

Information Conversion

Introduction

If information has any longevity to it, it will inevitably need to be transformed someday into another form. Either it will need cleansing to be made more consistent, or enhancement to provide additional value, or it will simply be transformed to work in a new environment. We typically think of these types of processes as data conversion. But there are really many different aspects to conversion, enough that it is useful to clarify what we mean and define some terms. Throughout this chapter we will talk about conversions, migration, translation, filtering, extractions, and even some other processes that are similar but fairly unique.

The tasks required to convert data from whatever form it happens to reside into SGML can be daunting. There are so many things that need to be done that it can be a management and organizational nightmare. This is the case with any conversion, whether SGML is involved or not. You can probably be assured, however, that a conversion to SGML is probably the last one you will do.

Because of the complicated tasks required for converting data, this chapter contains an section titled *Anatomy of an SGML Conversion* on page 153. In this section, you will see what is required to get data from a foreign format into SGML.

Related Topics

- *The Power of SGML Databases* on page 11
- Chapter 2, *Evolution of Publishing Systems* on page 23
- *Working in an SGML Environment* on page 44
- Chapter 5, *Document Analysis* on page 65
- *The Document Analysis Team* on page 67
- *Formatting and Structure* on page 87
- *Capture* on page 105
- *The Holy Grail* on page 108
- Chapter 7, *Implementation Planning* on page 121
- *Legacy Information Conversion* on page 140
- *Determine Granularity* on page 202
- Chapter 10, *Understanding SGML* on page 215
- *Markup* on page 219
- *Declarations* on page 223
- Chapter 11, *Building the DTD* on page 275
- *DTD Version Control* on page 283
- *Common Elements* on page 288
- Chapter 12, *Tipniques and Pratfalls* on page 301
- Appendix 8, *SGML Resources* on page 445

The Need for Conversion

We were performing data conversions long before there was SGML. But the development of SGML has reduced the need for some types of conversions by allowing us to define our data better and to improve the automated processes we use to transform data.

Data conversion can be very expensive due to the need for human intervention to resolve ambiguities and incompleteness in the data. In spite of the high costs of conversion, there are many situations where the costs are justified by the return on investment potential. Data is converted using a mixture of automated and manual processes.

TERMS

For the purposes of a consistent discussion, we will refer to the process of taking data from one type of coding format to another as conversion. That is to say, if we are in the process of moving data from one proprietary typesetting coding structure, a specific markup language, to a structured language such as SGML, and the process will require some manual resolution of data ambiguities, we are converting the data.

Taking a file from one system to another, analyzing and improving all the processes used to create and update that information, and creating a new database of enhanced information, is called migration. It usually involves a considerable investment in new software, workstations, and networks, and will require training of personnel in a whole new way of doing things. Conversion is the process of enhancing data to work with new, better tools, and is one step in the process of migration.

The process of moving information between word processing formats might be a conversion, except that the tools that are used to perform this process are often called filters, so maybe that is filtering. But when we filter water, we remove impurities, take something out. Perhaps filtering is the process of simplifying the coding to a less sophisticated form, such as taking richly encoded data and producing a plain ASCII text file. The industry commonly refers to this as "filtering".

Moving between formats entirely automatically is referred to as "machine translation", or just "translation", which should not be confused with natural language translation. Either way, filtering or translation, is not conversion since data is transformed to an equal or less sophisticated form, and is usually done without human intervention. Conversion involves raising data to a higher form.

So, to clarify, conversion is the process of enhancing data, which usually requires some manual processes to be completed. Migration is the entire process of implementing a new system, of which conversion (or translation) might be a single sub-process. Translation and filtering are the automated processes used to move data from one environment to another that is equally or less sophisticated.

Anatomy of an SGML Conversion

For data to be used and processed in an SGML-based system it must first be converted to an SGML format. This format is defined in the DTD, and the data must be marked-up according to the language and rules defined in this DTD. The process of converting data from plain ASCII, proprietary markup, or other forms can be range from simple to extremely complex and expensive.

The basic conversion of, for instance, a typesetting file for a single-volume book to a basic novel DTD may be done using very simple tools such as word processing macros or AWK scripts and require only one or two passes at the data. More richly encoded data, such as technical documentation with detailed information (part numbers, complex structure, graphics, etc.) will most likely require a more complex set of tools and many more steps in the conversion process.

This section provides an overview of a simple conversion project to illustrate the basis process that all conversions will most likely require. Specialized details or richly encoded data will require specialized processes and process flows, sophisticated tools, and, perhaps, outside resources. The issues related to a more complex conversion project are described in more detail throughout the balance this chapter.

THE BASIC CONVERSION PROCESS

All data being transformed from raw text or text with proprietary markup to more detailed SGML markup is in the process of being enhanced. These enhancements may require more detail to be added to the explicit coding in the text to support automated processes that was previous done manually, such as the generation of tables of contents or tables of figures. Another enhancement may be that once the data is converted, it may be validated to ensure that it complies with a consistent set of structure rules. Enhancing data almost always means that programs or utilities will be applied to the data conversion for most of the process, but that a small amount of ambiguous data will need to be completed by humans. The basic conversion processing steps are shown below:

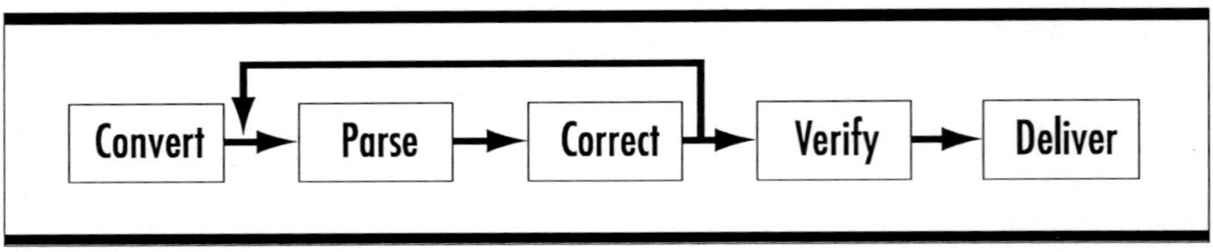

Figure 49. *Basic SGML Conversion Process.*

The Convert step may involve programs designed to change existing source data coding or characters into the target SGML markup, the use of search-and-replace tools or macros in software editors or word processors, utilities such as AWK scripts, or may be done entirely manually. Factors that dictate how this processing may be done include size of the file, complexity of the coding (both source and target), consistency of source coding or characters, and available skills and tools.

Parsing is the process of using an SGML parser to check the markup and structure of your converted file against the target DTD. A validating parser will report any errors it finds in the data instance (and the DTD). These errors messages usually describe the type of error condition and the location of the error. Conversion processing personnel can use these error messages to locate and correct the errors in the data. Once corrections are made, the file will need to be parsed again. This process is repeated until all errors are eliminated and the file is compliant with the target DTD.

Once the data is converted and successfully parsed, you will need to perform quality assurance activities to ensure the conversion was conducted properly beyond the control and reporting that parsing gives you. Even after a file parses without errors, you still have to verify that the content was correctly marked up, that no necessary data is missing, and that other problems did not occur during the conversion processing. This verification step is similar to proofreading. It involves a person comparing the converted SGML data to the source and checking that the correct tags were applied. It is different from proofreading in that the person doing the verification is not necessarily checking every word or character and it may progress much faster than proofreading.

The last step above, Delivery, indicates that there may be some activity related to delivering the data that is compliant. These activities may include combining files that were broken into small run units for manageability, or simply transferring the files to another location on a network and recording their completion in a log.

The process described above is extremely simple compared to what most conversions really entail. Areas that will require special attention and processing include tabular material that appears in text, text that is in a very inconsistent form, and other complex structures such as illustrations, equations, and specialized elements such as part numbers or cross-references.

FINDING CLUES IN SOURCE DATA

Source data will include coding and other clues that will be converted to the target markup. Conversion to SGML is almost always more complicated than simply translating one set of codes to equivalent SGML markup. There are often conditions where several codes may be used in conjunction with other codes or surrounding text in order create the desired SGML markup. This is shown in the following example where the following markup:

```
:h2.Chapter 2. Dogs
```

Is transformed into the following SGML markup:

```
<chapter number='2'><name>Dogs</name>
```

In this example the old source markup `:h2.` is interpreted as a heading, in this case a Chapter heading. The conversion program or regular expression command would need to then search the following text to find the number and insert it into the attribute `number` when it builds and outputs the SGML markup. Finally, in this example, the period may be used to indicate the end of the numerical value and the beginning of the text that will be marked-up as a `name` element. In OmniMark it would be expressed as:

```
find
  ":h2.Chapter "
  digit = ChapNum
  ". "
  letter+ = Name

  output "<chapter num='%x(ChapNum)'><name>%x(Name)</name>"
```

Of course your conversion programs will include many more rules such as the one illustrated above, and will be specific to your source data format, target data format, processing tools, and conversion system design. Converting to SGML can become very complex. Sometimes even the available markup and surrounding characters alone may not be sufficient to identify some SGML elements unambiguously. You may need to track the context in which things are found, the order in which they are found, or other information during conversion processing to be able to apply the appropriate markup. There are almost no completely automated conversion processes, and the ones that can run as smoothly and automatically as a filter, such as the filters used to translate between word processing formats, are probably not very complex or detailed.

CREATING A CONVERSION SPEC

If you have created a DTD and want to instruct a programmer to create a conversion program or a conversion house to convert your data you will need to create a conversion specification document, commonly called a "conversion spec". The conversion spec should be organized in a logical format to make it easy to locate the information for referencing and updating. You will find during a conversion project that the spec will need to be continually updated to include information found in the data instances after the initial specification was created. Just as a DTD will be continually updated during the first conversion process, so will the conversion spec and other documentation describing your document model.

A conversion spec, especially one that has been continually updated for completeness and accuracy, is extremely useful when you want to start the second conversion project. You will be able to reuse much of the information learned during the conversion, especially subtle nuances about the legacy data and coding, unusual features, common elements, and a more thorough list of all the variations of coding that has most likely not been prepared consistently.

Small or simple conversion projects may not require much if any conversion spec. More complex projects where several departments are involved in the overall development of the system and the data will depend on a clear and accurate spec for conversion.

Conversion instructions are not necessarily limited to simply stating what each code is in the legacy data and describing what it should be converted into. In fact, it is better to start by describing the target structures and coding and then give a complete list of all "clues" found in text that will be needed to build these structures. By organizing the document around the target, instead of the source coding, you will find updating and locating information much easier, as well as providing a useful way to keep the document model in mind when creating the specification. If the spec is written by from the perspective of the source data, it is easily limited to the coding and other clues found in the source data, and, after all, converting to SGML is all about inferring additional information about the data that was not explicit in the legacy format.

A conversion spec can be closely related to the DTD itself, or even be an annotated form of the DTD. Provide extensive examples of markup and surrounding text. Show how tags may be used several different ways to account for optional (`#IMPLIED`) attributes and defined allowed attribute values. Show how general entity references might occur in text. Describe how text elements are to be reorganized, broken into separate elements, and what text will need to be removed since it is implied by the markup and will be generated by the rendering application. Describe naming conventions for files and how work-in-progress data should be managed and handled.

Provide procedures for resolving anomalies— there will be many anomalies—through the conversion process. Use a structured approach that employs numbered problem resolution requests, since there may be many problems each day. Lastly, describe the conversion processing to be applied during the conversion and at later steps in the data migration process. A better view of the entire process will assist developers and conversion service bureaus in resolving questions.

Tracking the Conversion Process

A project with a significant amount of data to be converted will require at least some basic production management concepts to succeed. For instance, a large source file may need to be broken into several, or many, "run units" or "bite-sized chunks" to allow several people to work on converting different pieces of it at the same time. If the conversion is fairly complex, the convert step may need to be broken into several sub-steps, and may even need parsing several times along the way. Perhaps the first sub-step finds and makes consistent the obvious structural elements, and the second step uses the markup from the first step to specify context when doing more complex detailed markup. Maybe another step is used to reorganize the data. Footnotes may need to be merged to an in-line position in the SGML data, and this step may require that all footnote references be converted first to make the merge program run smoothly.

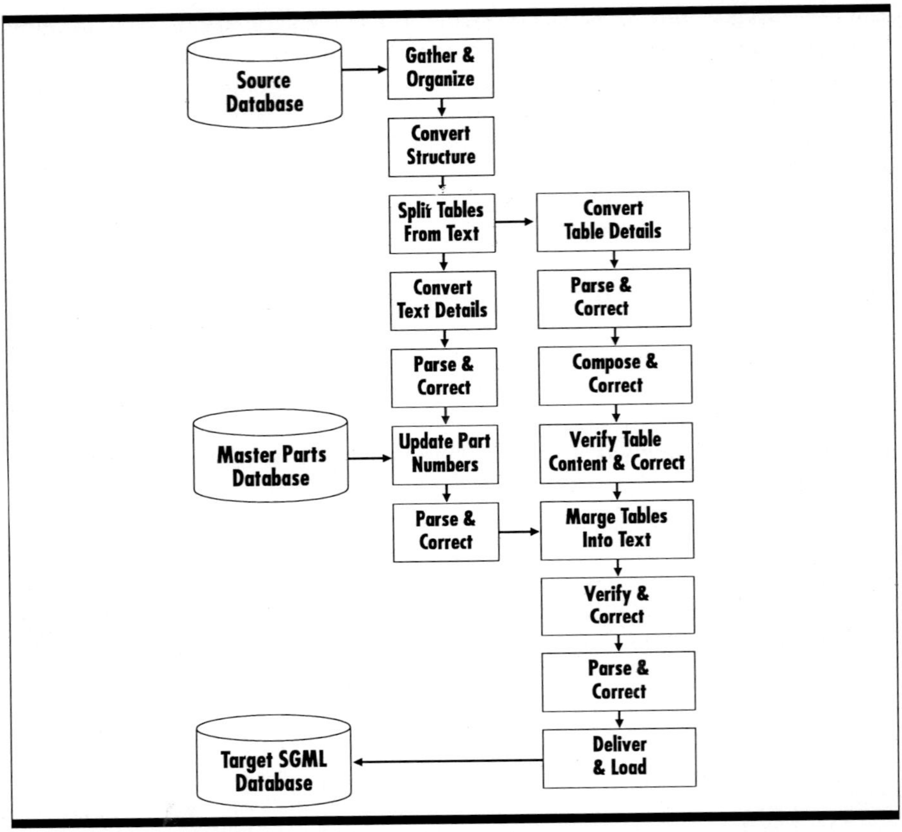

Figure 50. *Process Flow for a Typical SGML Conversion Project.*

If a conversion project requires many run units to be processed through several conversion processing steps, a method of tracking this work is recommended. A common form of tracking is to use a log with steps on one axis and run units on the other, as illustrated below:

Unit	Conv1	Conv2	Parse1	Conv3	Parse2	Verify	Deliver
chap1	dw 3/11	dw 3/11	dw 3/11	dw 3/11	dw 3/11	kl 3/12	
chap2	bt 3/11	bt 3/11	bt 3/11	bt 3/11	bt 3/11	lm 3/12	
chap3	dw 3/12	dw 3/12	dw 3/12	dw 3/12	dw 3/12		
chap4	bt 3/12	bt 3/12	dw 3/12	bt 3/12			
chap5	dw 3/13						

Figure 51. *Conversion Processing Log showing partial completion of conversion of five chapter run units.*

This log sheet includes a list of the run units, in this case the chapters of the book, along the vertical axis and the conversion steps along the horizontal. This log was created using a computer spreadsheet. In each cell at the intersection of a step and a run unit, the project manager has recorded the initials of the person who completed the step for that unit and the date it was completed. At a glance, the project manager can track the progress of the conversion project.

In the above example, there are three conversion sub-steps; given the names `CONV1`, `CONV2`, and `CONV3`. Each sub-step focuses on bringing the data to a slightly higher level in the conversion process that the previous form it was in, and may involve one or more programs. If several programs are included in a single step, it is likely that they have been streamed together using a script to make the processes of executing them easier. In this scenario, the results of the first sub-step, `CONV1`, will not be sufficient enough to allow the operator to parse the output successfully. Even so, `CONV1` may produce an error log or one or more reports, as might each step along the way. The chart below illustrates this and may be useful to the operator running the conversion programs for finding the right output and or error log.

Process Name	Program Names	Input File Ext.	Output File Ext.	Error Log Ext.	Report File Ext.
CONV1	STRUCT	.raw	.out	.lg1	
	TEXT	.out	.txt	.lg2	.pct
CONV2	PARTNO	.txt	.prt	.lg3	.pno
	XREFS	.prt	.xrf	.lg4	.xrp
PARSE1		.xrf		.lg5	
CONV3	MRGFN	.xrf	.sgm	.lg6	.fnr
PARSE2		.sgm		.lg7	

Figure 52. *Example of a conversion processing tracking sheet showing details of the entire process, including program names, reports, logs, and file extension naming conventions used in a DOS/LAN environment.*

In this scenario processing is done in a DOS environment and programs are streamed together or executed from DOS batch files that prompt for file names. A single run unit will keep the same DOS file name, but will have different file extensions when new versions are output by each process. In the chart above you can see how the first process actually runs two programs; `STRUCT`, which converts structural elements, and `TEXT` which converts the paragraphs and other text elements. These elements are used to determine context for finding part numbers and cross-references in the second process, `CONV2`. The output of `CONV2` is parsed by invoking the parser from a command line whose variables and have been gathered and/or specified by the DOS batch file. After parsing using `PARSE1`, the operator will check the file for that run unit with the `.lg5` extension and apply corrections to the file with the `.xrf` extension. Once successfully cleansed and parsed, the file will be run through the footnote merger program `MRGFN` by invoking the `CONV3` batch file. Finally, the file is reparsed to make sure that `MRGFN` did not introduce errors. There are several reports that are generated, such as the report showing footnotes that did not merge correctly (with the `.fnr` extension), and the report of all part numbers found and tagged (with the `.pno` extension). These reports may be used in verification or other quality assurance activities before the data is delivered.

The specific scripts or batch routines are dependent on your operating system, the tools you use and how you organize your conversion process. The types of reports you will need are dependent on the complexity of your data, the amount of quality assurance you need, and other processes that may be run later that depend on information gathered during the conversion. This example is a fairly simple process that has been well organized to allow it to run smoothly. A project that will involve the conversion of a very large volume of data will need to be well organized to prevent confusion and to track progress.

SUMMARY. This brief description of a conversion project barely scratches the surface of the material that can be covered regarding converting to SGML. The balance of this chapter delves into the topic much more thoroughly, but, again, since every situation has unique requirements, every project will be different.

Data Conversion Planning and Implementation

So you want to convert to SGML. If you have never done it before there are a few things about converting your data, your information resource, that you should know. A good strategy can make the difference between making budget and breaking the bank.

This discussion assumes you intend to convert more than one publication, perhaps all, or a significant portion of your company's information resources. The ideas in this discussion can be scaled up or down depending on your volume and complexity.

This discussion is oriented toward the commercial publishing field. Some ideas may need to be re-examined for how they apply to government agencies, defense contractors, and publishers that support another process, perhaps manufacturing, which is their business' primary activity.

PLANNING

What may seem obvious, but often is overlooked, is developing an overall plan of what and how you intend to convert, in what order, and using what resources. The first part of the implementation process is setting the scope of the entire migration; which titles, users, and sites. You will need to prioritize your titles on criteria that you deem necessary to your particular project.

No matter what your overall needs are, it is always a good idea to break a conversion plan into three phases:

1. prototype
2. critical need, and
3. follow up.

Prototype Phase

The prototype phase is your test, your shakedown cruise. After deciding what system tools you will be implementing, you will need to test their success and allow your developers and users a period of adjustment during the early part of their learning curve. You can also learn a lot about conversion techniques and the structure of your data during this phase and still have time to make adjustments before you commit to an irreversible and flawed direction (*i.e.*, one that is prohibitively expensive to correct).

Choose one or two titles that are representative of the types of products you will be converting in the critical-need phase (discussed below). Do not select the toughest one. Avoid the easiest unless you intend to do at least one more title that is fairly typical of the data types and work processes that are part of your overall system. The goal here is to test your design, test your tools and the applications you have developed under them, and to test your work flow and process flow before you commit the company's flagship products (or most critical assets) to the upheaval of migration to a new processing system.

Build an evaluation task into your plan that will allow you to identify problems, devise solutions, and make adjustments to your data design, applications, and work flow accordingly before converting your entire database.

Critical-Need Phase

The critical-need phase involves addressing the conversion of the titles based on your specific needs. Once you are satisfied that you have gotten critical bugs out of the process during the prototype phase, you will need to address the products that are critical to your objectives. These objectives, the goals of the project, are the reason you are involved in this project in the first place and should be addressed up front. If your objective is to convert your entire product line, then you will need to find some meaningful order in which to convert.

Perhaps there are several titles that are in terrible shape. They may be difficult to produce, or have fallen into disrepair and need to be reorganized or even rewritten. You might prioritize on trouble areas.

Maybe you need to develop electronic versions of key titles in order to reduce the cost of documentation or to open up a new product revenue opportunities. The cost of producing multiple versions of a product from the same information can be significantly cheaper if the data is maintained in a structured format. You might chose to prioritize on cost saving or revenue enhancement opportunities.

Another way to slice it might be on the impact implementation may have on the organization. You should consider the disruption caused by the implementation of any new system. It may even be a high priority consideration in a situation where work functions or product line responsibilities are fragmented. A driving force may be the need to get a grip on the product line or production process. Work performed in a process or by a particular group may be your first target for improvements.

The titles selected for the critical-need phase will represent a significant portion of the expected benefit for the implementation. Often you will find the big money makers (or high cost items) leading this list, especially if you are hoping to get considerable cost savings as a result of this effort. Other good candidates for the critical-need phase are titles that are parent publications with other titles that are dependent on them.

Reuse of data and sharing information across titles is also a candidate for the critical-need phase since there is more opportunity for realizing project goals by implementing this approach. If you have been publishing many books that include a parts list and parts information, you might consider creating a shared database where this information will be maintained once and used in many places. This shared database should be created in the critical-need phase, otherwise you will have converted the parts information in many publications and later thrown it away when the parts database is created.

Follow-Up Phase

You will eventually get around to doing all of the legacy titles included in the scope of your implementation. Whether you get around to the follow up phase titles right away or over an extended period of time depends on your overall strategy.

Taking a clean sweep approach, whereby all titles are converted as quickly as possible, offers both advantages and disadvantages. The advantage of attacking the entire list of publications in a short period is that you quickly move off the old system and onto the new one. People will not need to work in two environments and you can throw away the old system components along with their maintenance costs and other overhead. The disadvantage is that it might be more expensive and/or disruptive to be so aggressive.

One alternative is to address the critical-need titles aggressively, and then fall back into a more leisure pace, converting the remaining titles over a longer period of time. The advantage of this approach is that conversion costs may be lower and the process can be easily managed at a more sane pace. The disadvantages are that you will extend the period where you are running and maintaining two separate systems. Also, by putting the follow-up titles in a lower priority mode, you run the risk of never getting around to them, since we all tend to get caught up in the crisis *du jour*. You may wind up running both systems for a very long time. It is usually better to press ahead and follow up on converting the balance of titles as quickly as you can.

CONVERSION PROCESSING

The first rule of conversion processing is to expect errors that will affect the DTD, the conversion programs, and just about every other aspect of the conversion process. Even if you have done exhaustive analysis and testing, unless you actually convert every bit of data, you will not encounter every possible instance that may affect your design. Oh well, accept it and plan for it.

Communication is very important while converting the data. Let the people who are developing the formatting and database management facilities know of all DTD changes. Remember that the developers of these tools will also be encountering situations that may affect the DTD and every other process. Expect feedback from everyone and do not convert any data until you are sure all developers and users have had at least one thorough walkthrough of the DTD and system designs.

Once all the conversion processes have been coded and tested the conversion processing can begin. If you are processing large volumes of information, you will probably stagger the actual conversion to allow portions of the data to progress to the next step while other portions are still in the previous step. Staggering the conversion requires effective management of the data as it flows through the process and careful change management.

MANAGING DTD CHANGE

Once data is being converted, changes to the design can be either restrictive or relaxing. An example of a relaxing change to a DTD is making a required element optional. This relaxes or loosens the model. A relaxing change may be as soothing as it sounds since all data converted and validated before the change would still parse after the change. No data would need to be re-parsed.

A restrictive change is one where the model becomes tighter as a result of the change. An example is making an optional element required. Restrictive changes can be troublesome if made after you start to convert your data. All data previously parsed should be reparsed to ensure their validity. The parsing validation step is labor intensive. For this reason, care should be made during the design of the DTD to anticipate as much of the details of the DTD as possible and to try to err in favor of a model that is slightly tighter and can be loosened up if needed in the conversion process.

DATA CLEANSING AND VALIDATION

The cleansing process is an expensive manual clean-up designed to finish the work that either a program can't do or it would not be cost effective to spend the time to do it. Most of the clean-up involves clarifying ambiguities that exist in the data since it was not created in a controlled, structured environment, but new requirements, such as translating to electronic products using automated translation routines, now require the data be stored and managed more stringently.

Once a programmatic conversion has been applied to a set of data, error resolution and other clean up will need to be done in order that the data will be fully parseable. Some composition systems can compose data even though it does not parse against the DTD to which it was converted. There are several reasons why data should be completely cleansed and validated before you consider the conversion task complete. These include avoiding problems in translating to electronic products, reusing data in other publications or databases, loading databases, and using tools such as SGML-smart editors.

After a file is run through a conversion program(s) it is parsed and the errors are corrected by a human familiar with the document, the DTD and SGML concepts. This person needs to be familiar with SGML concepts and jargon because most parser error messages can be confusing to the uninitiated.

Clean-up parsing is usually an iterative process. When an error is found during parsing that is severe enough to cause the parser to stop, parsing may not continue past that point in the file until the error is resolved. Some parsers try to find a point where it can start validating again called a re-synchronize point. Errors tend to compound upon themselves, leading to dozens or even hundreds of useless errors being reported.

If the converted data is managed in large chunks, the processing time will be significant due to this iterative process because the earlier portions of the data will be reparsed several times until a pass is made through the entire file without an error. Conversion data should be managed in reasonably smaller, more manageable chunks or run units that are clearly identified so that they can be programmatically put back together when needed.

Any changes made should promptly be documented and communicated. Catch-up work caused by surprises in the data can cause missed deadlines weeks after the converted data is delivered.

CONVERSION STRATEGIES

Conversion Through Attrition

There are several typical steps involved in executing the processes to convert data from an unstructured, proprietary format (*e.g.*, a typesetting language) to a structured format such as SGML. They are illustrated below:

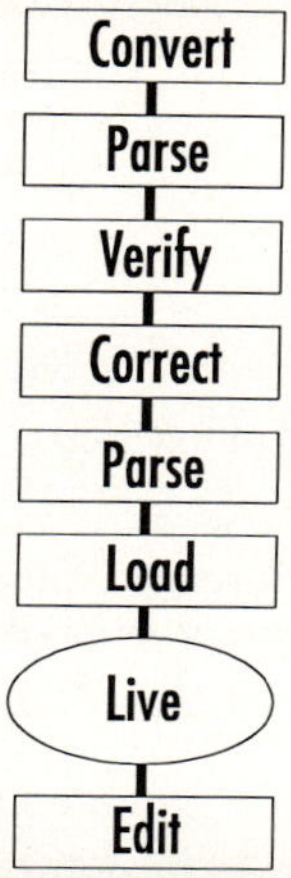

Figure 53. *Typical conversion steps where data is validated before being placed into a production editing environment*

These steps show how data can be taken from one format, converted to another, validated, and loaded into the editing environment where it is finally "live" (available for editing). Each organization may have unique specific steps that they will need to include. One example might be merging data that was previously stored separately (perhaps footnotes or supplements). Another example might be to reorganize the data into an entirely different form such as taking data stored in a traditional linear book format where everything is stored in the sequential order it appears in the printed book, and rearranging it to fit a more logical database model where related information is stored together regardless of the order in which it is published. Floating elements may be moved back in-line to the place from where they were originally referenced. The possibilities are too plentiful to be included in a simple process flow diagram such as the one we are using above to discuss the basic steps to converting data.

The following chart illustrates how costs increase dramatically after the programmatic conversion process stops and the human clean-up starts.

In some situations it is possible to avoid the higher costs of cleansing the data, or at least putting it off until it actually will be needed. By putting off the clean-up and parsing of data until after it has gone live, data can be loaded and be available for editing sooner. The theory is that much of the expensive manual clean-up costs can be deferred, or even avoided. These costs, illustrated below, rise significantly over time compared to programming costs since programs, once developed, can be run against large quantities of data achieving a better economy of scale.

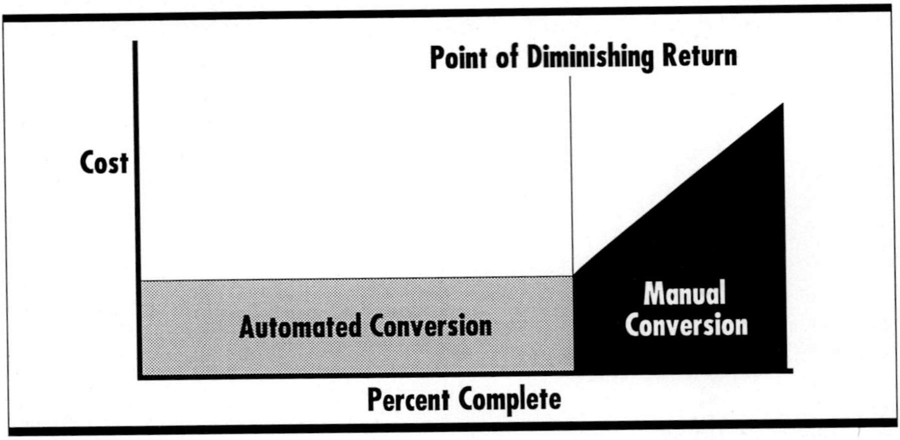

Figure 54. *Increased costs associated with final manual cleansing during conversion*

If you programatically convert 80-percent of your data, you might double or triple your costs while manually converting or cleaning up the balance. If a publication is going to be fairly heavily revised in the near future, it does not make sense to cleanse the parts of the book that will be rewritten or even thrown out. That's a waste of money. But if you don't know which parts will be kept and which will be changed, you cannot only cleanse the parts that will be kept.

Also, if the book is not going to be republished for some time, it might make sense to not do the cleansing as part of the conversion. Instead, let the authors clean up any problems when they open a portion of the publication for their normal updates. By cleansing the data through attrition, as it is normally edited, you can avoid a significant portion of the manual conversion costs.

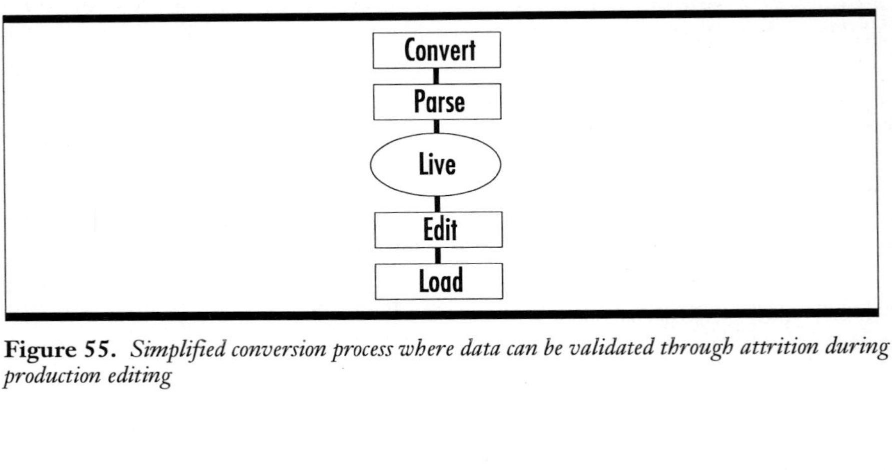

Figure 55. *Simplified conversion process where data can be validated through attrition during production editing*

Using this approach of cleansing through attrition is not practical if the data will be needed for reuse in other products or other versions such as CD-ROMs. The processes used to collect data and translate it into these by-products may not be capable of dealing with only partially cleansed data. If you have these requirements, you should bite the bullet and clean up the whole lot up front.

Conversions Using the Rainbow DTD

As you can see from reading this chapter, conversion to SGML can be a complex and expensive task. In an effort to reduce the complexity and cost of some conversions, the Rainbow DTD was developed by Electronic Book Technologies, Inc. and has been incorporated into at least two interactive conversion tools, sometimes referred to as "tree-transformation tools".

Rainbow is a flat, format-oriented DTD designed to get documents from many popular word-processing and text processing formats into a common format. Rainbow was not designed to be a model in which information would be managed on an on-going basis, but rather an intermediate step in the conversion process. The idea is to provide many "Rainbow Makers", or conversion utilities that convert common formats into the Rainbow format. After that, other conversion utilities could be built that would convert the text to other SGML DTDs.

If an organization has the need to convert data from three different word processing formats into a customized SGML application, they would most likely need to develop three conversion systems to accomplish it. If, on the other hand, these formats were supported by public domain Rainbow Makers, the conversion developers would only have to create one conversion system to support converting text from Rainbow to their custom DTD.

This approach can expedite conversion since it limits the number of incoming source formats for which conversion systems would need to be developed. Also, since Rainbow is a DTD, there are some opportunities to use SGML techniques, such as context sensitivity, during the conversion to the customized DTD and to increase the accuracy of that process.

Several products have been developed that provide interactive access to the conversion process (at the time of this writing, two utilize the Rainbow DTD. PowerPaste from ArborText and DynaTag from Electronic Book Technologies, Inc.. During processing, the application prompts an operator when it encounters a coding event that has not been accommodated in the conversion rules being applied. The interface application allows the operator to instruct the application on how to deal with that event type, to either treat it as a variation of another rule or to create a new rule. These types of product, as well as the whole Rainbow approach to conversion, are relatively new and unproven but hold much promise. This optimistic view is especially true for conversion projects that either do not involve large amounts of data, or are run regularly (like daily capture of outside authored information), or both.

Pre-conversion Testing

The only way to analyze every possible design issue that will be encountered during a document analysis and information conversion effort is to actually convert all the data. Even analyzing as much as half the pages still leaves the other half to present surprises during conversion processing. These surprises result in unexpected changes to the DTD and conversion programs and documentation. Users and conversion personnel will need to be notified. The result is a potential for delays, accuracy problems, and even the need for severe change that could require reconverting some or all of the completed data, all costly problems. Conducting data analysis, and even pre-conversion testing, against a scientific sampling of a representational cross section of all data types will provide useful feedback to the conversion programmer and allow for less problems during the production conversion processing.

If your information is going to be very valuable, it will need to be very rigorously or richly encoded, or both. The cost of converting data to this level of sophistication warrants as much analysis as possible to prevent delays and higher costs than necessary. A strategy to expedite a very precise conversion is to convert all or most of the data once, make a lot of notes on what is missing, throw away the converted data, modify the DTD and conversion programs, and then convert the data again. Introducing a pre-conversion process will improve the accuracy and completeness of the data analysis, make the programming more precise and thorough, and allow significant changes to be implemented at a point where they can be easily accommodated, before the data has begun to be converted for keeps.

We suggest that conversion programs be designed to allow as much conditional logic to be applied to anticipated states, and that all ambiguity be tagged as such with a `<problem>` tag to be resolved during the pre-conversion pass. For instance, every known state and content of a paragraph could be anticipated and coded for accordingly. When a condition occurs that is not provided for in the conversion code, a `<problem>` tag is applied and the conversion program applies the `</problem>` tag wherever it can recover (if at all). The contents of the `<problem>` element should be analyzed to determine what actions are needed; either a modification to the DTD or slight rewrite of the content, or both.

Several iterations may be needed for some areas where the `<problem>` tag was applied. Some problems will be so unique that they will hardly be worth coding into the conversion programs. These should be left for the manual clean-up. Eventually, most of the problems, and, more importantly, the design issues, will be resolved, thus expediting the conversion processing and subsequent manual clean-up effort.

CONVERSION RESOURCES

As you may have figured out by now, conversion of information, or rather enhancing information into a richer, more structured form, may not be such an easy process. There are conversion service bureaus that might be useful. There are also DTD designers that are available on a contract basis. But we feel the best approach to managing the conversion process is to do it yourself if you have the resources.

Writing conversion specifications without running into some sort of difficulty is nearly impossible. You could easily spend as much time writing conversion specifications, keeping them up to date, and checking up on the vendor as you would sitting down and developing the conversion programs yourself. Being once removed from the problem, the vendor is at a disadvantage when it comes to resolving problems and making decisions that might affect other processes. Changes need to be communicated quickly and with as little distortion as possible.

Working without conversion specifications or with an incomplete set increases ambiguity, and therefore, the potential for incorrect results. Even vendors with the best intentions who are honest have run into situations where the customer had a different idea of what was to be delivered than the vendor did. Nobody was trying to cheat or was being lazy, but the appearance remained that the vendor did not do a good job (the customer is always right).

Of course many conversion jobs have been done successfully by many vendors. The key to the success of the jobs is either a clear specification (written and/or verbally communicated) or wide tolerance in what would be accepted upon delivery, and planning on doing the finishing touches yourself after delivery.

Converting data yourself can be difficult as well. The advantages are that you will be closer to the problem and have a better idea of what answers there might be to question you come up with, or at least who should be contacted. One phone call and you might have your answer and approval to make a change. Another advantage is that you might be able to do it cheaper since you are not in the business of data conversion and not trying to maintain a profit margin. But, ironically, since you are not in that business, you might not have the skills, tools, or experience that would make doing it yourself cost effective.

Another reason you may elect to do the work yourself, even if it turns out to be more expensive and take longer than contracting, is if the information is internally confidential, or if you are under some kind of governmental or contractual agreement to keep the data secure.

Traditional programming shops have developed a very structured approach to programming that may not do well in converting data to SGML due to the short life-spans of most conversion programs and the higher cost of the structured methodology. In the structured approach, a programmer takes detailed specifications from an analyst and implements and tests them to ensure that they perform as specified. Since you can expect the specifications to require constant modification as the conversion progresses, you will need a super programmer analyst who can both make decisions and write effective code. Resolution of conversion issues must be done with close attention to DTD changes (See *Managing DTD Change* on page 163).

Another useful skill is knowing when it is overkill to build an elaborate routine which is only going to be used once. Unless you have a large library of very consistent publications, most conversion programming will be throw-away code. It will be used only once, or at least will not be useful for other publications without a lot of modification. Actually, a very effective approach to writing conversion programs is to continually write new routines as you encounter new issues and to allow the data to evolve as it is processed by each routine. Each routine is designed to perform a specific part of the conversion and can be utilized as needed. Everything from very powerful programming languages to simple utilities and macros can be applied *ad hoc* as the need for a particular function arises.

No matter which approach to conversion resources you use— in-house or outside—you will need some documentation beyond the DTD. The DTD is just a start. It is the target. You will also need to know how the existing markup works in order to convert it, whenever possible, to SGML markup. When there is no one-for-one relationship between existing markup and SGML markup, instructions on how to find and/or interrogate the content will be extremely useful. If, for example, part numbers are not identified as such in the legacy data, and now you want to identify and tag them, instructions—about where they might occur, what standardized text may precede or follow them, what to do to make this text, how to parse the sub-elements—would be essential for building an effective conversion program. Do not expect the "standardized text" specified by style guides to be consistent in the real world. Without programmatic enforcement, humans are capable of creating many variations. After all, this is one of the reasons you selected SGML.

The simplest form of conversion documentation will be the many pages of notes taken during face-to-face meetings with the programmers, the DTD developer, and other key players during a conversion walk-through. In a walk-through you should examine as much of the existing published data as possible and make decisions on how to handle the details.

It would be nice if we could lock an editor and a technical person (the super programmer/analyst) in a room and not let them out until the data is converted, thus avoiding having to write any specifications at all. But since this is unlikely, a second choice is to develop real software engineering and SGML design skills into a person who can communicate well and who can manage their own time and workload effectively. This mix of skills allows a level of ambiguity to remain that can expedite the progress of the conversion, but not at the expense of the required accuracy. A person who is too structured cannot handle this type of ambiguity and probably won't be able to think on his or her feet in order to swiftly resolve problems. A person who is too unstructured may make decisions too quickly causing errors and/or delays to the conversion effort.

EXISTING CONVERSIONS THAT MAY BE HIGH-COST AREAS

In many publishing systems in use today, there are many subsystems that attempt to assist the creation, capture, and conversion of information that is being managed in an unstructured form. This data presents opportunities for cost reduction and process streamlining through the application of structured data management techniques and tools. Typically we find three types of processes that can be significantly improved or even totally automated with the adoption of SGML and/or database techniques, including:

1. Ongoing data capture
2. Ongoing production feeds
3. Content extraction/generation.

Ongoing Data Capture

When we think of data conversion, typically we think of the one-time migration process that occurs when a new system is adopted and installed. But even in a production situation, there may be a continual need to convert new information that is part of the regular process of capturing data from external feeds or authoring sources and massaging it for use in publications and databases. This is called "ongoing data capture".

Eventually, most information that needs to be collected may be made available in a rigorous form such as SGML. This is the goal of many industry initiatives: to reduce on-going conversion costs and difficulties. Until then, organizations that count on data coming from external sources will need to develop a mechanism for continually converting data. This process is nearly identical to a one-time conversion, except that it usually involves much smaller quantities of data and will need to be performed on an ongoing basis.

Some industries may have regularly scheduled update cycles, such as the annual release of information in the automotive industry that is tied to new year car models. Other industries will have a less cyclical schedule, such as legal publishing where the laws may be passed at just about any time of the year and will need to be rapidly incorporated into the database as soon as they are passed. In the legal world, a publisher cannot afford to delay the collection and conversion of new information from outside sources, and therefore, usually builds a mechanism for data capture.

With the advent of industry initiatives to develop a consistent rigorous model for information interchange, many organizations will be able to realize the goal of getting information delivered in a form that is immediately usable. Although the industry-wide DTD may not be identical to the DTDs in use inside of the using organization, the fact that the data is delivered in a rigorous and predictable form will greatly improve the ability of the user to incorporate it into their database upon receipt. This will greatly simplify the on-going data capture process, but may not alleviate the need for a conversion-like data enhancement and clean-up step to be conducted on an ongoing basis.

If you depend on data from outside sources over which you have little control, you will need to develop processes that will allow you to convert this data in a manner that is timely and accurate enough to suit your business needs. There are many issues that need to be addressed by each implementor. Accuracy may need to be compromised for expediency if the data is of a time-critical nature. Perhaps a simpler DTD can speed up the process of data capture for initial inclusion in the database. Or, if timeliness is not as important as the accuracy and level of detail needed for the data to be useful and the business objectives to be satisfied, manual clean-up may be necessary, and may need to be conducted at a moment's notice. A sufficient resource, internal or external, should be developed and maintained to provide the conversion and clean-up services.

Ongoing Production Feeds

Another type of conversion emerged with the advent of electronic delivery tools such as CD-ROM. Typically, databases maintained for creating typeset pages could not feed the processes used to produce the electronic versions of the same data. Usually data was not coded in sufficient detail to support requirements for electronic products, such as hypertext linking. Therefore, additional steps had to take place where the data was enhanced in order to produce the electronic product. These steps could be manual or automated or a mixture of both. These steps may also include conversion processing to get the data into another coding scheme to support the electronic delivery environment.

Hypertext links were often coded using programs, but nearly always required manual cleansing and verification if any degree of detail and accuracy was required. Other processes were also required for electronic products that are not needed for print publication production due to the inherent differences in the way the data was packaged, delivered, and used. For instance, some data that would make sense in a print publication, such as tables of contents, front matter, and indices, might not be useful in an electronic product where other searching mechanisms are provided. Also, data need not be stored in the sequential form used in the print publication when organizing it for an electronic product.

In order to produce electronic products from databases designed to produce print products, a separate, additional production path is created. At some point in the process of creating the print product, a copy of the data would be extracted and converted and fed into a parallel database used for the electronic product. This linear production process is called an ongoing production feed and is illustrated below:

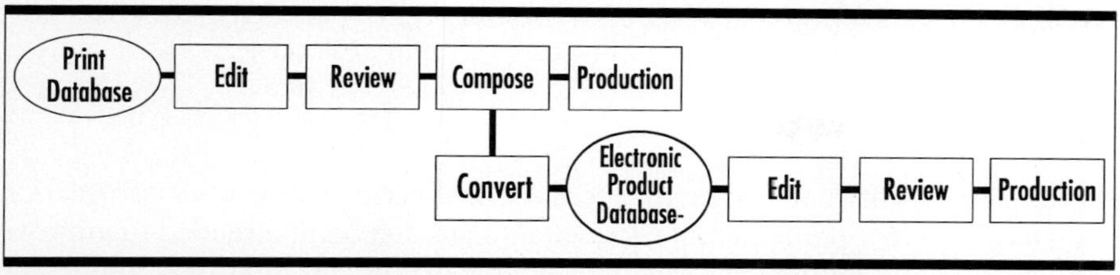

Figure 56. *Ongoing production feed with second path to create electronic products.*

The linear production process has been split into two paths, one for print and one for electronic products. Although the initial preparation of content may be done in early steps that are shared among the two processes, the electronic product requires additional steps and a duplicate database to keep synchronized with the print database. Also, the process of getting the data from a specific typesetting language into a form usable for the electronic product creates a need for a conversion step (either directly to the electronic product coding scheme or first to SGML, and then down to the electronic product coding). In this illustration, that step follows the composition process because that is the point in the process at which the data has been corrected enough to be useable in the electronic product. It could have been an earlier step in the process, but splitting the process at an earlier point may have created additional editing and reviewing steps that would need to be duplicated along the two paths.

Note that feedback may be given from any step in the electronic product creation path to the print product editorial and review steps, thus increasing the complexity of the overall process and creating iterations between steps. If a significant problem was found in the electronic product production, it could require that data be reworked in the print product steps and be reconverted and fed to the electronic product database.

This approach, although widely used, is cumbersome and has other built-in drawbacks, the solution to which has been to develop single SGML database capable of feeding multiple outputs (See *The Power of SGML Databases* on page 11). The main drawbacks to this approach are the timing issues related to the order of the steps in the process flow, and the cost of having to conduct the additional conversion processing to feed the electronic product. By design the electronic product produced in the flow will be delivered later than the print product. The timing and cost issues should be quantified when making the business case for adopting an SGML database.

In spite of the drawbacks of this approach, there may be compelling business reasons in your organization for it to continue for some time until a better method can be developed; perhaps upstream information creators are not willing to change their print-oriented information creation process. If so, you will continue to perform a conversion to feed the electronic product. Eventually, through the adoption of an integrated SGML database system, this process can be replaced with an automated translation from a richly encoded master database. Content

Generation/Extraction

Some elements of a publication or electronic product are really other information that has been reorganized and processed into another form intended to improve access or use of that same information. A table of contents is entirely implied by the content itself. In fact, many unstructured processing environments have added enough structure to allow the generation of these types of elements, albeit in a proprietary and less transportable way.

Tables of contents, figures, and tables, as well as indices and cross reference tables, end notes, footnotes, hypertext links, and other elements can and should be generated from information stored in content in order to improve accuracy and to reduce costs and processing time associated with manual or cumbersome automated steps. SGML markup is easily defined to support these processes. Through the use of detailed content-oriented tagging applied to the source of this information, the data can be processed to produce these elements partially or completely automatically.

To understand the benefits that can be achieved, we should explore the processes in use and the alternatives that are being adopted through the use of structured information techniques using SGML. The basic process is to interrogate the content of a publication to find elements that are relevant to a particular process, extract what is available, and record the location for inclusion in the resulting table or link process (footnotes or hypertext). In this way, content can be generated instead of created manually as a separate part of the document. But, a computer-based tool is only as good as the underlying design and the tools it utilizes, as well as the effective coding of the data.

The basic process for content extraction and generation is as follows:

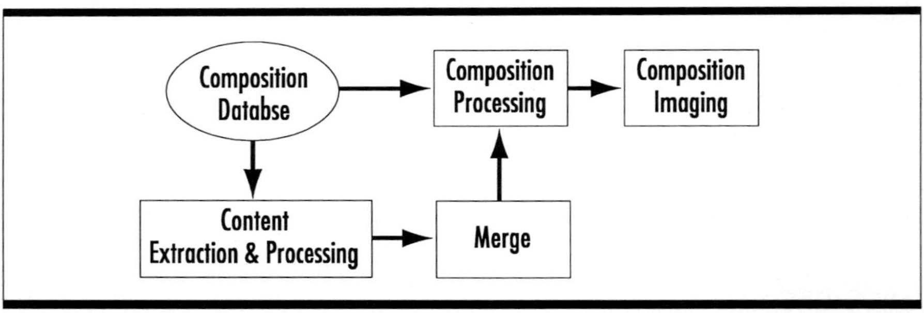

Figure 57. *Extraction of data for use as content*

If the content is rigorously defined in sufficient detail, the extraction and processing can be done entirely automatically (a feature commonly supported in word processors for creating tables of contents). Otherwise, one or more manual steps take place during these processes. Also, the resulting extracted elements can be easily placed into the appropriate position in the data stream or database if the detail of the information structure is of sufficient granularity and the processing tools are powerful enough to support this.

The content extraction/generation process is very similar to an ongoing production capture or one-time conversion process, especially if there is little rigor in the data to rely upon during the extraction process. If programs must sift through text looking for clues to the information buried therein, the process will be very much like a conversion from a non-rigorous form to an enhanced form such as SGML markup.

If the data is prepared in a way that allows quick and unambiguous identification of the implied content, otherwise known as detailed content tagging, then the process can be entirely automated and will not suffer from the costs and extended schedules associated with an enhancement conversion.

TYPES OF SGML CONVERSIONS

Data conversion is one of the biggest cost areas in any migration to SGML. Since conversion can represent such a significant investment, the conversion process should be carefully planned and the various means available to conduct the conversion considered.

Conversion of any type can be done using a number of techniques or combinations of techniques. We often hear stories of programmatic conversion of electronic source data, and bulk keying of data that only exists in hard-copy form. There are several approaches to converting data to SGML (one-time data migration as well as ongoing data capture and content extraction/generation).

There are many factors that dictate what approach to conversion is best suited for a specific set of data or processing requirements. These approaches to conversion will be discussed along with the types of problems each can solve.

Manual Conversion

Manual conversion is simply the process of opening a file and interactively converting the existing codes and data to another form. You start at the top and change any existing codes, or other clues, to tags in accordance with the target DTD. You must also add coding in places where none existed previously since you are probably enhancing the markup. This can be accomplished by working through a file and typing in a code wherever one would be required by the DTD, and removing the unneeded, old typesetting codes. Since many elements, such as paragraphs and headings, occur many times, you will quickly realize that manually converting a file is very boring and can be expedited through the use of search and replace tools, especially if they support regular expressions (for instance wild card characters and Boolean logic indicators for grouping).

Even with the help of smart search and replace tools, manual conversions are very time consuming, and, when labor rates are significant, very expensive. But, manual conversions are extremely useful when analyzing incoming source data to determine what coding has been used and what variations of the coding actually exist in the data. Manual conversion is also very useful for smaller files that would require more programming development time than it would take to simply convert the file by hand. Also, when working with data that is very inconsistently coded, perhaps coded using several composition systems and coding styles, manual conversions may be the only way to deal with the electronic source files. A strength of the manual conversion approach is that it is interactive and uses the human operator as the decision maker as needed.

Manual conversion is inappropriate for very large, consistently coded data. The speed of a computer in conducting redundant tasks quickly exceeds a human when facing these conditions. If the input coding is well known and consistent, manual conversion will be considerably more expensive.

Manual conversion may be combined with other approaches, perhaps as a finishing step to allow a human to take over where a program cannot continue. For instance, if the programs were built to handle the 90-percent of coding that was regular and predictable, a human could finish the conversion of the unusual or irregular coding. Also, a human can handle all the problematic areas where the programs fail. If a program senses the occurrence of an elements, but also senses that insufficient information exists to complete all required attributes, the program can be designed to insert the tag along with a standardized message to a human to resolve the ambiguity (perhaps a `<problem>` tag). Once the programmatic portion of the conversion is complete, a human can open the file and search for the message (and remove it) and resolve the ambiguities one-by-one. The combination of the expedience of the programmatic conversion and the intelligence of manual conversions can be combined to provide the lowest cost conversion with the required accuracy.

Interactive Assisted Conversion

Interactive assisted conversion is similar to manually converting a file in a software editor, except that the editor in use would use an integrated parser or parsing mechanism to assist in the identification of content and resolution of tagging errors, and assist in the application of markup. Any SGML-smart editor that has a parsing or validation function can be used. Periodically during the manual tagging, the operator can execute the parsing function to determine if any errors exist in the coding that has already been applied.

Again, since this is really only a variation of manual coding, all of the constraints and advantages of manual conversion apply. If a file is too large, one of the programmatic conversion methods described below should be considered.

Programmatic Conversion Against Proprietary Coding

Once you attempt to convert information manually, you will quickly realize that there is a lot of redundancy to conversion that can be better handled by programs. Text is made up of many occurrences of a very few items or elements, and very few occurrences of many elements. Twenty-percent of the data will cause you 80-percent of the effort and problems.

Typesetting coding is not usually very rich since it is limited to the number of variations that looks reasonably well on a page. Even when data is created by many different people over many years, it may be encoded with as few as a dozen codes. If the legacy data is of a considerable size you will find many thousands of occurrences of the same basic codes, and a lesser number of the more unusual codes.

As discussed earlier, there are situations where some or all of the data may have to be converted manually. When data is very inconsistently coded, or not coded at all, a large portion of the data may not be able to be converted strictly using procedural programming tools. Since text is much more free flowing and unstructured than traditional databases, it will contain more anomalies than, let's say, a financial database or data from a payroll system. Typesetting files, the most typical input source in an SGML conversion project, are encoded to provide a very limited set of instructions to a device that manages mostly the physical appearance of the information. Many things that are really different from an intellectual perspective can be assigned the exact same formatting coding since they will look the same on a printed page. A third-level heading may have the same appearance as the caption to a figure or the name of a table. For purposes of identification you may want to identify them as different elements and may have to find some way to differentiate them during the conversion process. An example of a clue that might help differentiate them is the word "Figure" appearing at the beginning of the line, which would indicate that it should be converted to a `<figure>` tag instead of `<head3>`. If this differentiation cannot be done programmatically, a manual step will need to be included after the programmatic step to finish the conversion.

There are a number of programming languages and utilities available for use in conversion (See the discussion in Chapter 4, *The SGML Environment* on page 43 regarding the kind of tools that are available). Some tools are even optimized for converting text to SGML by including powerful text manipulation features such as regular expressions and a parser to perform validation of the SGML-encoded data. Other tools offer less functionality but may be sufficient if your programmers are already familiar with them and adept in their use. There is no single perfect tool, but you should consider traditional programming languages such as Basic and COBOL as unsuitable since many text manipulation features that already exist in other tools, such as text sorting routines or pattern-matching features, would have to be built from scratch when using these languages. Languages that are fairly common that have text handling capabilities include LISP, SNOBOL, PERL, and AWK. Specialized languages that are designed for text and have SGML parsers integrated in them include Exoterica Corporation's OmniMark and Balise from AIS Berger-Levrault. Refer to Appendix 8, *SGML Resources* on page 445 for a complete listing of conversion tools.

Since you are most likely enhancing the data with additional detail, your programs may need to store information in buffers as it encounters it, and apply it in tags at a later point in the document. For instance, you may need to store the chapter number for use later in enhancing the sub-chapter elements that are contained in each chapter.

There are many text manipulation tools available today. Some utilities, such as AWK, exist in the public domain and are available for free. But AWK may not be powerful enough to build an industrial strength conversion program. You may be better off investing in an industrial strength, SGML-aware conversion language such as OmniMark or Balise if you have to convert a lot of complex data and expect to do a lot of conversion programming. There are many other tools available between the extremes discussed above, and some offer unique functionality or an unusual approach.

Programmatic Content Interrogation conversion

It is especially true in converting text from typesetting files to SGML that you will not have a corresponding typesetting code for every SGML element in your DTD. You will have to rely on other clues that are part of the content to programmatically find where some of the SGML tagging will have to go. Some of these clues may be explicit, such as the word "Note:" at the beginning of a paragraph indicating that it is probably a likely place to apply the `<note>`tag instead of the `<para>`tag.

Other instances may not be as obvious. For instance, you may have to parse (in a more traditional language sense) through an element to find sub-elements. A part number might have a certain nomenclature that is almost always found. But in some cases there might be variations that must be accounted for in your conversion programs. Authors may have entered information inconsistently. Eventually you may want to give up trying to add every possible occurrence of these inconsistencies to your program and finish the last part of the conversion manually.

Fielded data

If your source of data to be converted is stored in a structured database, some of the fields may convert entirely or partially to SGML elements. Since the data already has some structure to it, you will want to retain it where it is consistent to your SGML model. Even fielded data may need to have content interrogation techniques and manual cleansing applied to it to complete the conversion since data definition tools support different functionalities than SGML.

Visual recognition

There are tools that work against visual clues in the data when attempting to determine the appropriate location for tagging during a conversion (these are discussed in See Chapter 4, *The SGML Environment* on page 43). Visual recognition is really a mixture of programmatic conversion against existing coding and implied by presentation.

Visual recognition is most suitable for elements of information that are highly dependent on their physical structure, such as tables and equations. Visual recognition is very capable for identifying the structural elements of the information, such as headings and lists, and can work with the presentational markup available, such as indentation and position on the page. Currently, visual recognition tools are not as strong in some of the more sophisticated text manipulation features found in text transformation languages. Even so, they are very strong tools for converting text, especially when there are a lot of tables involved.

Standardized or Context Conversion

Standardized coding conversion relies on the incoming source data to be coded in SGML. The fact that it is already in SGML greatly improves the ability to recognize elements in context. For instance, a bold phrase immediately following the element `<table>`could easily identified as the table caption since from the perspective of a structured tool it could be interpreted as being part of a table.

If the structured transformation tool has a parser integrated into it, it can check the rules in a DTD for what could occur inside of a table. If nothing is allowed inside of the table after the end of the table itself, then the conversion tool could interpret the bold phrase as a heading. If a table caption is allowed at the end of a table element, the conversion tool could tag the bold phrase as a table caption. Or, maybe it would then look for clues in content to determine whether it was a head or a table caption, a subroutine that could be avoided if a caption was not allowed, thus speeding up the conversion process.

Standardized coding conversions are different than translation of SGML data into a specific language; composition processing, for example. Standardized coding conversions are very powerful ways of enhancing your SGML-encoded data even more. As new automated processing tools are developed, such as extraction programs, you may need to conduct an enhancement conversion against your SGML.

AUTO-TAGGING. The process of adding SGML tags has been called "upward transformation" or "auto-tagging". This is not a trivial process, and there has been much interest in making this type of transformation accurate, inexpensive, and easy-to-do. One might say accurate auto-tagging of SGML is the "holy grail" of the industry (Refer to *The Holy Grail* on page 108 for an in-depth discussion on this topic in a word-processing environment). We always expect conversion to a rich SGML structure to require some manual cleansing after automated processing for some time.

The main problem with tagging information according to its content and hierarchical structure is caused by the advanced pattern recognition capability of the human mind. When you read a document, be it a newspaper, novel, or virtually any other type, you make certain assumptions about the structure of the data by noticing the way in which various objects are placed about the page (although some documents come with instructions on how to read them that include references to the formatting). You can tell the difference between a title and a list item; between a paragraph and an example, so some ambiguity is allowed in presentation. Most people who read have been stumped by a poorly laid-out page, or an inconsistent structure. The importance of human visual recognition is realized by noticing how difficult it is to navigate a poorly designed document.

Thousands of years of experience with communicating by some written form has forced us to develop conventions and recognize such clues. Life-long exposure to these clues, along with our evolved minds, have allowed us to read a newspaper and consume the ideas therein without a users' manual.

As long as information was distributed visually, this paradigm worked fine. When an author wanted to break his work into structured pieces, he would add a subtitle, or underline the text, or place it further towards the margin, and the reader would figure it out. This implicit structure was communicated successfully.

Computers don't yet have the evolutionary heredity that we do, so we must add markup that tells the computer about the structure, since it will not know otherwise. Researchers are trying to build such intelligence into computer programs, so that they can do the work of adding these markers. The job is very difficult, since it involves encoding subtle rules from thousands of years of written communications.

The most important thing to know when evaluating auto-tagging software is to realize that there is no magic. Reading some vendors' advertisements would lead one to believe that their product will take any word processor document and convert it to a intelligent SGML document with no human intervention. While this might be true for some simple forms of SGML, it is rarely the case when dealing with legacy documents.

TREE-TO-TREE TRANSLATION (TRANSFORMATION). When converting from one form of SGML to another, or when converting from some other form of hierarchical text to SGML or back, a tree-to-tree translation tool can be used.

Tree-to-tree translation is a type of auto-tagging, since the tags are inserted by the program. However, it deserves its own category since the process can usually be done without operator intervention if the two models have well-defined structures.

The most common use for a tree-to-tree transformation is to convert data between two users who use different structures in production. For example, two divisions of a company may need to use the same information in very different applications. They could capture and store the data twice in two different databases, or create translation tools to do the structure translation automatically from each other's databases and models as needed.

Notice how this differs from auto-tagging. Tree-to-tree translation is designed to be completely automated; as part of the import/export function, where auto-tagging is usually performed once per document as it is loaded into the system. There are programs which combine the two to achieve more effective tagging of legacy material.

DOWNWARD TRANSLATION (TRANSFORMATION). An SGML file by itself is not of much use in communicating information to an end-user. The data is in a sequential file form and can be read easily, but it is easy for a person to miss the structure of the document just by looking at the sequential file.

Downward translation is the process of rendering an SGML file in another form. Common output forms are:

1. typesetting files that are read by a commercial typesetter for the purpose of creating printed pages,
2. hypertext-tagged input files for the purpose of creating electronic delivery products via CD-ROM or on-line services,
3. "intelligent" electronic documents that incorporate executable programs that lead the user, interactively, through a series of procedural steps,
4. data repositories that can be populated with large collections of structured information in a simplified form to support research.

The process of down translation is a fundamental piece of an ongoing SGML system. While the data will need to be converted into SGML only once, there is an ongoing need to translate the SGML structure into some other useable form.

RE-KEYING VERSUS ELECTRONIC SOURCE FILES. Keying data, even large amounts of data, can be done cost effectively, especially with the availability of data entry houses in countries with low labor rates (but these sources may have their own collection of problems, such as language and time zone differences). See Appendix 8, *SGML Resources* on page 445.

If the data has been kept up to date, is in fairly consistent condition, and is readily available in electronic form, it will most likely be easier to start with the electronic files. But if pieces are missing or out of synch with the set of master pages, or if the data is very old and has many years of coding from several different compositions systems, you might want to consider rekeying at least some of the data.

Summary

Converting data to SGML can be an expensive proposition. But there are ways to manage these costs and control the risk. Plan your conversion using a strategy that fits your company, the goals of the project, and your available resources and skills. Recognize where it is useful to be structured and necessary to be flexible.

Effective and timely communication is essential, as is the ability to think on your feet and react to anomalies in the data without compromising the overall use of it.

CHAPTER • NINE

SGML Data Management and Workflow

Introduction

In order to manage a database of SGML data, you must incorporate some kind of database manager. This can be anything from a tree-based file system to a sophisticated object-oriented database manager.

The homogeneous system illustrated in *Figure 14, The SGML Environment* on page 44 requires that the data contained in an SGML database system somehow be accessible to all processes, users, and other data. Only then can highly defined SGML data reach its full potential.

The process of getting data into and out of an SGML-based data management system and doing something with it is called "workflow". Workflow is not a new concept; no organization can exist without it. What is new, however, is that there are now tools available to automate workflow functions and integrate them with your SGML database. The functionality of these tools is also covered in this chapter.

Related Topics

- *The Power of SGML Databases* on page 11
- Chapter 2, *Evolution of Publishing Systems* on page 23
- Chapter 3, *Desktop Publishing and Professional Publishing Systems* on page 37
- Chapter 4, *The SGML Environment* on page 43
- *The SGML Environment* on page 44
- *Formatting and Structure* on page 87
- Chapter 6, *The SGML Application* on page 101
- Chapter 7, *Implementation Planning* on page 121
- *Using SGML to Restructure Processes and Information* on page 124
- *System Development* on page 139
- *Generation/Extraction* on page 174
- *The SGML Document Model* on page 216
- *The Hub File Concept* on page 324

The File System as Database Manager

There is a tendency to think that an SGML system cannot be implemented unless you are willing to spend many thousands of dollars on a centralized commercial database manager. This is only partially true.

While a centralized database storage manager will enable you to make maximum use of the data for many applications, it is certainly possible to make a perfectly functional SGML-based system using only the file system on your computer. In fact, this book was produced using these concepts. There are several tools and techniques that can be used to achieve such a system:

1. Entity Management
2. Version Control
3. Network Functionality

Each of these is covered in this section.

Entity Management

In the SGML Standard, an entity is defined as "A collection of characters that can be referenced as a unit."[1]. In order to manage entities as system-specific units, the ENTITY declaration was developed. As described in *The Entity Declaration* on page 250, the ENTITY declaration can be used to define anything from single-characters to the entire known world. How, then, can we manage our data, which most likely falls somewhere between those two extremes?

The key to successful entity management is to break a document into logical pieces, which can be managed independently, while maintaining their identity in a particular document or set of documents. This can be done using a "hub file".

You can think of a hub file as a collection of reference pointers to the actual data. An entity declaration is created for each physical file that is to be included into the document, then entity references indicate to the parser where the entity is to be placed.

Suppose you had a document that consisted of front matter (table of contents, introduction, foreword), body matter (chapters), and back matter (appendices, index, glossary). A hub file could be created to manage the assembly of the whole document by defining a set of entity declarations and entity references.

```
<!DOCTYPE techman SYSTEM "techman.dtd" [
<!ENTITY    frontm
         SYSTEM 'frontm.sgm'        >
<!ENTITY    chap1
         SYSTEM 'chap1.sgm'         >
<!ENTITY    chap2
         SYSTEM 'chap2.sgm'         >
<!ENTITY    chap3
         SYSTEM 'chap3.sgm'         >
<!ENTITY    chap4
         SYSTEM 'chap4.sgm'         >
<!ENTITY    backm
         SYSTEM 'backm.sgm'         >
]>
<techman>
 &frontm;
 &chap1;
 &chap2;
 &chap3;
 &chap4;
 &backm;
</techman>
```

1 ISO8879, definition 4.120

The example above shows entity declarations that point to system identifiers to find the separate entity files. `PUBLIC` identifiers could be used just as easily, as long as the appropriate mapping mechanism was applied (See *Public Identifier Mapping* on page 260). The hub file approach is also discussed in *Managing Documents using "Hub Files"* on page 324.

This is the start of a database management system using just the file system as the storage medium. This approach works as long as you build-in the proper precautions that will assure data validity. What you lose when using a file system instead of a central database manager is central control; in a database management environment, nothing goes into or out of the database without the manager knowing. The database manager becomes a central point where security, version control, transaction tracking, and many other things can be controlled and monitored.

In using a file-system approach to data management, you must be sure that these issues are addressed. For example, to replace the security aspect of database control, a network operating system can be configured to allow only certain users or processes to access certain files. Version control can be managed by a stand-alone program (See *Version Control* on page 186), and transaction tracking can be controlled manually or by using network file access control logs.

Database management using a file system can be a cheap way to get an SGML system implemented, as long as you take the appropriate precautions.

Version Control

Version control is the process of tracking changes made to a file. It is also called revision control, effectivity control, configuration management, and probably other things, as well. Each of these things mean different things to different people. In this chapter, we will refer to the entire process of tracking changes to a file as version control.

There are several version control systems available, from free utilities, such as RCS, the revision control system from the gnu software foundation, to multi-user, networked packages containing workgroup functionality and integrated database support (Intersolv PVCS and Microsoft SourceSafe are our favorites).

VERSION CONTROL BASICS

A version control system stores files in the host computer file system, and allows for checking a file out, then back in after it has been changed. The check-out/check-in model allows for some security control, but it should not be trusted to keep unauthorized people out of the files.

The version control system maintains a certain control over files by creating a base file plus changes, instead of storing every character in every version that is made. These changes are called "deltas", and allow the system to make efficient use of machine resources.

In order to create a version-controlled file, it must first be checked in as an initial revision. Most version control software adds header information that the system uses to track subsequent changes. When the file is checked out, the system assures that the requester has appropriate authority to access the file, then delivers it.

When checking the file back into the system, the version control system compares the changed file with the one that was checked out, then creates a delta containing only the changes. On check-in, the user can be prompted to enter a few words about the nature of the changes. This description is only needed for human reading, since the system knows exactly what changes were made at the character level. These descriptions provide a helpful way to track the progress of a document, and should be entered.

By default, only the latest revision will be checked out. This is called the "head" or "trunk". It is possible to check out any earlier revision by using a command-line switch.

REVISION NUMBERING

There are two parts to the version number. The nomenclature varies from implementation to implementation. We will call the two parts the version number and the revision number, separated by a decimal point. Every time a file is checked in, the revision number is incremented. Say revision 1.3 is checked out. When it is modified and checked back in, the new revision will get marked as revision 1.4.

VERSIONS

At some point in the life of the document, some milestone will be reached. In the case of a technical manual, changes will be made to the document in the process of creating the product, then the product will finally ship to customers. At this point, the document should be frozen, because customers and support personnel have the document in the field. We will call this a new "version" of the program. When a version is created, all deltas that have been applied to the original document are applied, and a complete document is stored as the new version. This increases the size of the file, but speeds access. Some systems use a "reverse-delta" storage methodology, where the most recent revision is stored intact, with deltas noting the differences between it and prior versions. This allows for fast access to the current version while maintaining all versions in the database.

Versions increment the number to the left of the decimal. If the document is numbered 1.4 when the product ships, you would probably mark the new version as revision 2.0. Revisions made to that document will increment the revision number (2.1, 2.2, etc.).

BRANCHING

When a past revision is accessed and changed, the new version cannot be given the next revision number, because that might conflict with an existing revision. For example, suppose a document exists with revisions 1.1, 1.2, and 1.3, and revision 1.2 needs to be modified for some reason. On check-in, it cannot be marked as revision 1.3, since that revision already exists. The version control software will recognize this conflict and give the revision the number 1.2.1. This revision now has a life of its own, and will be tracked independently.

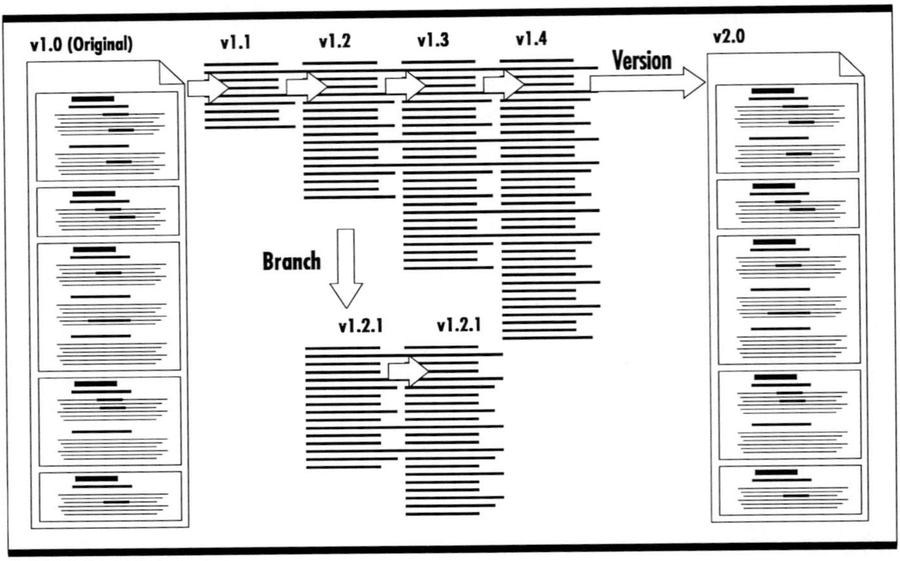

Figure 58. *Branching in a Version Control System*

Branching is used in the case of a document that has shipped with a product and the product has changed, requiring modification to the document that existed at the time of the delivery.

RECONCILIATION

One problem in any editing environment is in dealing with the issues surrounding reconciliation of similar versions. One of the basic tenants of version control is the ability to keep two people from editing a single document at the same time. This tends to limit the need for reconciling two dissimilar versions that might have existed without such control. With branching, however, reconciliation might become necessary because the branch has a personality distinct from the base from which it sprouted.

Unfortunately, there is no easy way to reconcile different versions of a document automatically. We don't yet have computers that can interpret human writing and make the kind of decisions necessary to do such reconciliation[1].

About the best we can do is identify which parts of a document are different, and to provide tools for a human to read two versions and come up with a single version.

Later in this chapter, we will discuss database tools that can track differences at a very small level. These tools can be combined to make the reconciliation task less painful.

EDITIONS

An "edition" is a collection of separately managed revisions that comprise a complete set. Suppose a technical manual is managed as a collection of chapters. Each chapter is a separate file managed independently by a version control system. At any point in the editorial process, each chapter could be at a different revision level. A delivery of the technical manual as a whole will probably be required at some point. At such a time, a version control system can retrieve the latest revision (head) of each chapter in order to create the master document. Once this document goes out, however, the chapters will continue to be modified, changing the meaning of the latest revision. There should be some way of getting to the collection of files that comprise the document that was distributed, however. We will refer to this as an "edition".

In many file-oriented version control systems, like rcs, there is no explicit provision for tracking the relationships between files. If you have a requirement for such functionality, it can be built, but it will be outside the realm of the version control software. The concept of editions is used in the version control area of a centralized database manager.

REPORTING

Most version control systems provide some rudimentary capability for displaying revision history and statistics like file size and delta fragmenting. The most common report is to show the revision history of a file. The system generates this report on demand.

```
Logfile:          C:\user\book\sgml\sgml\working\wflow.sgv
Workfile:         wflow.sgm
Owner:            btravis
Last trunk rev:   1.3
Locks:
Rev count:        4
Attributes:
```

1 It's probably a good thing for the authors, because if computers could do reconciliation, they could probably write books about implementing SGML also!

```
   WRITEPROTECT
   CHECKLOCK
   NOEXCLUSIVELOCK
   EXPANDKEYWORDS
   TRANSLATE
   NOCOMPRESSDELTA
   NOCOMPRESSWORKIMAGE
   COMMENTPREFIX = "   "
   NEWLINE = "\r\n"
Version labels:
Description:
Workflow and Version Control

-----------------------------------
Rev 1.3
Checked in:     09 Mar 1995 01:42:58
Last modified:  09 Mar 1995 01:42:58
Author id: btravis     lines deleted/added/moved: 42/6/0
Moved "Implementation Considerations" to implementation
chapter. They belong there, along with all of the other
implementation factors. Put plenty of cross-references here
to that chapter.
-----------------------------------
Rev 1.2
Checked in:     03 Feb 1995 01:41:48
Last modified:  02 Feb 1995 01:41:48
Author id: btravis     lines deleted/added/moved: 2/7/0
Added references to graphics for "Workflow in Action" section.
Need to build the graphics so they can be put in the file.
-----------------------------------
Rev 1.1
Checked in:     19 Dec 1994 01:39:54
Last modified:  18 Dec 1994 01:39:54
Author id: btravis     lines deleted/added/moved: 12/21/0
Modified description of a project manager. Clarified the
difference between the person and the software package. A
Project Analyst is the person in charge of managing a
project, a project manager is a piece of software the
Project Analyst uses.
-----------------------------------
Rev 1.0
Checked in:     12 Nov 1994 01:36:22
Last modified:  12 Nov 1994 01:36:22
Author id: btravis     lines deleted/added/moved: 132/3/0
Initial revision.
===================================
```

GRAPHICAL INTERFACE

It is more common to see a graphical front-end for systems that have traditionally been command-line oriented. Version control systems are no exception. Microsoft SourceSafe has a native graphical front-end in the Windows, Windows NT, and Macintosh versions. This graphical front-end makes it easy to see the structure of a project or group of text files, and to view the current status.

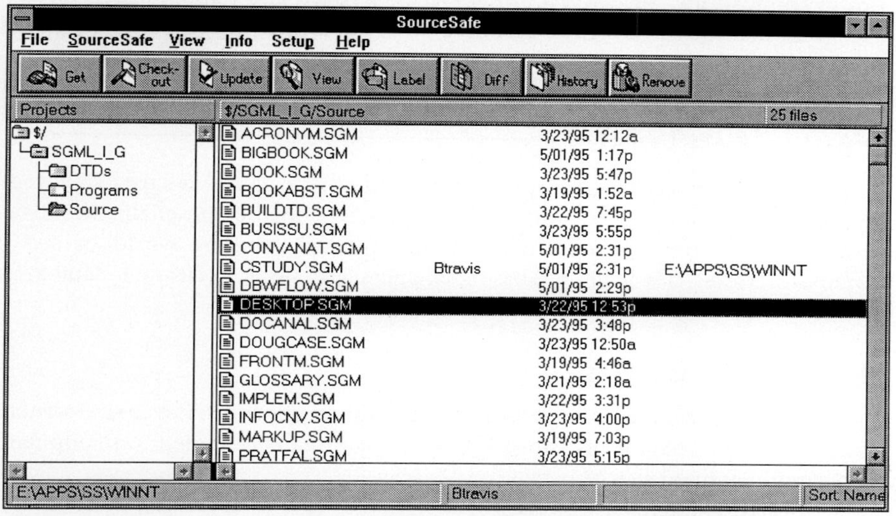

Figure 59. *Graphical interface for Version Control System (Microsoft SourceSafe)*

IMPLEMENTATION FACTORS

Stand-alone version control systems were originally designed to manage computer program source files. Because of this legacy, they generally work at the line level; if a single character in the line is changed, the whole line is considered changed. This line-oriented nature is fine for source code, which tends to be formatted on a line-by-line basis. However, text that exists in "thoughts" can transcend line boundaries and still convey the same meaning; the text in this book could be set in a narrower column width and still convey the same meaning.

The problem, in a version control environment, is that some editing programs take liberties in "re-flowing" text such that the version control software might see that many lines in a file have changed when, in fact, the underlying data has not changed. A version control program that uses line-based logic to compare versions will show that much more has changed than has really changed.

Network Functionality

Even with the best entity management and version control functionality, a stand-alone system is not much good if more than one person is to be working on the documents. Network functionality can be as simple as a physical connection between two machines, or as complex as a multi-server system with workgroup applications. Security, multiple-access to data, and remote access of data are issues that the network can be called on to do. Some version control systems make calls to the network to coordinate such activities.

Database Managers

Most database implementations use some kind of manager to assure data integrity, allow common access, support multi-process control, and enable the database administrator to perform other administrivia. In the world of SGML databases, three types of database managers are used: relational databases, full-text databases, and object-oriented databases.

RELATIONAL DATABASES

Relational databases have been around for many years, and serve as the cornerstone of modern data processing. They were originally designed to manipulate very rigidly defined sets of data.

Relational databases were not designed to deal with variable-length text. The relational model is so well-conceived and widely implemented that some vendors have added text storage on top of existing relational database systems. One way this is done is to use the relational database manager to track identifiers and other information about the textual objects. The text itself is stored elsewhere, maybe in a file system or some other easily accessible location.

When a user wants to query the text, he submits a query to the relational database, which returns pointers to the actual text. The system returns the text as whole objects, ready to be used.

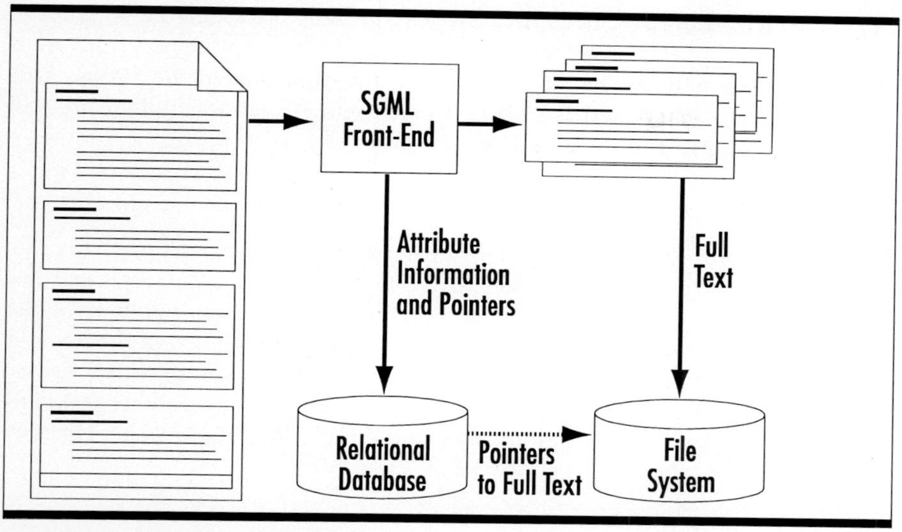

Figure 60. *Relational database loading text*

For example, suppose an automobile manufacturer keeps all of its repair manuals in such a system. Each chapter has its own unique identifier. When a document is loaded into the database, the database manager creates a record containing this identifier, along with other parameters like the authors name, load date, chapter title, and so on. The document is stored separately, with a pointer in the relational data table pointing to where the text ended up.

A user, wanting to create a repair manual for a particular car, requests that the system return all of the chapters necessary to create that manual. A database query is sent to the database manager, and the application fetches the text from its storage place.

This scenario, while sort of a kludge, works well as a storage and retrieval system, but it lacks some of the data integrity and hierarchical advantages available in systems that are better suited for the task.

Relational databases have been in use for many years and, as such, have a proven track record. Relational database managers are well-known by many programmers and analysts, and there are many on the market to choose from.

FULL-TEXT DATABASES

Flat storage

A full-text database is generally a specialized version of a relational database. When a document is loaded into a full-text database, all words are loaded into an index, along with positioning information like sentence location and proximity to other words. A list of "stop words" can be used to keep unwanted words out of the index.

Such systems have been used for years to keep track of large volumes of text. In fact, IBM developed their text storage and retrieval system to track all of the legal documents created as part of their anti-trust suit in the 1960s. This product was later marketed as STAIRS. Large users of such technology are still using them to store and retrieve legal case material.

Structured Storage

In addition to full-text databases, there are databases that allow the user to access the document structure in addition to the text. Consider a database that has several books on diseases. The book on Parkinson's Disease might have the phrase "Parkinson's Disease" in the title, but throughout the rest of the book, it may be referred to simply as "the disease", and the reader knows which disease is being discussed by its context within the document. If a researcher wants to search this database for to find out how antibiotics effect Parkinson's Disease, the query might look like:

```
find all paragraphs that contain Parkinson's Disease and
antibiotic
```

However, since the word Parkinson's is only found in the title, the researcher probably will not get the material he needs. On the other hand, if he placed the query:

```
find all paragraphs that contain Disease and antibiotic
```

the system would return paragraphs about AIDS, spinal meningitis, cancers, and many others. In this case, so many hits would be returned that the user would find it daunting, if not impossible, sift through the query results to find the document he needs.

A full-text database that stores the structure of text along with the text itself can be used to rectify this situation. In such a system, every object is stored with more information, such that the following query could be placed:

```
FIND para where #PCDATA INCLUDES
"antibiotic" AND #PCDATA
IN title OF ANCESTOR book INCLUDES
"Parkinson's Disease"
```

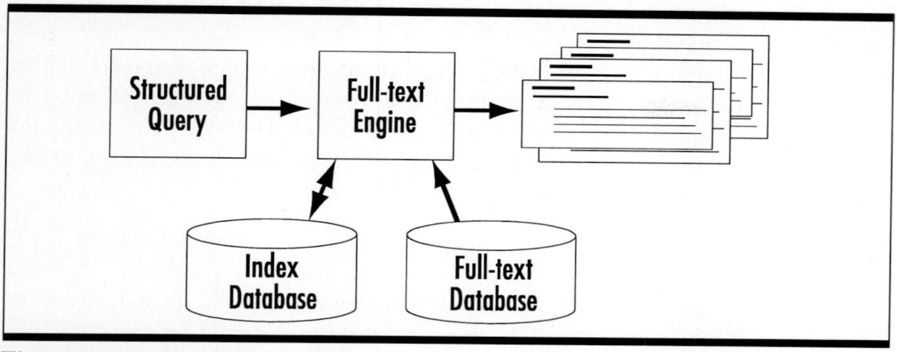

Figure 61. *Full-text database query*

Often, the value of a text database query process is how much irrelevant data is **not** returned. In full-text databases, this is called "relevance" and "precision".The effect of the process above greatly improves the two desired results: getting the data required, and not getting the useless data.

Using SGML to load such a system provides these benefits automatically, since the structure of the document is already declared and known by the application. The application will know, for example, that all occurrences of the word "disease" are in the context of a book with the word "Parkinson's" in the title.

OBJECT-ORIENTED DATABASES

Object-oriented databases provide an elegant way to describe and store different types of data objects. An object is generally defined as "an individual, identifiable item, unit, or entity, either real or abstract, with a well-defined role in the problem domain[1]", and "anything with a crisply defined boundary[2]" An object can also be defined in terms of its description: "An object has state, behavior, and identity; the structure and behavior of similar objects are defined in their common class; the terms instance and object are interchangeable[3]". In other words, an object is anything that can be identified and defined.

There are some basic concepts behind object-oriented databases. Since object-oriented database products that handle SGML are relatively new, there are

1 Cox, Brad J. Object-Oriented Programming, An Evolutionary Approach. Addison Wesley.

2 Ibid.

3 Grady Booch. Object-Oriented Analysis And Design With Applications, 2nd Ed. Benjamin Cummings. ISBN 0-8053-5340-2.

many different approaches that vendors are using to integrate the object model into the SGML model.

This section provides a brief description of the concept of objects to give you a feeling for what is happening under the covers. This tutorial will not give you enough information to build a system from scratch, but will give you an idea of the concepts of object-oriented databases as they relate to SGML so you can select a product that fits into your environment.

History

Objects were first formally used in the Simula programming language, and were created to describe things found in the real world, not just computer variables and data. Other programming languages also used the concept of objects to define the world. These languages had the ability to describe objects as a collection of attribute information the methods that operate on them.

The problem was that, once the program ended, the objects perished with the working memory. The users thought it might be nice to be able to save these objects between processing runs, so the concept of "persistent objects" was created. A persistent object lasts longer than the process using it. This was usually accomplished by creating some kind of non-volatile form into which objects could be saved and retrieved later. This requirement formed the basis of object-oriented databases.

Diverse data types

Object-oriented databases, also called object databases, are inherently designed to manage diverse kinds of data. In an object database, there might be several different data types that all have something in common. An object-oriented database can manage each piece of data independent of its data type.

In an SGML environment, the same database can hold text, graphics, sounds, and any other type of data that can be stored. Each object type can be completely different from the others, but is identified accurately enough for the SGML application to do something intelligent with it.

Hierarchical Storage

The object model allows for the hierarchical storage of things. Objects can contain other objects of the same or different type, and can be contained by other objects. The ability to store hierarchical structures, along with the ability to store diverse data types, makes the object model a natural storage medium for SGML data.

In an SGML environment, hierarchical storage is not enough. It is important to note that the order of the data must be maintained, as well. This is possible with object-oriented database managers, but is very difficult when using the relational model.

SGML Loading

Before loading an SGML document into an object-oriented database, the class library must be created. This process will vary depending upon the product used, but involves creating a class for every element type. This corresponds strongly to the content model in the element declaration.

Loading an SGML document can be illustrated with the following diagram:

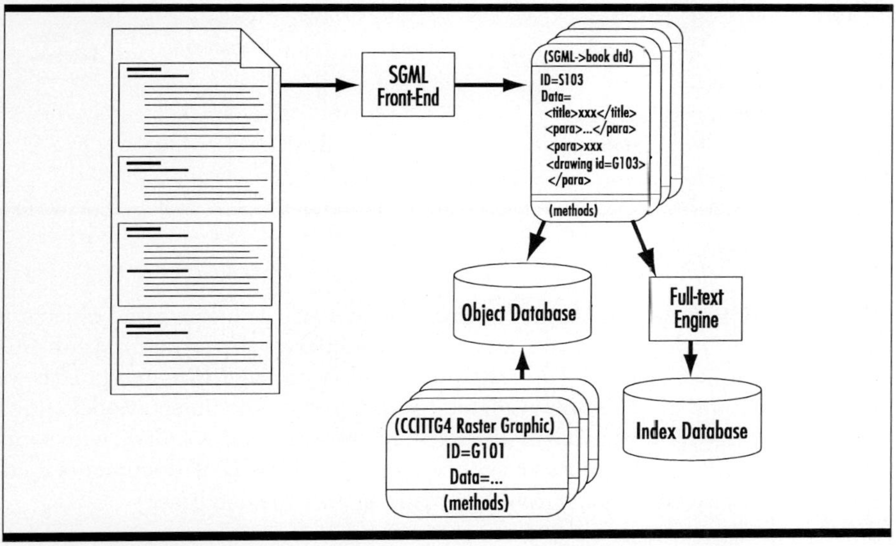

Figure 62. *Object-oriented database with SGML front-end*

This illustrates a document passing through the SGML front-end, which, with the help of the DTD and instructions from the database, break the document into pieces and instantiate a series of objects. These objects are stored into the object database as is. With the right software, an index database could also be loaded with the words for searching.

Notice, also, that non-text information like graphics, tables, multimedia objects, are stored alongside the text information. This homogeneous storage of all objects required to create the SGML database is the main advantage of using the object database model.

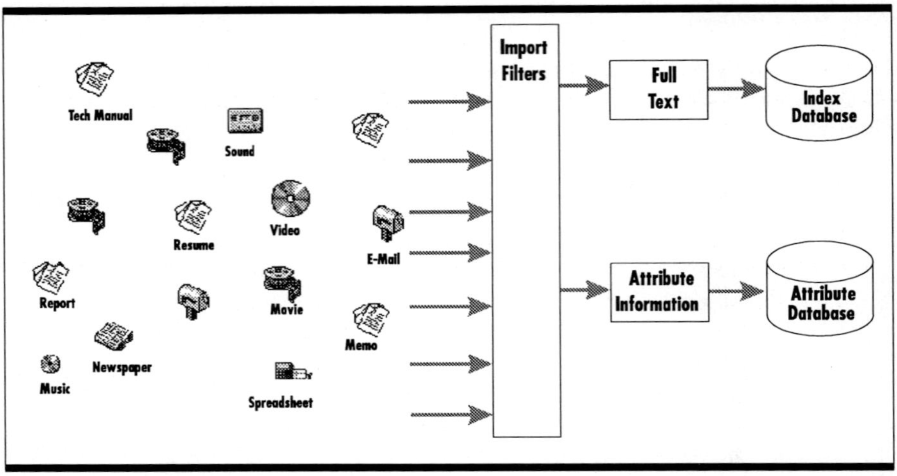

Figure 63. *Object-oriented database objects*

QUERY. Once the data is loaded into the database as instantiated objects, a query can be made against the data. This is similar to the structured full-text model shown in *Figure 61, Full-text database query* on page 195, except that we have all attribute information available for the query. The object model allows the user to place queries based on the attribute information, as well as, with some systems, the full text. Suppose an agency wants to declassify all documents up to 1946. A parameterized query could be made against the database:

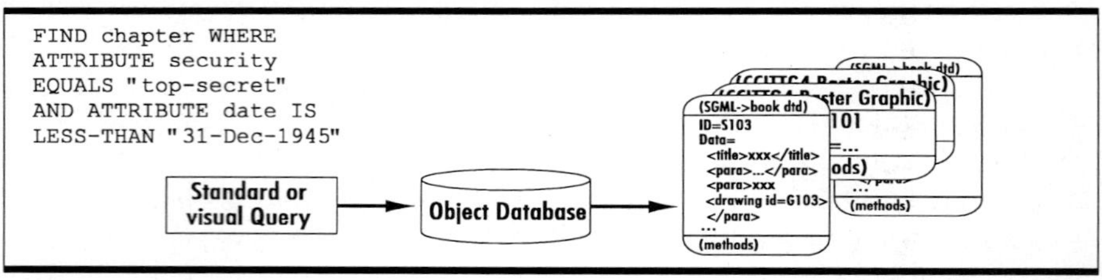

Figure 64. *Parameterized search*

ACCESS. Any object can be accessed for edit (checked-out) by issuing the appropriate query to the database:

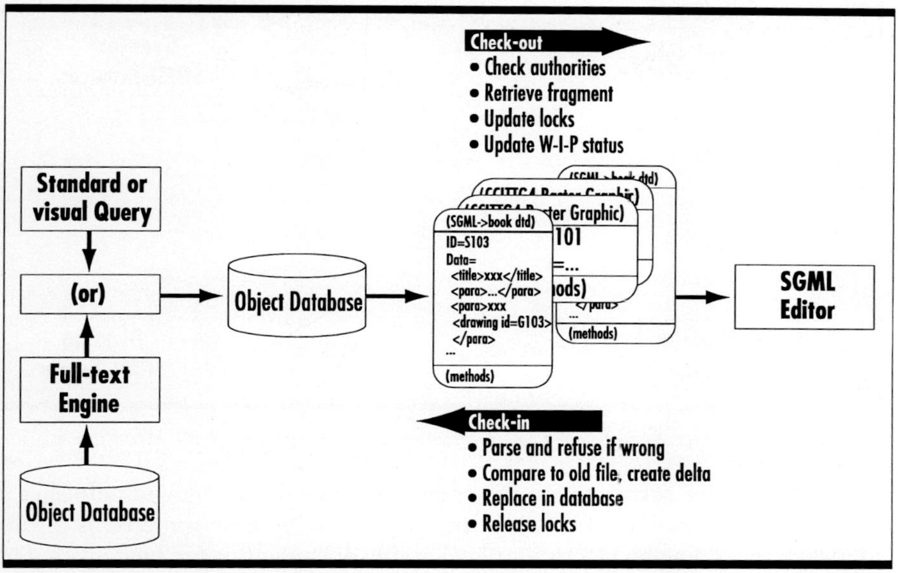

Figure 65. *Check out for edit*

The author finds the object required, either by providing address information ("Give me object I2235"), or accessed via a full-word or parameter query of the database. The object manager assures that the object in question can be checked out by the person requesting it, then updates locks and give the object to the requester.

The object requested might refer to other objects in the database. In such a case, the object manager can also provide those to the user, following the same authority checking and lock updating as for the base object.

When the user is finished, he will check the document back into the database, which will parse the document to assure that it is a valid SGML document. If not, the application can be instructed to refuse the check-in until it is correct.

If the file is valid, the object manager will update the lock status and create a delta file for version control purposes.

OBJECT DATABASE IN ACTION. One application of object-oriented databases is in the area of electronic review. A typical application is illustrated below.

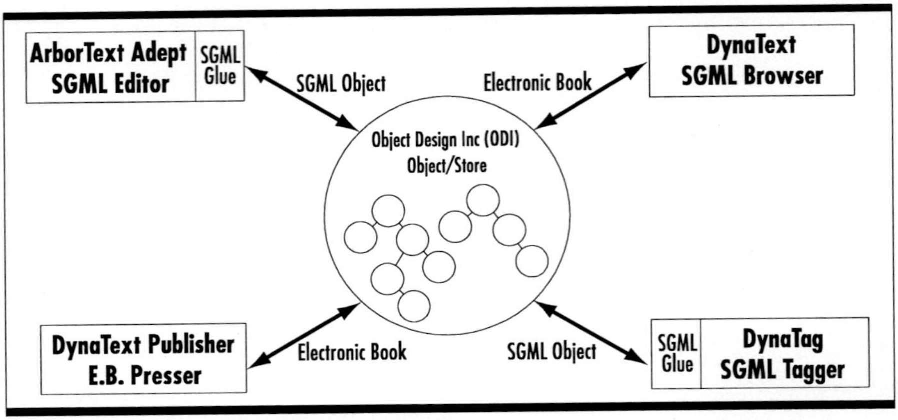

Figure 66. *Elecronic Review using object-oriented database manager (EBT DynaBase)*

In such an environment, the author creates a document and publishes it using an electronic book publisher tool, DynaText by Electronic Book Technologies, Inc. Being an electronically viewable document, it can be delivered to the reviewers over a network or other electronic means.

The reviewers use the workgroup-oriented annotation feature of the electronic book tool to make editorial suggestions to the book, then send it to the author with all editorial remarks attached.

The author reviews the annotated book and finds areas that need to be changed. Since the electronic book is just one instantiation of the real data in the database, the author must check out each object to be modified. He does this by using a special menu item that only his copy of the electronic book viewer has. The product places an object request to the database manager, which checks access rights and locks the document.

On receiving the checked-out object, the integrated system loads the document into an SGML editorial workstation, Adept•Editor by ArborText. The author makes the necessary changes and puts the document back into the database, where the status is updated and locks are removed.

After all changes have been made, the book is re-pressed, using the electronic book pressing facility.

The advantage here is the concept of only retrieving what is necessary. Since each element is stored as an individual object with its hierarchy known, any level in the hierarchy can be retrieved for modification. So, if the author only wanted to modify a paragraph, then it, along with any children such as lists and quotes, would be retrieved and locked from use by others. If another author wanted to modify another paragraph in the same section, he would not be prohibited from doing so because the entire section is not locked.

This raises the concept of granularity, which is discussed in *Determine Granularity* on page 202.

Choosing an SGML-enabled Database Manager

When shopping for a database manager to include into your SGML environment, there are certain things you should consider.

DOCUMENT ASSEMBLY

Can the system build a document from its objects? How does it handle SGML entity management? Can a document be built based on the results of a query? Does the system support an output specification language, like DSSSL or FOSI?

GRANULARITY OF LOCKING

At what level does the system allow the implementor to lock objects? Can every element be locked, or does the implementor need to specify ahead of time the granularity?

VERSION MANAGEMENT

Does the system have version management capabilities built-in? At what level are versions tracked? Does the system have the ability to mark a particular set of objects as an "edition"? Does the system allow for revision branching? Is there any capability to automate the reconciliation of two branches?

Does your organization track document effectivity? If so, does the database system have effectivity tracking? The same goes for configuration management.

PROGRAMMABILITY

Can the system be custom-programmed to fit into your environment? Is there an API available? Does the system allow for command-line access to structures? This is important if it is to be integrated into an existing environment.

TOLERANCE OF INVALID SGML

Does the system require all SGML data to be valid before saving it in the database? If so, is there a way to save invalid data as a work-in-process function? Is there a way to save partial objects for which there is no `DOCTYPE` declaration?

TRANSACTION PROCESSING

Does the system support transaction processing? What kind of reporting is available to track transaction commits and failures? Is there a way to capture transaction rollback events?

QUERY

Does the system support queries? Does it support full-text, parameterized, or structured query capabilities? Can the system accept queries that "go back in time" to a particular release by using its version control capabilities? This functionality is important in an environment where there are multiple configurations of documents that are active at once.

BLOBS

Can the system handle large binary objects (BLOBS)? Are there any size limitations? What kinds of NDATA formats are supported? Can the system perform full-text queries across binary data? Some graphics formats contain words that might be useful in a search. If your system can read the words inside graphics, it might be more valuable for certain types of research.

DIRECT INTEGRATION TO SYSTEM

What kind of SGML-specific support is provided? Does the system support other tools in your environment? DynaBase by EBT has a module to perform direct electronic book pressing. Texcel Information Manager has the ability to fire off a build process to any electronic book creation tool, such as Folio Views or DynaText.

Database Implementation Factors

DETERMINE GRANULARITY

The most important factor when implementing an SGML-enabled database is to determine the level at which the document information will be split. This is usually called "granularity", and each piece is called a "grain" or "atom".

Grains are typically chapters or parts, but we have seen implementations where each paragraph is stored separately.

Setting the grain size too large may cause unnecessary data access overhead. If a part consists of chapters, and the grain is set to the part level, the author will probably need to check out an entire part to make a change. This takes longer to extract from the database, load into the editor, and save than does checking out a smaller piece. Also, when the author has the entire thing checked out, others cannot make changes to other chapters.

Setting the grain size too small causes problems, also. If the grain is set at the paragraph level and an author needs to make global changes to a chapter, he must check out and modify each paragraph individually, or use some utility that works on a range of paragraphs. This creates its own resource problems, and is frustrating to the author.

A hierarchical storage methodology can help this somewhat. By setting the grain size on the smaller end of the scale, an intelligent front-end can effectively present a larger piece to the author by checking out and managing the smaller pieces internally. So, if the grain size is the paragraph, and an author wants to make global changes to all paragraphs in a chapter, the author would select the appropriate chapter from the intelligent front-end, and the system would do the dirty work of extracting all of the child pieces. Conversely, on check-in the system would be responsible for breaking the chapter back up into paragraphs.

For these reasons, we tend to suggest a smaller grain size for more flexibility. Determining the proper level of granularity is largely a matter of how the data is structured, and what its purpose is in the enterprise. Users will also have opinions as to the level of granularity. In one implementation we have seen, the grain is the entire document. The reason for this is that the users had been dealing with the document for twenty years, and were not about to change their way of doing business just to make the thing more elegant. They had developed internal procedures for knowing who was currently editing the document, and the system worked fine.

Sometimes, the level of granularity is self-defining. A common way is to break by chapter or sub-chapter. It is the level at which the author is likely to work. In many situations, even if a book has several authors or maintainers, a chapter will be owned by a single person. By setting the grain size to this object, the database reflects what the users do naturally.

In one implementation, a library of paragraphs was maintained for the purpose of building insurance policies. Each state has requirements for insurance companies to assure that the correct things are covered in each policy. Every paragraph is created with this in mind, and a policy document is built on-the-fly according to rules set forth by the states.

In this implementation, each paragraph was authored separately, and went through a gauntlet of lawyers, regulators, and production people. The level of granularity in this system was easy to determine. In yet another implementation, the grain is the lowest common division of both the intellectual structure and the physical page structure needed for looseleaf publishing. See Appendix 1, *Case Study: RIA TIGRE System* on page 371.

There are also technical factors to keep in mind when determining granularity. There is a certain amount of database overhead for each object. If each word were tracked, the overhead could easily be more than the actual data. Even in a system with paragraph-sized grains, the overhead could exceed the content of the data. But if it is necessary for data management, this overhead is just the price you need to pay. Be sure to keep in mind the storage requirements and the performance penalties when determining data granularity.

APPLICATION DEVELOPMENT

In creating applications in a database environment, the most important thing to consider is the ownership of the data. For a database system to be effective in managing the data, there must be a single point of control of the data content and internal and external links.

A single owner also provides a central location to assure that access is granted only to those individuals or process that posses appropriate security clearances.

The applications in a database environment usually query a central manager for all access to the data.

Database load

Getting data into the system is usually the first application designed and developed. It is here that the database manager builds the internal structure tables and stores the data and indexes.

A database loader in an SGML-enabled system contains some kind of "atomizer" that breaks the source document into the grain-sized pieces mentioned above. The loader also makes available to the database parameterized information that can be used later to search and retrieve the appropriate objects.

Such parameter information is object identifiers, author names, creation and modification dates, and perhaps some keywords. Most of this information can be obtained by querying the attributes on the element tags in the content of the document object. This parameter information is one more thing that should be determined in the document analysis stage of system implementation (See Chapter 5, *Document Analysis* on page 65).

External system interconnect

Most databases do not exist in a vacuum. The system designer must create the ability to access data and systems external to the database. This might include notation processors, enterprise-wide applications, or other databases.

At the very least, applications to allow for check-in and check-out from the database.

Administrative functions

In a single-owner system, the database manager is completely responsible for tracking objects, their relationships, security access privileges, and many other things. Since the idea behind the data owner is to prevent uncontrolled access to the data, the owner has a lot of power.

Inevitably, something will go wrong. If the owner loses a link between two pieces of data, or, worse, loses a pointer to a piece of data in the system, data integrity will be compromised.

A set of administrative tools must be built to allow for low-level access to the database to fix this sort of problem. These tools should be accessible only by the most trusted and competent of the system administrators, since they allow for unchecked access to the data. One tactic would be to encrypt the applications such that it requires two keys to unlock and run.

Workflow

A workflow management tool has its basis in project management[1]. There are many project management tools available that allow a project analyst to design and track the progress of a project as it flows through the company. Workflow, as defined in this chapter, goes one significant step beyond traditional project management tools in that it is integrated with the information database. This integration allows a workflow management tool to provide information to the person assigned to each task as it is needed, and in the form that is most appropriate for the person.

Workflow is the process of executing one task after another until a particular result is obtained. A task can be dependent upon zero or more tasks and can have other tasks dependent upon it.

Workflow management is an essential part of implementing an SGML documentation system. The simplest workflow management is done in someone's head: "First I must pick up the paper, then put it in the typewriter, adjust it so it is square, position the roller to the top of the page, then type the first character." This is a workflow. If there was not a piece of paper around the roller, there would be no point in positioning it to the top of the page. We have a set of dependencies that must be executed in a particular order to achieve the final result.

The examples used in this chapter are representative of commercially available workflow management systems, but are shown mainly to illustrate the capabilities of such systems.

A computer-based workflow manager deals with "projects". It links together and controls the movement of "tasks" from inception of the project to its completion. Along the way, it reports the status of the project. A task is defined by the user: "wash the car", "proofread introduction chapter", "run for president". Each of these can be broken down into subordinate tasks, which can be further defined until the project becomes manageable. The level of this breakdown is dependent upon the users who will be doing the work. For example "wash the car" can have sub-tasks such as "connect the hose to the water source", "prepare the soap bucket", and "close the windows". Personally, we simplify the project by defining the task: "drive to the car wash".

---

1 A "project analyst" is a person who manages projects. In an organization, this person is usually called a "project manager". We use "project analyst" to differentiate the person from project management software.

At any point in the process, the flow of work can take different paths depending upon the outcome of a decision. The task "wash the car" can take different paths depending upon the answer to the questions, "do we have soap?", or, "is it raining?"

Connectors link these tasks and decision points and create the flow. The connectors show the user and the system what path to take depending on the results of the task, or the outcome of a decision.

Commercial workflow managers provide a graphical tool for the creation of projects. Creating a project with such a tool involves drawing a flow consisting of tasks, decisions, and connectors.

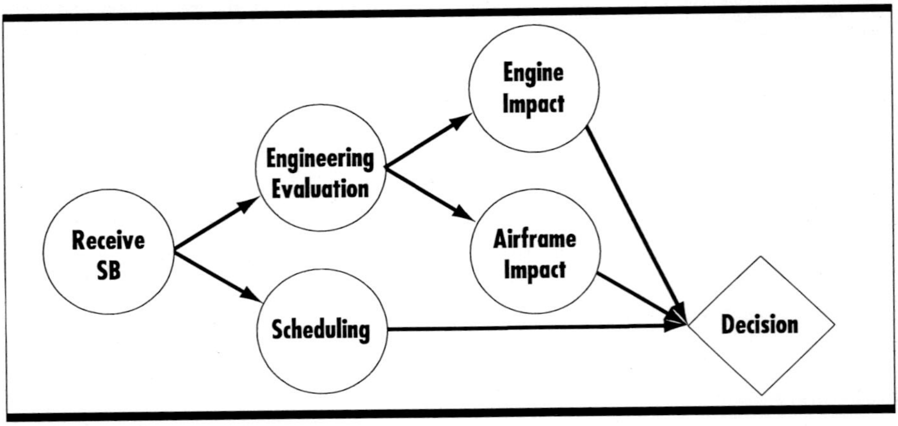

Figure 67. *A workflow shown graphically*

Once the initial flow is done, subordinate tasks can be created and edited in the same way. The workflow editor allows the entry of the description of the task itself, along with parameters like resources required, estimated time to complete, security level required, and other user-defined items.

WORKFLOW IN ACTION

The power of a workflow management tool in a documentation environment is its ability to provide to each resource everything it needs to complete the task. Consider the scenario of a manufacturer of automobile brakes. The manufacturer is under federal mandate to replace the lining with a non-asbestos material.

Several tasks must be performed to complete this project. First, someone from the legal department must be consulted to interpret the meaning of the federal order. Based on the outcome of this report, the engineers must investigate alternatives to asbestos lining. Upon receipt of an engineering specification, the production people must determine if the design is able to be implemented using the company's equipment.

All along the way, the legal department must be consulted to determine if the proposed design and implementation adhere to the edict.

The person assigned to each of these tasks requires some kind of information in order to complete the task. In a traditional workflow "system", the corporate counsel would retrieve or be given a stack of papers from many sources to review. He would write a report and hand that, along with the background information necessary, to the engineer. The engineer would search his own files for the information he needs.

This research and transfer of paper is time-consuming and takes the person's attention away from the task at hand. With computer-based documents, we still see people working with "virtual paper", in that they might have their information on a computer network, and send these files to each other via e-mail or some other sort of inter-company transfer. On a conceptual level, this is no different from passing actual paper; it still takes a person's mind off the task at hand, and requires knowledge of the locations of the necessary information. It also does not gather documents and data as needed, leaving that research up to the next person in the process.

A workflow management system, on the other hand, can automate this "paper chase" by providing a central manager whose job it is to see that information gets where it needs to, when it needs do.

CREATING A PROJECT

In the federal mandate example above, an analyst would be assigned to the task of creating a workflow template. In a graphical environment, the analyst would drag task objects onto a task design field, and connect them with lines indicating work flow.

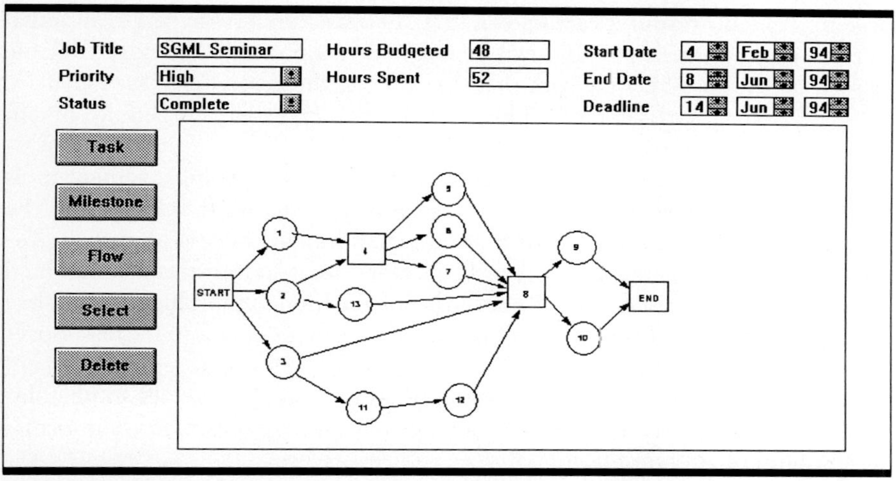

Figure 68. *Workflow Manager — Job Profile Editor*

"Behind" each task is information about resources, authorities, time and money estimates, and data needed to complete the task.

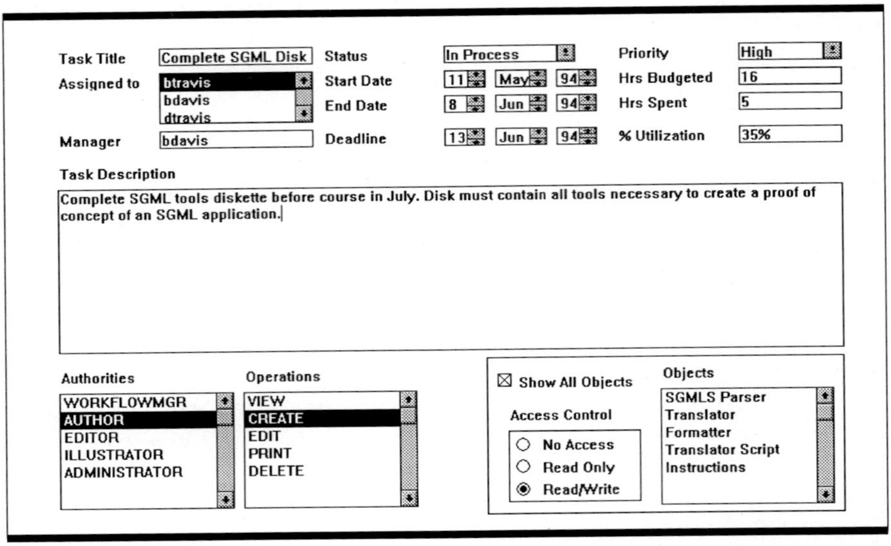

Figure 69. *Workflow Manager — Task Editor*

The top part of this screen is similar to many project management tools. It is here that the analyst indicates the resources required, estimated time, and dates to complete the task. Since the workflow management tool is part of an integrated system, available resources are known to it. The task can be assigned to an actual person, or to a "position". If a task is assigned to a position, the next available person on the list of people with that title will get the task when it is ready.

A description is entered. This is for the human reader, and should contain enough guidance to complete the task.

The bottom section of the screen is where workflow management tools differ from non-integrated project management systems. It is here that the project analyst specifies what kind of information and process objects are required to complete the task. Also, it specifies what authorities the assigned resource must possess in order to access the information. An intelligent workflow management tool will assure that all authorities are in order before the task moves to the resource.

By completing one of these for each task, the analyst creates an unambiguous set of tasks that the workflow management system uses to move information around the organization.

In addition to this project, the organization has other project analysts creating work-flows for their projects. Each of these analyst has a pool of resources upon which to draw, and assigns tasks to them as required.

ASSIGNING TASKS

When a person who is a resource arrives at work, the workflow management system presents him with a screen listing all of the tasks to which he has been assigned.

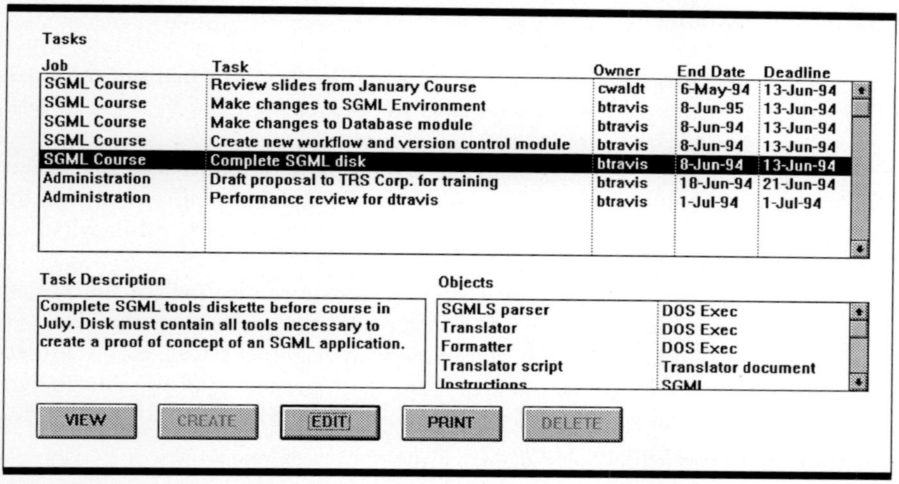

Figure 70. *Workflow Manager — Job Task Screen*

The tasks are sorted according to their importance and deadline.

In a typical scenario, the user would select a task and see the description of it and items required to complete the task. This is where the benefits of a workflow management system is most easily seen. Upon selecting the task, the workflow manager makes all of the information available to the user, either by copying it to a user's task directory, or making network connections to the information where it is.

A workflow management tool can be seen as a thoughtful concierge, providing everything to its master, and endowed with the authority to get the job done.

In the federal mandate example above, consider the engineer's task of designing a new brake lining. In order to complete the task, he might need the following items:

1. the report sent by government regulators,
2. the analysis report prepared by the legal department,
3. specification sheets from third-party brake-lining suppliers
4. the existing design documents

In addition, he needs access to his CAD (computer-aided design) software to do the actual re-design.

The workflow management system will provide all of these items to the engineer, allowing him to start work immediately instead of searching for information and the tools he needs.

Notice that the bottom of the screen contains certain "actions" that are appropriate for the task selected. In this case, the engineer can view, edit, or print the documents at hand.

After completing an initial design, he marks the task as complete, which signals the workflow manager to note time and budget information, then pass the task and required resource objects to the person assigned to the next task: the production department.

At this time, a new task is added to the production analyst's task screen. This task, the review of the initial design for production ability, contains the initial design created by the engineer in the previous task, **plus** whatever information is required for the production analysis.

The project flows, task by task, to a decision point, where the project analyst can determine which path to take, or until the project is complete.

The difference between a workflow management tool and a project management tool is in the data-centered approach of the workflow management tool. A project management tool might require the worker to take the following steps in order to complete a task:

1. determine what to do today,
2. track down the information required,
3. retrieve the information,
4. perform the task,
5. determine who is responsible for the next task,
6. pass the information to that person,
7. access the project management system and report time spent and resources used.

On the other hand, a workflow management tool is integrated with the resources and information objects, as well as the project details. So, the steps to be taken are more straightforward:

1. select task from task list,
2. perform the task,
3. mark the task as complete.

It is not difficult to see that productivity and accuracy can be greatly increased with such a system, because the user is not concerned with administrative details such as deciding and adjusting priorities, notification of completed tasks, and delivery of the goods to the next resource.

USER AUTHORITIES

Each user resource in the system has certain tools for which they have the training to use. In certain situations, tools and information is available only to certain users based on security guidelines.

The system is linked to a user database that contains such authorities. When a user selects a task, the appropriate tools are loaded according to the task and the user's abilities.

For example, of a task is to review and comment on a policy statement, the task window will indicate that one of the actions is "view". Based on this user's authority database, the system knows that he has received training on two different document viewers, but that the user prefers one over the other. So, clicking on the "view" action loads the appropriate viewer and the document to be reviewed.

SYSTEM MANAGEMENT

Now that an integrated system is in charge of all data and flows in the organization, a tremendous amount of management information can be provided. At any time, the project analyst can query the system to find out how far the project has progressed, where the bottlenecks are, and how the budget and time estimates compare with actuals.

The project template is a dynamic entity that can be modified along the way. If some unexpected event occurs, the project analyst can modify the tasks and connectors in a project template to reflect the new situation.

IMPLEMENTATION CONSIDERATIONS

Certain things should be kept in mind when implementing a workflow management system.

Full access

The most important aspect of a successful workflow management system is that the system has access to all information required to complete the project. If the information is not available to the system, it cannot make maximum use of the human resources.

It is unlikely that all information for a given project will be directly accessible in an electronic form. For example, the federal mandate above might have come in the form of a paper document, with a box of supporting documentation.

A well-designed workflow management system will account for this by creating pointers to physical documents. For example, a project analyst could create a task of reviewing the government documents by placing, behind the "view" action, a message for the engineer to call the librarian and request a certain document number, or will refer him to a particular drawer in a particular filing cabinet. Another approach is to create a task for a secretary to fetch the paper documents and give them to the engineer.

Network and Security

A networked environment is a fundamental requirement for implementing a workflow management system. The actual workflow manager software must have access to all data in the system in order to make the required objects available to the task resource.

Moreover, in a classified environment, the workflow management tool must have sufficient security clearance to make the information available.

E-mail

Electronic mail can be integrated in to a workflow management system to allow for communication between the task resources and the project analyst. Such messages can be copied into a repository in the workflow management system as a record of the project as it progresses.

E-mail can also be used as a bridge to communicate with employees, customers, and vendors who are not attached directly to your system resources.

PART • III

Part III / The Language

CHAPTER • TEN

Understanding SGML

Introduction

This chapter is a reference manual for SGML syntax and use. While we have made every attempt to be comprehensive, there are areas that are in the standard that we feel are not necessary to cover in depth. This book is about SGML implementation, so we have concentrated on those areas of the standard that the real-life SGML implementor will find useful. If there is a feature or subject area that is not covered in-depth here, you can read more about it in the SGML standard itself, or in the technical resources listed in Appendix 8, *SGML Resources* on page 445.

This chapter provides detailed descriptions and explanations of the constructs of SGML. Many examples of markup and declarations are provided and minimization features are described.

Related Topics

- *The Problem with Unstructured Information* on page 4
- *The Power of SGML Databases* on page 11
- Chapter 4, *The SGML Environment* on page 43
- *SGML Parser* on page 46
- *DTD Development Tools* on page 58
- Chapter 5, *Document Analysis* on page 65
- *The Document Model* on page 75
- *Formatting and Structure* on page 87
- *Defining a Markup Language — The Recipe* on page 92
- Chapter 6, *The SGML Application* on page 101
- *Translation to non-SGML applications* on page 111
- *Data Design and DTD Development* on page 140
- Chapter 8, *Information Conversion* on page 151
- *Managing DTD Change* on page 163
- Chapter 9, *SGML Data Management and Workflow* on page 183
- Chapter 11, *Building the DTD* on page 275
- *Organizing a DTD* on page 276
- *Specific vs. General DTDs* on page 285
- *DTD Documentation* on page 286
- *Common Elements* on page 288
- Chapter 12, *Tipniques and Pratfalls* on page 301
- Chapter 9, *SGML Data Management and Workflow* on page 183

The SGML Document Model

An "SGML document entity" consists of three basic parts:

1. the SGML declaration
2. the prologue
3. a document instance set

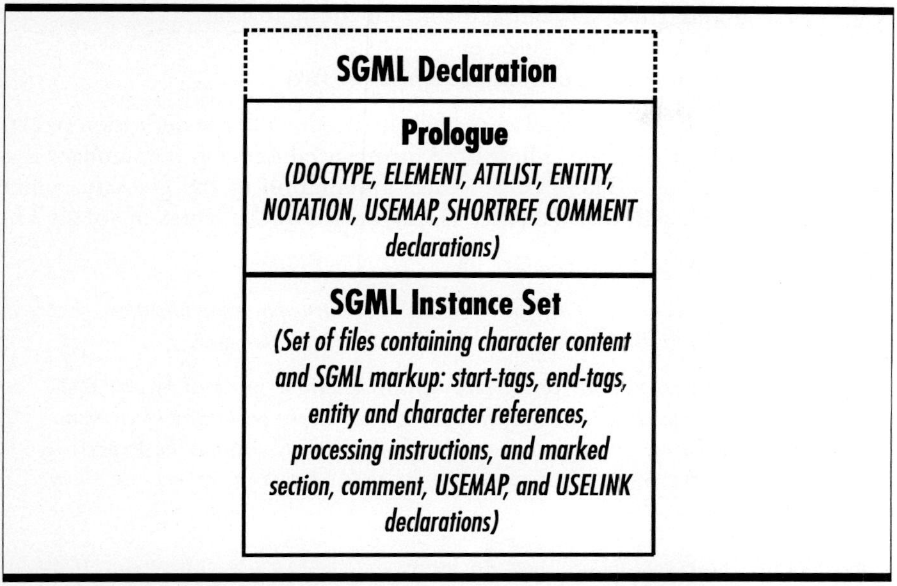

Figure 71. *The SGML Document Model*

SGML DECLARATION

The SGML declaration, although required as a piece of the SGML document entity model, can be implied by the application. That is, some applications will have defaults for all of the items required in the SGML declaration, making its explicit existence unnecessary.

The SGML declaration defines, among other things, the character set to use, the characters that are to be recognized as markup, and various capacities, quantities and features that are used. The SGML standard defines a base set of defaults for these values: the reference concrete syntax. See Appendix 6, *Fully Commented SGML Declaration* on page 425 for two versions of the SGML declaration.

The Prologue

The prologue contains the document type declaration[1]. The document type declaration contains:

1 Technically, the prologue can contain more than one document type declaration (if the optional feature CONCUR is used) and one or more link type declarations (if the optional feature LINK is used). These features are not widely supported, and we do not cover them in-depth.

1. a set of rules that define the document model, or
2. a pointer to these rules, or
3. in some cases, a combination of these two.

This set of rules is popularly called the document type definition (DTD). This is not entirely accurate. There is no formal production in the standard that states what is a DTD. There is, however, a definition in the glossary, which indicates that only part of the DTD can be expressed by the syntax of SGML. The definition is as follows:

> *4.105 document (type) definition: Rules, determined by an application, that apply SGML to the markup of documents of a particular type.*
>
> *Note that part of a document type definition can be specified by an SGML document type declaration. Other parts, such as the semantics of elements and attributes, or any application of conventions, cannot be expressed formally in SGML. Comments can be used, however, to express them informally.*

This would indicate that the DTD consists, not only of the "formal" declarations that we will learn about in this chapter, but also contains an "informal" part that defines further the semantic and application-specific descriptions of the document model. This underscores the importance of DTD documentation described in *DTD Documentation* on page 286.

In this book, we will use the more informal definition of a DTD as "the set of SGML declarations that describes the document model". While this is not entirely accurate, it is easier for the implementor to work with.

The DTD also contains descriptions of, special characters that the document uses, external pieces that are necessary to process the document, and some other information about the document. We will be covering all declarations in this chapter.

SGML Document Instance Set

The document instance is what is typically referred to as "the document itself". It contains the text and markup that make up the document.

The SGML document instance can exist only after a set of rules, the DTD, has been defined. It is important to note that "without the DTD, it isn't SGML". This is not to say that the DTD needs to be physically attached to the top of the document instance, but it must be available to the application that processes the instance in order that it know what the rules are. See *The Document Type Definition* on page 228.

Versions of SGML

The original version of SGML is referred to as "ISO 8879-1986" in the SGML declaration. Soon after the standard was adopted, there was an amendment containing some changes that were recommended as the result of the balloting and adoption process. The amended version is referred to as "ISO 8879:1986" in the SGML declaration (note that the hyphen is replaced with a colon).

Every five years, each ISO standard undergoes a review to determine whether the standard deserves to continue as an international standard, and what, if any, changes must be made so that it remains useable. The first quinquennial review took place in 1991-92. The special working group that reviewed the standard made assurances to the SGML industry that any changes would not render existing documents obsolete.

Markup

There are several forms that SGML markup takes. Throughout this section, we will be using the default characters that are defined in the standard as part of the "reference concrete syntax". These characters can be changed to fit most any environment.

The following table shows all of the different markup items that can exist in an SGML document instance.

Name	*Description*	*Example*
Start-tag	Notes the start of elements that are defined in the DTD.	<title>
End-tag	Notes the end of an open element.	</chapter>
General Entity Reference	Used to indicate substitutable text or external files to be expanded.	ĉ
Comment	Used to indicate information to some person or process reading the data.	<!--Bob, please check these numbers -->
Processing Instruction	Used to provide some processing information directly to the application.	<?indent 5em>
Character Reference	Inserts a single character by its numerical value in the host system.	-
Marked Section Declaration	A special area that can change how the parser looks at the data.	<![IGNORE[<chapter>...]]>
Short Reference Use Declaration	Indicates when a new short reference mapping is to be initiated.	<!USEMAP dvorak>
Link Set Use Declaration	Indicates when a particular link set should be used.	<!USELINK #RESTORE booklink>

Table 6. *Markup allowed in an SGML document*

The following describes to each of these forms of markup.

START-TAG

The most common forms of markup are the start-tag and end-tag. The start-tag is used to indicate the start of elements that are defined in the DTD.

The start-tag is not always required. There is a set of features in SGML called "minimization features". These allow for the omission of start- or end-tags when they are not required to indicate structure. There are more minimization features (See *Minimization Features* on page 266).

In addition to the name of the element, the start-tag can contain information about the element. This additional information is called an "attribute". Attributes can be used to indicate additional information for processing. For example, although the creation date and author may never be printed in any form from this document, this information might be needed in order to load a database or decide which elements are to be included in a particular rendering. In this case, the start-tag for `chapter` might look like this:

```
...
<chapter date='940721' author='btravis'>
```

In this example, there are two attributes declared: date and author. The SGML parser can assure that, for example, the date consists only of numbers, and the author starts with a letter, but it is up to the application to decide what to do with this information.

END-TAG

The end-tag indicates the end of an element. Elements are hierarchical and can contain data and other elements nested within. For this reason, it is important to indicate clearly the boundaries of elements, either implicitly or explicitly with end-tags.

Like the start-tag, the end-tag is not always required, based on minimization rules that might be in effect. If the element is a special type called an "empty element", the end-tag is not allowed. There is another special case, called "content reference (`#CONREF`)" when the existence of an end-tag will generate an error (See *#CONREF—Default Value* on page 246).

GENERAL ENTITY REFERENCE

General entity references are used to indicate substitutable text or external files to be expanded. At its simplest level, an entity reference will cause the parser to substitute replacement text that is declared in the DTD. For example, `&sgml;` can be defined to become "Standard Generalized Markup Language" when expanded.

Entity references provide a powerful tool for managing the various files needed to process the SGML-tagged data. An entity reference can be declared as a pointer to an external data set that the application will insert into the document at the point of the entity reference. In fact, those entities that are inserted can have entity references themselves. Entity references can also point to non-SGML data such as graphics, sounds, video, and the like.

COMMENT DECLARATION

Comments are allowed almost everywhere in the SGML document. They are ignored by the parser, so they do not affect the output, but can be used to communicate with other people or processes who are editing the document.

For more information on the comment declaration, See *The Comment Declaration* on page 262.

PROCESSING INSTRUCTION

Processing instructions provide a way of passing commands directly through the parser to the application. You might think that the mere existence of a processing instruction might seem to violate all of the things we have been saying about generalized markup and system-independent data. You would be right. However, although we are setting the groundwork for a completely generalized database of valuable data, it is still necessary to produce books to run the company and, therefore, sometimes pragmatic concerns will require the use of system-specific coding to support an essential feature. Processing instructions allow the inclusion of system-specific encoding in such a way that is easily distribguished from the more "pure" generalized coding defined as elements, attributes, and other constructs. As the DTD gets more accurate and the applications learn to deal with the generalized databases, the need for processing instructions will diminish.

Processing instructions are passed to the application untouched by the parser. The use of processing instructions is deprecated by the standard. The standard warns against the use of processing instructions because they reduce the portability of the document. For example, a document containing processing instructions that have codes that are specific to a particular typesetter will be difficult to process for use with a different typesetter or CD-ROM engine.

Processing instructions provide a standard way to describe system-dependent processing information. In this way, it is preferable to a situation where every implementor creates his own means to insert such information.

Even the people who created the language conceded that what they were doing was of a questionable nature, as indicated by the character used to represent a processing instruction: a question mark.

A processing instruction looks like this:

```
<?CD-ROM JL:Jump, ITIT-CPP-1>
```

In this example, everything between "<?" (processing-instruction open — PIO) and ">" (processing-instruction close—PIC) will be sent to the application, with some indication that the system data came from a processing instruction.

Processing instructions do not need to be declared, but they can be part of a special entity called a "processing instruction entity". See *PI - Processing Instruction Entity* on page 255

Processing instructions are passed through the parser intact, to be used by the application in whatever way it deems necessary, from ignoring them to passing them un-hindered to the output stream. Whatever is done with processing instructions by the application, the parser will remain out of the way.

We have seen some very good uses for processing instructions over the years. We have also seen many abuses, those that the developers feared might happen. See *Using Processing Instructions the "Right Way"* on page 333 and *Use Processing Instructions for Inter-application Communication* on page 348.

Character Reference

A character reference is used to insert a single character by its numerical value. It is usually used to represent a character not available on the keyboard. However, the use of these, like the use of processing instructions, should be monitored by the application, since they could render a document unportable.

A better way to deal with characters that are not available from the keyboard is to declare them as `SDATA` entities with a mnemonic name. This will allow the document architect to change the value of the entity based on the current system. It will also make it easier to read, since a name for the character can be used instead of its numerical value.

Marked Section Declaration

Marked sections provide a way of indicating to the parser the type of data that comprises a particular block. A marked section declaration is placed around a block of text to indicate whether or not it is to be ignored by the parser or treated as character data or replaceable character data. The marked section declaration is described in *Marked Section Declaration* on page 264.

Short Reference Use Declaration

A short reference use declaration is used to indicate when a new short reference mapping is to be initiated. This is only used when short reference mappings have been declared. Short references are a form of minimization that allow certain characters to indicate markup. See *Using Short Reference Minimization* on page 330 for real-world use of short references.

LINK Set Use Declaration

A link set use declaration can be placed in the instance to indicate which link set is to be active. We do not discuss the use of the `LINK` feature in this book. Refer to *The SGML Handbook*, in Appendix 8 / SGML Resources on page 494 for more information about link.

Declarations

SGML defines the declarations shown in *Table 7, Declarations in SGML* on page 225

Declaration	*Description*	*Example*
SGML	The SGML declaration is the "bootstrap" section where character sets and features are specified.	<!SGML ISO 8879:1986...>
Document Type	Contains declarations that make up the formal, structural piece of the document type definition (DTD).	<!DOCTYPE book [...]>
Element	Names structural elements, indicates their content, and specifies minimization rules.	<!ELEMENT chapter - - (title, abstract, para+)>
Attribute Definition List	Declares attribute names and permissible values for a given element.	<!ATTLIST section date NUMBER #REQUIRED>
Entity	Establishes a link between a symbolic name and its replacement text or a pointer to an external data set. There are two kinds of entities: parameter entities and general entities.	<!ENTITY chap01 SYSTEM "/usr/pubs/TM5007/chap01.sgml">
Short Reference Mapping	Associates a particular character with an entity.	<!SHORTREF paratext '"' qtag>
Short Reference Use	Maps a previously defined short reference map in a particular context.	<!USEMAP paratext p >

Declaration	***Description***	***Example***
Comment	Contains only comment text.	<!-- The following declarations form the table subset -->
Marked Section	Hides or makes visible content and markup from the parser, or to change the character handling of entire sections	<![IGNORE[...]]>
Notation	Attaches an external process to a piece of text.	<!NOTATION eqn SYSTEM "/usr/bin/equproc">
Link Type	Associates the link type name with the link process definition	<!LINKTYPE style general #IMPLIED [...]>
Link Set	Provides a name to a set of link rules.	<!LINK online title [text=red] para [text=norm]>
Link Set Use Declaration	Indicates when a particular link set should be used.	<!USELINK #RESTORE booklink>
ID Link Set	Overrides the link set that would otherwise be current for particular element instances.	<!IDLINK ex01 example [type=12pt] ex02 example [type-10pt]>

Table 7. *Declarations in SGML*

THE SGML DECLARATION

The SGML declaration is where the system finds out about the various characters used to indicate data, markup, and control information. It also specifies which characters should be "shunned" from processing because of some system limitation.

There are two categories of customization defined by the SGML declaration: defining a concrete syntax, and setting optional features. In this section, we will not attempt to describe every value in the SGML declaration. Rather, we will explain those areas of the declaration that you are most likely to modify. For a complete description of the SGML declaration, refer to <TAG>, The SGML Newsletter[1]. See Appendix 6, *Fully Commented SGML Declaration* on page 425 for a fully commented SGML declaration.

Concrete Syntax

The designers of SGML defined a default set of values to act as a minimum base for conforming SGML systems. This default set is called the reference concrete syntax. This defines what characters are to be used to delimit tags, what character set is to be used, the maximum sizes of names, and so on.

Most SGML applications comply to this set of defaults, because it handles most users' documents. In fact, some SGML applications do not allow you to modify the values in the SGML declaration, but instead force you to use the reference concrete syntax.

Any change to the reference concrete syntax constitutes some customization of the SGML environment. There are several publicly available variant concrete syntaxes that have been written over the years for particular uses. For example, the U.S. Department of Defense CALS program has requirements that have forced it to modify the reference concrete syntax to handle the large names of entities and attributes, among other things. This variant is published and available widely, as are others.

Capacities

The designers of SGML felt that it would be helpful if parsers knew what kind of horsepower was required to process a particular document. With this information available before parsing the document, a parser could stop and issue a warning before commencing a processing run that it could not complete.

The idea of the `CAPACITY` section of the SGML declaration is to inform the parser about the amount of memory needed to parse the document. Capacity limits seem to be unnecessary with the increased power and resources of most computers today. Many implementors have increased the values of capacities to values much higher than defined in the reference concrete syntax to prevent error messages from occurring where they do not necessarily indicate an error.

Quantities

The SGML declaration defines several quantities that you might want to change:

---

1 The DTD May Not Be Enough: SGML Declarations. Three-part article: Volume 5, Issue 10 (October, 1992), Volume 5, Issue 12 (December, 1992), Volume 6, Number 2 (February, 1993), <TAG>, The SGML Newsletter.

Quantity	*Default*	*Description*
ATTCNT	40	Number of attribute names and name tokens in an attribute definition list.
ATTSPLEN	960	Normalized length of a start-tag's attribute specifications list.
BSEQLEN	960	Length of a blank sequence in a short reference string.
DTAGLEN	16	Length of a data tag.
DTEMPLEN	16	Length of a data tag template or pattern template (undelimited).
ENTLVL	16	Nesting level of entities (other than primary).
GRPCNT	32	Number of tokens in a group.
GRPGTCNT	96	Grand total of content tokens at all levels of a content model (a data tag group is three tokens).
GRPLVL	16	Nesting level of model groups (including first level).
LITLEN	240	Length of a parameter literal or attribute value literal (interpreted and undelimited).
NAMELEN	8	Length of a name, name token, number, etc.
NORMSEP	2	Used on lieu of counting separators in calculating normalized lengths.
PILEN	240	Length of a processing instruction (undelimited).
TAGLEN	960	Length of a start-tag (undelimited).
TAGLVL	24	Nesting level of open elements.

Table 8. *Quantities in the SGML Declaration.*

There are a couple of quantities that you will probably want to modify. The most common are `NAMELEN` and `LITLEN`. SGML names are used in many different places. The most common places are element names, attribute names and entity names. We have found that eight characters is not enough to mnemonically identify the elements. Using eight characters forces strange names like `bodymat`, `abbrsect`, `applicab`, and so forth. The `NAMELEN` quantity is used to specify a different maximum length for SGML names.

Parameter entity names are limited to one character less than the NAMELEN quantity, because the PERO delimiter (%) is counted. If PERO is defined to be more than one character, the length of a parameter entity name is shortened by the length of PERO.

LITLEN defines the maximum length of literals. Literals are used in many places in an SGML system. The most common place is in the replacement text for a general entity and the value of attributes. This number is usually increased if the implementor wants to have long replacement text, as in the case of boilerplate text inside an entity or very long attribute values.

Optional Features

There are a number of features that a particular application can use. These features are defined in the standard, but remain optional because there is no need for an application to be burdened with supporting them all if they are not going to be used.

The following table shows eleven optional features that can be defined in the SGML declaration.

Feature	*Description*
CONCUR	Turns on processing of concurrent document type instances
DATATAG	Allows data tag minimization
EXPLICIT	Allows explicit link process definitions to be used
FORMAL	Forces public identifiers to conform with a defined structure
IMPLICIT	Allows implicit link process definitions to be used
OMITTAG	Allows omitted tag minimization
RANK	Allows the use of rank suffix minimization
SHORTREF	Allows the use of short entity references
SHORTTAG	Allows unclosed, empty, and omitted tags to be used as minimization
SIMPLE	Allows simple link process definitions to be used
SUBDOC	Allows the use of nested subdocuments

Table 9. *Optional features in the SGML declaration*

THE DOCUMENT TYPE DEFINITION

The document type definition is a collection of rules describing all documents adhering to a particular document type. The standard does not address the document type definition as a structural piece of the document model. Instead, the DTD is seen as a collection of element, attribute definition list, entity, notation, entity, short reference, and comment declarations contained within the document type declaration, in an area called the "document type declaration subset".

In some cases, the word "document" is an abstraction; a document type definition could be written to describe only a part of what a final document consists of. For example, a collection of declarations that describe the structure of equations could be written and included into a larger set by entity reference. This type of construction is usually called a "DTD fragment", since it is meant to be included in larger DTDs, and will probably never stand alone.

THE ELEMENT DECLARATION

The element declaration is the cornerstone of structural definition. Elements can contain other elements, character data, or nothing.

Element declarations define:

1. the name of the element
2. start- and end-tag minimization that can be used
3. content

An important part of the element declaration is the content model. It is here that the document architect indicates the order and occurrence of other element or character data. Each element type is given a unique name.

The various parts of the element declaration are illustrated in *Figure 72, The element declaration* on page 230.

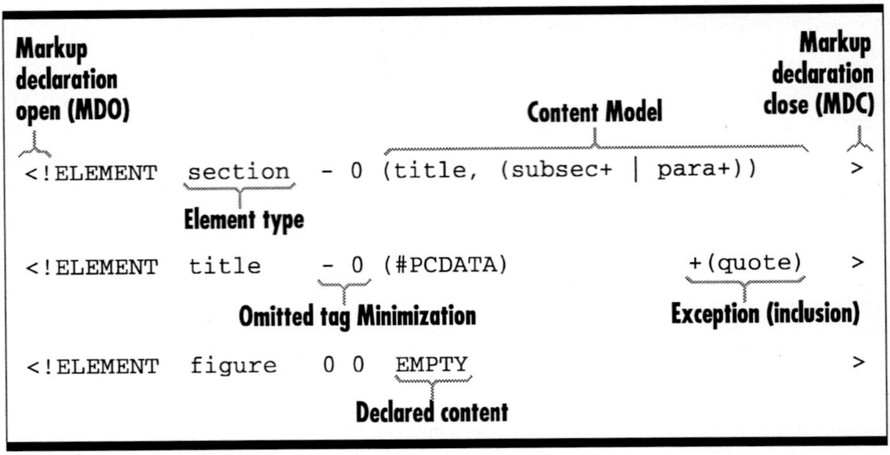

Figure 72. *The element declaration*

Element Type

The element type is the name of the element being defined. It is properly known as a generic identifier (GI), but most people call it a "tag name". This is the user-defined name of the element. It must start with a name start character, followed by zero or more name characters. A name start character is a letter (A through Z and a through z). A name character is a name start character or a number or a hyphen or period. All of these characters can be modified or changed by making the proper modifications to the SGML declaration.

Case is insignificant by default for elements, so `Paragraph` and `paragraph` are identical generic identifiers. In order to make case significant, `NAMECASE GENERAL` in the SGML declaration must be set to `NO`. This is probably not a very good idea, since most implementations assume case insensitivity in tag names and it can be confusing to a user if `List`, `LIST`, and `list` are used to mean different element types.

Omitted Tag Minimization

The minimization field consists of two characters, "start-tag minimization" and "end-tag minimization", separated by one or more parameter separators (white space: tab, newline, or space). Each field has two possible values, a hyphen or the letter `O`. A hyphen indicates that the start- or end-tag is required. A letter `O` indicates that the tag is omissible.

The minimization fields are not considered by the parser to determine whether a tag was omitted. It is only used to generate an error message when the tag was omitted improperly. This is an area with which first-time users have difficulty. The parser will process the document without any notice of the minimization fields. It is only the error-generation logic that will do something if an element is omitted improperly.

Notes on tag minimization:

1. Minimization is only allowed if the `OMITTAG` feature is set to `YES` in the SGML declaration. This is the default defined by the reference concrete syntax.
2. Regardless of what is specified in the minimization fields, tags can only be omitted if the feature is enabled.

Content Model

The content model is where the structure of the element is defined. Content models indicate order of sub-elements, and how many times they may be specified.

There are two types of content models. The first is one that starts with a model group—a parenthetical list of elements, separated by "connectors" and marked with "occurrence indicators".

```
(title, abstract?, paragraph+)
```

This content model indicates that the element that uses it contains a single mandatory title, followed by an optional abstract, followed by one or more paragraphs.

In addition to a model group, this form of content model can have an optional area where exceptions (inclusions and exclusions) are declared. We will describe these in *Exceptions* on page 237.

The second type of content model is the keyword `ANY`, which means that the element can contain character data or any other element declared in the same document type definition. This can be used for development, but should not appear in the final version of your DTD, because of the loose nature of the `ANY` content model. This can be used for development, but, due to the loose nature of `ANY` should not appear in production DTDs.

CONNECTORS. A connector is placed between any two elements in a model group to indicate how they are to appear in the structure.

Connector	*Description*
`,`	Sequence: followed by
`|`	Or: one or the other
`&`	And: both are required in any order

Table 10. *Content model connectors*

Occurrence Indicators. Occurrence Indicatorsare placed immediately after each generic identifier in a model group to indicate how many times the element may appear in the structure.

Occurrence indicator	*Description*
?	Optional: The element may occur once or not at all.
+	Required and repeatable: The element must occur one or more times.
*	Optional and repeatable: The element may occur one or more times, or not at all.

Table 11. *Content model occurrence indicators*

If there is no occurrence indicator, the element must appear exactly once.

Group open and group close. Content model groups can be nested further by putting groups inside parentheses. This can help with the readability of the content model, and is required to prevent mixed connectors in a single group. Only one kind of connector can occur in a single model group (but a model group nested within it could have a different connector).[1]

For example, suppose a chapter consists of a title followed by both an abstract and an author, in any order, followed by a body. The following content model has two different kinds of connectors, and is, therefore, marked as an error by the parser.

```
(title, abstract & author, body)  <!-- error -->
```

In order to rectify the situation, a model group must be parenthetically grouped to indicate what is really meant:

```
(title, (abstract & author), body)
```

Examples. Consider the following content models and their "plain language" equivalent descriptions that follow each example.

A memo:

```
(to+, from+, subject, date?, para+)
```

1 ISO 8879:1986 11.2.4.1 Connector

One or more required to, *followed by one or more required* from, *followed by a single required* subject, *followed by an optional* date, *followed by one or more required* para.

An e-mail header:

```
(path+, message-id, (to & from & subject & date), body)
```

One or more required path, *followed by a single required* message-id, *followed by a single required occurrence of the following elements in any order:* to, from, subject, date, *followed by a single required* body.

A lesson:

```
(title, intro, objective+, paragraph+ (question, answer)+)
```

A single required title, *followed by a single required* intro, *followed by one or more required* objective, *followed by one or more required* paragraph, *followed by one or more required sets of a single required* question *and a single required* answer.

An illustration:

```
((graphic, caption) | example)
```

Either a graphic *followed by a required* caption, *or a* example.

The body of a chapter:

```
(paragraph+ | section+)
```

Either one or more paragraph, *or one or more* section.

Note in this last example that, once either a paragraph or a section is specified, it must be repeated, and not mixed with the other. In order to mix paragraphs and sections, use the content model below:

The body of a chapter:

```
(paragraph | section)+
```

One or more section *or* paragraph *in any order*

#PCDATA. At some point in the document hierarchy, actual words will usually need to appear. Characters are noted in the content model by the special word `#PCDATA`[1], which means "parsed character data".

Because this type of data is parsed, each character is viewed by the parser to determine if it is markup or data. Within parsed character data, all markup is recognized and processed appropriately. That is, all start- and end-tags, entity and character references, marked sections, comments, certain declarations, and comments are processed according to the rules of SGML.

Examples. Content model for a paragraph:

```
(#PCDATA)
```

Contains parsed character data

List item:

```
(#PCDATA | list)+
```

Contains parsed character data or `list` *in any order.*

MIXED CONTENT. An element contains "element content" if it contains no `#PCDATA`, which means it can contain sub-elements, processing instructions, and other markup including general entity and character entity references and marked sections. An element's content is called "mixed content" if it is allowed to contain data characters. That is, if it is defined by `ANY` or has a model group including `#PCDATA`. The term "mixed content" suggests elements that can contain either data characters or sub-elements. However, SGML uses this term even for elements that can only contain data characters. Elements can appear here through the use of inclusions.

There is a subtle problem that some model groups using both `#PCDATA` and sub-elements can cause. The standard therefore recommends mixing them only in a particular way. See *Mixed Content* on page 312.

---

1 The hash mark (#) is called the "reserved name indicator" (RNI), which indicates that the word has special meaning to the parser, and is not to be considered a user-defined word. You could actually have an element called PCDATA (with no hash mark). The result would be clear to a computer, but it could be quite confusing for someone reading the DTD for the first time.

AMBIGUOUS CONTENT MODELS. The term "ambiguous content model" is defined by the standard as: "A content model for which an element or character string occurring in the document instance can satisfy more than one primitive content token without look-ahead". Note that the word "ambiguous" is used here as it is defined in the standard, and should not be confused with the English adjective of the same name.

During development of the standard, it was suggested that ambiguous content models could be resolved by the parser by looking ahead at future content, but this was discarded as unworkable.

An example of an ambiguous content model is the content model for a chapter, which consists of an optional abstract paragraph, followed by an optional title, followed by one or more paragraphs in the body. Such a content model would look like this:

```
  ...
<!ELEMENT chapter      - -          (paragraph?, title?,
                                    paragraph+)             >
  ...
```

This generates the following error:

```
valid.sgm:4:15:E: content model is ambiguous: when no tokens
have been matched, both the 1st and 2nd occurrences of
`PARAGRAPH' are possible
valid.sgm:10:20:E: end tag for `CHAPTER' which is not finished
valid.sgm:10:20: open elements: CHAPTER (PARAGRAPH[ 1])
```

Almost any ambiguous content models can be resolved by simply re-arranging the model to make it unambiguous. The above example could be written as:

```
  ...
<!ELEMENT chapter      - -          (abstract?, title?,
                                    paragraph+)             >
<!ELEMENT abstract     - O          (paragraph+)            >
  ...
```

See *Ambiguous Content Models* on page 315 for more information on ambiguous content models.

DATA TAG GROUPS. One method of markup minimization is called "data tag". Data tag allows for data to be both markup and content simultaneously.

The data tag feature is not supported by very many parsers, and, due to the potential for confusing or unpredictable results, we have never used data tag in a production environment. We will not, therefore, attempt to cover the details in this section. Refer to the standard or *The SGML Handbook*, in Appendix 8 / SGML Resources on page 494 for complete information about data tag.

DECLARED CONTENT. Instead of specifying a structured model of an element's content, the content can be declared as a particular type of data. There are three types of declared content:

Declared Content	***Description***
`EMPTY`	No content at all
`CDATA`	Character data
`RCDATA`	Replaceable character data

Table 12. *Declared content*

Each of these types of declared content is described below.

EMPTY. Some elements do not contain anything at all. Consider a non-text graphic. Such an element might not contain any character data, but instead will indicate where the application should place some external file that contains a bit-mapped image.

Another use of an empty element is to provide information that the application will use to access an external database. Both of these examples rely on the use of attributes, which are covered below. After the attribute discussion, we will give examples of empty elements. See *Uses for Empty Elements* on page 321.

CDATA. Some elements contain only character data that should not be interpreted by the parser. Take this book as an example. In a book about SGML, there will be plenty of examples of `<markup>` embedded in the text. These examples should be printed as literals, and not interpreted as element tags.

`CDATA` is used in such a situation to ignore all markup except for something that looks like an end-tag, but not necessarily the end-tag for the current element.

The following element declaration uses `CDATA` declared content to avoid interpreting markup:

```
  ...
<!ELEMENT example      - -          CDATA                    >
  ...
```

The following example shows how this might be used in the text:

```
  ...
<example>
for (i=1; i<x; i++)
    {
    printf ("Month: %s\n", MonthName [ i] );
    }
```

```
</example>
```

If example was not declared as containing only CDATA, the parser would have generated an error indicating that it could not find an element for x, since it looks like a start-tag to the parser. However, because of the CDATA declared content, the parser is only looking for an end-tag, and all other characters are passed through as literals.

RCDATA. In addition to CDATA, there is another declared content that can be used to indicate non-parsed elements. Replaceable character data, RCDATA, is "slightly parsed". That is, the parser, upon encountering an element with declared content of RCDATA, will, as with CDATA, look for an end-tag, but it will also replace any general entity references according to their declarations in the DTD, and will replace character references. Consider

Consider the following example showing a mathematical formula with markup characters that should not be replaced, and entities, which should be replaced. The following markup is used:

```
...
<!ELEMENT formula      - -          RCDATA                    >
...
<formula>Result &equal;<X&sub2;>
</formula>
```

The parser replaces the entity reference, but keeps the angle brackets:

```
Result = <X2>
```

Notice that declared content is not contained in a parentheses as is a content model. Because it is not in the content model, it does not require a reserved name indicator (RNI, #) (See *Using CDATA and RCDATA Elements* on page 315).

EXCEPTIONS. The content model contains an optional field that specifies a list of elements that can be either included or excluded at any point in the element. This field is called "exceptions", and comes in two flavors: inclusions and exclusions.

Exception	*Description*	*Example*
Inclusion	The elements listed can occur anywhere in the element being defined, or in any of its descendants.	`+(footnote)`
Exclusion	The elements listed is no longer included or, if specified as optional in the content model, is no longer allowed in this element, or any of its descendants.	`-(note)`

Table 13. *Exceptions*

Although the words "exclusion" and "exception" sound similar in English, they mean different things in SGML. All exclusions are exceptions, but some exceptions are inclusions.

Exclusions are sometimes used to indicate that a previously included element cannot be included within itself. For example, a `warning` element might be defined as an inclusion to a `paragraph`, which would allow it to be included anywhere in `paragraph`, including any descendant of `paragraph`. If `warning` is included in `paragraph`, it becomes a descendent, and, therefore, the inclusion is valid. In order to prevent the possibility of allowing `warning` inside another `warning`, `warning` can be excluded from itself:

```
 ...
<!ELEMENT para       - O        (#PCDATA)      +(warning) >
<!ELEMENT warning    - -        (#PCDATA)      -(warning) >
 ...
```

NOTES ON CONTENT MODELS.

All elements in all content models should be declared. Some parsers will issue a warning if an element that is included in a content model is not also declared, but it is not an error. However, when the document instance is processed, an error is reported if the element has not been declared.

Extra elements can be declared. Any number of elements can be declared in the DTD, even though they are not required for any content model. Some parsers provide informational messages alerting the DTD developer if it finds an undeclared element specified in a content model.

Parameter separators. Parameters are separated by newlines (or carriage returns), tabs, or spaces called "parameter separators". Different separators are equivalent and may be used together. Adding separators can make declarations easier to read. Consider, for example, the following complex content model. Separators can be added to make the groups clear:

```
(
    title,
    (
        (
            note, caution, (paragraph | list | note)+
        )
        |
        (
            (paragraph | list), (paragraph | list | note)+
        )
    )
)
```

This alignment of the parenthetical groups makes it easier to see what is happening.

Exception Notes.

- You cannot exclude an element that is in the current content model.
- At any point in a document instance, if an element is both an applicable inclusion and an exclusion, it is treated as an exclusion.

Quantities. The element declaration is affected by some quantities:

1. The level of nesting in a content model is limited by the `GRPLVL` quantity.
2. The grand total of content tokens cannot exceed the `GRPGTCNT` quantity
3. The length of a parameter literal in a data tag pattern cannot exceed the `DTMPLEN` quantity

If the groups in your content models or the length of your parameter entity references become large, you may need to increase these quantities in the SGML declaration.

THE ATTRIBUTE DEFINITION LIST DECLARATION

Attributes are used to convey extra information about an element. There has been much debate concerning when to use attributes and when to declare a particular piece of information as an element. Our general rule is that an element contains information that is to be published or appear in the rendered output forms, while attributes are used to further describe that information (information about the information). This is just a general rule, and we find ourselves breaking it from time to time. Our best advice is just to say that experience in defining elements and attributes, and experience in the eventual processing of the tagged data are the best way to know what should be defined as an element and what should be defined as an attribute (See *Organizing Elements and Attributes* on page 279).

The attribute definition list declaration (ATTLIST) specifies the following information:

1. The element names for which attributes are being defined
2. The name of each attribute
3. A list of possible values or the type of data the attribute can contain
4. The default value of the attribute

More than one attribute can be defined for a given element, but only one attribute definition list declaration is allowed for an element. The keyword `ATTLIST` is used in the declaration to indicate the declaration of an attribute definition list.

The various parts of the attribute definition list declaration are illustrated below.

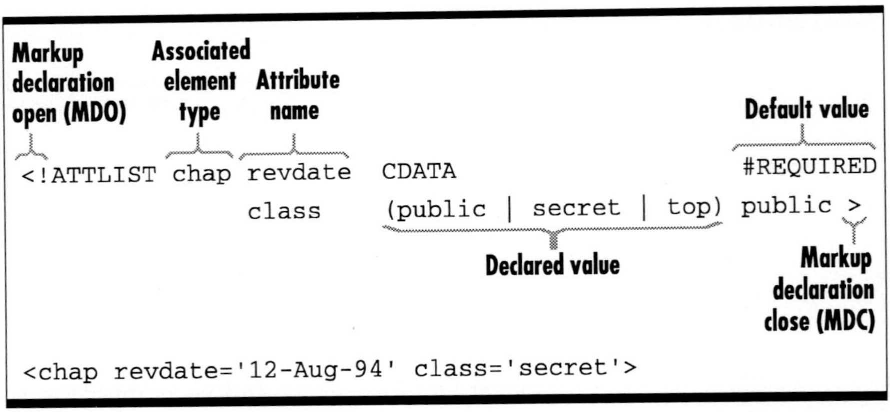

Figure 73. *The attribute definition list declaration, also called* `ATTLIST` *declaration, and an example of markup adhering to this declaration*

Associated Element Type

The first field in the attribute definition list declaration is the name of the element type for which the attributes are being declared. This can also be a list of element types, enclosed in parentheses and separated by connectors. In this case, all attribute definitions apply to each element type.

Attribute Definition List

The attribute definition list consists of one or more attribute definitions, Each attribute definition in turn has the following three parts: attribute name, declared value, and default value.

Attribute Name

This is the name given to the attribute defined in this attribute definition list. It must be an SGML name, meaning it must start with a name start character, followed by zero or more name characters. A name start character is a letter (A through Z and a through z). A name character is a name start character or a number or a hyphen or period. All of these characters can be modified or changed by making the proper modifications to the SGML declaration.

The name should be meaningful to the user, and must be unique among all attributes listed in the declaration.

Declared Value

The next field in the attribute definition list defines the values that can be specified in the attribute. This can be a list of allowed values (a "name token group") or one of the following keywords:

Keyword	*Description*	*Example*
`CDATA`	The attribute value is character data.	`<chapter author='brq'>`
`ENTITY`	The attribute value is the name of a general entity which must be declared as a data entity before it is used.	`<figure name=chevy>`
`ENTITIES`	The attribute value is a list of entity names, separated by spaces.	`<part source='chap01 chap02 chap03'>`
`ID`	The attribute is an `ID` value. Each one must be unique within the current instance.	`<appendix id=I1002>`

Keyword	*Description*	*Example*
IDREF	The attribute is an ID reference value. There must be an element with the same ID somewhere in the document.	`<xref reference=I1002>`
IDREFS	The attribute is an id reference list, which is a list of id reference values separated by spaces.	`<multixref ref='I1002 I2004 I4931'>`
NAME	The attribute is an SGML name.	`<figref type=graphic>`
NAMES	The attribute is a name list, which is a list of names separated by spaces.	`<chapter type='sales techman'>`
NMTOKEN	The attribute value is a name token.	`<command arg='-r'>`
NMTOKENS	The attribute value is a name token list, which is a list of name tokens separated by spaces.	`<command arg='-b 10m -v'>`
NOTATION	The attribute value is the name of a notation that identifies the notation of the element's content. The notation must be declared in the DTD.	`<equation type=tex>`
NUMBER	The attribute value is a number.	`<paragraph date=940722>`
NUMBERS	The attribute value is a number list, which is a list of numbers separated by space characters.	`<recipients phone='2487 2489 2494'>`

Keyword	*Description*	*Example*
NUTOKEN	The attribute value is a number token (begins with a number and can contain any name character thereafter).	`<graphic perspective='3D'>`
NUTOKENS	The attribute value is a number token list, which is a list of number tokens separated by spaces.	`<recipients ssn='565-21-4181 352-55-3192'>`

Table 14. *Declared values*

In addition to the keywords above, the declared value can be a list of name tokens separated by a connector.

```
(top-secret | classified | public)
(yes | no)
(generated | keyed)
```

Although any connector (`&`, `|`) can be used, it is more intuitive to use the "or" bar, since the declared value requires that only one choice be made from the ones in the list.

Remember that a name token is one or more name characters; a name such as `first_class` is not allowable unless the underscore is added to the list of name characters in the SGML declaration.

Default Value

The default value of an attribute can be one of the items in the name token group if the declared value is a name token group, or can be a string or number as appropriate. There are several other possible declared values and any allowable corresponding value is a possible default. The default value parameter in an attribute definition can either define the default value, or be an SGML reserved name that indicates that the attribute does not have a default value.

Keyword	Description
#REQUIRED	The attribute must be explicitly specified on the start-tag. It is not an error to declare an element with a required attribute to be start-tag minimizable, but some parsers generate a warning. It is an error, however, to declare its start tag as being omissible for such an element in the instance.
#IMPLIED	The attribute value is implied by the application, and need not be, but may be, specified in the start-tag. If no value is specified in the start-tag, it is up to the application to determine what the value is.
#CURRENT	The attribute value, if not specified, assumes the value of the most recently specified attribute with the same name.
#CONREF	The attribute value, if specified, renders the element EMPTY.
#FIXED	The attribute value is always the same value.

Table 15. *Default values*

#REQUIRED—Default Value

A default value of #REQUIRED is pretty self-explanatory; the parser will issue an error if the attribute is not specified.

#IMPLIED—Default Value

A default value of #IMPLIED can be thought of as "optional" because the application will infer its value if the author does not specify it.

#CURRENT—Default Value

The following example illustrates the use of #CURRENT. Refer to the normalized output that follows.

```
  ...
<!ELEMENT chapter      - -          (title, paragraph+)          >
<!ELEMENT appendix     - -          (title, paragraph+)          >
<!ATTLIST (chapter | appendix)
                       print        (yes | no)          #CURRENT >
<!ELEMENT paragraph    - O          (#PCDATA)                    >
<!ATTLIST paragraph    print        (yes | no)          #CURRENT >
<!ELEMENT title        O O          (#PCDATA)                    >
```

```
<!ATTLIST title       print        (yes | no)        #CURRENT >
 ...
<chapter print='yes'>
<title print='yes'>
This Title Will be Printed
</title>
<paragraph print='yes'>
This paragraph will be printed.
</paragraph>
</chapter>
<!-- note that there is no print attribute on chapter          -->
<chapter>
<title>This Title Will be Printed
</title>
<paragraph print='no'>
This paragraph will not be printed.
</paragraph>
<!-- nor is there one here                                      -->
<paragraph>
This paragraph will also not be printed.
</paragraph>
</chapter>
<!-- note that there is no print attribute on the appendix    -->
<appendix>
<title>This Appendix Will be Printed
</title>
<paragraph print='no'>This paragraph will not be printed.
</paragraph>
</appendix>
```

The output from the parser looks like this:

```
(BOOK
APRINT TOKEN YES
(CHAPTER
APRINT TOKEN YES
(TITLE
-This Title Will be Printed
)TITLE
APRINT TOKEN YES
(PARAGRAPH
-This paragraph will be printed.
)PARAGRAPH
)CHAPTER
APRINT TOKEN YES
```

```
(CHAPTER
APRINT TOKEN YES
(TITLE
-This Title Will be Printed
)TITLE
APRINT TOKEN NO
(PARAGRAPH
-This paragraph will not be printed.
)PARAGRAPH
APRINT TOKEN NO
(PARAGRAPH
-This paragraph will also not be printed.
)PARAGRAPH
)CHAPTER
APRINT TOKEN YES
(APPENDIX
APRINT TOKEN YES
(TITLE
-This Appendix Will be Printed
)TITLE
APRINT TOKEN NO
(PARAGRAPH
-This paragraph will not be printed.
)PARAGRAPH
)APPENDIX
)BOOK
C
```

Note that the inheritance only happens at the same element level. That is, the parser, upon encountering the print attribute in the title tag, does not care what the value of the print attribute in the chapter is.

The first time an attribute with a default value of #CURRENT is encountered, it is treated as if it had a default value of #REQUIRED; an error is generated if the value is not specified at the first occurrence. Beware of using #CURRENT in a database where objects are extracted in a random order, since one object, when it was originally parsed, might have inherited the #CURRENT attribute value from an earlier sibling, only to be missing that sibling now.

Notice the attribute declaration that declares both chapter and appendix with a #CONREF attribute. By declaring the attribute like this, both elements can share the value of the attribute. That is, the appendix will inherit the value of print from the most recently defined value in the chapter tag, as is shown in the example.

#CONREF—Default Value

The default value of #CONREF allows the inclusion of structural elements if the content existed somewhere else. Suppose three authors are creating chapters for a book, but one of the authors is in charge of maintaining the structure of the entire book. The author-in-charge-of-structure will create a document that contains all of his chapters, as well as the other structural information required by the book.

The attribute definition list declaration for the chapter tag is as follows:

```
...
<!ATTLIST chapter       author      CDATA           #REQUIRED
                        location    ENTITY          #CONREF  >
...
```

For the chapters written by the author maintaining the book, the location attribute is not specified, and the content of the chapter is complete according to the content model. For the chapters written by the other authors, the location attribute contains an entity reference that points to some external file containing the co-author's works. For these chapters, the parser assumes the chapter has a declared value of EMPTY.

Another use for #CONREF is in the area of change processing. In a loose-leaf publishing system, if an element is deleted, it does not necessarily disappear without a trace. If, for example, subsection 3.4 is deleted, only the pages on which the subsection appeared will be replaced, but subsection 3.1, 3.2, 3.3, 3.5, and 3.6 are still in the document. That is, the higher-numbered elements are not necessarily renumbered to reflect the state of their fallen brother. If 3.4 is removed, users will think they are missing a section, and could flood the documentation distribution center with phone calls.

What is desired, in this case, is to put some kind of notification that 3.4 has been deleted, but remove all of its content. This can be done by leaving the subsection tag in place, but the DTD might require that certain sub-elements exist, which all must be specified in order to assure a valid document. This might be cumbersome for the authors and confusing for the application developers.

By using #CONREF, the content model for the subsection element magically changes to a declared content of EMPTY.

```
...
<!ELEMENT subsection    - -         (title, abstract?,
                                    paragraph+)             >
<!ELEMENT (title | abstract | paragraph)
                        - O         (#PCDATA)               >
<!ATTLIST subsection    number      CDATA           #REQUIRED
                        status      CDATA           #CONREF  >
...
```

Before the subsection is deleted:

```
...
<subsections>
<subsection number='3.4'>
<title>Fight for the Right to Arm Bears
</title>
<paragraph>
...
</paragraph>
</subsection>
<subsection number='3.5'>
<title>...
</title>
<paragraph>...
</paragraph>
</subsection>
```

After the subsection is deleted:

```
...
<subsections>
<subsection number='3.4' status='deleted'>
<subsection number='3.5'>
<title>...
</title>
<paragraph>...
</paragraph>
</subsection>
```

In this case, the application might output something like "Section 3.4 deleted".

Note: If the `#CONREF` attribute is specified, it becomes an error to have an end-tag, and any content is considered what would normally follow the element according to the DTD.

The value of the `status` attribute is not important in determining whether the parser should ignore the content; the only fact that matters is that it is specified.

#FIXED—Default Value

When the default value is specified as `#FIXED`, the attribute value is always the same value, specified as a literal immediately following the `#FIXED` keyword. The DTD designer can specify a constant that will always be sent to the application.

It is an error to specify the value for a `#FIXED` attribute that is not the same as the fixed value.

```
...
```

```
<!ELEMENT process      - O          EMPTY                   >
<!ATTLIST process      system       CDATA
                                    #FIXED           'Windows NT'>
  ...
<!-- parser encounters:                                     -->
<process>
<!-- parser sees:                                           -->
<process system='Windows NT'>
<!-- parser encounters:                                     -->
<process system='Windows NT'>
<!-- parser sees                                            -->
<process system='Windows NT'>
<!-- parser encounters:                                     -->
<process system='Macintosh'>
<!-- parser generates an error                              -->
```

The following error log is generated by the SGML-S parser:

```
valid.sgm:17:37:E: value of fixed attribute `SYSTEM' not equal
to default
valid.sgm:17:37: open elements: PROCESSES (PROCESS[ 1] )
```

Quantities

The total number of attribute names and name tokens cannot exceed the `ATTCNT` quantity in the SGML declaration.

Omitted Attribute Specification

SGML enforces a rule that prohibits the use of the same name token in more than one group in an attribute definition list. This is done to allow for attribute name omission to reduce the size of files and keystrokes to create it.

Consider the following SGML document:

```
<!DOCTYPE contact-info [
<!-- Error!                                              -->
<!ELEMENT contact-info - O       EMPTY                    >
<!ATTLIST contact-info phone     (yes | no)      'yes'
                       fax       (yes | no)      'yes'
                       e-mail    (yes | no)      'yes'    >
]>
<contact-info phone='no'>
```

This causes an error, as shown below:

```
valid.sgm:6:26:E: token `YES' occurs more than once in attribute
definition list
valid.sgm:6:26:E: token `NO' occurs more than once in attribute
definition list
valid.sgm:7:29:E: token `YES' occurs more than once in attribute
definition list
valid.sgm:7:29:E: token `NO' occurs more than once in attribute
definition list
```

There has been much debate over the usefulness of this feature, because it restrains the DTD designer in favor of reducing keystrokes or storage space, which might not be an issue in this day of powerful and cheap workstations and storage media. But it is defined that way in the standard and must be observed. See *Omitted Attribute Specifications* on page 319 for a trick to get around the limitations imposed by this feature of the standard.

THE ENTITY DECLARATION

Entities provide a very powerful function to the SGML environment. An entity defines a replacement object. Anything from a single character on up can be defined with a single entity.

There are two basic types of entities, general and parameter. Parameter entities are only allowed in declarations, and are usually used to make a DTD more readable or to control processing. General entities are used in a document instance. There are several different types with specific intended functions.

General Entities

The general entity declaration associates an entity name with some kind of replacement text or non-text object. The entity must be declared before it is used or an error will occur if there is no default entity declared.

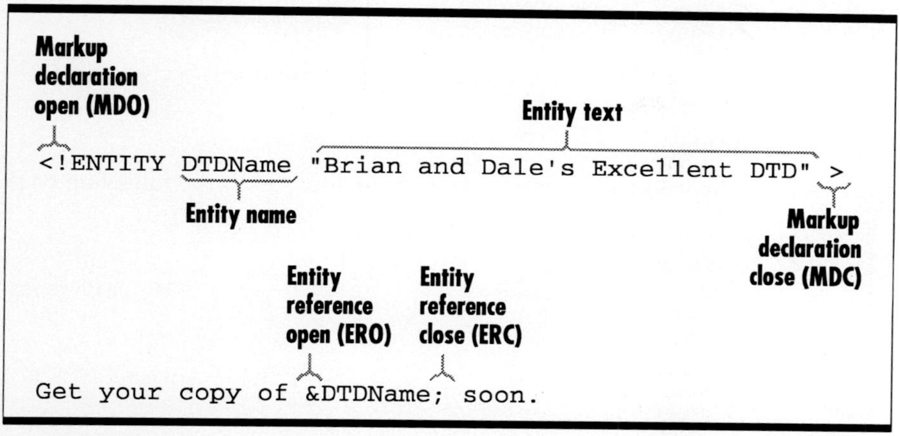

Figure 74. *The general entity declaration*

An entity can be declared more than once. An error is not generated, but the second and subsequent declarations are ignored; the first entity declaration for a given entity name is the one that counts.

```
  ...
<!ENTITY    gibralter   'granite, quartz, and other hard stuff'>
<!ENTITY    gibralter   'pumice, sand, and other sqishy stuff' >
  ...
The Rock of Gibralter is made of
 &gibralter;.
  ...
```

Results in:

```
The Rock of Gibralter is made of granite, quartz, and other
hard stuff.
```

If an entity is declared in the document type declaration subset of a file that contains an SGML instance, it will be read first, rendering any other declarations of the same name impotent. This can be used to override certain values locally, as is shown in the following example:

```
<!DOCTYPE chapter [
<!ELEMENT chapter      - -          (title, paragraph+)        >
<!ELEMENT (title | paragraph)
                       - O          (#PCDATA)                  >
<!ENTITY    company-name           'Information Architects, Inc.'>
]>
<chapter>
<title>Welcome to
```

```
 &company-name;!
<paragraph>We are glad you have chosen
 &company-name; to start your career in the exciting world of
SGML.
</chapter>
```

To override the value of `&company-name;` at the local level, the following could be done:

```
<!DOCTYPE chapter SYSTEM "local.dtd" [
<!ENTITY    company-name                         'SGML University'>
]>
<chapter>
<title>Welcome to
 &company-name;!
<paragraph>We are glad you have chosen
 &company-name; to start your career in the exciting world of
SGML.
</chapter>
```

Now, the following is generated:

```
(CHAPTER
(TITLE
-Welcome to \n SGML University!
)TITLE
(PARAGRAPH
-We are glad you have chosen \n SGML University to start your
career in the exciting world of SGML.
)PARAGRAPH
)CHAPTER
C
```

EXTERNAL ENTITIES. In addition to simple string replacement, entities can be used to access external resources like data files and executable processes. This is done by using external entities.

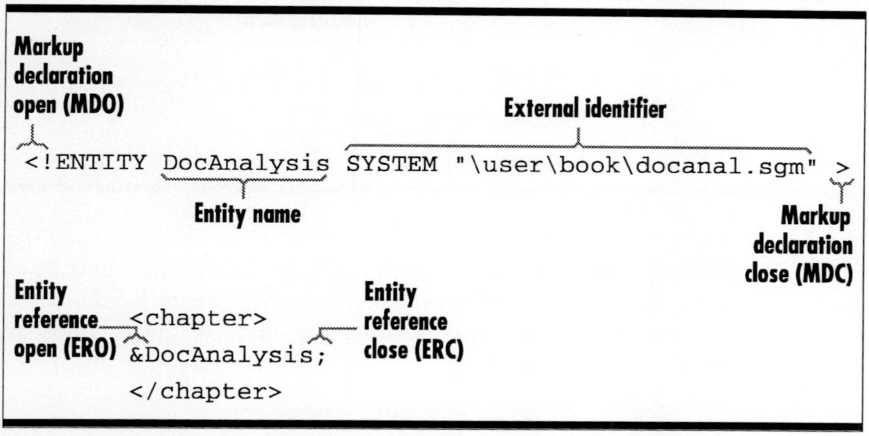

Figure 75. *The external entity declaration (*SYSTEM*)*

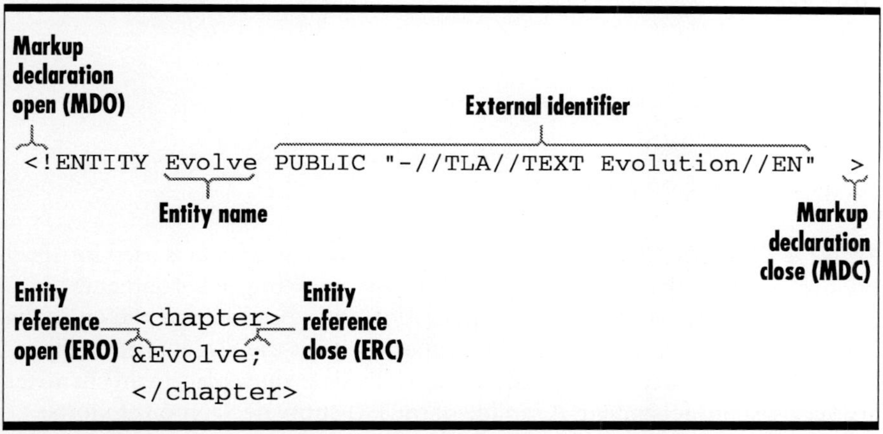

Figure 76. *The external entity declaration (*PUBLIC*)*

An external entity is an entity with the keyword SYSTEM, followed by a system identifier, or the keyword PUBLIC followed by a public identifier. See *System and Public Identifiers* on page 257

DATA TEXT ENTITIES. Data text entities are always treated as character data. There are three types of data text entities, each differing in how they are treated by the parser.

Type	*Description*
CDATA	Character data
SDATA	Specific character data
PI	Processing instruction

Table 16. *Data text entities*

CDATA - Character Data Entity. As with CDATA attributes, CDATA entities can contain character and entity references, which are interpreted by the parser. These are mainly used if you want to insert markup characters in an entity and have the parser ignore them.

```
<!ENTITY  TelCo   'AT&T'   -- error! -- >
```

Produces an error stating that entity T cannot be found because &T looks to the parser like a general entity, which is ERO (&) followed by a name start character.

```
 ...
<!ENTITY    telco      CDATA 'AT&T'                           >
 ...
 &telco; Test
```

Produces the desired result.

SDATA - Specific Character Entity. Specific character data is used for specifying characters that might vary in different operating environments. Most parsers will make available to the application an indication that the entity has been declared as SDATA so the application can process the text appropriately.

The ISO entity sets use SDATA extensively, since the replacement characters are very system-dependent. A sample of the ISO entity declarations follows:

```
<!ENTITY aacute SDATA "[aacute]" --small a, acute             -->
<!ENTITY Aacute SDATA "[Aacute]" --cap A, acute               -->
<!ENTITY acirc  SDATA "[acirc ]" --small a, circumflex        -->
<!ENTITY Acirc  SDATA "[Acirc ]" --cap A, circumflex          -->
<!ENTITY agrave SDATA "[agrave]" --small a, grave             -->
<!ENTITY Agrave SDATA "[Agrave]" --cap A, grave               -->
<!ENTITY aring  SDATA "[aring ]" --small a, ring              -->
<!ENTITY Aring  SDATA "[Aring ]" --cap A, ring                -->
<!ENTITY atilde SDATA "[atilde]" --small a, tilde             -->
<!ENTITY Atilde SDATA "[Atilde]" --cap A, tilde               -->
<!ENTITY auml   SDATA "[auml  ]" --small a, dieresis/umlaut   -->
<!ENTITY Auml   SDATA "[Auml  ]" --cap A, dieresis/umlaut     -->
<!ENTITY aelig  SDATA "[aelig ]" --small ae diphthong         -->
```

```
<!ENTITY AElig  SDATA "[AElig ]" --cap AE diphthong         -->
```

The advantage of this approach is that it normalizes the entity declaration files, making the document instance system-independent. The application can replace the bracketed replacement text according to the current output device.

This example shows the use of `NAMECASE ENTITY NO` in the SGML declaration. With this setting, which is the default, the parser discriminates with case when evaluating an entity name. Therefore `Agrave` and `agrave` are distinct entities.

PI - Processing Instruction Entity. A processing instruction entity provides some advantages, but is mostly useful to differentiate "good" processing instructions from "bad" ones.

By declaring a processing instruction entity, the document designer has indicated that there is a good reason for it, as opposed to the author putting a processing instruction anywhere in the file he pleases.

Therefore:

```
 ...
<!ENTITY    pagebreak  PI '.pa'                          >
 ...
 &pagebreak;
```

produces the same output as:

```
<?.pa>
```

This use of a processing instruction entity indicates that document analysts have determined that there is a valid use for this processing instruction. There are some limited uses for such rigid definition of system-specific processing. We think that, in most cases, if there is a valid reason for institutionalizing a processing instruction in the DTD, there is probably a valid reason to create an element and put it in a proper place in the structure.

BRACKETED TEXT ENTITIES. Bracketed text is for declaring entities that contain markup. We have not been able to find a use for this type of entity, since it is possible to accomplish the same effect in other ways, but are including it here for completeness:

Type	Description
STARTTAG	start-tag
ENDTAG	end-tag
MS	Marked section
MD	Markup declaration

Table 17. *Bracketed text entities*

The following . . .

```
...
<!ELEMENT para          - O          (#PCDATA)                   >
<!ENTITY    startpara   STARTTAG 'para'                          >
<!ENTITY    endpara     ENDTAG 'para'                            >
<!ENTITY    markedsec   MS 'CDATA[ This is a marked para</para>' >
<!ENTITY    elementdec  MD '<!>ELEMENT para - O (#PCDATA)'       >
...
```

. . . provides the same output as:

```
...
<!ELEMENT para          - O          (#PCDATA)                   >
<!ENTITY    startpara    '<para>'                                >
<!ENTITY    endpara      '</para>'                               >
<!ENTITY    markedsec    '<![ CDATA[ This is a marked para</para>]]>'>
<!ENTITY    elementdec  CDATA '<!ELEMENT para - O (#PCDATA)>'    >
...
```

The main advantage of using bracketed entities is in their use to communicate the author's intentions.

Parameter Entities

Parameter entities are only used inside of declarations. They are mostly used to make oft-occurring text inside of content models and attribute definition lists, making them easier to manage. In *Figure 77, Parameter entity declaration* on page 257, an entity is declared containing all elements that can float inside of a particular element. Later in the DTD, the entity is referenced inside an inclusion. See *Naming Parameter Entity References* on page 303

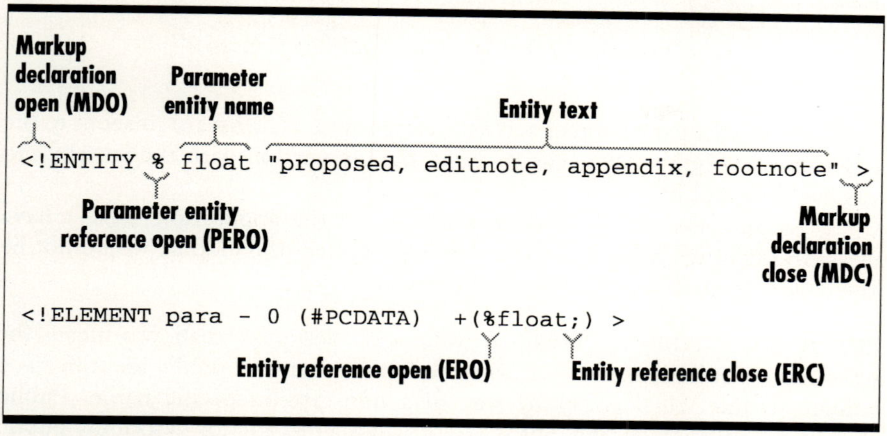

Figure 77. *Parameter entity declaration*

Parameter entities can also be declared with public identifiers or system identifiers or both.

QUANTITIES. A name in a parameter entity cannot exceed the NAMELEN quantity in the SGML declaration, including PERO. That is, if PERO is % and NAMELEN is 8, then the longest parameter entity name possible is 7 characters.

System and Public Identifiers

In addition to straight replacement text, the entity text can contain references to files that exist outside of the current entity (external identifiers). An external identifier can contain what is called a system identifier or public identifier or both.

SYSTEM IDENTIFIERS. A "system identifier" indicates that the replacement text contains some system-specific string (*e.g.*, physical file, external address, hypertext link) that the system can understand. It is primarily used to introduce into the current entity another entity that is managed as a separate operating system object. For example, a bit-mapped graphic file might reside on another system that is accessible using a url[1] address to access information on the World Wide Web. In order to place it in your document, you need to specify an address that means something to the application and operating environment.

. . .

1 Uniform Resource Locator

```
<!ENTITY     crashburn   SYSTEM
          'http://www.jpl.gov/Jupiter/FirstPic.tiff'          >
  ...
```

When the parser comes across a reference to `&crashburn;`, it sends to the application everything it needs to make the connection with the system and retrieve the graphic.

System identifiers are system-specific. If the application doesn't have access to http sites when the document is processed, the graphic would not be found, and an error would probably be issued.

PUBLIC IDENTIFIERS. Public identifiers are designed to allow a means for attaching a symbolic name to a physical data structure. A public identifier is a pointer to the actual entity by way of a non-system-specific name. Public identifiers can be any string, but SGML provides a method for describing public identifiers in a way that the rest of the world can use. This type of public identifer is called a "formal" public identifier. All public identifiers must be defined in this formal format (described below) if the `FORMAL` feature is set to `YES` in the SGML Declaration (See *Fully Defined SGML Declaration* on page 427).

A `FORMAL` public identifier is a precisely structured string that contains certain fields.

1. **Owner identifier**. Identifies who owns the public identifier. The options are shown below:

   a. **ISO owner identifier**. Indicates that ISO owns the identifier. The value indicates the ISO number.
      Example: `ISO 8879:1986`
   b. **registered owner identifier**. Indicates that the owner of the public identifier has registered the identifier with the public registrar. As of this writing, there is no registrar.
      Example: `+//IAI, Inc.`
   c. **unregistered owner identifier**. Indicates that the owner of the public identifier has not registered the identifier.
      Example: `-//IAI, Inc.`

2. **//**. A double solidus (two slashes) separates the fields.
   Example: //
3. **Text identifier**. A multiple-field entry indicating the type of entity and the owner's identifier for the entity. The fields are listed below:

   a. **public text class**. Identifies which one of the 13 SGML constructs that is allowed to be made public:

      i. `CAPACITY`. capacity set
      ii. `CHARSET`. character data
      iii. `DOCUMENT`. SGML document

iv. `DTD`. document type declaration subset
v. `ELEMENTS`. element set
vi. `ENTITIES`. entity set
vii. `LPD`. link type declaration subset
viii. `NONSGML`. non-SGML data entity
ix. `NOTATION`. character data
x. `SHORTREF`. short reference set
xi. `SYNTAX`. concrete syntax
xii. `SUBDOC`. SGML sub document entity
xiii. `TEXT`. SGML text entity

Example: `DTD`

b. `SPACE`. a single space character
c. **unavailable text indicator**. Optional indicator. Its presence indicates that the text is unavailable to the public.
   Example: -//
d. **public text description**. A description of the material found in the object
   Example: `Equation Tags`
e. **//**. A double solidus (two slashes) separates the fields.
   Example: //
f. **public text language or public text designating sequence** .
   i. **public text language**. A two-character name indicating the natural language of the public identifier. This must conform with ISO 639
      Example: `EN`
   ii. **public text designating sequence**. An alternative to the public text language field. This field identifies the designating sequence defined by ISO 2022
      Example: `ESC 2/8 4/0`
g. **//**. A double solidus (two slashes) separates the fields. Only required if the next, optional, field is specified.
   Example: //
h. **public text display version**. Used to differentiate between public text that would be identical except for system dependencies. Optional.
   Example: `BSD Unix`

Putting it all together, the following entity declarations show valid public identifiers:

```
  ...
<!ENTITY    example1
          PUBLIC 'ISO 8879-1986//ENTITIES Greek Symbols//EN'    >
<!ENTITY    example2
          PUBLIC '-//TLA, Inc.//TEXT Your System is Broken//EN' >
<!ENTITY    example3
```

```
          PUBLIC '+//SoftQuad//ELEMENTS Table Elements//EN'     >
...
```

The value of the FORMAL feature in the SGML declaration determines whether the parser verifies that public identifiers conform to the rules of FORMAL public identifiers. Otherwise, these identifiers have much less rigorous rules to follow. We have found that it is usually best to keep FORMAL set to YES, as it forces the proper use of public identifiers.

Public identifiers are used to include publicly available entity sets into the DTD.

PUBLIC IDENTIFIER MAPPING. Ultimately, the SGML application needs to know how to get to the physical entity. In an environment where entity files are saved as physical collections in the operating system file system, the public identifier must be mapped to a name the system can resolve. In an environment where the entity is stored in some location on a wide-area network or the Internet, the same requirement for accessing the file applies.

At some level, is possible to create an association with a physical entity by manipulating the public identifier. For example, changing all double slashes to single slashes and spaces to underscores. This methodology might be sufficient to make a public identifier look like a path name to the operating system, but does not provide very much freedom in entity storage.

Any application that supports public identifiers must provide a mapping function to allow the system to find the physical entities.

The SGML standard does not provide a standard way of indicating mapping, so each vendor's approach is a little different. The SGMLOpen consortium has developed a standard entity mapping strategy that uses a common catalog format.

In an environment that supports more than one vendor's applications, a mapping file will probably need to be kept for each. See *Generate Public Identifier Mapping Files* on page 327 for an approach to managing multiple public entity mapping files.

Empty Elements

Empty elements are special elements that contain nothing. In order to talk about empty elements, we had to cover the element declaration, the attribute definition list declaration, and the entity declaration, since empty elements almost always have attributes, and many call external entities. See the following topics for examples of how empty elements are used:

- *Cross-references* on page 293
- *Graphics* on page 297
- *Uses for Empty Elements* on page 321
- *Cross-references* on page 322
- *Formatting Information* on page 324

Default Entity

All entities must be declared before they are referenced. If an entity is referenced before it is used, the value of the `#DEFAULT` entity will be used instead. If there is no `#DEFAULT` entity declaration, most parsers will issue an error message and ignore the entity reference.

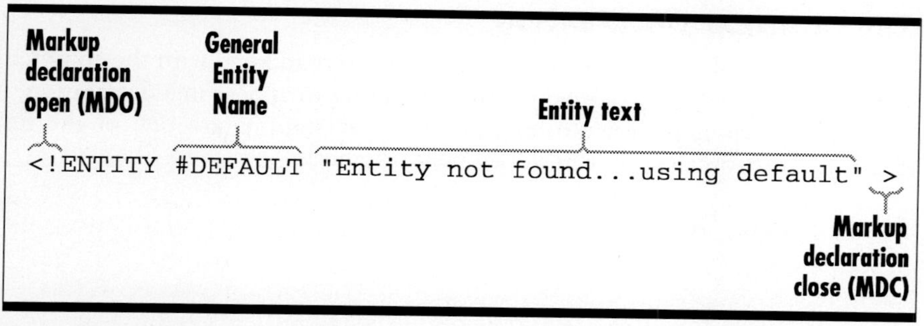

Figure 78. *The default entity declaration*

The `#DEFAULT` entity can be declared to avoid parsing errors and to insert some text in the output stream to notify the user that an entity has not been declared. However, since an error is not generated in such a case, it is possible for a semantically invalid document to pass the validation step.

```
<!DOCTYPE chapter [
<!ELEMENT chapter      - -          (title, paragraph+)         >
<!ELEMENT (title | paragraph)
                       - O          (#PCDATA)                   >
<!ENTITY    #DEFAULT            '!! Error: entity not declared !!'>
]>
<chapter>
<title>Welcome to
 &company-name;!
<paragraph>We are glad you have chosen
 &company-name; to start your career in the exciting world of
SGML.
</chapter>
```

This produces the following:

```
(CHAPTER
(TITLE
-Welcome to \n !! Error: entity not declared !!!
)TITLE
(PARAGRAPH
```

```
-We are glad you have chosen \n !! Error: entity not declared !!
to start your career in the exciting world of SGML.
)PARAGRAPH
)CHAPTER
C
```

There is no default allowed for parameter entities.

THE COMMENT DECLARATION

Comments are allowed in any declaration, and start and end with the comment delimiter (COM, --). If a comment is the only thing to appear in a declaration, it is called a comment declaration. Comment declarations are one of the few declarations that can appear in a document instance.

In the SGML Declaration

```
FEATURES    -- only OMITTAG and SHORTTAG --
    MINIMIZE
    DATATAG NO
    OMITTAG YES
    RANK NO
    SHORTTAG YES
```

IN THE DTD.

```
  ...
<!-- grammatical paragraph                                      -->
<!ELEMENT p             - O           (#PCDATA)                  >
<!-- structural paragraph                                       -->
<!ELEMENT para          - O           (#PCDATA)                  >
  ...
```

For examples of using comments, see See *Comment Your DTD* on page 277 and *Using a Comment to Avoid Entity Misinterpretation* on page 354.

IN THE INSTANCE.

```
  ...
<p>
Next quarter's numbers are estimated to be between 12,000 and
14,000 units
<!-- Bob, please check these with the forecasting people       -->
</p>
```

THE DOCUMENT TYPE DECLARATION

The document type declaration defines the set of rules the document instance is to adhere to. It can take several forms, depending on the requirements of the application.

The document type declaration can be wrapped around the set of declarations that comprise the formal part of the document type definition. See *The Prologue* on page 217 for an explanation of the formal and informal part of the DTD.

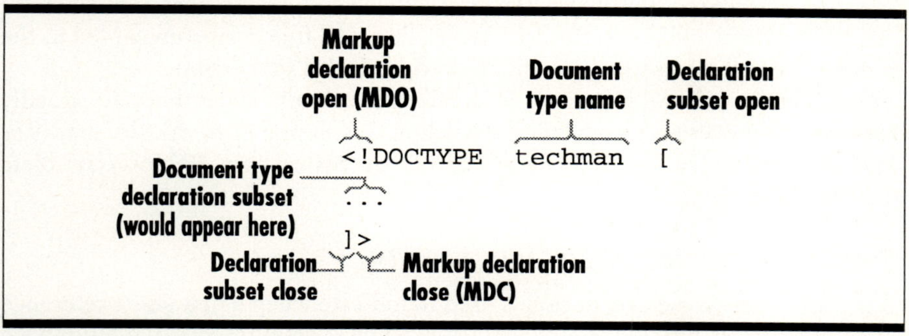

Figure 79. *Document type declaration (in DTD)*

The document type declaration subset contains all of the element, attribute definition list, entity, notation, and short reference declarations.

The document type declaration can also appear in the document instance with an external identifier pointing to the DTD.

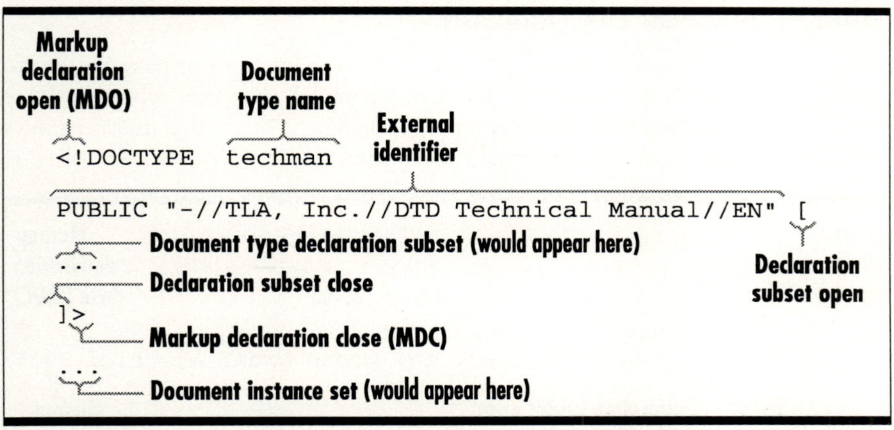

Figure 80. *Document type declaration (in instance)*

In this case, the document type declaration subset can only have entity declarations and short reference declarations; no element or attribute definition list declarations can appear here. The declaration subset is not required unless there are entity or short reference declarations required.

However it is used, it is important to note that exactly one document type declaration be part of the processing run. That is, if there is a DTD in a file with a `DOCTYPE` declaration wrapped around it, then there cannot be a `DOCTYPE` declaration in the instance file. See *Managing Documents using "Hub Files"* on page 324.

LINK-RELATED DECLARATIONS

`LINK` is an elegant solution to the problem of adding semantics and certain processing functionality to the document. The `LINK` functions were added to the standard to provide a standard way to do rules-based processing.

We do not describe `LINK` in detail in this book, since there are usually application-specific ways of doing what link was designed to do. Refer to *The SGML Handbook*, in Appendix 8 / SGML Resources on page 494 for a complete description of `LINK`.

SHORT REFERENCE USE DECLARATION

A short reference use declaration is used to indicate when a new short reference mapping is to be initiated. This is only used when short reference mappings have been declared. The short reference provides a form of minimization that allows certain characters to indicate markup. A typical example of short reference mapping is the case where a quote character (") can be defined to generate or be interpreted as a `<quote>` tag at the beginning of the element and a `</quote>` tag at the end of the element. See *Using Short Reference Minimization* on page 330.

MARKED SECTION DECLARATION

The marked section declaration is used to hide content from or pass content to the parser, or to mark a chunk of data as a particular character type. They are very useful in creating flexible documents that can be processed in different ways depending upon current environment variables.

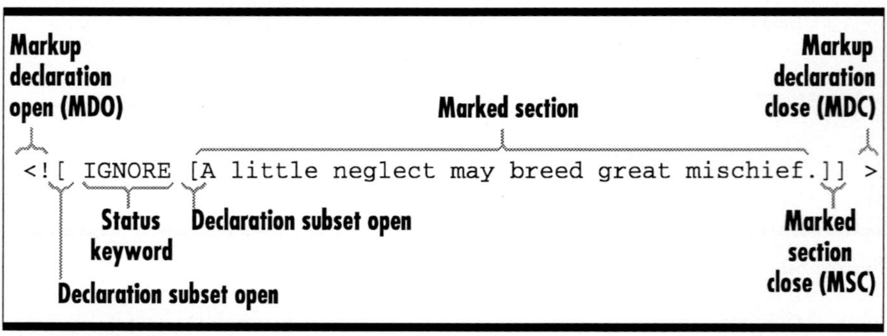

Figure 81. *Marked section declaration*

Status Keywords

The status keyword is used to indicate the type of marked section being declared:

Status Keyword	*Description*
`IGNORE`	The text is ignored by the parser
`INCLUDE`	The text is included.
`CDATA`	The text is seen as character data
`RCDATA`	The text is seen as replaceable character data.

Table 18. *Marked section status keywords*

IGNORE. The contents of the marked section are ignored by the parser. The data is not passed through to the application, as if it was not part of the input stream. If any other marked section is inside an ignored marked section, it is also ignored.

INCLUDE. The contents of the marked section are passed to the output, with any indication that it was in a marked section stripped. That is, the data is passed to the application, but the marked section declaration information is stripped.

CDATA. The contents of the marked section are considered to be character data. That is, all character strings except the end of the marked section that would otherwise be interpreted as markup are considered to be data and are passed to the application as data by the parser.

RCDATA. The contents of the marked section are considered to be replaceable character data. That is, all markup except the end of the marked section is passed through to the application by the parser and entity references are resolved.

TEMP. In addition to status keywords, the marked section can be specified with the keyword status specification of `TEMP`, which indicates that the marked section is a temporary part of the document, which may need to be removed at a later date. Marked sections with `TEMP` are treated as if they were declared with the status keyword `INCLUDE`. See *Using Marked Sections* on page 335.

NOTATION DECLARATION

SGML can work with certain types of data, mostly referred herein as "text". How does the system access "non-text" data like graphics, sounds, databases, and so forth? The answer is found in the notation declaration.

There are two main classes of notations: character data and non-SGML data. Character data consists of natural language objects, scientific notations, and formatted text. Non-SGML data consists of characters undefined by the current character set, binary objects like graphics, sounds, and movies, and binary objects mixed with character data.

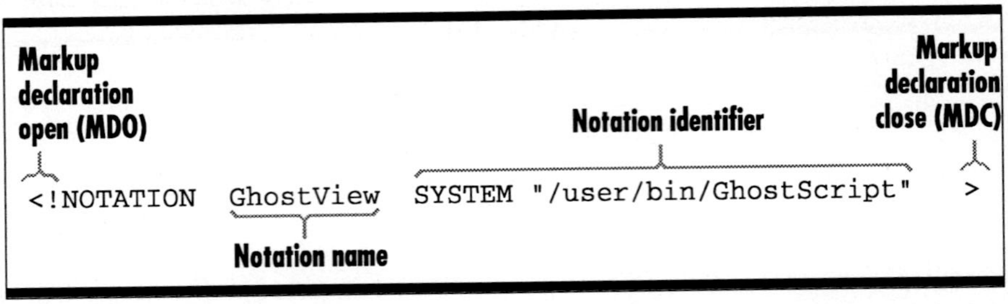

Figure 82. *Notation declaration*

A notation declaration must be created for each notation processor. The notation identifier can be a system identifier or public identifier. See *Using NOTATION for External Tables* on page 338.

Minimization Features

SGML was developed when the state-of-the-art for computers was 64K of memory and very limited storage by today's standards. The developers spent much time developing techniques to keep the size of the files to a minimum and to speed input. Also, SGML-smart editorial workstations were not available, so most SGML entry was done with text editors. If the parser could determine the structure without having the start- and end-tags explicitly specified, then why should the author be required to enter them?

Now there are much more powerful machines and many SGML-smart applications to assist in the creation and maintenance of SGML files. The importance and usefulness of minimization techniques is lessened because these applications shield the user from the markup. In fact, minimization techniques could cause confusion to users because they hide some markup from the user.

However, there is an advantage to minimization, even today. Many companies have documents in paper form that they want to load into their SGML databases. In many cases, the text is hand-keyed from the paper copy. Minimization techniques can be created to save keystrokes, thereby limiting the costs of conversion.

Another area is in the creation and maintenance of highly structured data. It is possible, through the use of these minimization techniques, to create and maintain documents that don't have a single angle bracket, but are actually parseable SGML documents. These minimization techniques can be used to maintain these files using an inexpensive text editor, while maximizing their usability.

OMITTED TAG MINIMIZATION

Omitted tag minimization allows the start-tag, end-tag, or both to be omitted when it would otherwise be redundant. The `OMITTAG` keyword must be set to `YES` in the SGML declaration in order to use this feature.

In the following example, both the start- and end-tag of chapter are required, neither the start- or end-tag for title are required, nor is the end-tag for para:

```
  ...
<!ELEMENT chapter      - -          (title, para+)          >
<!ELEMENT title       0 0           (#PCDATA)               >
<!ELEMENT para         - 0          (#PCDATA)               >
  ...
```

So, the following input is valid:

```
  ...
<chapter>The Aristocracy of Pull
<para>The calendar in the sky beyond the window of her office
said: September 2.
<para>She had looked at that distant page every evening in the
months behind her.
</chapter>
```

Notice that the title tag is not explicitly specified in the instance. It is perfectly unambiguous to have it omitted, since it is the only thing that the first letter following the chapter tag could start. This is referred to as "contextually required". Consider a chapter with the following content model:

```
  ...
<!ELEMENT chapter      - -          (title?, para+)         >
<!ELEMENT title       0 0           (#PCDATA)               >
<!ELEMENT para         - 0          (#PCDATA)               >
  ...
<chapter>The Aristocracy of Pull
<para>The calendar in the sky beyond the window of her office
said: September 2.
<para>She had looked at that distant page every evening in the
months behind her.
</chapter>
```

Optional elements cannot be start-tag minimized, because they are not contextual required by the parser. Now, when the parser comes along the first word after the chapter tag, it assumes it is the start of the first required tag in the model that contained data. In this case, it generates the following error:

```
valid.sgm:7:20:E: start tag for `PARA' omitted, but its
declaration does not permit this
valid.sgm:7:20: open elements: CHAPTER (PARA[1])
```

It is important to note that the parser does not consider the omit tag minimization fields in the element declaration when deciding what the element is. Omit tag minimization is only used by the error-generation logic. Logic determines what is impliable and what must be explicitly provided. In the above content model for chapter, the first character after the close of the chapter tag may be either a title (which is optional), or a para. It is ambiguous unless the author enters the markup explicitly.

In the above example, it is tempting to declare the title with the start-tag required, so that the parser could see that the text following the chapter tag is actually a title and not a paragraph. After all, a logical case could be made for that sequence of processing, couldn't it? So, the DTD would look like this, using the same instance above:

```
<!DOCTYPE chapter [
<!ELEMENT chapter     - -       (title?, para+)        >
<!ELEMENT title       - O       (#PCDATA)              >
<!ELEMENT para        - O       (#PCDATA)              >
]>
<chapter>The Aristocracy of Pull
<para>The calendar in the sky beyond the window of her office
said: September 2.
<para>She had looked at that distant page every evening in the
months behind her.
</chapter>
```

But the parser reports this error:

```
valid.sgm:7:20:E: start tag for `PARA' omitted, but its
declaration does not permit this
valid.sgm:7:20: open elements: CHAPTER (PARA[1])
```

and continues along with this view:

```
 ...
<chapter>
<para>The Aristocracy of Pull
</para>
<para>The calendar in the sky beyond the window of her office
said: September 2.
</para>
<para>She had looked at that distant page every evening in the
months behind her.
</para>
```

```
</chapter>
```

which is the same error generated before the `title` start-tag was declared omissible. The parser interpreted the first text character as a `para` element, since `para` is required, and skipped the `title` element since it is optional, or not contextually required. The minimization field is only for the reporting of errors. The markup must be rich enough to avoid ambiguity regardless of how the minimization has been declared.

It is never wrong to insert a start-tag before an element when the start-tag is declared omissible.

It is an error to declare an element to be start-tag omissible when there is an attribute definition list declaration that contains a #REQUIRED attribute.

It is never wrong to insert an end-tag in an element where the end-tag is omissible, with the two following exceptions:

1. if the element is declared as EMPTY, or
2. if the element contains a #CONREF attribute that is specified.

Some applications do not support OMITTAG. These applications expect a so-called minimal SGML document, which means, among other things, that all start- and end-tags are in place.

SHORT REFERENCE MINIMIZATION (SHORTREF)

The short reference minimization feature uses characters as markup instead of complete tags. These characters are mapped, via the entity structure, to start- and end-tags. This can be a great saver of space and keystrokes, and even make the data more readable. Short reference minimization uses certain characters to indicate the start and end of an element, and can be mapped to produce different results depending upon the current context.

A set of pre-defined short reference delimiters are defined in the SGML declaration. In order to add delimiters, the SHORTREF area of the SGML declaration needs to be modified. This area looks like this:

```
DELIM
SHORTREF SGMLREF
```

meaning that the defaults are used. Default short reference delimiters (those defined by the reference concrete syntax) are:

Delimiter	***Description***
&#TAB;	Horizontal tab
&#RE;	Record end
&#RS;	Record start

Delimiter	***Description***
&#RS;B	Leading blanks (record start followed by one or more spaces).
&#RS;&#RE;	Empty record
&#RS;B&#RE;	Blank record
&#B&#RE;	Trailing blanks
&#SPACE;	Space character
BB	Two or more blanks
"	Quote mark
#	Number sign or hash mark
%	Percent sign
`	Apostrophe
(	Open parenthesis
)	Close parenthesis
+	PLUS sign
,	Comma
-	Hyphen
--	Two hyphens
:	Colon
;	Semicolon
=	Equals sign
@	Commercial at
[	Left square bracket
]	Right square bracket
^	Circumflex, or caret
_	Underscore
{	Left brace
}	Right brace

Delimiter	Description
*	Asterisk
~	Tilde

Table 19. *Default short reference delimiters*

In order to add characters to the short reference delimiter set, the SGML declaration must be modified by listing the new characters after the SGMLREF keyword.

```
DELIM
    SHORTREF
        SGMLREF
        "\"
        "!"
```

This example adds the backslash and exclamation mark to the list of default short reference delimiters shown in *Table 19, Default short reference delimiters* on page 271.

If you want to specify all characters and not depend upon the previously defined characters in the SGML reference delimiter set, use the NONE keyword, followed by the characters you want to use:

```
DELIM
    SHORTREF
        NONE
        "["
        "]"
        "!"
```

The main advantages to using short reference minimization is that you can create useable, native SGML input. The short reference delimiter characters that are used in the input text are part of the natural language characters used every day. The main problems with short reference minimization are that it is difficult to define in the DTD, and sometime difficult to debug if a user does not key in just the right thing. See *Using Short Reference Minimization* on page 330.

SHORT TAG MINIMIZATION (SHORTTAG)

While omit tag minimization is used to completely eliminate the keying of start- and end-tags, short tag minimization is used to minimize keystrokes for tags that must be specified. Short tag minimization takes several forms.

Unclosed short tag

When two tags are next to each other, the closing of the first tag is redundant. So the following are equivalent:

```
<section><para>A brief section.</para></section>
<section<para>A brief section.</para</section>
```

Elements with attributes specified can also have unclosed start-tags.

Empty start-tag

SHORTTAG minimization also allows for the use of empty start-tags. That is, a start-tag with no generic identifier.

```
<list>
<item>Buckle my shoe
<>Shut the door
<>Pick up sticks
</list>
```

When such markup is encountered, the parser inserts the most recent generic identifier (tag name). Actually, what is inserted depends upon the setting of OMITTAG in the SGML declaration.

The empty start tag was originally put in the standard for the same reason as most of the minimization features (to save space and keyboarding costs), but carries a higher risk that the wrong generic identifier will be inserted without the applications designer knowing. Also, the document structure could change drastically just by changing the setting of OMITTAG in the SGML declaration. For these reasons, we strongly discourage the use of the empty start tag.

Empty end-tag

It is possible, using short tag minimization, to create an end-tag with no element name. This is called an empty end-tag. An empty end-tag ends the most recently started open element. So, the following lines are equivalent:

```
May the <q>force</q> be with you.
May the <q>force</> be with you.
```

Empty end-tags may be confusing, especially when used with minimized start-tags.

Null end-tag (NET) and NET-enabling Start-tag

Maximum minimization can be achieved by using a special form of tag minimization called the NET-enabling start-tag. This allows the close markup character to be omitted from the start tag, and the open- and close-markup characters from the end tag to be omitted. The NET-enabling start-tag appears in this form:

```
Do you want <emphasis/maximum/ minimization?
```

It can also be used when there are attributes:

```
This shows the <acronym type=glossary/NET/-enabled start-tag.
```

Attribute minimization

Because all tokens in an attribute definition list are required to be unique, the name of the attribute can be omitted, as long as the attribute has a token list in the declared value field:

```
  ...
<!ATTLIST memo        status        (draft |
                                     final)        #REQUIRED>
  ...
<memo status='draft'>
<memo draft>
```

See *Omitted Attribute Specifications* on page 319 for more information on attribute minimization.

OTHER MINIMIZATION FEATURES

Two other minimization features, data tag and rank, are not supported by many parsers. We only mention them here for completeness, but have found little use for them in most implementations. Our belief is that, had the standard been approved six months later, at least one of these would have disappeared. We do not recommend the use of either of these features.

Data Tag

The data tag minimization feature allows content to act like data and like a tag at the same time. It is similar to short references, except in a short reference, content is consumed and replaced with a tag. It was created early in the development of the language as yet another way to reduce character overhead, and is largely replaced by the easier-to-use and more versatile short reference.

RANK

Rank provides a short-hand way to indicate nesting levels. It, too, was created early in the development of the language, and is largely unsupported.

CHAPTER • ELEVEN

Building the DTD

Introduction

There are logical techniques to organizing a DTD that make it easier to develop, understand, and maintain. The techniques discussed in this chapter include the order in which declarations may appear, use of comments and white space, and naming conventions, as well as techniques for DTD management, testing, and versioning. Also included are examples of techniques that provide a head start for defining common elements that occur in nearly every DTD.

Related Topics

- Chapter 4, *The SGML Environment* on page 43
- *DTD Development Tools* on page 58

- Chapter 5, *Document Analysis* on page 65
- Chapter 6, *The SGML Application* on page 101
- *Vendor-Supplied Applications* on page 117
- *Data Design and DTD Development* on page 140
- *Data Conversion Planning and Implementation* on page 160
- *Managing DTD Change* on page 163
- *Conversions Using the Rainbow DTD* on page 167
- Chapter 10, *Understanding SGML* on page 215
- *The SGML Document Model* on page 216
- *Declarations* on page 223
- Chapter 12, *Tipniques and Pratfalls* on page 301
- Chapter 9, *SGML Data Management and Workflow* on page 183

Organizing a DTD

Assuming you have read this book in order, you have learned about document analysis, and you have worked your way through the meaty chapter about the SGML constructs. Now you have to write a DTD using the SGML syntax to express the structure you find in a document analysis sessions.

Writing a DTD is a fairly straight-forward task if you approach it logically. Understand that your average end-user is not going to look at a DTD. The audience for a DTD is usually somewhat SGML literate and fairly technical. Even so, you should create an organized, consistent DTD, to aid the ongoing updating that it will require and to allow developers to read it in the process of developing tools that will utilize it. Many of the same practices used in writing good programs—documentation, testing, orderly layout —apply to creating a good DTD.

If you took good notes, recording them into a DTD should be easy. In fact, the best way to record these notes is to create the DTD as you perform the document analysis. The DTD is the only expression comprehensive enough to record the rules you identify in document analysis without ambiguity.

NAMING CONVENTIONS

Consistency in the names you create for elements, DTD attributes, and entities will enhance the usability of your application. You must exercise care when assigning names. A little far-sighted thinking will yield great results over the long run.

In the early days of implementation, we went through the growing pains of learning what makes a good DTD, and sometimes our experiments were less successful than others. A naming convention should be developed and adopted throughout the entire development team. It will simplify development by making understanding the design quicker.

Naming Element Types

We do not recommend that you strictly adhere to the reference concrete syntax requirement of name length being limited to eight characters. (Although some applications do not allow modifications to the default lengths via variant concrete syntaxes). Many DTD developers have chosen to increase the allowed length and have created names that are very mnemonic and easy to understand and learn to use. After all, the names you give your elements should be based on the names the users use when referring to things in the data (unless they are used to using format-oriented composition commands). And many names in use may be more than eight characters in length and may not easily shorten to an abbreviated form.

Many DTD developers have used names that are as short as possible, even less than eight characters whenever possible. The only justification that remains for this is for applications where bulk keying will be used quite heavily and the keying is paid for by the keystroke. It is easy to forget what a short name refers to when looking at unformatted SGML data.

Longer names allow the use of naming conventions within the names. For instance, some DTD developers have chosen to show that some related elements belong to a group by adding a prefix, perhaps separated with a hyphen or period (both are `NAME CHARACTERS`). All of the elements in a table, for example may start with a `t.` prefix.

The use of prefixes is useful when DTD fragments are reused. For instance, you will most likely create one table DTD fragment and reuse it in all of your DTDs. See *Entity Management* on page 184. If you need to allow a paragraph in your table, and it has a different content model that the ubiquitous paragraph element used in text, you will need to maintain separate element declarations and use different names. You could assign `para` and `t.para`. The use of the common root `para` would help associate the two elements as belonging to the same class of information. The developers of HyTime have created a concept called architectural forms that formalized this classification of similar elements used in a single domain.[1] For instance, by associating elements from DTDs of data from different sources into a single class using architectural forms you could greatly enhance the ability to conduct context-sensitive searches across large data collections.

1 For more information on Architectural Forms refer to the HyTime standard (ISO 10744). Also see the article SGML Architectural Forms by Ludo Van Vooren and Eric Seversen, <TAG>, The SGML Newsletter Volume 5, Number 2, February, 1992.

COMMENT YOUR DTD

You should lace your DTD liberally with comments, either as separate comment declarations or by using the comment delimiters somewhere in the declarations themselves. Comments serve to clarify subtle information about the DTD, hard to remember details, and clues to the organization of the DTD.

Comments can be used to create divisions and headings that serve to ease navigation and understanding of the DTD. Some choose to add a comment with a long row of asterisks or hyphens to provide a visual break between groupings of related declarations.

Many DTD developers include a plain language name and brief notes on the use of the element and/or attributes directly in the declarations defining them. Some prefer to use a separate comment declaration in front of the element to make reading the DTD easier, as seen in the following example:

```
...
<!-- List: my be bulleted or numbered                        -->
<!ELEMENT   list     - O (item+)                             >
<!ATTLIST   list     type     (b | n)    'b'                 >
<!ELEMENT   item     - O (#PCDATA)                           >
...
```

Comments can also be inserted inside of the declarations to point out specific details. These are delimited by the comment delimiters, two hyphens, for both start and end of the comment, as seen below:

```
...
<!ELEMENT   list     - O (item+)                             >
<!ATTLIST   list     type     (b | n)    'b'                 >
<!ELEMENT   item     - O (#PCDATA)   --  'b' = bulleted
                                         'n' = numbered  -->
...
```

Comments act as a good place to store details about decisions made in the way you define things in your DTD since they can be kept right where the DTD developer needs them when analyzing the DTD and considering changes.

A common convention used is to store a collection of comments at the top of the file containing your DTD after the Document Type Declaration. Some developers record information in plain language about the DTD, a version number, and even copyright information at the very top. This information is sometimes followed by a list of changes made by the DTD developer during the document analysis and DTD development process. A list of changes can be kept in the order in which they were implemented. Some DTD developers include a brief description of the change, why it was needed, a date, and their initials to aid in tracking changes. This technique is helpful because it keeps the version tracking and change information with the DTD. Anyone who needs a copy of the current DTD will also receive this useful information to aid in reading how the design came about.

After a complex DTD has been developed for a while and many changes made and tracked, it is interesting to read these comments and see how the model it described has changed. These comments can be useful in developing a house style for common elements and approaches to solving information modeling and DTD development issues.

There are no official requirements on how a DTD should be commented. Comments can be difficult to maintain if too complex of a methodology is employed. Or they can be all but useless if not done consistently and kept up to date. You will need to come to some agreement with the development team members about what would constitute enough, but not too much, commentary in your DTD.

Although comments are ignored by the parser, we expect to see more applications use comments to aid in processing. An example of this is how Microstar Software Ltd.'s DTD development environment Near&;Far uses carefully placed comments to create reports for tag documentation.

SEQUENCE

DTDs should be logically organized to assist in reading and updating them. The standard has few rules on what order declarations should occur. An important rule to remember though is that entity references cannot be referenced until after they have been declared. A common approach is to declare all of your entities, parameter and general, first, then the other declarations as needed. Other than that, you can just about do what ever way you think suits the needs of your development team.

The DTD will be read often by many people involved in developing applications. More often than not, the most commonly looked up declarations are element, attribute list, and entity declarations since they form the structure and naming components of markup, and are the basis of many other types of declarations. We suggest that these declarations come first in the DTD, and are followed by the more esoteric declarations. However you organize your DTD, you should, for the most part, group all like declarations together.

Even within groups of a declaration type, you may develop sub-groupings. For instance, within entity declarations, you may group all of the parameter entities together, and the general entities together. Within parameter entities you may group the ones that define content models together, and others that are used in attribute list declarations in another grouping. In general entities your groups may be special character, system entities, boiler-plate text, etc.

A good exception to grouping declarations by type is that element and attribute list declaration should be intermixed.

ORGANIZING ELEMENTS AND ATTRIBUTES

Some people like to organize their DTD with all the element declarations sorted together in one area, and all the attribute list declarations sorted in another area. Other people like to group the attribute list declaration with the element declaration with which it associated. There are advantages and disadvantages to both techniques.

Keeping the associated declarations sorted together makes it easier to understand what the markup will look like. Changes can be implemented more easily if they affect both declarations. One problem with keeping them together occurs when more than one element type appears in a single attribute list declaration. With which element declaration should the attribute list declaration be grouped?

Keeping the associated declaration separate is less common. This technique solves the problem raised in the previous technique, but raises some other issues. For instance, in order to understand what the markup will look like, the person reading the DTD will need to look in two places. Comments about the element and attribute may need to be repeated in both places.

You can organize your DTD just about any way you wish. The attributes can be declared before or after the element declaration with which they are associated.

There has been much discussion concerning whether to use an element or an attribute to capture information in SGML. The rule of thumb is to keep content in elements, and information about content in attributes. During the document analysis process, the developer may ask that some of the content be maintained as attributes to aid processing. See *Elements vs. attributes* on page 304

Also, attributes can have declared values that can be used to make the information more consistent. Another consideration for the use of attributes is to provide a place to store specialized information regarding formatting. Although the inclusion of format-specific information is to be avoided in your DTD, some situations may require a judicious use of it. For example, math and tabular constructs may not be possible without some formatting information in the form of attributes or even elements.

GROUPING ELEMENT DECLARATIONS

It is a good idea to group different kinds of element declarations together (along with their associated attribute list declarations). For instance, common text level elements that are widely used throughout the DTD may need to be frequently accessed by people reading the DTD. It may be best to group these together under a commented heading. Structural elements may be another good group to use. Front matter and rear matter elements may be grouped together as well.

If your information is heavily cross-referenced or "linked" and you have many different specific cross-reference elements, they should be managed together in a group. For instance, legal publications may have dozens of different types of legal citations which will be used to create hypertext links and cross reference tables. Each of the citation types requires a separate tag since they have varying structures that need to be enforced in order to support the hypertext linking. But, since they are all "citations", they can be grouped under a commented heading labeled "citations" to ease in locating them in the DTD.

ALPHABETICAL OR SEQUENTIAL

The simplest method for writing a DTD is to start with the highest level element and work your way down the tree structure, branch by branch, traversing one branch to its lowest level, then moving to the next branch and repeating the process until you have identified all your elements. Along the way you will need to make decisions about when to use an attribute, when to enter something in the content model of one or more elements, and when to use inclusions and exclusions, short references, and other features. During the document analysis process you will have been faced with the need to make some of these decisions based on how the information will be managed, created, updated, and processed.

An alternative is to list all of the elements as you find them and sort them alphabetically by element names when you create the DTD. Alphabetically sorted DTDs make finding a particular element easier when reading a DTD. A drawback is that the structure is harder to track if the reader has to move around a lot in the DTD to trace through it. In contrast, some people feel that organizing a DTD by the sequence in which the elements are used makes it hard to locate element declarations and is, therefore, harder to read.

With the advent of new DTD development tools like MicroStar Software Ltd.'s Near&Far, this debate becomes somewhat moot. While viewing a DTD in Near&Far, the reader can locate a specific declaration very easily and can generate reports about the DTD as well as the DTD itself. Near&Far also stores documentation information and can track updates and suggestions from developers through the use of a Lotus Notes Database Template. See *Near&Far*, in Appendix 8 / SGML Resources on page 456.

We suggest you adopt whatever approach your entire development team feels comfortable with. They will be using the DTD the most. We prefer the sequentially organized DTD with logical groupings (discussed above), liberally commented, and recommend you use this style to ease access and maintenance of your DTD.

WHITE SPACE

Since the Standard allows liberal use of white space in a DTD, you can use it to your advantage to improve the presentation of the DTD. White space includes, spaces, tabs, and carriage returns.

Many DTD developers have successfully used a combination of white space, comments and alignment to make a tidy, easy to read DTD. Consider the following set of declarations (not a complete DTD):

```
<!ENTITY amp '&' >
<!ENTITY dtd 'Document Type Definition' >
<!ENTITY % paratext    'paragraph | art | quote' >
<!ENTITY % incs 'footnote | quote' >
<!ENTITY % number.atr 'number CDATA #REQUIRED' >
<!ELEMENT chapter - O (name, abstract, (%paratext;)+,
subbchapter*, appendix*, bibliography?)   +(footnote | quote) >
<!ATTLIST chapter %number.atr;
security (public | secret) 'public'>
<!ELEMENT subchapter - O (name, (%paratext)+ )>
<!ATTLIST subchapter %number.atr;>
<!ELEMENT abstract - O (name,(%paratext;)+)   -(art) >
<!ELEMENT note - O (#PCDATA)>
<!ELEMENT name - O (#PCDATA)>
<!ELEMENT paragraph - O (#PCDATA)>
```

Now consider the readability of the same declarations with a little white space, a few comments, and some alignment rules:

```
<!--  **************************************************   -->
<!--  ENTITY REFERENCES                                    -->
<!--  **************************************************   -->

<!--  GENERAL ENTITY REFERENCES                            -->

<!-- Ampersand                                             -->
<!ENTITY    amp        '&'                                  >
<!-- DTD                                                   -->
<!ENTITY    dtd        'Document Type Definition'           >

<!--  PARAMETER ENTITY REFERENCES                          -->

<!--  Content Models/Groupings                             -->
<!-- Text                                                  -->
<!ENTITY  % paratext   'paragraph | art | quote'            >
<!-- Common elements                                       -->
<!ENTITY  % incs       'footnote | quote'                   >
<!--  Attrbute Definitions                                 -->
<!-- Req. number                                           -->
<!ENTITY  % number.atr 'number CDATA #REQUIRED'             >

<!--  **************************************************   -->
<!--  ELEMENTS AND ATTRIBUTES                              -->
<!--  **************************************************   -->
```

```
<!--  STRUCTURE                                             -->

<!--  Chapter Division                                      -->
<!ELEMENT chapter    - O  (name, abstract, (%paratext;)+,
                          subchapter*, appendix*,
                          bibliography?)  +(footnote | quote) >
<!ATTLIST chapter    %number.atr;
                     security  (public | secret) 'public'     >

<!--  Subchapter Division                                   -->
<!ELEMENT subchapter - O  (name, (%paratext)+ )              >
<!ATTLIST subchapter %number.atr; >

<!--  TEXT ELEMENTS                                         -->

<!--  Chapter Abstract                                      -->
<!ELEMENT abstract   - O (name,(%paratext;)+)   -(art) >

<!--  Inline Note                                           -->
<!-- Generates "NOTE:"                                      -->
<!ELEMENT note       - O (#PCDATA)                           >
<!ELEMENT name       - O (#PCDATA)                           >
<!ELEMENT paragraph  - O (#PCDATA)                           >
```

Of course, the attempt made above at making things line up only works with monospaced fonts (tabs would work when using proportional fonts).

ADVANCED FEATURES

Extra care should be taken when using some of the more advanced features of SGML such as short references and marked sections. These features are discussed in more detail in Chapter 10, *Understanding SGML* on page 215

You need to consider the impact of using these features in addition to the potential benefits. Sometimes simpler is better. For instance, marked sections, although supported by most SGML-smart editors, may require cumbersome markup and can be difficult to explain to users. Short references can become confusing, even to the experienced DTD developer.

If you do feel that there is sufficient benefit to using one of these features, be sure your elements and associated attributes are well-defined before implementing them. Be sure you understand the implications that a change in an element declaration might have to, for example, your short reference mapping.

Some features are worth avoiding altogether. You may find that the parser and processing tools you choose to employ may not support features such as SUBDOC, RANK, or LINK.

DTD VERSION CONTROL

Aside from documenting changes in the comments of your DTD, there are strategies to managing the changes in a DTD that might keep you from becoming overwhelmed. During the early development and conversion phases of implementation, you should expect many changes. DTDs tend to evolve rapidly during these phases.

Using a version and release numbering system similar to software release management techniques is essential (See *Version Control* on page 186 for more information on version control concepts). We recommend that during development, you use release 0 and incremental releases for each changed draft that gets distributed to the development teams. For instance, the first draft written by the DTD analyst and distributed at the beginning of the team review process would be version 0, revision 1 (or 1.1). Every time a change is implemented and the DTD re-issued, the release number should be incremented. You should expect dozens of change releases in a single version for a DTD of any significant size or complexity, so use a numbering nomenclature that supports two-digit releases. When significant events occur during the evolution of the DTD, perhaps major overhauls or release of the production versions of the DTD, you should increment the version number.

If you include comments in the DTD that track changes, you should group them by the version number under which the changes were made. We have seen examples of DTDs that have had hundreds of individual changes recorded in the comments under dozens of numbered versions.

DTD CHANGE STRATEGY

You should expect the DTD to change frequently during conversion and development. During conversion, you will encounter situations where the data instance just doesn't match the DTD, and a DTD modification will be required. During application development, an approach that a developer was going to take on a specific process might prove to be too slow or difficult. A slight change in the DTD, for instance requiring end tags for a specific containing element, might make it easier for the process to run smoothly. You may deem it more feasible to change the DTD than other options available to you.

We recommend that you try to enforce as much stringency up front that you think you will need, and hopefully, as you make changes, you will be making the model more relaxed rather than more stringent. It is easier to loosen up a rule than to tighten it up when you are half way through development or conversion. For instance, if you had the following element declaration:

```
...
<!ELEMENT chapter      - O          (name?, paragraph+)          >
...
```

and you decided half way through your conversion that the name should have been required, you would have to go back and check all the data previously converted to ensure that it complies with the new, more stringent rule. But, if your initial model was:

```
...
<!ELEMENT chapter       - -            (name, paragraph+)            >
...
```

and you decided to allow name to be optional, then all of the previously parsed data that adhered to the stricter rule would still comply with the more relaxed rule. The same concept is true for the minimization rules expressed in the two declarations above. In the second one, the end tag for chapter became required. You would have to re-parse and cleanse any data that has already been converted to ensure compliance.

It is usually easier to change from a more stringent DTD to a more relaxed DTD than the other way around. But, it is sometimes impossible to anticipate just how stringent you need to make some rules. That is why you need to perform extensive of review of the DTD before starting your conversion.

Specific vs. General DTDs

There are several general-purpose DTDs that exist. Some are industry-specific applications, others are intended to be used by all types of publishing organizations.

Before considering using a general purpose DTD instead of developing your own, you need to consider several things. What business problems are you trying to solve? Will the general purpose DTD solve these issues? What is the purpose of the general DTD? Was it designed, for example, to improve interchange but not editing and electronic product production? Database management? Context-sensitive searching? Does it satisfy your information processing requirements? Are the tools and applications that exist that utilize this DTD rich enough to handle your processing requirements? How much customization will be needed?

One of the great strengths of SGML is in customization. The need for customized applications is very powerful. The benefits available through customization are great. You may want a customized version of an industry-specific DTD for internal use, and perform down or cross translates to the general DTD for interchange only.

There exists a logical dilemma when customizing a general purpose DTD. At what point does it stop being the general-purpose DTD and start being a customized DTD. That point, we believe is when enough information is removed to make it difficult to translate into the general DTD. Just as there are many flavors of Unix, there are probably many flavors of the ISO DTD for standards or another general-purpose DTD. Slight customization is often necessary to achieve processing efficiency using the tools in your shop. But there is a cost to customizing, and that may be the need for automated, or even manual, transformation processes to facilitate interchange.

It may be useful to start with a general-purpose DTD to reduce the amount of design work required up-front. A DTD such as the EPSIG[1] DTD could be the basis for your development. Once it is heavily customized, it is no longer the EPSIG standard, but development of routines at the composition house or another editorial office may be minimal compared to a those required to process a DTD created entirely from scratch.

Test Your DTD Against Reality

Before you can evaluate your DTD you need to understand the purpose and uses for which it is being developed. You need to test your DTD constantly as you develop programs for processing your data. You need to conduct sanity checks with users to make sure that the information model you are developing accurately reflects what is useful to the users. You need to determine if external requirements for interchange can be met either by using the DTD as is or by performing a translation into another expression.

Always test against real data; the more the better. You will be surprised how many details emerge when you begin to encode data with the DTD you have developed, even if you conducted extensive analysis during the document analysis process, interviewed all developers and users, referred to editorial style guides and external requirements, and parsed the DTD until no more errors were reported.

It is better to have tested a DTD thoroughly against data before starting your conversion, than it is to find a critical error half way through your conversion that will require reconverting work already completed. Granted, you will not find everything that could possibly be considered a critical error, but thorough testing reduces the risk.

DTD Documentation

Documenting your DTD, and your entire application, is becoming increasingly important. DTDs are not created in a vacuum. As companies formalize their information model, it will need to be communicated to users, developers, and

1 The Electronic Publishing Special Interest Group DTD is the enhanced version of the original Association of American Publishers (AAP) DTD, the first general purpose DTD to exist. The EPSIG DTD is an official ISO Standard (ISO 12083). The Graphic Communication Association Research Institute has assumed management of EPSIG.

outsiders. Often, these people will not want to read a DTD. So another form of expressing the rules expressed in the DTD may be needed.

Another situation that increasingly demands good documentation is the industry initiative and standardized DTD. As the SGML world grows up, methodologies for developing good documentation will be developed or improved.

Each application of SGML seems to have its own style of documentation. This diversity may be acceptable if each set of documentation is thoughtfully, and logically prepared and is current with the DTD. We offer the following list as a minimal set of documentation that must be maintained to support understanding the DTD:

1. Application Overview
2. Alphabetical element cross reference lists
3. Alphabetical tag name cross reference lists
4. Tag Documentation
5. Sample encoded files and pages
6. Copy of the DTD complete with comments

APPLICATION OVERVIEW

A description of the overall system, including all data repositories, editorial workstations, and other applications, should be prepared. This document should give a general overview of the different processes that will be performed, including, how the editing will be done, how the data will be managed, and what types of output will be supported and the specific requirements of each. Understanding the purpose of the information model is essential in understanding decisions made in the developing the DTD.

The application overview should be just that, an overview. Do not describe every little detail. You will need to determine what information about the system is needed to describe the goals of the DTD and the model it expresses.

TAG DOCUMENTATION

Users of the system, as well as developers of the system processes, will need more information about the elements, attributes, and entities that is normally contained within the DTD as text comments. It is, therefore useful to prepare a plain-language description of each element, its associated attributes, and the details on the contents of each. A master list of entities is also useful, as well as any other aids to understanding the DTD.

These details can be organized in any way that is easy to access and use. Typically, tag documentation is prepared much like a dictionary with the following headings and information for each element:

1. Element name in plain language
2. Generic Identifier and sample markup
3. Description of associated attributes and their usage

4. Textual description of the element, it's purpose and relationships to other elements, and
5. Description of special processing such as generating text, details on granularity needed to support hypertext linking, etc.

Keeping tag documentation up to date can be difficult, especially if the information being kept is very complicated.

You may find that you need more (or less) information than described above. Make sure to have tag documentation requirements and drafts reviewed by users and members of the development team.

Common Elements

In our experience, we have found that there are certain types of elements that are found in most applications. This section is here to discuss some ways to deal with these elements, and some suggestions on processing.

TABLES

Tables are entirely a function of formatting. A table is one representation of a set of data. Any information contained in a table can be expressed in another form. A tax table could be printed as a series of paragraphs:

> *If your income is between US$15,010 and US$16,810, and your filing status is single, your taxis US$1,420. If your income is between US$15,010 and US$16,810, and your filing status is married, your tax is US$1,380. If your income is between US$15,010 and US$16,810, and your filing status is head of household, your tax is US$1,172.*

This kind of output can get tedious very quickly, but it contains the same information as the corresponding table.

Format vs. Content

There are several different approaches to tables. The most common is to treat the object as a series of rows and columns. Most publicly available DTDs have a table construct that reflects this thinking. The basic structure is:

```
table information
    column widths
    border information
    spanning information
table head
    row+
        cell+
table body
    row+
        cell+
table notes
```

Usually, there is some means of indicating horizontal (and sometimes, vertical) spanning, where adjacent cells are combined into a single cell. Some models contain a way of indicating which columns constitute the "stub", or that which must be duplicated if the table breaks across a page.

The allure of a format-driven table is that any type of data can be fit into the model. A format-driven table can easily be rendered onto a piece of paper, since that is the foundation for the model in the first place.

The problem with a format-driven table is the same as the general problem of format-driven elements as a whole. That is, the original meaning of the data is lost. The following three examples illustrate the exact same data:

City	*Denver*	*Rochester*	*Palm Springs*
Population	850,000	240,000	48,000
Annual Snowfall	23"	88"	0"

Table 20. *Snowfall in Various Cities*

City	*Population*	*Annual Snowfall*
Denver	850,000	23"
Rochester	240,000	88"
Palm Springs	48,000	0"

Table 21. *Snowfall in Various Cities*

The city of Denver has a population of 850,000 and an annual snowfall of 23 inches. The city of Rochester has a population of 240,000 and an annual snowfall of 88 inches. The city of Palm Springs has a population of 48,000 and an annual snowfall of 0 inches.

The first two examples are identical, except the rows and columns have been transposed. Both are two-dimensional renderings of the same data. The third example is the same information, expressed in a single-dimensional manner.

The shorthand notation allowed by tables is the main attraction for their use. The number "850,000" is not just a number. Rather, it's identification is defined by its relation to the horizontal and vertical axes on which it resides. So, "850,000" is the "population" of "Denver" This is obvious to us as humans reading this, but it is not so obvious to a computer attempting to search for certain data.

This is the problem with a format-oriented approach to tables. Without sophisticated analysis, a computerized data query tool would have a difficult time trying to find the "population" of "Denver"

One way to create a more intelligent table structure would be to make a table model specific for each data set. In the example above, the DTD would look something like this:

```
...
<!ELEMENT cities        - O         (city+)                    >
<!ELEMENT city          - O         (name, population,
                                    snowfall)                  >
<!ELEMENT (name | population | snowfall)
                        - O         (#PCDATA)                  >
...
```

Using this DTD fragment, the application programmer can render the information in any of the three ways. Also, a query like "list the population of cities that have more than 35 inches of snowfall" is possible.

The drawback to this approach is specific to each data type. If an author wants to illustrate a point by creating a two-dimensional table, he would need to create a new structure in the DTD to accomplish this.

Another approach, which is gaining in popularity, is to create a generalized row-and-column structure, but place additional information in the structure to indicate the semantic purpose of the data, as illustrated using the type attribute in the colspec element.

```
...
<!ELEMENT table         - O         (colspec+, thead?, tbody)
                                                               >
<!ELEMENT colspec       - O         EMPTY
                                                               >
<!ATTLIST colspec       width       NUMBER          #REQUIRED
                        type        CDATA           #REQUIRED>
<!ELEMENT (thead | tbody)
                        - -         (row+)                     >
```

```
<!ELEMENT row          - O          (cell+)                  >
<!ELEMENT cell         - O          (#PCDATA)                >
  ...
```

The first example of the city table would be tagged like this:

```
  ...
<table>
<colspec width='5' type='City'>
<colspec width='3' type='Population'>
<colspec width='2' type='Annual Snowfall'>
<thead>
<row>
<cell>City
<cell>Population
<cell>Annual Snowfall
</thead>
<tbody>
<row>
<cell>Denver
<cell>850,000
<cell>23"
<row>
<cell>Rochester
<cell>240,000
<cell>88"
<row>
<cell>Palm Springs
<cell>48,000
<cell>0"
</tbody>
</table>
```

With this kind of construct, the author can still create a random table and have all of the formatting options required by completely format-driven models, but can provide enough semantic information to the application designer so intelligent queries can be done.

For some other examples of dealing with tables, See *Using NOTATION for External Tables* on page 338 and *Using #CONREF to enable External Table Processing* on page 352.

Electronic Delivery Considerations

We have identified two basic classifications of tables. There are tables whose purpose is to answer a particular question. For example, the tax table published annually by the U.S. Internal Revenue Service is around a dozen pages long. It contains columns indicating filing status, and rows containing income earned. The intersection of these axes is the amount of tax you owe. There is a single number in this table that each taxpayer is interested in. Once that number is retrieved, the tax table ends up at the bottom of the bird cage. This is a classic example of a "reference table".

The other type of table is used to illustrate a particular point. A policy analyst might pore over a table looking for trends by comparing the values in a cell with values in the cells around it. In this way, the analyst is using the table as a picture, and is not just using it to get a particular piece of data. We call this an "illustrative table"

When information is presented on a non-interactive, two-dimensional medium such as paper, both types of tables appear similar in their format. However, they can be treated differently when delivered electronically.

In the case of a reference table, an electronic delivery tool can be programmed to ask the user to select a filing status and enter his income. The intersection of the two is presented immediately, without the user scrolling through screens full of data looking for the number.

On the other hand, users who are accustomed to viewing tables as illustrative matter will be taken aback if they are handled the same way as reference tables are.

In both cases, it is important to recognize the purpose of the table, how the user will use it, and the processing capabilities your applications.

EQUATIONS

Like tables, equations are largely format-oriented. It is possible to think of equations in typographical terms. Equations are usually difficult to typeset, because they could contain many levels of super-scripting and sub-scripting, **plus** non-standard characters and symbols. However, most typesetting languages provide the functionality to set complex equations through complex movement of the typesetter's imaging field.

By creating a format-oriented image of an equation, you are satisfying the requirements of paper publishing, but you are losing the opportunity to provide a valuable level of functionality for the user of an electronic product.

There are languages used to typeset math formulas (eqn and TeX, to name two) and languages used to interpret algebra (Maple and Mathematica). If a mathematical formula is described in typesetting terms, without capturing the underlying logic, a two-dimensional rendering is all that will ever be possible. By capturing the semantics of the equation, however, an electronic delivery tool can be programmed to accept from the user variables, and can interpret the equations and produce a result. Of course, the equation will be rendered in a standard way, as well.

This can be achieved, either by defining a DTD with equation semantics as elements, or by using SGML's notation construction to call an external processor. If you define the structures as SGML elements, you will need to translate the instances to some kind of output language when the document is rendered. The AAP and Euromath DTDs are good places to start, since they already have mathematical structures defined.

CROSS-REFERENCES

Cross-references (See *Cross-references* on page 293) are used to indicate to the reader that there might be other information available on the topic at hand. Cross-references have been around since the beginning of writing. In modern computer terms, these are sometimes called "hyperlinks".

In SGML, we usually use an empty element to indicate a link to some other part of the document. The `ID` and `IDREF` declared values for attribute definition lists are used to assure uniqueness (in the case of `ID`) and valid reference (in the case of `IDREF`) within the document.

Brian and Dale's Excellent DTD(See Appendix 5, *Brian and Dale's Excellent DTD* on page 411) contains the following element and attribute list declarations for cross-references:

```
...
<!ELEMENT xref       - O         EMPTY                   >
<!ATTLIST xref       refid       IDREFS        #REQUIRED
                     see         (see |
                                 nosee)        'see'
                     refer       (refer |
                                 norefer)      'norefer'
                     number      (number |
                                 nonumber)     'number'
                     autotext    (autotext |
                                 noautotext)   'autotext'
                     page        (page |
                                 nopage)       'page'    >
...
```

In addition, each element that can be a target has an attribute called "id" that has a declared value of `ID`:

```
...
<!ATTLIST chapter      id        ID            #IMPLIED >
<!ATTLIST section      id        ID            #IMPLIED >
<!ATTLIST illustration id        ID            #IMPLIED >
<!ATTLIST table        id        ID            #IMPLIED >
<!ATTLIST question     id        ID            #IMPLIED >
...
```

In the instance, the cross-reference is placed at a point in the text where the author wants to refer to an object.

```
...
<section id='i68'>
<title>Cross-references
</title>
<para>Cross-references
<xref refid='i68' see='see'>are used to indicate to the reader...
...
```

Some implementations use different cross-reference elements to generate different text. For example, the element <tableref>might generate the text "See table 1 on page 45", and the element <figref>might generate the text "See figure 4". In some uses, this might make it easier for the user to understand how the text will be formatted in the output version, but such distinctions are not necessary from the standpoint of SGML. In the example of our book, there is a single cross-reference tag used for all occasions. It is the responsibility of the application to generate the appropriate text for the type of element that is being referenced.

There are three more attributes on the xref element: type, page, and number. These attributes allow the author to specify the type of text that he wants generated by the system. In this example, there are 16 possible combinations, some of which don't make sense. The following table shows what an application might produce given some combinations of values:

Type	*Number*	*Page*	*Autotext*	*Text generated*
see	number	page	autotext	(See figure 5 on page 38)
see	number	nopage	autotext	(See figure 5)
see	nonumber	page	autotext	(See page 38)
see	nonumber	page	noautotext	38
see	number	nopage	noautotext	5
see	nonumber	nopage	noautotext	(semantic error!)
refer	number	page	autotext	(Refer to chapter 12 on page 421)

Table 22. *Cross-reference (*<xref>*) Attribute values*

The autotext attribute is used to generate the standard reference text. It is possible that an author wants to insert the number of an illustration directly in the body of the text, without having the system generate the “see” or “refer” information.

```
  ...
<!ATTLIST figure      id          ID                #REQUIRED>
  ...
<!ATTLIST xref        refid       IDREF             #REQUIRED
                      type        (see |
                                  refer)            'see'
                      number      (number |
                                  nonumber)         'number'
                      autotext    (autotext |
                                  noautotext)       'autotext'
                      page        (page |
                                  nopage)           'page'    >
  ...
<para>As you can see by looking at the example in figure
<xref refid='meaning-of-life' number nopage noautotext>on page
<xref refid='meaning-of-life' number page noautotext>, life does
have a meaning.
</para>
```

This will generate the text:

> *As you can see by looking at the example in Figure 48, Implementation Enthusiometer on page 148, life does have a meaning.*

Notice that the combination of nonumber, nopage, and noautotext is an application error. SGML does not have the facilities to validate this type of condition, so the application must check for it and notify the user at run time.

QUOTES

A typographical quote is different than the single and double “ticks” found on most keyboards. In addition, the typographical character for a start quote and the one for an end quote are different. In order to produce acceptable start and end quotes, some kind of character reference must be output to the typesetter. In addition, the character used to begin and end the quote inside of quoted material must change to a single quote (in American English).

A entity references could be used to satisfy this requirement:

```
  ...
<!ENTITY    ldq        '\LeftDoubleQuote'                  >
```

```
<!ENTITY    rdq         '\RightDoubleQuote'                    >
<!ENTITY    lsq         '\LeftSingleQuote'                     >
<!ENTITY    rsq         '\RightSingleQuote'                    >
  ...
```

And referenced in the text as appropriate:

```
  ...
<para>He said, &ldq;She said, &lsq;I understand.&rsq;&rdq;
</para>
```

Another common rule of quotes is that, if the quoted material will take up more than three lines in the output, it should be set-off from the text, indented on both sides, and printed, without quote marks, in a smaller point size and possibly italicized.

Some implementations use an element called "long quote" to specify such extended material. In keeping with the concept of device-independent output, however, the author does not know if the quote will be longer than three lines, since the line length is known only at rendering time.

There is also the problem with generating different characters based on the area of the world the document will be read. In some parts of Europe, the "french quote" is used.

The elegant way to resolve all of these issues is to use a quote tag that can contain other quote tags. Then, it is up to the application to determine the characters to use and the formatting considerations. The following declarations illustrate this:

```
  ...
<!ELEMENT paragraph    - -         (#PCDATA)         +(quote) >
<!ELEMENT quote        - -         (#PCDATA)                  >
  ...
</title>
<paragraph>Para Text
</paragraph>
  ...
```

Note that the quote is an inclusion at the paragraph level, so it can be included in any of paragraph's descendants, even if that descendant is a quote. Because the quote is not excluded from itself, a quote can contain quotes, which is what we are trying to achieve.

The example above becomes:

```
  ...
</title>
<paragraph>He said,
<quote>She said,
<quote>I understand.
```

```
</quote>
</quote>
</paragraph>
  ...
```

If the quote gets too long to be rendered in-line, the application can issue the appropriate codes, at process-time, to carry out the style guidelines set forth by the document designer. Note that the quote element declared above only contains #PCDATA and other quotes, and therefore will not cross the start and end boundries of other elements. If two paragraphs in a row are part of the same quote, they will have to be treated as two separate quotes. This may cause problems with leaving the end quote characters of the first paragraphs as is the custom of some styles.

GRAPHICS

Graphics (*i.e.*, bitmap pictures, vector illustrations, etc.) are usually stored outside the document because they contain non-text information. We usually use an empty element to indicate the placement of a graphic, and use attributes in the element to indicate the name of the graphic and formatting considerations, as necessary.

A typical declaration set for graphics follows:

```
  ...
<!ENTITY    workflow   SDATA
         'http://www.sgml.com/usr/SGMLguide/graphics/workflow.tiff'>
<!ELEMENT illustration O -          (graphic+, caption)        >
<!ATTLIST illustration id           ID               #IMPLIED >
<!ELEMENT graphic      - O          EMPTY                      >
<!ATTLIST graphic      name         ENTITY           #REQUIRED
                       crop         CDATA            #IMPLIED
                       scale        CDATA            #IMPLIED >
<!ELEMENT caption      O -          (#PCDATA)                  >
  ...
<illustration id='wflow-funda'>
<graphic name='workflow'>
<caption>Workflow fundamentals
</caption>
</illustration>
```

Notice the declared value ENTITY in the name attribute of graphic. For each graphic in the instance file, we must declare an external entity that points to the appropriate physical file on the system.

When the application gets this instance, it knows everything it needs to know in order to fetch the graphic and render it. See *Notation Declaration* on page 265

FOOTNOTES

A footnote is a note placed at the bottom of a page of a book or manuscript that comments on or cites a reference for a designated part of the text[1]. Some might argue that the fact that footnotes appear in your DTD indicates that you have not yet mastered content-tagging. This is a valid point, because most of the content of footnotes (bibliographic references, legal citations, editorial asides) can be tagged as such, and just rendered at the bottom of the page. The concepts in this section (rendering, inclusions) are applicable to those types of element names as well.

Footnotes in an SGML environment are usually placed in-line with the document. There are several reasons for this:

1. the author is thinking about the contents of the footnote, and should not be concerned with moving somewhere else to enter the text,
2. if the paragraph containing the footnote moves, the footnote moves with it,
3. the application designer has freedom to place footnotes at the end of the page, at the end of the chapter or as sidebars on the page.

Footnotes can generally appear anywhere text can, so they are usually defined as inclusions at some level high in the document hierarchy.

```
...
<!ELEMENT chapter      - -        (title, para+)  +(footnote) >
...
```

Remember that the nature of inclusions is that they are appropriate for the element in which they appear in the content model (chapter, in this case), and in all subordinate elements (title and para). As such, if a footnote appears in a paragraph, it is a subordinate element, and can have footnotes, itself. While this might be desirable in some implementations, it is not usually what the document designer intended.

In this case, the declaration for footnote should have an exclusion:

---

1 An endnote is similar in use, except that endnotes generally appear collected at the end of the chapter or document. The difference between footnotes and endnotes is the way they are rendered; they both are used by the author in the same way but appear at different positions in the document after output. This is important to note in an SGML implementation, because footnotes and endnotes can be treated the same, as far as authoring goes.

```
...
<!ELEMENT footnote     - -          (#PCDATA)       -(footnote) >
...
```

Note: at any point in a document instance, if an element is both an applicable inclusion and an exclusion, it is treated as an exclusion.

INDEXING

Indexing documents is a science. Determining which words should appear in an index—and how they are to be related—has been the subject of essays and theses, and the work of professional indexers, for generations.

Aside from the issues of how the indexed words are selected, the process of creating an index for a document in an SGML environment is an issue that the document designer and application developer must deal with.

Some systems have "authored" indexes, where a person collects appropriate words from the document and actually creates the index pages. This task can be assisted by the composition engine by providing page number references, but it is largely a manual task, because the same text may be indexed very differently for different audiences.

Indexing theory can be used as a guide in developing automated indexing procedures. There are two important factors to consider when developing index procedures:

1. index entries can be hierarchical
2. index entries can refer to other index entries

The element declaration for index-item in Brian and Dale's Excellent DTD (See Appendix 5, *Brian and Dale's Excellent DTD* on page 411) looks like this:

```
...
<!ELEMENT index-item   - -          (#PCDATA)                    >
<!ATTLIST index-item   type         (sub-item |
                                    see |
                                    see-also |
                                    base)          'base'
                       text         CDATA          #IMPLIED
                       print        (print |
                                    noprint)       'print'   >
...
```

Once a word has been identified as an indexed term, it is tagged with the <index-item>tag. The four attributes are used to indicate how it will appear in print and in the index. This paragraph is tagged as follows:

```
...
Once a word has been identified as an <index-item
sub-item text='identified'>indexed term</index-item>, it is
tagged with the <start-tag gi=index-item> tag. The
four <index-item see-also text='attribute list
declaration'>attributes</index-item> are used to
indicate how it will appear in print and in the index. This
paragraph is tagged as follows:
```

To see how this manifested itself in the index of this book, check out the index entries for "indexed term" and "attribute".

The tagging does not actually create the index; that it the job of the application. It is the job of the `<index-item>`tag to indicate to the application which items are to be indexed, and how they are to appear.

WARNINGS, CAUTIONS, AND NOTES

Warnings, cautions, and notes are notices that there is something described in the text that could be injurious to life or property. They appear most often in technical manuals that describe procedures. In military documents, warnings are created for things that could be injurious to life or limb. Cautions indicate things that are less severe, but still could pose a problem. A note is less severe then a caution, but is still something the operator should be aware of. Other organizations may have more extensive, yet similar text that is usually set off with a highlighted leading phrase or other visual clues.

Like footnotes, cautions, warnings, and notes are usually authored near the text where the danger is described. Unlike footnotes, cautions and warnings need to be observed before the procedure is attempted.

To illustrate this, we use the fictional procedure for how to defuse a bomb:

> Step 1: Cut the red wire
> Step 2: **Warning!** If there is a blue wire, cut it first

It is clear from this example that the warning, even though it directly concerned the second step, the operator should have known about it before executing the first step.

For this reason, warnings, cautions, and notes usually float to the top of the procedure, chapter, or section in which they are declared, just so the user is forewarned.

In some military documents, warnings and cautions are collected in a section in the front of the book, then repeated near the text that the warning describes. Since this is an intelligent SGML system, the actual warning text does not need to be created and stored twice. Rather, the application can automatically process the warning text appropriately in both places.

CHAPTER • TWELVE

Tipniques and Pratfalls

Introduction

For the new user, SGML presents many complex situations and problems that can be confusing and difficult to solve. Over the years, we have developed many techniques to solve problems we have encountered. Also, we have found some areas where new (and seasoned) users tend to get in trouble.

This section contains some tips and techniques (tipniques) and pitfalls and practices (pratfalls) that we have encountered. There are many ways to solve one problem. This is especially true due to the fact that every application is potentially different. What we have done here is to share the experiences of the many applications we have built. As our collective understanding of SGML grows we find even better solutions to these problems.

Our thanks to <TAG>, The SGML Newsletter for allowing us to adapt some of these items for this book.

Related Topics

- *The Power of SGML Databases* on page 11
- Chapter 4, *The SGML Environment* on page 43
- Chapter 5, *Document Analysis* on page 65
- *Discovering the Information in Documents* on page 75
- Chapter 6, *The SGML Application* on page 101
- *Publication-specific Development* on page 111
- *System Development* on page 139
- Chapter 8, *Information Conversion* on page 151
- *Conversion Strategies* on page 164
- Chapter 9, *SGML Data Management and Workflow* on page 183
- Chapter 10, *Understanding SGML* on page 215
- Chapter 11, *Building the DTD* on page 275
- *Common Elements* on page 288

Using Parameter Entity References

Parameter entity references were designed originally as a tool to make the preparation of DTDs easier. By being able to group common constructs and providing a simple, easy-to-remember name, the tool would make DTDs easier to read and maybe at times easier to modify and/or update. For example, if the construct:

```
fnref | quote | partno | bookttl
```

was used frequently in the DTD a parameter entity declaration could be used to accomplish the following:

```
  ...
<!ENTITY  % text        'fnref | quote | partno | bookttl'     >
<!ELEMENT para         - -          (paratext | %text; |
                                    latphrse)                  >
<!ELEMENT title        - -          (hdtext | %text;)          >
  ...
```

At a later time we decided that we could also use the tool to be able to make minor modifications to an existing DTD in the same fashion as modifying general entity references. That is, if the DTD developer wanted to allow a user to redefine something in the DTD, the use of a Parameter Entity could be used to allow for this. For example, if one department prescribed that a memo was to consist of the following:

```
...
<!ELEMENT memo          - -           (to, from, subject, date,
                                      body)                    >
<!ELEMENT (to | from | subject | date)
                        - 0           (#PCDATA)                >
<!ELEMENT body          - 0           (para+)                  >
<!ELEMENT para          - 0           (#PCDATA)                >
...
```

and another wanted to do it as:

```
...
<!ELEMENT memo          - -           (from, to, subject, date,
                                      body)                    >
<!ELEMENT (to | from | subject | date)
                        - 0           (#PCDATA)                >
<!ELEMENT body          - 0           (para+)                  >
<!ELEMENT para          - 0           (#PCDATA)                >
...
```

Then a parameter entity declaration could be used to allow the otherwise identical DTD to serve both departments:

```
...
<!ENTITY  % who             'from, to'                         >
<!ELEMENT memo          - -           (%who;, subject, date,
                                      body)                    >
<!ELEMENT (to | from | subject | date)
                        - 0           (#PCDATA)                >
<!ELEMENT body          - 0           (para+)                  >
<!ELEMENT para          - 0           (#PCDATA)                >
...
```

This way the department that wanted to use the other construct could pass the revised parameter entity declaration in front of the DTD and thus effectively change the DTD.

NAMING PARAMETER ENTITY REFERENCES

Following is an example of a convention we developed to identify the purpose of parameter entity references used to manage attribute definitions:

```
...
<!-- Number Attribute Optional                                -->
<!ENTITY  % number.ato  'number NUMBER #IMPLIED'               >
<!-- Number Attribute Required                                -->
```

```
<!ENTITY   % number.atr   'number NUMBER #REQUIRED'                >
<!-- Security Attribute (token list)                               -->
<!ENTITY   % security.at      'security (public | secret) public'>
  ...
```

These parameter entities can be easily interpreted by humans reading the DTD and result in attribute list declarations like the following:

```
  ...
<!ATTLIST chapter
%number.atr;
%security.at;         >
<!ATTLIST subchapter
%number.ato;          >
  ...
```

Another example of using a parameter entity reference is to manage content models or groupings within content models. The following example shows how a parameter entity reference for a class of similar documents can simplify the expression of a content model group that occurs frequently throughout the DTD and may be subject to many changes as the DTD is developed.

```
  ...
<!-- Paragraph elements                                            -->
<!ENTITY   % paratext     'para | list | art | quote | equation' >
<!ELEMENT chapter      - 0          (name, abstract,
                                    (%paratext;)+)              >
<!ELEMENT abstract     - 0          (name, (%paratext;)+)
                                                        -(art) >
  ...
```

This example shows how many elements can be grouped in a parameter entity reference and used in more than one place, simplifying reading and updating. Understanding is enhanced by a consistent naming convention. Note how the `art` element was excluded from the `abstract` element. This exclusion essentially changes the meaning of the `%paratext;`, but allows the same name to be used to mean two different things.

Using a consistent naming convention in conjunction and parameter entity references for content models, attribute definitions, and other parts of the DTD can result in concise, easy to read DTDs if implemented judiciously.

Elements vs. attributes

It is usually difficult for the beginner to determine the best way to specify the structure of a document. One area of confusion is whether to call a piece of information an element or an attribute. Consider a chapter that consists of a `title` followed by one or more `paragraph`. There might be a need to capture the author of the chapter and the last time it was updated. Which of the objects just described should be declared as elements and which should be included in the attribute list. Making them all elements would result in the following tagging:

```
 ...
<chapter>
<author>Bonnie Hurt
</author>
<updated>23-Jul-94
</updated>
<security>public
</security>
<title>Six ways to Leave an Impression
</title>
<paragraph>. . .
</paragraph>
</chapter>
```

Making all objects attributes results in the following tagging:

```
 ...
<!ELEMENT chapter      - O          (paragraph+)            >
<!ELEMENT paragraph    - O          (#PCDATA)               >
<!ATTLIST chapter      author       CDATA           #REQUIRED
                       updated      CDATA           #REQUIRED
                       security     (top-secret |
                                    classified |
                                    sensitive |
                                    public)         #REQUIRED
                       title        CDATA           #REQUIRED>
 ...
<chapter author='Bonnie Hurt' updated='23-Jul-94'
security='public' title='Six ways to Leave an Impression'>
<paragraph>
...
</paragraph>
</chapter>
```

Both of these examples are equivalent as far as their ability to express the required information. Neither one is a better solution for this instance. There are some rules to follow when deciding which will work the best in particular instance.

1. Elements should contain information
2. Attributes should contain information about the information
3. Attribute values can be validated by the parser

4. Elements can contain other elements, attributes cannot contain elements
5. System and process limitations may dictate which one to use

Using the above as guidelines, we would use the following tagging:

```
  ...
<!ELEMENT chapter       - -          (title, paragraph+)          >
<!ATTLIST chapter       author       CDATA               #REQUIRED
                        updated      CDATA               #REQUIRED
                        security     (top-secret |
                                     classified |
                                     sensitive |
                                     public)             #REQUIRED>
<!ELEMENT (title | paragraph)
                        - O          (#PCDATA)                    >
  ...
<chapter author='Bonnie Hurt' updated='23-Jul-94'
security='public'>
<title>Six ways to Leave an Impression
<paragraph>...
</chapter>
```

The paragraphs and the title contain the actual information. The author, date, and security classification might never be rendered for the user to see, so they constitute information about the information, and are handled as attributes. This data, if managed consistently as attributes with declared values, could ease their use. For example, the application would be able to extract only those chapters that have a particular security classification, or to extract those that were authored by a particular person.

Consider the "security" attribute. The only allowed values for this attribute are defined in the DTD as `top-secret`, `classified`, `sensitive`, and `public`. If managed as attributes with these declared values, the parser will not allow the user to assign any other value to this attribute.

Suppose a footnote were required inside of the title. Attributes cannot contain elements, so putting the title in an attribute would make it impossible to put a footnote in the title.

Another example is a cross-reference. Consider the requirement to create a link to an on-line database containing legal citations. The name of the citation must be rendered on the screen in a different color and underlined, which informs the user that the item is associated with an external link. Either of the following approaches will work:

```
  ...
<citation num='10-289' name='Directive 10-289'>
```

```
<citation num='10-289'>Directive 10-289
</citation>
```

Notice that the unique number of the citation is contained in the "num" attribute. This will be used to access the database, while the actual name of the citation is stated separately. Either one of these approaches will work. The environment should be considered to determine which will work best. With a sufficiently powerful application, it is possible to indicate just the num attribute, and have the application query a citation database for the text to be inserted. See *Organizing Elements and Attributes* on page 279.

Parameter Entities

Parameter entities provide a powerful means to develop the DTD in an organized manner. Consider a document database that contains information about a new car. Contained in this database is technical information about building the car, repair information, sales and marketing data, and user maintenance information.

At some point, various documents will be produced using the information in the database. Much of the information is shared among the various documents, so each has an attribute that specifies which document or documents it belongs to.

This attribute is called "type", and is a list of names stating which documents it belongs to. For example:

```
  ...
<chapter type='sales techman'>
  ...
<paragraph type='sales'>
```

Since all of these elements contain the same attribute definition, a parameter entity is used to build and maintain the DTD:

```
  ...
<!ENTITY  % types       'type NAMES #IMPLIED'                  >
  ...
<!ATTLIST chapter      date         CDATA           #IMPLIED
                       %types;
                       author       CDATA           #IMPLIED >
<!ATTLIST paragraph    %types;                                 >
  ...
<chapter>
```

This eliminates redundant coding, and simplifies maintenance. Care should be taken, however, to check the use of parameter entities; the first-time reader of the DTD might spend a considerable amount of time moving between the parameter entity reference and its declaration to determine what the value is. As always, clear documentation will assist in this process.

DTD Fragments

Certain element structures are shared by many different documents. Things like tables, equations, and graphics could have a common structure throughout the organization. It is possible to maintain a library of such structures and call them by reference in each DTD that needs them.

An example is the inclusion of a company-wide general table DTD fragment:

```
<!DOCTYPE sales-manual [
<!ELEMENT sales-manual - -          (title, chapter+)          >
<!ELEMENT title        - O          (#PCDATA)                  >
<!ELEMENT chapter      - -          (title, paragraph+)        >
<!ELEMENT paragraph    - O          (#PCDATA)        +(table)  >
<!ENTITY   % table-fragment                              SYSTEM
           '\user\book\sgml\table.DTD'                          >
 %table-fragment;
]>
  ...
```

Care should be taken to assure that there are no elements declared in the fragment that are also declared in the body of the DTD. It is just as important to make sure that all elements in the fragment are declared either there or in the DTD body. In other words, all common elements that should be declared are declared only once.

Start-tag Omission

The ability to minimize markup, actually leave out tags that can be implied, can sometimes be more of a problem than it is worth. In the early days before SGML-smart formatting editors took care of typing and hiding tags, a lot of markup in your documents seemed burdensome to enter and sift through while reading the text. The Standard developers were very smart to allow tag minimization to solve this problem. The need for minimization is lessened somewhat by the tools now available to apply and manage the tags. In fact, many SGML-smart editors do not support minimization.

Start-tag minimization can be especially problematic in that using it makes your application more complex. Resolving parsing errors can sometimes be difficult because of minimized start tags. Until you are familiar with the Standard, the results of minimized start tags may seem unusual.

In the following example, the DTD designer has chosen to make the `<name>` element both start- and end-tag minimizable. It seems obvious that the first thing that will, and must, occur in the chapter is a name. It is required, so its start-tag can be omitted. Start-tags can only be omitted from required elements. So in the DTD, the designer has set start tag-minimized to "O" for ommitable. (Note: the start-tag minimized indicator only tells the parser whether to report an error if the tag is missing. It does not change whether the tag is omissible or not. That is determined by the logic of the content model(s) in which the element is used. See *Omitted Tag Minimization* on page 230 for more information on the use of this feature.)

Since the start-tag for name can be omitted, the author created a document instance with two chapters, both without the <name>start-tag. But, the second <name>start-tag caused unexpected results. This is due to the <e>start-tag occurring immediately after the <chap>start-tag before any #PCDATA occurred.

```
<!DOCTYPE book [
<!ELEMENT book      - -      (chap+)          >
<!ELEMENT chap      - O      (name, p+)  +(e) >
<!ELEMENT name      O O      (#PCDATA)        >
<!ELEMENT p         - O      (#PCDATA)        >
<!ELEMENT e         - -      (#PCDATA)        >
]>
<book>
<chap>Name Text
<p>Paragraph text.
<chap>
<e>Bold
</e>Name Text
<p>Paragraph text.
</book>
```

A start tag is implied by the occurrence of what it contains, in this case, #PCDATA. The parser recognized the <e>to be included in chap, not name. The following is what the parser saw:

```
(BOOK
(CHAP
(NAME
-Name Text
)NAME
(P
-Paragraph text.
)P
)CHAP
(CHAP
(E
-Bold
```

```
)E
(NAME
-Name Text
)NAME
(P
-Paragraph text.
)P
)CHAP
)BOOK
C
```

This is not an error, but it might be a problem if your application is treating emphasized text differently in chap than in name. You can see how easy it is for start-tag minimization not to work as you might first expect. We suggest the following advice—when in doubt, do not leave it out.

In this example, you could require that authors enter the start tag only where the first thing inside of the name is an emphasized phrase that begins with the <e> tag. This rule is, however, hard to explain and enforce. A better solution would be to not allow start-tag minimization for the <name> element.

Another solution is to put the inclusion lower in the hierarchy. By moving it to the name and p elements, the correct result is obtained:

```
<!DOCTYPE book [
<!ELEMENT book       - -        (chap+)              >
<!ELEMENT chap       - O        (name, p+)           >
<!ELEMENT name       O O        (#PCDATA)       +(e) >
<!ELEMENT p          - O        (#PCDATA)       +(e) >
<!ELEMENT e          - -        (#PCDATA)            >
]>
<book>
<chap>Name Text
<p>Paragraph text.
<chap>
<e>Bold
</e>Name Text
<p>Paragraph text.
</book>

(BOOK
(CHAP
(NAME
-Name Text
)NAME
(P
-Paragraph text.
```

```
)P
)CHAP
(CHAP
(NAME
(E
-Bold
)E
-Name Text
)NAME
(P
-Paragraph text.
)P
)CHAP
)BOOK
C
```

Recursion

Recursion is the repeated nesting of elements inside of each other. For instance, a paragraph may contain lists, and lists contain list items, and list items may contain paragraphs. This nesting cannot be indefinite; the number of open elements cannot exceed the TAGLVL quantity defined in the SGML declaration.

It is good to allow recursion in some instances, such as the example above. But unintentional recursion can cause problems. For example, in the DTD below footnotes have been included into the paragraph element. And, since footnotes contain paragraphs in this example, that means a footnote can contain a footnote. This recursion is probably not a good idea, unless your model really does allow footnotes inside of footnotes.

```
<!DOCTYPE section [
<!ELEMENT section     - -        (para+)              >
<!ELEMENT para        - 0        (#PCDATA)      +(fn) >
<!ELEMENT fn          - -        (para+)              >
]>
<section>
<para>Paragraph text.
<para>Paragraph text with footnote
<fn>
<para>Paragraph text in a footnote.
<fn>
<para>Paragraph text in a footnote in a footnote
(two levels deep, probably an error).
</fn>
<para>More paragraph text in a footnote
```

```
</fn>text.
</para>
</section>
```

Aside from the logical considerations, there is a more insidious and subtle issue with this example. If a user were to leave off the end footnote tag for a footnote, the following material would erroneously be considered part of the footnote. If that material is tagged as paragraphs, it would not cause a parsing error since paragraphs are allowed in the footnote in this DTD. The parser would not report an error until it encounters an element that is not allowed in a footnote, which could be much later. The users might not even notice the error until they had a chance to look at composed pages, and even then it is not guaranteed that they will notice it at all.

The footnote in the third paragraph would be a footnote in a paragraph in a footnote in a paragraph. You could build a program that counts footnote start and end tags and if it comes up with two different numbers go hunting for the problem. Or you could design this program to report when two footnote start tags occur without an end tag somewhere in between them. Or you could let the parser do this. If you add an exclusion to the footnote that excludes footnote from itself, as seen in the following example:

```
 ...
<!ELEMENT fn          - -          (para+)          -(fn) >
 ...
```

The parser will report an error when the second <fn>occurs:

```
valid.sgm:7:15:E: start tag for `PARA' omitted, but its
declaration does not permit this
valid.sgm:7:15: open elements: PARA FN (PARA[ 1] )
valid.sgm:8:15:E: end tag for `PARA' omitted, but its
declaration does not permit this
valid.sgm:7:15: start tag was here
valid.sgm:8:15: open elements: PARA FN PARA[ 1]
```

The error, however, will not be reported if a footnote end tag is not required and the footnote occurs near the end of the instance.

Another approach would be to assign a different name to the paragraph inside of footnotes, perhaps <fnp>would work. This type of solution increases the number of elements, which may prove undesirable if you have a lot of areas where recursion can occur.

Mixed Content

An element is said to have element content if its declaration has a content model and the special token #PCDATA does not appear in the content model. The content of such an element can include sub-elements, processing instructions, and various forms of markup such as general entity references, character entity references, and marked sections.

The standard defines "mixed content" as content consisting of data characters, elements, or certain declarations.

Mixed content is warned against frequently due to the unexpected results that may be encountered[1] Clause 11.2.4 of the standard recommends that "...`#PCDATA` be used only when data characters are to be permitted anywhere in the content of the element; that is, in a content model where it is the sole token, or where **or** is the only connector used in any model group". It goes on to say "This recommendation is made because separator characters, which are recognized as separators in element content, are treated as data in mixed content". In other words, when this recommendation is not followed, there are elements in which separator characters (spaces, tabs, and carriage returns) are considered to be errors in contexts in which they would be ignored if they were permitted. The resulting error can be very confusing.

The following example illustrates the mixed-content problem:

```
  ...
<!ELEMENT para          - O           (title, #PCDATA)          >
<!ELEMENT title         - -           (#PCDATA)                 >
  ...
<para>
<title>Getting Started
The first step in the analysis is choosing the appropriate
people to perform the task.
```

Notice the content model for `<para>`. It shows that a `title` is followed by parsed character data. The parser will issue three errors for this[2]:

1. The title start tag was implied by the data, but was not minimizable.
2. A title tag was encountered out of context.
3. The title end tag was implied by the data, but was not minimizable.

Why? The problem is the newline between the `<para>`and `<title>`tags. The parser interprets this as character data, which is not allowed in a paragraph before the title (remember, in mixed, content, space characters are recognized

1 Mixed content issues are described in detail in Element Content vs. Mixed Content, by John McFadden and Ronald Hater, page 12, Issue 5 of <TAG>, The SGML Newsletter.

2 Actually, the standard does not specify an error recovery strategy, so any error after the first is not possible to predict. However, most available parsers have some form of recovery, and they seem to work in predictable ways.

as data). So, the parser thinks the newline is `#PCDATA` for `title`, which generates the first error. The parser generates its own `title` tag. Then, when the actual `<title>`comes along, the `title` part of the content model has been satisfied and the parser notes that title is not allowed twice in a row.

There are at least three ways to get around this problem:

1. **Make sure there are no data characters between the para and title tags**. This is often difficult to achieve, since there could be various applications that might process the data and inadvertently put a newline there.
2. **Modify the content model so that it is a repeatable "or" group**. This will solve the mixed content, but it might not give you what you want.

```
  ...
<!ELEMENT para        - 0        (title | #PCDATA)+       >
  ...
```

In this case, the content model has been loosened to allow multiple titles and data, interspersed in any order:

```
  ...
<para>
<title>Getting Started
</title>
The first step in the analysis is choosing the appropriate
people to perform the task.
<title>Doing the analysis
</title>
As you analyze the documents, make sure that a dictionary of
terms is available.
</para>
```

This is probably not what you want, since the original content model stated that a paragraph contains a single title followed by words. By loosening the DTD, the mixed content problem is avoided, but the application might have trouble dealing with multiple titles in a single paragraph.

3. **Get rid of the mixed content altogether**. By introducing another level of structure (and another element), you can avoid the mixed content problem and still describe the structure properly.

   The DTD and instance:

```
<!DOCTYPE para [
<!ELEMENT para        - 0        (title, text)            >
<!ELEMENT title       - 0        (#PCDATA)                >
<!ELEMENT text        0 0        (#PCDATA)                >
```

```
]>
<para>
<title>Getting Started
</title>
The first step in the analysis is choosing the appropriate
people to perform the task.
```

Notice the addition of a new element, text. This is declared as start- and end-tag omissible. By doing this, the input is exactly the same as it was in the first instance, but, by adding the extra element, the mixed-content problem is fixed, and the structure is what was originally intended. For a warning, see *Start-tag Omission* on page 308.

We recommend against the use of mixed content when possible. In many situations another solution may exist. You should explore other possibilities before using mixed content.

Ambiguous Content Models

Consider the following content model for a chapter. The designer wanted to force the authors to insert a caution if a note was the first thing following a title. Inside the chapter, however, paragraphs, lists and notes are allowed in any order:

```
(title, (note, caution)?, (paragraph | list | note)+)
```

This is an ambiguous content model because the first note that appears could be interpreted as either being the one before the caution or the one in the body of the paragraph.

There is always a work-around for ambiguous content models. In the case above, the content model could be re-written to take the two possibilities into account. If a note is the first element, then a caution must follow it. If a list or a paragraph is the first item, no caution is required:

```
(title, ((note, caution, (paragraph | list | note)+) |
((paragraph | list), (paragraph | list | note)+)))
```

Notice the parentheses around each group. This is to avoid the error of using different connectors at the same level. Now, if the parser sees a note first, the first "or" group will be used. If it sees a paragraph or a list first, the second "or" group will be used.

Ambiguous content models are sometimes very difficult to detect, and even harder to fix. In order to correct the problems, it is necessary to break down the desired content into its primary pieces, and build the model from there. It might be necessary to create new elements to avoid the problem, or, as above, create two groups, separated by an "or", which provides an unambiguous path for the parser.

Using CDATA and RCDATA Elements

For both CDATA and RCDATA, any text that looks like an end tag will close the element

```
<!DOCTYPE example [
<!ELEMENT example      - -          CDATA                    >
]>
<example>
<para>This text will be passed by the parser untouched
<footnote>That is, until it reaches the footnote end tag
</footnote>
</example>
<!-- error!                                                -->
```

The following errors are reported:

```
valid.sgm:8:21:E: end tag for element `FOOTNOTE' which is not
open
valid.sgm:8:21: open elements: EXAMPLE
```

The occurrence of an end-tag open (ETAGO) caused the parser to report an error, even though the CDATA element that was open was the example.

One way around this is to use RCDATA and declare an entity for the end tag open string: (</):

```
<!DOCTYPE example [
<!ELEMENT example      - -          RCDATA                   >
<!ENTITY    etago       '</'                                 >
]>
<example>
<para>This text will be passed by the parser untouched
<footnote>That is, until it reaches the footnote end
tag
 &etago;footnote>
</example>
```

Notice that declared content is not contained in a parentheses like a content model is.

Using Glue to Hold an SGML System Together.

CONVERT PROLOGUES FROM ONE FORM TO ANOTHER

The SGML standard allows several different methods for defining the prologue. Any SGML application is free to pick which of these to use. Inevitably, the two vendors you choose will pick incompatible methods.

A glue program that sits between these two programs can convert the files between the two formats. Consider the following tagged instance, which was created by a conversion program:

```
<chapter>The Moratorium on Brains
<para><quote>Where have you been all this time?</> Eddie Willers
asked the worker in the underground cafeteria, and added, with a
smile that was an appeal, an apology and a confession of
despair,
<quote>Oh, I know it's I who've stayed away from here for
weeks</quote>.
```

This is a chapter that is to be contained in a part in side of a book. However, without the DTD, it is impossible to know this. An SGML editor must know where the prologue is in order to process the file. So, a glue program is required to add it:

```
<!DOCTYPE chapter "book.dtd" [
<!ENTITY apos "'" >
]>
<chapter>The Moratorium on Brains
<para><quote/Where have you been all this time?/ Eddie Willers
asked the worker in the underground cafeteria, and added, with a
smile that was an appeal, an apology and a confession of
despair,
<quote>Oh, I know it&apos;s I who&apos;ve stayed away from here
for
weeks</>.
```

In this case, the glue program also noticed that there was an entity reference in the file that was not contained in the prologue. It created an entity declaration for this, and put it in the generated prologue.

This type of manipulation is easy to undo by just removing the generated prologue. Some types of processing, like normlizing and some pre-processing, are not so easy to undo.

NORMALIZE SGML INSTANCES

Refering to the example above, notice that the file has some minimization. If this file is to be loaded into an application that does not support minimization, it must be normalized. A glue program can do this easily.

```
<!DOCTYPE chapter "book.dtd" [
<!ENTITY apos  "'" >
]>
<chapter><title>The Moratorium on Brains</title>
<para><quote>Where have you been all this time?</quote> Eddie
Willers asked the worker in the underground cafeteria, and
added, with a smile that was an appeal, an apology and a
confession of despair, <quote>Oh, I know it&apos;s I
who&apos;ve stayed away from here for weeks</quote>.</para>
</chapter>
```

Pre-process Files for a Future Step

Glue can be used to add additional information to the SGML file that is to be processed by a program that lacks the intelligence. For example, a loose-leaf system has strict requirements to assure that material that is added or deleted maintain the proper paragraph and title labels. A section added between 1.2 and 1.3 becomes 1.2a. A typesetter that uses FOSI instances might have difficulty generating title labeling in a loose-leaf environment. A glue program that has the intelligence to do this processing can manipulate the file so that it can be sent to the typesetter.

```
<!DOCTYPE chapter "book.dtd" [
<!ENTITY apos  "'" >
]>
<chapter label='VII' revision-level=3><title>The Moratorium
on Brains</title>
<para><quote>Where have you been all this time?</quote> Eddie
Willers asked the worker in the underground cafeteria, and
added, with a smile that was an appeal, an apology and a
confession of despair, <quote>Oh, I know it&apos;s I
who&apos;ve stayed away from here for weeks</quote>.</para>
</chapter>
```

Entity Management

An entity in an SGML system is anything from a character to the entire system. Managing entities is a task that can be made easier by using glue. Consider a database that contains hundreds of chapters on a particular topic. Consider a publisher who wants to create a book designed for a particular segment of the market. The publisher queries the database and determines that five chapters need to be pulled out to create the book.

A glue program can create a "hub file" that puts together these five chapters for a single processing run.

```
<!DOCTYPE book "book.dtd" [
<!ENTITY  chap1  "/usr/chaps/id-3112.sgm"                    >
<!ENTITY  chap2  "/usr/chaps/id-4626.sgm"                    >
<!ENTITY  chap3  "/usr/chaps/id-3458.sgm"                    >
<!ENTITY  chap4  "/usr/chaps/id-9845.sgm"                    >
<!ENTITY  chap5  "/usr/chaps/id-4717.sgm"                    >
]>
<book><title>The Utopia of Greed</title>
&chap1;
&chap2;
&chap3;
&chap4;
&chap5;
</book>
```

See *Managing Documents using "Hub Files"* on page 324 for more information on hub files.

Omitted Attribute Specifications

SGML enforces a rule that prohibits the use of the same name token in more than one group in an attribute definition list. Consider the following attribute definition list declaration and markup:

```
<!DOCTYPE section [
<!ELEMENT section      - O          ANY                          >
<!ATTLIST section      type         (userman |
                                    techman |
                                    salesman)        'techman'
                       status       (draft |
                                    final)           #REQUIRED
                       printable    (yes | no)       'yes'       >
]>
<section type='userman' status='final'>
```

However, using attribute name omission, the name of the attribute is not required, as long as the declared value is a token list. Note that the same tagging could be achieved using the following markup, which employs attribute specification omission:

```
  ...
<section userman final>
```

The reason all name tokens must be unique can be illustrated with the following attribute definition list declaration:

```
    ...
<!-- illegal ATTLIST declaration                                          -->
<!ATTLIST appendix    tocentry     (yes | no)          'yes'
                      verified     (yes | no)          'no'
                      fullwidth    (yes | no)          'no'     >
    ...
```

If this was possible, the markup, with omissible attribute names, would look like this:

```
    ...
<appendix yes yes no>
<!-- error!                                                               -->
```

The following errors are reported by SGML-S

```
valid.sgm:7:29:E: token `YES' occurs more than once in attribute
definition list
valid.sgm:7:29:E: token `NO' occurs more than once in attribute
definition list
valid.sgm:8:30:E: token `YES' occurs more than once in attribute
definition list
valid.sgm:8:30:E: token `NO' occurs more than once in attribute
definition list
valid.sgm:10:29:E: duplicate specification of attribute
`TOCENTRY'
valid.sgm:10:31:E: duplicate specification of attribute
`TOCENTRY'
```

Since attributes can be listed in any order, it is not clear to the parser which attributes are yes and which are no. We have seen people get around this limitation by coming up with synonyms for yes and no, in order to achieve the same effect:

```
    ...
<!ATTLIST appendix    tocentry     (yes | no)          'yes'
                      verified     (yup | nope)        'nope'
                      fullwidth    (da | nyet)         'da'     >
    ...
<appendix>
```

There is a better way to do this, without the requirement for creating silly values. The trick is to change the "question" being answered by the attribute value:

```
    ...
```

```
<!ATTLIST appendix   tocentry    (tocentry |
                                 notocentry)      'tocentry'
                     verified    (verified |
                                 noverified)      'noverified'
                     fullwidth   (fullwidth |
                                 nofullwidth)     'nofullwidth'>
...
```

The attribute definition list declaration looks funny, but the markup can be minimized, giving the reader a meaningful tag:

```
...
<appendix notocentry verified fullwidth>
```

Uses for Empty Elements

External Graphics

An empty element can be used to indicate the placement of an external file at a particular point in the document instance. Consider the following:

```
...
<!ELEMENT illustration - -     (artwork, title)         >
<!ELEMENT title        - O     (#PCDATA)                >
<!ELEMENT artwork      - O     EMPTY                    >
<!ATTLIST artwork      id      ID             #REQUIRED
                       name    ENTITY         #REQUIRED >
<!ENTITY    implant    SDATA
        '/usr/pics/dental/implant.tiff'                 >
...
<illustration>
<artwork id='D1005' name='implant'>
<title>Dental implants
</title>
</illustration>
```

The `artwork` element is declared as `EMPTY`, but contains two important attributes:

1. **id**. The unique identifier for the element, which will be used in the next example, and
2. **name**. an entity attribute that points to an external data file.

Upon encountering this markup in the document instance, the application produces code to produce the following output:

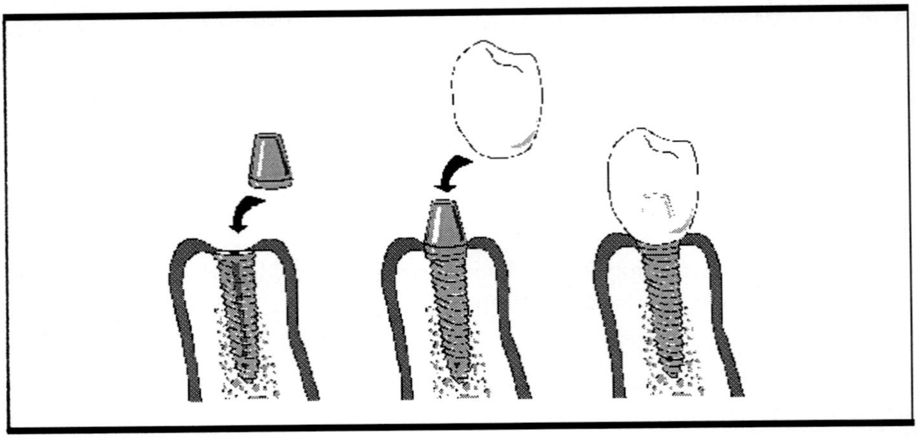

Figure 83. *Dental implants*

The application would need to perform the following tasks to produce this output:

1. use the information in the entity declaration to retrieve, in this case, a physical TIFF file (`/usr/pics/dental/implant.tiff`) and place it in the proper position,
2. increment the figure counter and outputs the caption line,
3. make a note of the value of the `id` and the `title` and the fact that it is figure 83 on page 322.

The application is doing all of the work of retrieving the graphic and remembering the position, but the parser is giving the application everything it needs in a very portable manner. In keeping with the device-independent nature of SGML, the processing is kept separate from the instance file.

CROSS-REFERENCES

When referring to elements in the same document, an author could place the text directly in-line:

See Figure 83, Dental implants, on page 322 for more information.

However this requires that the author print the book first, in order to get the page number and figure number. Then, if something should cause one of those numbers change, for example, the re-ordering of graphics, the author would need to correct the reference text. What often happens in these situations is that the latter does not get done properly, and the reference ends up pointing to a page with no graphic.

An empty element can be used to provide a pointer for the application so that it can generate the appropriate output. Consider the use of a cross-reference that prints the name of the figure and its title:

```
  ...
<!ELEMENT xref        - 0        EMPTY                  >
<!ATTLIST xref        ref        IDREF         #REQUIRED>
  ...
See
<xref ref='D1005'> for more information.
```

The following can be generated by the application:

See Figure 83, Dental implants, on page 322 for more information.

The application would need to perform the following tasks to produce this output:

1. access the IDREF attribute ref and look up the corresponding value saved in the previous example,
2. use the saved information to generate the replacement text.

Again, the application is doing the work of outputting the reference text, but the parser is making the information available, and assuring that there is a valid ID with the value specified.

Part Numbers

In a technical manual, it is important to assure that certain items be accurately defined. A part number is an example of something that, if it is mis-keyed, could cause anything from a minor annoyance to a major catastrophe.

Most organizations that have parts have some kind of database where the information about parts are kept. Information such as description, quantity on-hand, pricing and warehousing locations may be standardized. An empty element can be used to generate the appropriate text and assure that the part number is valid by allowing the application to query the database.

Consider the following:

```
<!DOCTYPE step [
<!ELEMENT step        - -        (#PCDATA)       +(part) >
<!ELEMENT part        - 0        EMPTY                   >
<!ATTLIST part        n          NUTOKEN       #REQUIRED >
]>
<step>Insert
<part n='630-112A'>
into bone.
</step>
```

The application provides the following output:

Insert threaded foundation pin into bone.

The application would need to perform the following tasks to produce this output:

1. access the n attribute and formulate a query of the appropriate database,
2. query the database, asking for the description of the part, and
3. replace the empty element tag with the results of the query.

This example shows the power of SGML in its ability to pass enough information to the application to perform such a feat. If the query returns an error, the application could be instructed to halt processing or write something to an error log indicating a bad part number.

Another advantage of this approach is that it puts the intelligence where it is most appropriate: in the structured markup. Suppose the company replaces the "threaded foundation pin" with a new, improved "threaded titanium foundation pin". If the name of the part was maintained as text in the SGML instance, it would need to be changed everywhere. By using the technique described here, only the name of the item in the database would need to be changed. Then, the next time the document is printed, the application will place the new name in the output stream.

FORMATTING INFORMATION

Some formatting information can be captured using empty elements. A common use is in the area of loose-leaf publishing, where an indication that a page is starting must be kept in the instance.

In a typical case, the page-break tag contains a page number in order to provide the loose-leaf publishing system with a starting point:

```
<pagebreak n='5-12.1' squeeze-factor='85%'>
```

This tag also has an attribute that indicates the amount of tightening should be performed in order to keep recent additions from generating another page (point page).

Managing Documents using "Hub Files"

To ease in the management of an SGML document instance, it is possible to create a central document that uses entity references to include external files into a single processing run.

THE HUB FILE CONCEPT

Consider the following DTD for a novel:

```
<!DOCTYPE book [
<!ELEMENT book        - -        (title, intro?, chapter+)  >
<!ELEMENT chapter     - -        (title, para+)             >
<!ELEMENT intro       - -        (para+)                    >
<!ELEMENT title       O O        (#PCDATA)                  >
<!ELEMENT para        - O        (#PCDATA)       +(quote)   >
<!ELEMENT quote       - -        (#PCDATA)                  >
]>
 ...
```

And the following instance[1]:

```
<!DOCTYPE book SYSTEM "novel.DTD" [
]>
<book>The Strike
<chapter>The Aristocracy of Pull
<para>The calendar in the sky beyond the window of her office
said: September 2.
<para>She had looked at that distant page every evening in the
months behind her.
</chapter>
</book>
```

The parser uses the external identifier to load the proper DTD file and process the instance. Consider the situation where all of the chapters are being written independently and are located in separate files:

```
<!DOCTYPE book SYSTEM "novel.DTD" [
<!ENTITY    theme      SYSTEM
          '/usr/GreatAmericanNovel/TheTheme.SGML'              >
<!ENTITY    chain      SYSTEM
          '/usr/GreatAmericanNovel/TheChain.SGML'              >
<!ENTITY    topbottom  SYSTEM
          '/usr/GreatAmericanNovel/TopAndBottom.SGML'          >
<!ENTITY    immovable  SYSTEM
          '/usr/GreatAmericanNovel/ImmovableMovers.SGML'       >
<!ENTITY    climax     SYSTEM
```

1 From "Atlas Shrugged", Ayn Rand

```
          '/usr/GreatAmericanNovel/Climax.SGML'              >
<!ENTITY    exploit    SYSTEM
          '/usr/GreatAmericanNovel/Exploiters.SGML'          >
]>
<book>The Strike
<intro>
<para>What happens when the prime movers of the world go on
strike?
</intro>
 &theme;
 &chain;
 &topbottom;
 &immovable;
 &climax;
 &exploit;
</book>
```

This is what we call a "hub file". It is a small base file that contains all of the structure for the document, but refers to the bulk of the overall instance only by entity reference. This allows the chapters to be maintained separately and incorporated into the whole when necessary. If a chapter is not quite finished, it becomes easy in the hub file to comment-out one of the entity references:

```
<!-- %topbottom; -->
```

The chapters can be parsed separately using the same DTD by using the following technique:

```
<!DOCTYPE chapter SYSTEM "novel.DTD" [
]>
<chapter>The Sacred and the Profane
<para>She looked at the glowing bands on the skin of her arm,
spaced like bracelets from her wrists to her shoulder.
  ...
</chapter>
```

Notice that the document type declaration indicates that the parser is to begin with the chap tag, not the book tag. In other words, the document type name indicates where the parser is to start building its tree. And, since extra unused element declarations are allowed, there is no conflict with the book element declaration.

Note: If an element has an exception at a point in the DTD that is higher than the starting position, then the exception will not be known by the parser. Suppose the above example had a footnote element inclusion on the book tag:

```
<!DOCTYPE book [
<!ELEMENT book        - -          (title, intro?, chapter+)
```

```
                                                          +(footnote) >
<!ELEMENT chapter      - -          (title, para+)                    >
<!ELEMENT intro        - -          (para+)                           >
<!ELEMENT title        O O          (#PCDATA)                         >
<!ELEMENT footnote     - -          (#PCDATA)                         >
<!ELEMENT para         - O          (#PCDATA)             +(quote)    >
<!ELEMENT quote        - -          (#PCDATA)                         >
]>
<book>The Strike
<chapter>The Aristocracy of Pull
<footnote>Published 1957
</footnote>
<para>
The calendar in the sky beyond the window of her office said:
September 2.
<para>
She had looked at that distant page every evening in the months
behind her.
</chapter>
</book>
```

The instance could be coded like this:

```
<!DOCTYPE book SYSTEM "novel.DTD" [
]>
<book>The Strike
<chapter>The Aristocracy of Pull
<footnote>Published 1957
</footnote>
<para>
The calendar in the sky beyond the window of her office said:
September 2.
<para>
She had looked at that distant page every evening in the months
behind her.
</chapter>
</book>
```

Recall that inclusions are valid in the element in which they are declared, as well as any descendants of the element unless specifically excluded. The example above would not create an error, since the document started at the book level and the footnote occurred at the chapter level, which is a descendant of book. However, if the chapter was processed by itself— using a chapter document type as shown earlier—the parser would issue an error upon encountering the footnote, since the book element declaration is bypassed.

Generate Public Identifier Mapping Files

When an application uses public entities, some sort of mapping function must be provided to the application so it knows how to resolve the public identifiers into some kind of system equivalent. It is possible, in the `PUBLIC` identifier area of an external identifier, to indicate an equivalent system identifier:

```
<!DOCTYPE example PUBLIC "-//SIG//DTD Brian and Dale's Excellent
DTD//EN" "\usr\doctypes\excellent.DTD" [
]>
  ...
```

In the above example, the second string, `"/usr/doctypes/excellent.DTD"`, indicates that the application should use this as the system identifier to find the entity file. If the file cannot be found, the public identifier is used.

If a system identifier is not specified in the public identifier, some kind of mapping that is external to the SGML file is required. Without such a mapping, the application can not know where to find the physical representation of the entity described in the public entity.

The SGML standard does not provide a standard way to indicate such mapping, so each vendor's approach is a little different. In an environment that supports more than one of these applications, a mapping file must be kept for each environment.

The problem with this environment containing multiple configurations is that, if a mapping pair should change, all mapping files must be updated with the appropriate information. To avoid such a state, it is possible to configure some kind of master mapping database from which each vendor's mapping file is generated.

At its simplest, public entity mapping is a one-to-one correlation between a public identifier and its system equivalent. Most mapping techniques use this approach:

1. **Exoterica OmniMark**. The `library` declaration contains sets of public identifiers and the system equivalent.

   ```
   library
   "-//SIG//DTD Brian and Dale's Excellent DTD//EN"
       "excellen.DTD"
   "-//SIG//TEXT The SGML Implementation Guide//EN"
       "working\book.sgm"
   "-//SIG//TEXT Brian and Dale's Excellent Front Matter//EN"
       "working\frontm.sgm"
   ```

2. **SGML-S**. A catalog file adhering to the SGML Open Draft Technical Resolution on Entity Management.

   ```
   PUBLIC "-//SIG//DTD Brian and Dale's Excellent DTD//EN"
   ```

```
"excellen.DTD"
```

3. **ArborText Adept•Editor**. The `entities.map` file contains sets of pointers to the public identifier, followed by the public identifier.

```
../entities/iso-dia.gml
    ISO 8879-1986//ENTITIES Diacritical Marks//EN
../entities/iso-dia.gml
    ISO 8879:1986//ENTITIES Diacritical Marks//EN
```

4. **SoftQuad Author/Editor**. The `*.map` files provide a programmatic way of mapping external identifiers to system identifiers. SoftQuad uses a pattern-matching language that can resolve many public identifiers to a single system equivalent.

```
"ISO 8879-1986//ENTITIES Added Latin 1//EN" ~ isolat1.ent
"ISO 8879-1986//ENTITIES Added Latin 2//EN" ~ isolat2.ent
~ (.*)\.DTD \1.rls
".*" (.*)\.DTD \1.rls
```

It is straightforward, then, to create a generic mapping file that can be used to create all of the appropriate mapping files automatically whenever the maps are changed.

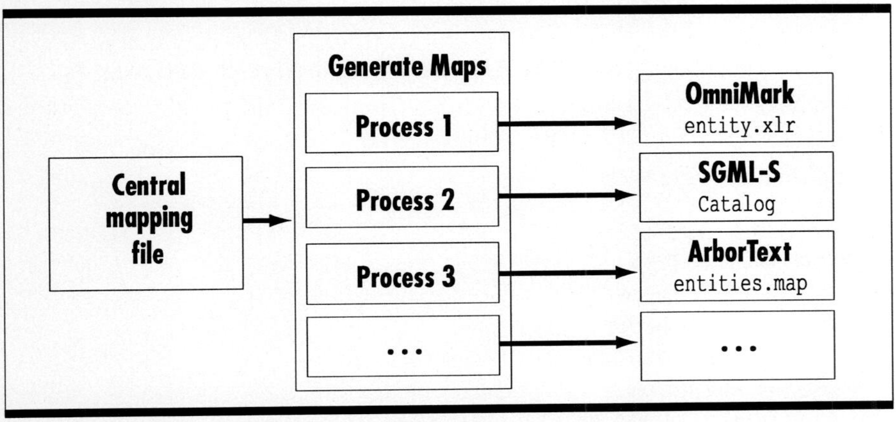

Figure 84. *Creating Multiple Entity Mapping Files*

The illustration above shows the system that tracks `PUBLIC` identifiers. A master "database" of identifier mapping pairs is kept in an easily maintainable form. When an identifier is added or changed, a program is run that reads the database and creates a mapping file for each SGML application in the form that the application requires.

The format of this central mapping file can be whatever you want it to be since only the map-generation program needs to work with it. It might make sense to choose the one that the SGML Open consortium is recommending, since that is probably what all vendors will use eventually.

There are schemes that use a pattern-matching language to create a more active mapping between identifiers. SoftQuad's Author/Editor uses such an approach. It is possible, using the technique above, to incorporate this type of ambiguous mapping, but beware that, unless all applications support this type of feature, the automatic generation of system identifier equivalents is more difficult.

Using Short Reference Minimization

Short reference minimization (SHORTREF) can be used to generate large amounts of detailed tagging without requiring the tags to be specifically entered in the instance. SHORTREF can be used, even when SGML editorial workstations are available, to maintain highly structured data with a minimum of markup.

QUOTES

One place where short reference minimization is used is in tagging quoted material. See *Quotes* on page 295.

In a document, the author keys the following:

```
 ...
<para>
In accordance with "The Takings-impact Analysis" the bill is
revoked.
</para>
```

Using the following DTD:

```
 ...
<!ELEMENT para          - O          (#PCDATA)          +(quote) >
<!ELEMENT quote         - -          (#PCDATA)                   >
<!-- begin quote                                                -->
<!ENTITY     q-tag         '<quote>'                             >
<!-- end quote                                                  -->
<!ENTITY     end-q-tag     '</quote>'                            >
<!SHORTREF        para-map         '"'     q-tag   >
<!SHORTREF        quote-map        '"'     end-q-tag       >
<!USEMAP para-map          para>
<!USEMAP quote-map         quote>
 ...
```

The tagging above is replaced by the following:

```
 ...
<para>In accordance with
```

```
<quote>The Takings-impact Analysis
</quote>the bill is revoked.
</para>
```

Two entities, q-tag and end-q-tag are created. These entities are assigned to the short reference maps para-map and quote-map. The USEMAP declaration indicates that, when in an element called para, the para-map is active. The SHORTREF declaration indicates that, when para-map is active, a quote character (") is to be replaced with the value of an entity called q-tag. The next USEMAP, declaration indicates that, when the parser is in an element called quote, the quote-map is active. The SHORTREF declaration indicates that, when quote-map is active, a quote character is to be replaced with the value of an entity called end-q-tag. This is how a single character (") generates one tag in one context and another in a different context.

This multiple-level mapping seems cumbersome in this example, but it is possible to assign a set of characters to a single map, which becomes active in a state declared by the USEMAP declaration. See *Tables* on page 331

The advantage of short references, aside from the fact that they save characters, is that the input file looks more readable, because the markup has been replaced by natural keying conventions. Also, now that the SGML instance contains rich tagging for quotes, the application designer can use whatever style guidelines required to publish the document (for example, using typographical quotes or french quotes).

TABLES

Simple table tagging consists of specifying rows and cells within those rows. For long tables that contain short entries, short reference mapping makes the data more readable and easier to edit.

Consider the following example:

```
<!DOCTYPE table [
<!ENTITY     row          '<row><cell>'                          >
<!ENTITY     cell         '</cell><cell>'                        >
<!ENTITY     end-row      '</cell></row>'                        >
<!ENTITY     amp          '&'                                    >
<!SHORTREF        table-map       '('     row
                                  '|'     cell
                                  ')'     end-row >
<!USEMAP table-map       table>
<!ELEMENT table          - -          (thead, tbody)             >
<!ATTLIST table          columns      NUMBER            #REQUIRED>
<!ELEMENT thead          O O          (row)                      >
<!ELEMENT tbody          O O          (row+)                     >
<!ELEMENT row            - -          (cell+)                    >
```

```
<!ELEMENT cell          - -          (#PCDATA)                    >
]>
<table columns='3'>
(Form    |Record Keeping    |Preparing Form    )
(1120    |68 hrs., 24 mins. |70 hrs., 38 mins. )
(1120-A  |43 hrs.,  3 mins. | 4 hrs., 41 mins. )
(Sch. D  | 6 hrs., 56 mins. | 5 hrs., 46 mins. )
</table>
```

The parser sees the following:

```
ACOLUMNS TOKEN 3
(TABLE
(THEAD
(ROW
(CELL
-Form
)CELL
(CELL
-Record Keeping
)CELL
(CELL
-Preparing Form
)CELL
)ROW
)THEAD
(TBODY
(ROW
(CELL
-1120
)CELL
(CELL
-68 hrs., 24 mins.
)CELL
(CELL
-70 hrs., 38 mins.
)CELL
)ROW
(ROW
(CELL
-1120-A
)CELL
(CELL
-43 hrs.,  3 mins.
)CELL
```

```
(CELL
- 4 hrs., 41 mins.
)CELL
)ROW
(ROW
(CELL
-Sch. D
)CELL
(CELL
- 6 hrs., 56 mins.
)CELL
(CELL
- 5 hrs., 46 mins.
)CELL
)ROW
)TBODY
)TABLE
C
```

Notice that blanks were placed before the vertical bar in order to make the columns line up in the input. These are recognized as literals, which might need to be stripped by the application.

The table, when typeset, might look something like this:

Form	*Record Keeping*	*Preparing Form*
1120	68 hrs., 24 mins.	70 hrs., 38 mins.
1120-A	43 hrs., 3 mins.	4 hrs., 41 mins.
Sch. D	6 hrs., 56 mins.	5 hrs., 46 mins.

Table 23. *Time needed to file business-tax forms*

Using Processing Instructions the "Right Way"

Processing instructions are deprecated by the standard, but they exist anyway. The developers of SGML realized that it is better to provide a standard, system-independent way for implementors to indicate non-standard, system-dependent information than not to provide any means at all.

Since the standard has been out, we have seen some very intelligent uses of processing instructions. We have also seen some inappropriate uses, but this is to be expected.

SGML EDITORIAL WORKSTATION

When an editorial workstation saves an SGML file, it is confident that the file adheres to the rules set forth in the DTD. However, when it reads a file, it must assure that the instance is valid, because it has no idea if the process that created the file actually parsed it.

Data load time is one of the critical performance areas of an editorial workstation, since the operator is sitting at the terminal waiting. If the editorial workstation had to parse the document every time it loaded it, the load time would be increased, sometimes substantially. However, if the editorial workstation knew that it was the last program that touched the file, and knew that it parsed it then, it would be able to avoid the redundant step of parsing the file again at load time.

To this end, one SGML editorial workstation product writes a special processing instruction at the end of the file containing the size of the file and an indication of whether it was parsed satisfactorily. Then, once the file has been loaded, if the number of characters counted equals the value in the processing instruction, no parsing is done. However, if the size is different, the editorial workstation software assumes someone else has touched the file and parses it.

The processing instruction looks like this:

```
<?Pub *0000351108 0>
```

The keyword "Pub" is used by this vendor to identify its processing instructions, and ignores any others that might be in the file. The file size and a character indicating whether or not the file was parsed is contained in the processing instruction.

SGML DATA PRE-PROCESSOR

Suppose a complicated process required that the nesting level of certain elements and their relationship to other elements at their level be known. With all of the processing that must be done with the program, a pre-processor could be written that only calculates the element nesting level and the relationship of each element to its siblings.

For example, if a list contained three items, the first is 1 of 3, the second 2 of 3 and the last 3 of 3. Processing instructions can be used to communicate this level and sibling information to the next program, which uses the information and strips the processing instructions from the file.

The processing instruction looks like this:

```
<?OM SIBLING=1/5 LEVEL=4>
```

The keyword OM indicates the owner of the processing instruction. All other programs ignore this processing instruction, and this program ignores all others that might be in the file. The processing instruction above indicates that this is the first of five siblings under a common parent, and that the level of nesting for the siblings is four.

TYPESETTING SYSTEM

Suppose a typesetting program has a table formatting language that can create very complex tables at high speed. In the process of converting data from this typesetting format to SGML, processing instructions can be used to convey to the typesetter information that is difficult or impossible to code using the elements defined in the DTD. Since this typesetter would still be used to format the document to paper, the conversion people may leave some typesetter codes in the form of processing instructions to do some of the more critical formatting:

```
<?XY TS;0;5p;6p;14p>
```

The application can read the first two characters from the processing instruction to determine that this typesetter owns the data, then passes the system data straight to the typesetter.

This approach, while providing the necessary information to the typesetter, is what the designers of SGML had in mind when they deprecated the use of processing instructions. The main problem here is the system-dependence of a critical piece of information. Should the owners of the data want to create another form (like CD-ROM) from this data, they will have a hard time translating the typesetter code into something the CD-ROM production process can understand.

In a case such as this, using processing instructions is acceptable, as long as there is a commitment to remove them over time.

Using Marked Sections

CAUTIONS WHEN USING NESTED MARKED SECTIONS

Any marked section inside of an ignored marked section is ignored, regardless of the nested section's status keyword.

Be careful when including a marked section inside of a CDATA or RCDATA marked section:

```
...
<para>
<![ CDATA [Marked sections are declared like this:
<![ INCLUDE [there is an included marked section within
]]>They can be used to mark sections of text
]]>
<!-- error                                              -->
```

This generates the following errors:

```
valid.sgm:11:11:E: marked section end not in marked section
declaration
valid.sgm:11:11: open elements: PARA (#PCDATA[1])
```

Remember that a character data marked section only recognizes the end of the marked section, so it does not recognize that another marked section is nested, only that the markup ending the "nested" marked section is what it is looking for to end itself. The next marked section end generates an error because the parser has already been satisfied.

This is what the parser sees:

```
(PARA
-Marked sections are declared like this:\n\n[ INCLUDE [ there is
an included marked section within\n\nThey can be used to mark
sections of text\n
)PARA
```

PARAMETER ENTITIES

Status keywords can be specified with parameter entities, since they are part of a declaration. The use of parameter entities provides a powerful way of making the document useful for more than one version. In this way, marked sections can work like"smart comments", excluding and including material based on some global value that can be changed.

In the Document

Consider an SGML file that contains sales information along with some company-confidential marketing information. The information is maintained as a single file, since most of the information is shared between the two documents. However, in order to print the public version, the confidential information should be suppressed. Throughout the document, marked sections are placed around the confidential material. Instead of one of the status keywords defined above, a parameter entity is placed in the field:

```
...
<para>The product can accelerate from a standing stop to 50
meters per second
<![ %CONFIDENTIAL; [ , assuming we can get the accelerator to
work,
]]>without
the operator even noticing.
</para>
```

Then, in the prologue, a parameter entity is created:

```
...
```

```
<!ENTITY  % confidential  'IGNORE'                             >
  ...
```

The value of the parameter entity depends upon the desired output. Putting it together for the public version:

```
<!DOCTYPE product SYSTEM "\usr\doctypes\product.DTD" [
<!ENTITY  % confidential  'IGNORE'                             >
]>
<product>
<para>The product can accelerate from a standing stop to 50
meters per second
<![ %CONFIDENTIAL; [, assuming we can get the accelerator to
work,
]]>without the operator even noticing.
</product>
```

produces the following:

> *The product can accelerate from a standing stop to 50 meters per second without the operator even noticing.*

Changing the parameter entity to:

```
<!DOCTYPE product SYSTEM "\usr\doctypes\product.DTD" [
<!ENTITY  % confidential  'INCLUDE'                            >
]>
<product>
<para>The product can accelerate from a standing stop to 50
meters per second
<![ %CONFIDENTIAL; [, assuming we can get the accelerator to
work,
]]>without the operator even noticing.
</product>
```

produces the following:

> *The product can accelerate from a standing stop to 50 meters per second, assuming we can get the accelerator to work, without the operator even noticing.*

This type of construct can get more complex, as the document contains more overlaid sections. Beware, however, that marked sections can be nested, but cannot end before all nested sections end. The syntax of the language prevents such a situation, but the author needs to understand what the parser sees in order to avoid confusion.

In the DTD

Parameter entities can also be used to control the processing of the DTD, as well. Consider an application that requires mathematic entity declarations. In some applications, a local version of the math entities is required, and in some cases an external set of entities is required. The following fragment illustrates the point:

```
  ...
<!ENTITY  % external-math  'INCLUDE'                            >
<![ %EXTERNAL-MATH; [
<!ENTITY  % mathpack    SYSTEM  '\usr\doctypes\math.entities'  >
]]>
<!ENTITY  % mathpack    PUBLIC
          '-//USA-DOD//DTD SUP MIL-M-28001 MATHPACK 900102//EN' >
 %mathpack;
  ...
```

Remember that the second and subsequent declarations of the same entity are ignored. In this case, if the parameter entity "external-math" is set to `INCLUDE`, the entity "mathpack" is declared as a system identifier, and the re-definition of the "mathpack" entity is ignored.

However, if the parameter entity "external-math" is set to `IGNORE`, the first entity declaration for "mathpack" is ignored, and the entity declaration with a public identifier is used.

Using NOTATION for External Tables

Notations can be used to provide a standard means of managing non-SGML data.

Consider a system that uses a spreadsheet to create and maintain tabular data. This data is not readable by the SGML system, since it contains non-SGML data. It requires some kind of application to read the spreadsheet and make it useable by the SGML application.

Suppose there existed a program that can query the spreadsheet and return information based on the result of the query. What is returned can be turned, by the SGML application, into typesetting code to render on the page, or into screen-fulls of table information for electronic delivery.

In the DTD:

```
<!DOCTYPE table [
<!NOTATION   SSHTP     SYSTEM 'e:\apps\XLPROC.EXE'          >
<!NOTATION   DATAP     SYSTEM 'e:\apps\ACCPROC.EXE'         >
<!NOTATION   TEXTP     SYSTEM 'e:\apps\ASCPROC.EXE'         >
<!ELEMENT table        - -         RCDATA                   >
<!ENTITY     list       SDATA
        'c:\usr\data\excel\filelist.xls'                    >
```

```
<!ATTLIST table          type        NOTATION           (sshtp |
                                     datap |
                                     textp)             'sshtp'
                         name        ENTITY             #REQUIRED
                         range       CDATA              #REQUIRED
                         columns     CDATA              #REQUIRED
                         extract     CDATA              #REQUIRED
                         sort        CDATA              #REQUIRED
                         hilite      CDATA              #REQUIRED
                         total       CDATA              #IMPLIED
                         format      CDATA              #IMPLIED >
]>
  ...
```

Notice the Type attribute of the table element. The special keyword NOTATION indicates that the value of the attribute must be one of the tokens listed in the declared value field for the attribute. Each one of these, in turn points to a notation processor defined in the notation declaration.

The instance looks like this:"

```
  ...
<table type='sshtp' name='List' range='file_list'
columns='File_Name [ Label=Subject] , Size, Date'
extract='Size>20000' sort='Size, order=d' hilite='File
Name=COMPUTER, Shade=3' total='Size, Underline=double,
Label=Total' format='Size=(align=right, number=comma)//
Date=(align=center, number=dd-Mmm-yy)//
#table=(Border=med-thick, align=center, Size=normal)//
#head-underline=thick, Highlight=bold, Size=large)'>
  ...
```

The result of all of this is that the parser returns valuable information to the application, which can then issue the proper query to the processor:

```
Notation: SSHTP e:\apps\XLPROC.EXE
Entity resolved: List SDATA c:\usr\data\excel\filelist.xls
```

The output from the application might look like this:

Subject	Size	Date
TALKENV	446,572	10-Sep-92
COMPUTER	37,627	15-Oct-91
SCIENCE	36,806	29-Nov-91
BUSINESS	23,676	30-Sep-91
ISSUES	22,670	28-Dec-91
Total	567,351	

Figure 85. *Sample output from notation application*

This table was created just by querying the spreadsheet; all of the information was external to the SGML file.

Tracking Information about Elements During DTD Development

Without getting into a debate about mixed content models, there are three basic kinds of elements: those that contain other elements, those that contain data, and those declared empty. An example of an element that contains other elements is:

```
...
<!ELEMENT coverpg      - O          (title, subtitle, author+)  >
<!ELEMENT (title | subtitle | author)
                       - O          (#PCDATA)                   >
...
```

An example of an element that contains data is:

```
...
<!ELEMENT title        - O          (#PCDATA)                   >
...
```

An empty element is:

```
...
<!ELEMENT glossref     - O          EMPTY                       >
...
```

While developing a DTD, we have found it helpful to identify which elements are containers, which are data, and which are empty. These distinctions are helpful when developing content models. By attaching some kind of suffix to each element name, creating a DTD becomes a little easier. For containing elements, you may want to attach a single hyphen (-) to the element name. For elements that contain data, attach a single period, and for empty elements, attach nothing. So, the above element declarations become:

```
  ...
<!ELEMENT coverpg-      - O          (title., paragraph.)
                                                +(glossref) >
<!ELEMENT title.        - O          (#PCDATA)              >
<!ELEMENT paragraph.    - O          (#PCDATA)              >
<!ELEMENT glossref      - O          EMPTY                  >
  ...
```

If the user finds the suffix annoying, a simple string replacement can be invoked to remove them from all element and attribute declarations and content models of the production version. It is a good idea, however, to maintain the original in case the DTD must be updated.

Using Ambiguity for Maximum Benefit

Certain situations require an ambiguous approach. A client had a number of documents with similar structure, but each document class had different names for each basic document element. In one document, a `book` contained `parts`, which contained `chapters` which contained `sub-chapters`. In another, a `book` contained `sections`, which contained `parts`, which contained `chapters`. There were dozens of variations, and the client did not want to invest in dozens of DTDs with their associated costs for development and maintenance. Another requirement was that more document classes would probably be defined, leading to more DTD development work.

Since all documents had similar hierarchical structure, a generic collective element called `<clump>`, could be used as a container for other `<clump>`elements or elements further down the hierarchy (like lists and paragraphs).

In use, authors will enter the `<clump>`tag with an attribute indicating which type of clump it is (chapter, part, section, etc.). This allows new document classes to be used without creating an entirely different DTD. A `#REQUIRED` attribute called `type` is used to indicate what type of element is being tagged.

The DTD looks something like this:

```
  ...
<!ELEMENT clump-        - O          (ttl?, (par | list |
                                     clump))                >
<!ATTLIST clump-        type         CDATA          #REQUIRED
                        id           ID             #IMPLIED
                        number       CDATA          #IMPLIED >
```

```
<!ELEMENT (ttl | par | list)
                    - -          (#PCDATA)           >
   ...
```

Other attributes are defined if references or unit numbers must be specified. The result of this effort is a single DTD that is able to define multiple documents accurately without requiring individual document analysis.

While this interim solution may seem to violate some fundamental concepts of SGML, in actual use this approach allows management to start capturing data in SGML. This approach is not meant to provide a long-lasting solution. Rather, it enables the documentation staff to analyze exactly what types of documents are currently being used, and to come up with a smaller set of structures to which editors will comply. In practice, this approach produced workable SGML files that could be translated to the formatting system for now, and a base of documents to use later when we want to normalize the structures and come up with a small set of customized DTDs.

A Tool to Assist in Accurate Document Analysis

Deductive reasoning involves going from the general to the specific. For example, "All dogs bark, Otto is a dog, therefore Otto must bark" is deductive. Inductive reasoning attempts to go from the specific to the general, and can be very inaccurate. Example: "Otto is a dog, Otto has spots, therefore all dogs have spots".

When analyzing documents for their intellectual elements, it may be difficult (or impossible) to use the more accurate form of reasoning, deduction, in order to define, categorize, and further define elements. We often settle for using scientific sampling of elements instead of examining every page or record in our analysis. Sampling results in a form of induction being applied, although the risk can be managed if done carefully and may outweigh the costs of deducing from a more thorough analysis.

When it is necessary to use a representative sample, we use a grid that lists all elements for the product class at hand and their occurrence in specific contexts. On one axis is the element name, and on the other is the context. Context may be publications within the class or scope of this DTD, or portions of a publication or data set that may use similar elements in different ways, as shown in the following simple example. The "X" indicates that an element occurs in that publication. The numbers indicate that there is an order in which the pubs occur. The indentation in element name indicates membership in a higher level element.

Element Name	*Pub A*	*Pub B*	*Pub C*	*Pub D*	*Pub E*	*Pub F*
Front	x		x	x	x	x
Preface	1		2	2	x	x
Intro	2		3	1	x	x
Credits	3		1		x	
Body	x	x	x	x	x	x
...	...	...	...	...	...	...

Table 24. *Deductive Reasoning in Document Analysis*

The grid tells us that if we intend to create an element declaration for front matter, we better look at Pubs A, C, D, E, and F. The DTD better allow them to occur in any order. We may need separate DTDs to specify a required order, or the order can be managed by database extraction.

A grid can be devised for many purposes. We may use a grid to categorize documents into types or classes, each class using the same DTD and composition and other processing modules (*e.g.*, Pub B may be excluded from this class if having no front matter is important). It is also a good way to establish the boundaries or scope of a project, *i.e.*, to explicitly list what information (publications) are included in this migration effort.

We have the authors or editorial assistants complete the grid since they know the rules for their information better than we do (*e.g.*, know if the order is required or not).

It is a way of downloading some institutional information that is useful for both DTD development and development of processes such as composition modules. One caveat, keep the list simple and do not try to create a tool that expresses everything a DTD does. That is the role of the DTD itself.

Use Table of Contents First

When doing document analysis, usually the best place to view the structure of an existing document is by looking at the table of contents of an existing book.

This will give not only the overall structure, but some indication of what words the author uses to describe each piece.

The Problems with Politics

In attempting to introduce SGML into an enterprise, the biggest problem is the contradictory agendas of the groups involved in the process.

We have seen far more implementation problems caused due to corporate politics and turf-saving than hardware, software, and system incompatibilities combined.

SGML provides a company with a means of saving or making a lot of money. Because of this, it is usually an easy sell to the financial and upper management people. However, getting the line employees to change the way they work is often difficult.

One key to successful implementation is to convince key people at each level of the benefits they will realize upon successful implementation. Then, let them be the evangelists for change.

Dealing with Floating Elements

When faced with the problem of dealing with looseleaf documents that are revised using change pages, there is an additional requirement in the publishing process that causes some SGML problems too. Because some elements may float to another page, they may appear in the printed document at a location that is not conforming to the DTD. This means that the DTD has to be modified to make these elements inclusions that can occur virtually anywhere. We've seen situations where a figure appears in the middle of a word because the word was hyphenated at the end of the page and the figure floated to the next page, before the rest of the hyphenated word.

Therefore we are faced with the problems of addressing the publishing requirements in our source file. It would be one thing if we just recomposed the segment again and allowed the float to happen naturally, but that would mean that we had to always use the same composition engine each time we prepared a change package. We also have to assume that we do not know why the element floated to a particular spot or in what the order of floated elements may be on a particular page, thus there is a requirement for an explicit indication of what the original composition system did to create the pages. While one solution is to make the elements that can float be an inclusion, this seems to be too much of a concession to the publishing process and could cause problems in other uses of the document source.

One solution we have used is to create an element that is allowed to occur anywhere in the instance, for example:

```
 ...
<!ELEMENT doc          - -          (front, body, rear?)
                                           +(location) >
 ...
<!ELEMENT location     - 0          EMPTY                >
<!ATTLIST location     idref        IDREF       #REQUIRED>
 ...
```

Here the element location can become a place holder that indicates where the element that is allowed to float actually occurred in the published document. In creating change pages, the location element can have text move around it when required for proper pagination. If a new version or revision is to be created, then the element would be ignored in the process and new ones created as needed.

While this is a concession to the publishing process, it seems a small price to pay since it preserves the original SGML DTD design and only adds one element, in this case the location element, to indicate pagination.

Using DOCTYPE ID to Fool Application

Elements that have an attribute with a declared value of `ID` and a default value of `#REQUIRED` will generate a parsing error if a unique value is not entered. An `ID` attribute is usually used as an anchor point that is referenced by an `IDREF` attribute. However, as a document is being authored, the value of a particular `ID` might not be known when the author wants to reference it.

Consider the following DTD and instance:

```
<!DOCTYPE idtest [
<!ELEMENT idtest      - O          (para | illus)+
                                                  +(illusref) >
<!ATTLIST idtest      id           ID             #REQUIRED>
<!ELEMENT para        - O          (#PCDATA)               >
<!ELEMENT illus       - O          EMPTY                   >
<!ATTLIST illus       id           ID             #REQUIRED
                      name         CDATA          #REQUIRED>
<!ELEMENT illusref    - O          EMPTY                   >
<!ATTLIST illusref    ref          IDREF          #REQUIRED>
]>
<idtest id='doc001'>
<para> This document illustrates the use of a #REQUIRED ID and
IDREF declared value.
<illus name='fig1' id='fig001'>
<para>As you can see in
<illusref ref='fig001'>, a #REQUIRED ID will cause a parsing
error if it is not present
</idtest>
```

Note that the id attribute in `idtest` and `illus` are both `#REQUIRED`, and that the ref attribute in `illustref` is `#REQUIRED`. Omitting any of these would generate a parsing error.

Now, suppose the author did not know the identifier of the illustration named `fig1` when he wrote the paragraph that pointed to it. He can do one of the following:

1. do not enter the ref attribute or enter the ref attribute as a null value (*e.g.*, `<illusref ref=''>`),
2. leave the `<illusref>` tag out altogether, or

3. enter a dummy value into the ref attribute

The first choice will generate a parsing error, which could possibly make it impossible to process through the application. The second choice will cause the document to parse properly, but there is a danger that the author will forget to add the tag once the id is known. The last choice is the best. By pointing to a dummy verbatim/id/, the parser will process the document properly. One easy way to do this is to use the one at the DOCTYPE level. Remember that all ID values must be unique, but there can be any number of IDREF values pointing to the same id. So, the <illusref> tag looks like this if the <illus>id is not known:

```
...
<illusref ref='doc001'>
```

By using this approach, the application can provide a list of attributes that point to the DOCTYPE id so the author can correct all missing values before the document is published.

Using Both LIT and LITA in an Attribute

SGML provides for two literal start or end delimiters, LIT and LITA, which are defined in the reference delimiter set as " (ASCII 34) and ' (ASCII 39), respectively. The purpose of these delimiters is to define when a literal starts and ends. For example, in an attribute, the value of the attribute must be contained between these delimiters if the value contains a space character. For example:

```
...
<dog type='German Shepherd'>
```

The reason there is an alternate delimiter is to make it easy to enter the other delimiter in the literal. For example:

```
...
<dog type="David's German Shepherd">
```

However, if an attribute literal contains both LIT and LITA, it is not as easy to contain the literal:

```
...
<dog type='German Shepherd' height='1'-6"'>
<!-- error!                                                -->
```

This produces the following error:

```
valid.sgm:9:49:E: `-6' is not a member of a group specified for
any attribute
valid.sgm:9:51:E: an attribute specification must start with a
name or name token
valid.sgm:9:52:E: character data is not allowed here
```

One way (albeit rather radical), is to re-assign the value of LIT and LITA to be something other than the defaults. This can be done by modifying the SGML declaration, and is valid for the entire document. As with all changes to the SGML declaration, caution is recommended, since not all parsers support such changes. See *Fully Defined SGML Declaration* on page 427 for how to change the SGML declaration.

Another way is to use an entity in the literal:

```
 ...
<!ENTITY    inch        '"'                                           >
<!ENTITY    foot        "'"                                           >
 ...
<dog type='German Shepherd' height="1&foot;-6&inch;">
```

Embedding Notes During Conversion Clean-up

During the conversion of data from a proprietary format to SGML, data might go through several passes before it is completely converted. For instance, the first pass might be to allow a conversion group to do as much of the tagging as possible, the second pass may consist of authors correcting content, and a third pass may be a query against a database to check all product names, part numbers or legal references. When an ambiguity or other problem is encountered in one of the conversion passes that must be resolved in a later pass, a note to the parties downstream may be embedded in the file. By altering the DTD slightly for the second pass, you can use the parser to find these notes. If the problem-identification notes are allowed in the first DTD but not the second one, the parser will flag as errors the location of every note in the second parsing pass.

One element that handles these types of notes nicely is borrowed from the little yellow pads that serve the same purpose in the three-dimensional world: the <postit> tag. Such a tag with certain descriptive attributes will allow easier resolution of the problem specified in the <postit> element. Some attributes to consider are userid, date, and a description of the problem.

The following example shows an IRS form that is mentioned in text without a required revision date. For some reason, the first conversion group did not have the date information available (it could have been implied by the content, or mentioned earlier in a section that was not available to the conversion group). In our hypothetical DTD, both form number and revision date are required attributes of the <irsform> element. The conversion contractor that did the initial conversion could insert the following tags:

```
 ...
<irsform n='1040' rev=''>
<postit userid='dcw' date='12/25/93' type='missing revision
date'> if you intend to itemize....
```

Once the data is received, a DTD that does not allow <postit>tags can be used to generate parsing errors and allow the customer to find all <postit>tags during a parsing pass.

Use Processing Instructions for Inter-application Communication

Processing instructions (PIs) can be used to facilitate communication between applications. Several SGML-smart editors use PIs to communicate formatting information for format-intensive objects like equations and tables. This is done to convey information that might not be included in the element or attributes of the tagged file.

Consider a data stream that goes from the author to a proofing system, then to a database and eventually imaged on CD-ROM. An author might want to communicate some process-specific information to the CD-ROM imager that other steps might not need to know about. For example, the author could be aware of a link that should be present but is not because of pending legislation or some other reason outside the scope of the information itself. If the CD-ROM is imaged and the link is not present, the end-user might receive an unintelligible error from the access software when the link is tried.

To tell the CD-ROM process that there might be a problem, a PI could be embedded in the source file with a unique identifier for the imaging process:

```
<!DOCTYPE case [
  ...
]>
<case id='TD 94-771'>
<?CD-ROM this link is not available because of pending legislation>
```

Each application that reads the file can be programmed to ignore or include the processing instruction based on its function. In this case, the CD-ROM imager might generate a dialog box for the user that includes the text of the PI.

This procedure could be carried out using marked sections, attributes, or some other legal method, but those all require changes to the DTD; a PI can be placed anywhere in the file. Beware that this use of PIs is still deprecated by the standard. It requires intelligent application of this powerful feature to keep out of trouble.

Using Attributes to Capture Essential Data for Processing

Content tagging, using very specific names instead of generic structural names, is a powerful way to differentiate similar looking things that may be used selectively in different processes. You can even sub-define elements to capture the sub-elements that make up the larger one to improve handling and processing. A part number, for instance, may have three sub-elements; model, number, and version. Instead of using the following style where only the start and end of the part number are identified:

```
<partno>5100-127a-93</partno>
```

consider defining the sub-elements thusly:

```
<!DOCTYPE partno [
<!ELEMENT partno        - -          (mod, no, ver)              >
<!ELEMENT mod           - O          (#PCDATA)                   >
<!ELEMENT no            - O          (#PCDATA)                   >
<!ELEMENT ver           - O          (#PCDATA)                   >
]>
<partno>
<mod>5100
<no>127a
<ver>93
</partno>
```

This will allow each sub-element to be more easily identified for processing such as building a key used for sorting by padding the fielded version of this information, as in the following example:

```
05100-00127a-1993
```

Short references (and start tag minimization) could be used instead of explicit tagging to indicate the boundaries of each sub-element to make the application of markup easier and easier to read. (In this case the hyphen would imply the start of each tag and could imply a different tag start based upon the context in which it occurs; when in <mod>inside of a <part>a hyphen (the first one in this example) becomes the start <no> tag, and so on.)

If there are rules for what type of data each of these fields can contain, such as numbers only or numbers and alphas, defining these sub-elements as elements will not allow the parser to validate that the entered data complies to these rules. A solution is to use attributes and an empty element instead of sub-elements for data that need validating. The following declarations:

```
 ...
<!ELEMENT partno        - O          EMPTY                       >
<!ATTLIST partno        mod          NUMBERS          #REQUIRED
                        no           NUTOKEN          #REQUIRED
                        ver          NUMBERS          #REQUIRED>
 ...
```

would allow the creation and validation of the following data instance:

```
...
<partno mod='5100' no='127a' ver='93'>
```

which could easily translate to the printed form or the sort key form described earlier.

FOSI hints

In an environment where files are created and edited using an SGML-smart editor, the editor uses PIs to place information in the file to speed-up the editing process and to provide functionality such as the location of the cursor the last the time the file was edited. As a courtesy to others who may want to place PIs in the file, the editor uses a convention that all their PIs begin with a three-character sequence. This then allows any application that will process this file in the future to ignore those PIs and possibly recognize others that the process may be interested in using. There is a naming convention that requires the identification of all PIs with a string that will identify which process is intended to use each PI.

One system in particular is used to compose loose-leaf pages according to a formatted output specification instance (FOSI). To provide the required information to the FOSI, the application assigns the string "os" (output specification DTD) to allow the FOSI process to identify those PIs meant for it. For example, if it is necessary to "squeeze" a few more lines onto a leaf to avoid the creation of a point page (an additional page required to contain extra text in a loose-leaf environment), the author inserts a PI to adjust the character size and leading as follows.

```
...
<para>
<?OS squeeze="95%">
```

or, to fill out an already-generated point page to avoid excess white space:

```
...
<para>
<?OS squeeze="110%">
```

An intelligent formatter should do this kind of page-based formatting at composition-time. However, a computer can only do so much, and the price to pay might be in very slow processing time. Also, the formatter still might not make right decisions, so some means could be provided to allow the operator to force a modification.

Protect Comments from the Parser

SGML comments of the form:

```
<!-- this paragraph needs some work -->
```

are ignored by the SGML parser. In our environment, an SGML file is pre-processed by an SGML application to remove chapter, section, and paragraph numbering in anticipation of making editorial changes.

In the process of parsing the file, all comments are removed from the file since the parser ignores them. This results in a loss of vital editorial information, since we use comments to pass information between authors.

One solution is this: as part of the pre-processing step, convert SGML comments to processing instructions, which are seen by the parser and passed on to the output file.

In the original instance file, an SGML comment might appear as follows:

```
...
<para label='475-3.2.4'>Now is the time
<!-- Better check the correct time                              -->
for all . . .
```

After the pre-composition process, it would appear as follows:

```
...
<para label='475-3.2.4'>Now is the time
<?USER comment="Better check the correct time">
for all . . .
```

A process was run after the first to convert the processing instructions back to SGML comments prior to the next editing session.

Protect Entity Names

In a loose-leaf environment, pages are managed by having the formatter place pagebreak tags in the proper locations. If an entity is expanded and composed, there is a chance that the formatter will break the page inside the entity. Therefore, entities must remain expanded, with their pagebreak tags in place, until the publication is revised. At revision time, all page breaks are stripped and the document is re-composed completely.

When we do a revision, we must strip out the entity text, since it is managed separately from the document, and replace the entity name where it belongs. For example, the original text might look like this:

```
...
<para>The
 &standard; is used as the . . .
```

When it is first published, a pre-composition process protects the entity name and expands the text as follows:

```
...
```

```
<para>The
<?USER ENTITY="standard" START>ISO Standard 8879, Standard
Generalized Markup Language
<?USER ENTITY="standard" END> is used as the . . .
```

This text is composed, with the formatter ignoring the processing instructions. The expanded text is treated like normal text in that is available for page breaks and other processing that the formatter might do to the rest of the file.

At revision time, a process is run that strips out the expanded text and replaces it with the entity name.

Using #CONREF to enable External Table Processing

Some applications that create output files to drive some kind of composition engine do not have the ability to deal with the complex issues surrounding table formatting. For this reason, external programs are sometimes used to format the tables, which are merged at the proper location to complete the conversion.

In a recent application, OmniMark was used to create files to be compiled into Folio infobases. The first step was to strip the SGML-coded tables from the input file and create a separate instance for each table. As the tables were stripped, a #CONREF attribute was specified and the table tag turned into an empty element.

After stripping the tables from the original input, the tables were formatted using an external composition engine and cleaned up manually to produce 78-column "screen-ready" images for presentation in a MS-DOS application.

The table element and attribute declarations look like this:

```
 ...
<!ELEMENT body          O O        (table+)                  >
<!ELEMENT table         - -        (colspec*, (tbody |
                                   tgroup+))                 >
<!ATTLIST table         id         ID              #REQUIRED
                        break      CDATA           #IMPLIED
                        col        NUMBER          '2'
                        colsep     CDATA           #IMPLIED
                        colwidth   CDATA           #IMPLIED
                        frame      CDATA           #IMPLIED
                        srt        CDATA           #CONREF   >
 ...
<!ATTLIST colspec       col        NUMBER          '2'
                        colwidth   CDATA           #IMPLIED  >
 ...
</table>
```

The srt attribute contains the name of the file that was created from the SGML-tagged content of the table itself. This will be used to insert the screen-ready table image into the output in the next step.

The original file looks like this:

```
  ...
<table id='exc610' frame='single' col='3'>
<colspec col='1' colwidth='*'>
<colspec col='2' colwidth='/$000,000/'>
<colspec col='3' colwidth='/($000,000)/'>
<tbody>
<row>
  ...
<entry col='3'>$40,000
</entry>
</row>
</tbody>
</table>
</body>
```

After stripping, it looks like this:

```
  ...
<table id='exc610' srt='T1778'>
```

The srt attribute contains a name created by the program. In this case, the name T1778 indicates that this table is the 1,778th one to be created. The ID could be used as a file name, but there are some implementation issues that could cause problems. For example, although the parser will guarantee that all IDs in a particular instance are unique, it will not assure that they are unique within all documents in a single run. If the ID was used as a file name in this instance, and another instance had the same ID, one would overwrite the other. By generating a unique name for each table, this potential problem is avoided.

Because srt is declared as a #CONREF attribute, when it is specified in the instance, the parser sees the table as an empty element, so parsing will continue properly after the content is stripped. This is a valid SGML instance, and can be read as input to the next step.

The transform into Folio reads the modified SGML file with the tables stripped and inserts the proper screen-ready image into the output stream.

Use Minimization to Keep Keyboarding Costs Down

Some conversion houses charge by the "k-char" or thousand-character block of keyboarded data. By making maximum use of minimization, the DTD designer can cut costs dramatically.

There are several easy ways to achieve minimization:

1. **Use omissible start- and end-tags**. Tag omission is covered in *Omitted Tag Minimization* on page 266.
2. **Use short tag names.** `<p>`instead of `<para>`, `<s>` instead of `<section>`. These can always be substituted later for more mnemonic names.
3. **Use the empty end-tag**. For in-line elements such as quote or emphasis, an end-tag usually cannot be omitted. In this case, it is possible to use the empty end-tag,

```
 ...
<!ELEMENT quote        - -          (#PCDATA)              >
 ...
<para>Marx said:
<quote>Time flies like an arrow, fruit flies like a banana
</>
```

Note that the empty end-tag ends the most recently started open element. Beware that if another element is placed before the empty end-tag, that element would be ended. This could cause unintended results.

4. **Use the null end-tag.** . For elements that have a short content, such as certain emphases or the like, the null end-tag (NET) can be used.

```
Make that a bottle of <emph/red/ wine.
```

In this case, at least two characters were saved. Be sure not to use the NET delimiter (in reference concrete syntax, the slash) in the content, or it will be mistaken for the null end-tag. See *Null end-tag (NET) and NET-enabling Start-tag* on page 272.

5. **Use short references.** . Short references use certain characters to imply markup. For example, you can assign two newline characters in a row to indicate the start of a paragraph. This makes input more readable and eliminates the need to enter the tag.

Using a Comment to Avoid Entity Misinterpretation

Comments are defined by the standard using the following two productions:

```
[ 91] comment declaration = mdo, (comment, (s | comment)*)?,
        mdc
[ 92] comment = com, SGML character*, com
```

SGML character is a character that is permitted in an SGML entity.

1. MDO. Markup declaration open (<!)

2. MDC. Markup declaration close (>)
3. COM. Comment start or end (<!--)
4. S. a separator character (*e.g.*, space, newline, or tab)

The following comments are legal according to the productions:

```
<!-- Include the stuff from engineering. -BET -->
<!-- Put figures here -BET -- -- Done -DCW -->
<!---->
<!>
```

Notice the last comment. We call this a 'null comment'. Most people who have been through SGML training have been told that a comment is separated by two hyphens at either end of the comment text. By looking at the productions above, however, we see that the existence of (comment, (s | comment)*) is optional.

Changing gears, a general entity reference is used to indicate where replacement text, such as simple boilerplate text or entire documents, is to be placed in the SGML input stream. The appropriate productions are:

```
[ 59] general entity reference = ero, name group?, name,
        reference end
[ 61] reference end = (refc | RE)?
```

The following characters and reserved words are specified here:

1. ERO. Entity reference open (&)
2. NAME GROUP. a group whose tokens are required to be names
3. NAME. is a name token whose first character is a name start character (*e.g.*, a-z)
4. REFC. is Reference close (;)
5. RE. is Record end character (ASCII 13)

Any name characters following ERO are interpreted by the parser to be an entity reference. However, if an ERO is followed by a non-name character, the parser sees it as a literal. So, using the reference concrete syntax, the ampersand in the text, 1234&5 is treated as a literal, since '5' is not a name-start character, but the ampersand in AT&T is interpreted as the beginning of an entity reference to the entity &T;.

One way of getting around this problem is to declare the following entity in the DTD:

```
 ...
<!ENTITY    ampersand    '&'                                  >
 ...
```

then using it in the text when required:

```
AT&ampersand;T
```

There may be a reason that you don't want to define such an entity, and the null comment declaration allows such a means. Remember that is possible for a comment to contain only MDO and MDC (<!>). Since < is not a name start character, the parser passes the & as a literal, then consumes the comment. The following example illustrates this:

```
<!DOCTYPE tip [
<!ELEMENT tip          - -          (#PCDATA)                >
]>
<tip>This is 1234&5, This is AT&T. This is AT&<!>T.
</tip>
```

SGML-S outputs the following:

```
(TIP
-This is 1234&5, This is AT This is AT&T.
)TIP
```

and reports the following error:

```
valid.sgm:5:43:E: general entity `T.' not defined and no default
entity
valid.sgm:5:43: open elements: TIP (#PCDATA[ 1])
```

Rendering Footnotes in Electronic Documents

Footnotes, and other objects that provide supplementary material in a document, have been used for hundreds of years. The nature of such objects is that they do not have a direct, in-line relationship to the text from which they are referred, but are used to further clarify what is said in the text, or to refer the reader to explanatory material.

As such, it is acceptable to place such material at the bottom of a page (as in footnotes), or at the end of a section or book (as in endnotes), and place a marker in the text that the reader can use if further information is required. In the case of footnotes, all the reader of a paper document need do is to glance down to get the information. Referring to notes placed at the end of a document requires a bit more effort, but there are reasons why some types of documents, such as legal texts, use endnotes instead of footnotes.

All of this is fine for paper documents. What, though, of electronic documents, where there is no concept of a page, and the end of a document might require complex mouse and cursor navigation to find?

One way that manufacturers of document browsing software have solved this problem is by placing some kind of marker in the text, and providing a means to display a pop-up window with the referenced text inside.

However, there is still much information that is rendered as plain ASCII text, and requires no more than a standard file browser to view. In the case of these documents, there might not be pages, and it could be hard to navigate between the current reading point and the end of the document, if that is where the notes are placed.

One solution is to place footnotes immediately following the end of the paragraph, preceded with the footnote marker [1] that is associated with the footnote. If there are multiple footnote markers in the paragraph, the list of footnotes [2] will follow it.

[1] This is an example of the usual footnoting mechanism used for plain-text books for print-impaired use.

[2] The numbering sequence is normally reset for each chapter, but other numbering schemes are acceptable.

Handling ID/IDREF when Deleting Elements

An interesting problem has arisen using the Military DTDs designed for processing technical manuals. The DTDs provide a mechanism to identify elements that have been deleted by setting an attribute on the element. This is used specifically for those elements that are numbered or labeled. It provides for the ability to carry placeholders for the numbers. In this system, a structural element is marked for deletion using the ArborText Adept•Editor, but is not actually removed. A later process removes the content of the element and sets a `#CONREF` attribute indicating that it has been deleted.

The problem is that, if a chapter that might contain a figure is deleted, that figure has an `ID` that is used as a cross reference elsewhere in the document. Because the chapter is not really deleted in the document instance (only the attribute is set indicating that it is to be removed later), the `ID` remains in the file, so that the editor's internal parser does not report that there is an error. However, once the post-processor deletes the chapter, the `IDREF`s pointing to it will generate an error.

One solution to the problem is to have the editing application automatically alter the `ID` of all elements included in the deleted text, such as pre-pending an "x" in front of the `ID`. This will enable the parser to detect the SGML error that there is an `IDREF` that does not have a matching `ID`. How automated this is will depend on the editing application. Another approach would be to have the post-process automatically alter the IDs and then parse to detect the errors. This would be one of what could be many semantic checks this post process performs to verify that non-SGML errors are caught prior to any additional processing.

Using Nested Quotes

A typographical quote is different from the single and double 'ticks' found on most keyboards. In addition, the typographical characters for a start quote and the one for an end quote are different. In order to produce acceptable start and end quotes, some kind of character reference must be output to the typesetter.

In addition, quoted material inside of quoted material must change to a single quote (in American English).

Entity references could be used to satisfy this requirement:

```
  ...
<!ENTITY    ldq         '\ldquote'                       >
<!ENTITY    rdq         '\rdquote'                       >
<!ENTITY    lsq         '\lsquote'                       >
<!ENTITY    rsq         '\rsquote'                       >
  ...
```

And referenced in the text as appropriate:

```
He said, &ldq;She said, &lsq;I understand.&rsq;&rdq;
```

Another rule for quotes is that, if the quoted material will take up more than three lines in the output, it should be set-off from the text, indented on both sides, and printed, without quote marks, in a smaller point size and possibly italicized.

Some companies use a separate element called "long quote" to specify such extended material. In keeping with the concept of device-independent output, however, the author does not know if the quote will be longer than three lines, since that is only known at rendering time.

There is also the problem of generating different characters based on the area of the world in which the document will be read. In some parts of Europe, the french quote is used.

The elegant way to resolve all of these issues is to use a quote tag that can contain other quote tags. Then, it is up to the application to determine the characters to use and the formatting considerations. The following declarations illustrate this:

```
  ...
<!ELEMENT chapter      - O          (title, paragraph+)
                                                +(quote) >
<!ELEMENT (title | paragraph)
                       - O          (#PCDATA)            >
<!ELEMENT quote        - -          (#PCDATA)            >
  ...
```

Note that the quote is an inclusion at the chapter level, it can be included in any of chapter's descendants, even if that descendant is a quote. Because the quote is not excluded from itself, a quote can contain quotes, which is the desired goal.

The example above becomes:

```
  ...
<paragraph>He said,
<quote>She said,
```

```
<quote>I understand.
</quote>
</quote>
  ...
```

If the quote gets too long to be rendered in-line, the application can issue the appropriate codes, at process-time, to carry out the style guidelines set forth by the document designer.

Three "Views" in one Branching DTD

Sometimes you will find you need to manage several similar document types in a single DTD. Maybe you need to enforce subtle differences yet allow the documents to coexist in a single application environment. Perhaps your editing software allows only one DTD at a time, but your users may work with two or three different subclasses simultaneously.

The following DTD fragment allows three types of memos to be enforced with different headers, but allows the text elements to be maintained once as a single DTD through branching into different subclasses, and then returning to the main text as a single element (in this case <body>). Certain rules can then be selectively applied to each subclass of correspondence. For instance, footnotes are not allowed in either memo or letter, but are allowed in the legal memo. The headers/greetings are different as well as the closing information. But, the main text portion is identical (except for exceptions). Applications development and maintenance may be simplified as a result without constraining users.

```
  ...
<!ELEMENT corr          - -          (memo | legal.memo |
                                     letter)           +(fn) >
<!ELEMENT memo          - O          (to+, from+, body)  -(fn) >
<!ELEMENT legal.memo    - O          (to+, from+, copy+,
                                     subject, index, body)    >
<!ELEMENT letter        - O          (address, salut, body,
                                     from)             -(fn) >
<!ELEMENT (to | from | fn | para | copy | subject | index |
address | salut)
                        - O          (#PCDATA)                >
<!ELEMENT body          - O          (para+)                  >
  ...
```

Using Titles in Subordinate Elements

In the case of multi-part objects, such as individual pages in a technical drawing, it is sometimes necessary to collect all objects under a common element in order to maintain the proper object structure.

Consider the case of technical drawings. Such a drawing can be a single graphic that appears somewhere on the output page, or it can contain several images, each of which is to appear on a separate page. Whether there are one or more drawings in a set, the document designer considers it a single object.

Rendering these objects, however, is more of a problem, since the writer of the output specification must deal with single- and multi-page drawings much differently. One difference is in the treatment of titles. A single-page drawing might be declared like this:

```
 ...
<!ELEMENT techdraw    - -          (title, graphic)         >
<!ELEMENT title       - O          (#PCDATA)                >
<!ELEMENT graphic     - O          EMPTY                    >
 ...
```

while a multi-page drawing might have sub-drawings, which would be declared like this:

```
 ...
<!ELEMENT techdraw    - -          (subdraw+)               >
<!ELEMENT subdraw     - -          (title, graphic)         >
<!ELEMENT graphic     - O          EMPTY                    >
<!ELEMENT title       - O          (#PCDATA)                >
 ...
```

Notice that, in the second case, `techdraw` does not contain a title. This may or may not work, depending upon the document's style. Sometimes, all pages in such drawings are assigned a common title, with "page 1 of 5" appended. In this case, a common title would be sufficient. Other documents might allow for separate titles for each page "Fuel Filter Flange, top view", "Fuel Filter Flange, cutaway view", and so on.

The following element declarations show one way to deal with both methods:

```
 ...
<!ELEMENT techdraw    - -          ((title, graphic) |
                                   (subdraw+))              >
<!ELEMENT subdraw     - -          (title, graphic)         >
<!ELEMENT graphic     - O          EMPTY                    >
<!ELEMENT title       - O          (#PCDATA)                >
```

```
...
<graphic>
</techdraw>
```

The problem comes in the case where both methods are used. ("Fuel Filter Flange, cutaway view, page 1 of 3"). In this case, the application must decide how to deal with the multiple paradigms. One way is to treat the `techdraw` title as a prefix to the subdraw title:

```
...
<!ELEMENT techdraw      - -          (title, (graphic+ |
                                     subdraw+))             >
<!ELEMENT subdraw       - -          (title, graphic+)      >
<!ELEMENT graphic       - O          EMPTY                  >
<!ELEMENT title         - O          (#PCDATA)              >
...
</title>
<graphic>
</techdraw>
```

The instance fragment would be tagged as follows:

```
...
<techdraw>
<title>Fuel Filter Flange
</title>
<subdraw>
<title>cutaway view
</title>
<graphic name='fff01'>
</subdraw>
<subdraw>
<title>top view
</title>
<graphic name='fff02'>
<graphic name='fff03'>
<graphic name='fff04'>
</subdraw>
</techdraw>
```

In this case, the application must count how many graphic elements are specified, and produce titles accordingly. The above instance might generate the following titles:

```
Fuel Filter Flange, cutaway view
Fuel Filter Flange, top view, page 1 of 3
Fuel Filter Flange, top view, page 2 of 3
Fuel Filter Flange, top view, page 3 of 3
```

Use #CURRENT Attribute for Ease of Entry

The attribute default value #CURRENT is not used very much, perhaps because its benefits are unknown or because everyone is using SGML-smart editorial workstations that make such minimization unnecessary.

The parser treats the first tag that appears in a document that has a #CURRENT attribute as if it is a #REQUIRED attribute. That is, if it is not specified, the parser will issue an error. The parser will treat subsequent instances of the tag as if the previously specified value were the default value. This is one of SGML's little trick that makes it possible to create intelligent applications with a minimum of keying. Reducing necessary keystrokes leads to greater productivity and less chance of error.

In a time-reporting system, each employee is to enter his or her time and expense information for each day. It is important to capture the employee number for each day, so the attribute should be declared with a #REQUIRED default value. However, every day for a particular SGML instance submitted to the accounting department will have the same employee. It is wasteful to require the employee to repeat the information for each day, so a #CURRENT default value is used.

The DTD and instance looks like this:

```
<!DOCTYPE report [
<!ELEMENT report      0 0         (day+)                     >
<!ELEMENT day         - 0         (hours, expenses)          >
<!ATTLIST day         employee    NUMBER           #CURRENT
                      day         NUMBER           #REQUIRED>
<!ELEMENT hours       - 0         (#PCDATA)                  >
<!ELEMENT expenses    - 0         (#PCDATA)                  >
]>
<day day='941028' employee='2234'>
<hours>8
<expenses>52.55
<day day='941029'>
<hours>0
<expenses>34.00
<day day='941030'>
<hours>0
<expenses>34.00
```

SGML-S creates the following output:

```
Line  1: (REPORT
Line  2: AEMPLOYEE TOKEN 2234
Line  3: ADAY TOKEN 941028
Line  4: (DAY
Line  5: (HOURS
Line  6: -8
Line  7: )HOURS
Line  8: (EXPENSES
Line  9: -52.55
Line 10: )EXPENSES
Line 11: )DAY
Line 12: AEMPLOYEE TOKEN 2234
Line 13: ADAY TOKEN 941029
Line 14: (DAY
Line 15: (HOURS
Line 16: -0
Line 17: )HOURS
Line 18: (EXPENSES
Line 19: -34.00
Line 20: )EXPENSES
Line 21: )DAY
Line 22: AEMPLOYEE TOKEN 2234
Line 23: ADAY TOKEN 941030
Line 24: (DAY
Line 25: (HOURS
Line 26: -0
Line 27: )HOURS
Line 28: (EXPENSES
Line 29: -34.00\n
Line 30: )EXPENSES
Line 31: )DAY
Line 32: )REPORT
Line 33: C
```

Notice that for `day=941029` and `day=941030`, the employee attribute (lines 13 and 23) was inserted by the parser even though the author left it out.

Using Attributes to Specify Semantic Information

Even though we stress the importance of doing complete and accurate document analysis and creating element structures that are oriented toward the meaning of the data in the elements, sometimes it is necessary to create catch-all elements that can collect data that does not fit anywhere else.

For example, during the document analysis phase, let's say you identified foreign words, emphasized words, part numbers, and legal citations, all of which should be tagged separately, but traditionally all appear italic when printed on paper.

Consider the woes of an author when he comes across a piece of slang. This should also be printed in italic, but there is no way to tag slang, since we did not find that during the document analysis phase. So the author tags it as a foreign word and completes the sentence. It works, but is it the best way?

One way to rectify this situation is to create a catch-all element for these items. Call it `<italic>`, and instruct authors to use it when nothing else fits.

We have not seen this work. In their haste, authors might have a tendency to tag all of the above items with the `<italic>`tag, and you are back where you began.

There is another way to create this escape route. This is done by defining classes of elements at authoring time. These classes define a class of element, and indicate whether the element is generally placed inline or blocked. The content of the definition explains what the class means so that you have more information about the class than simply the title or name. Here is a class for `slang`:

```
 ...
<!ELEMENT class-def     - O          (title, semantic)             >
<!ATTLIST class-def     class-name   CDATA                #REQUIRED
                        element-type (inline |
                                     block)               #REQUIRED>
<!ELEMENT title         - O          (#PCDATA)                     >
<!ELEMENT semantic      - O          (#PCDATA)                     >
 ...
<class-def class-name='Slang' element-type='inline'>
<title>Slang
<semantic>Identifies all terms which while generally understood,
at least in the community reading this document, is not a
formally correct or proper usage of the language.
</class-def>
```

These definitions could be placed in the doctype element as optional repeatable at the beginning of the document.

The following classes are candidates for this type of treatment.

1. Abstract Term
2. Fixed Term
3. Idiom
4. Technical Term
5. Slang
6. Emphasis
7. Example Annotation

8. Cliche
9. Acronym
10. Trademark

Notice that there is one called Emphasis still, which is reserved for words we would expect to hear with emphasis and for which no other class applied.

To use a defined class, there are two elements (<block>and <inline>):

```
Administrative tasks (sometimes referred to as
<ph class-name=slang/administrivia/) are often handled through
other
```

As you see[1], it doesn't require much more effort than marking emphasis in more traditional ways. It does require a knowledge of the different classes that an element may take and a willingness (in the case of emphasis) to figure out why you want to emphasize the material.

Why bother? One application that may be useful, if this approach were used consistently, is that it would flag certain phrases for human language translators (people, but maybe programs too) that a term or phrase needs special treatment. This in addition to the obvious application of changing the presentation style for different classes of phrase.

For another approach to this problem, see *Using Ambiguity for Maximum Benefit* on page 341.

Creating a Conditional Processing Language with SGML

SGML can be used to define conditional processing semantics in the same say as it can be used to define structural elements.

In such a system, variables are defined, either internal to the SGML document, or from some outside source available to the application. The following DTD and instance defines a structure where variables are defined inside the document, then checked by the application when invoked in an <ifblock>:

```
<!DOCTYPE doc [
<!ELEMENT doc        - -      (vars, para+)     +(ifblock) >
<!ELEMENT vars       0 0      (var+)                       >
<!ELEMENT var        - 0      (#PCDATA)                    >
<!ELEMENT ifblock    0 0      (if, elseif*, else?)         >
<!ELEMENT if         - 0      (condition, then)            >
```

1 Here, we make use of the null end tag and NET-enabled start tag.

```
<!ELEMENT elseif     - O    (condition, then)            >
<!ELEMENT then       - O    ANY          -(elseif | else) >
<!ELEMENT else       - O    ANY          -(elseif | else) >
<!ELEMENT condition  O O    (#PCDATA)                     >
<!ELEMENT para       - O    (#PCDATA)                     >
<!ENTITY    lt         '<'                                >
]>
<doc>
<var>StartYear=1994
<para>As you might know, <TAG> has been published for more than
eight years.
<ifblock>
<if>StartYear <= 1993
<then>
Thank you for your support over the years.
<elseif>StartYear > 1993
<then>Welcome to <TAG>. We hope you enjoy your subscription.
<else>We hope you have enjoyed your subscription so far.
</ifblock>
</para>
</doc>
```

The instance above produces the following normalized output:

```
<DOC>
  <VARS>
    <VAR>StartYear=1994
    </VAR>
  </VARS>
  <PARA>As you might know, <TAG> has
  been published for more than eight years.
    <IFBLOCK>
      <IF>
        <CONDITION>StartYear <= 1993
        </CONDITION>
        <THEN>Thank you for your support over the years.
        </THEN>
      </IF>
      <ELSEIF>
        <CONDITION>StartYear > 1993
        </CONDITION>
        <THEN>Welcome to TAG. We hope you enjoy your
        subscription.
        </THEN>
      </ELSEIF>
      <ELSE>We hope you have enjoyed your subscription so far.
      </ELSE>
    </IFBLOCK>
  </PARA>
</DOC>
```

SGML knows nothing about conditional processing, so it is up to the application to make sense of the variables contained in the `<var>` element, then test them against the conditions contained in the `<condition>` element. This is a simple example that has been edited for space. In an actual system the variables can be accessed by the application from a database, and the document instance processed for each set of variables. Sort of like a word processor's mail merge function.

This type of processing can also be done with marked sections and parameter entities that are set in the prologue, but an element approach offers advantages for some implementations:

1. the element approach will withstand the stripping of ignored marked sections done by the SGML parser.
2. SGML editors can use the element approach to present to the user a "conditional hierarchy", similar to the structural hierarchy that is usually displayed.

3. we have found that it is more intuitive than using the obscure syntax required to set and maintain parameter entities and call them out as marked section keywords.

PART • IV

Appendices

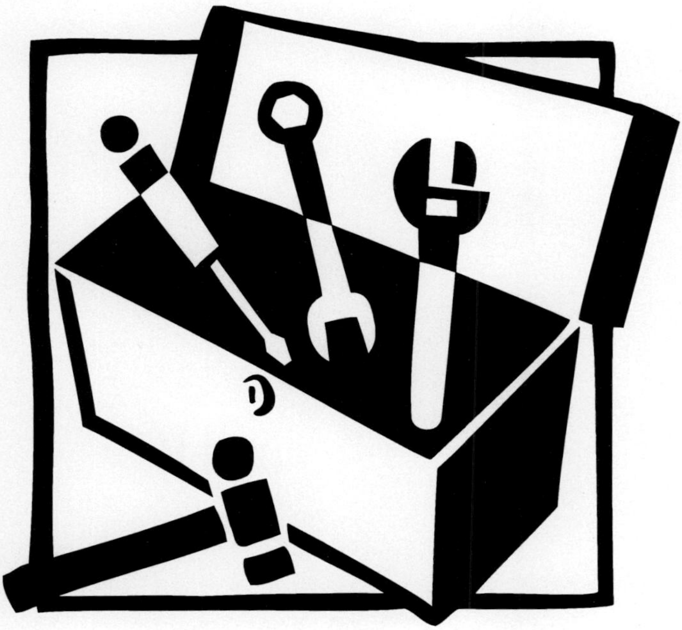

APPENDIX • ONE

Case Study: RIA TIGRE System

Introduction

This case study represents a large-scale enterprise re-engineering effort based on SGML that produced dramatic results to a company in a competitive market.

Background

The Research Institute of America (RIA) is a leading professional publisher focusing on tax products. RIA, based in New York City, is part of the much larger Thomson Corporation. Thomson is a collection of some of the best known commercial publishing companies in North America, and all around the world. Thomson companies include many newspapers, reference, financial, and professional publishing companies, and other non-publishing companies.

RIA produces some of the most respected publications covering US federal, state, and municipal tax laws, regulations, case law, and analysis. RIA has relied on internal resources for producing print products, mostly large loose-leaf publications, as well as CD-ROM products. Some RIA information appears in large commercial on-line database services.

Issues Faced by RIA

Increasing competitive pressures in the legal publishing world have lead to increased need to produce products that are competitive priced and contain content improvements in order to meet customer demand. On the other side, RIA was faced with increased pressures from competitors.

Although RIA products are generally regarded as being some of the highest quality products available to tax attorneys and accountants, management felt that the existing production costs and schedules could not be supported given the pressures in the industry for lower prices and more timely information.

Also, the need was recognized to improve the ability to create spin-off and specialty products to meet rising customer demand for more choices in how they receive their information. This demand increasingly included the requirement for CD-ROM versions of existing and new products. Early attempts at producing electronic products from what was primarily a print database proved to be inadequate. Schedules were too long and costs too high.

In 1991, RIA chose to develop a dramatically new system for producing information to be used in a wide array of products in both print and electronic forms. The goals of the development project were to reduce production costs and schedules and to facilitate the production of new products through the use of existing information.

Enabling Technologies Employed

The development team at RIA chose to utilize several enabling technologies in order to meet the goals of the system. At the top of the list was SGML for the encoding of their text data. Other enabling technologies that were to be instrumental in the successful completion of the development project were low-priced powerful workstation running client applications, networked resources including database and composition servers, and the use of customizable commercial software applications wherever possible.

SGML was chosen to create an intelligently encoded database that could be easily managed and manipulated by automated processing tools. Personal computers were felt to provide the best price/performance ratio and were networked to minicomputer servers. The distributed architecture of the system provided flexibility in application of computing resources, and the ability of workstations to continue working even if other resources were temporarily not available.

Off-the-shelf software provided the benefit of allowing development resources to be applied to the process of migrating product information and configuring applications for product processing instead of developing the tools that were employed. Commercial software is a way of leveraging internal development resources with those of the software developer.

System Components

For the database, BasisPLUS from Information Dimensions, Inc. was chosen for its ability to handle textual information efficiently. The composition functionality selected was the Pager composition system from Frame Technology Corp., due to it powerful batch processing capabilities which were felt would reduce composition schedules and cost by eliminating page inspection and correction steps.

OmniMark from Exoterica Corporation was chosen for data conversion, translation and manipulation due to its powerful SGML and text-manipulation capabilities. FastTag from Avalanche Development Company was chosen to assist in converting tabular materials that occur in text due to its powerful abilities regarding format-specific element tagging.

The SGML-smart editor chosen was WriterStation/PM, also from Frame Technology Corp. WriterStation was the only SGML editor available that could handle tagging minimization. Since most of RIA's products involve the handling and management of loose-leaf pages, it was anticipated that editors would need to work with document fragments that could not contain or have introduced complete minimal markup.

Workstations run OS/2 from IBM for two reasons; it is what WriterStation/PM runs under, and for the added benefit of the powerful pre-emptive multi-tasking capabilities of OS/2.

Client/server applications were implemented using TCP/IP. Servers for composition and database functionality run on VAX/VMS since that is the only environment that both Pager and BasisPLUS were available.

Critical System Features

Initially, the team performed a thorough requirements analysis and potential system evaluation and narrowed it down to one commercial system or building and integrating it on their own. The commercial system was the only one available that could support loose-leaf publishing and utilized SGML databases and editing tools. Even though it was one of the most sophisticated commercially available tools, RIA found several critical functions were not supported and chose to build their own system. They had experience in a previous system built in another part of Thomson from which many lessons were learned and ideas were reused.

SEAMLESS ACCESS

RIA developed the Thomson Integrated Generation & Retrieval Environment (TIGRE) system by integrating third-party commercial tools and internally developed systems to create a single integrated environment that supports all of the functions needed to produce print and electronic products.

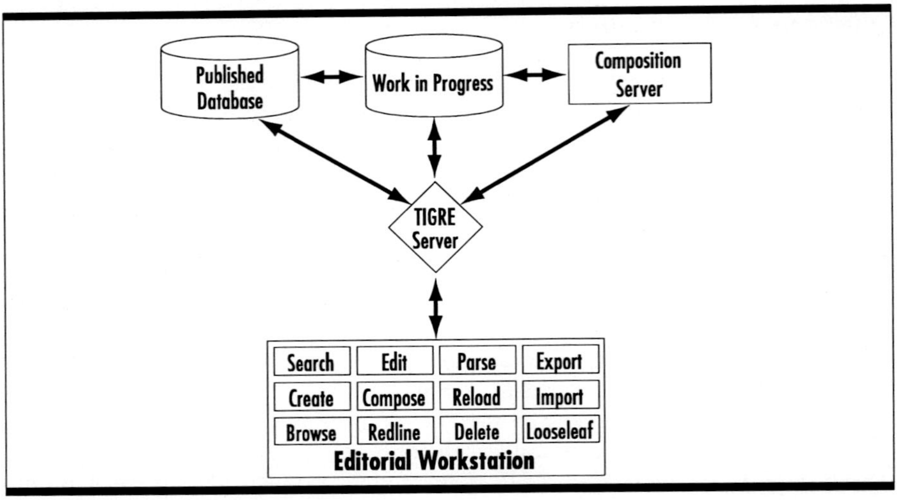

Figure 86. *TIGRE System Model*

In the TIGRE system, users select the function they wish to perform. Access and workflow timing are managed by the TIGRE Server.

CONFLICTING CONCURRENT STRUCTURES

Since the system is designed to facilitate the production of both electronic and printed loose-leaf products, multiple "views" of the data had to be supported; the physical structures of the loose-leaf page-pairs conflicted with the intellectual structures defined in SGML and the basis for editing and the organization of the information in the electronic products.

The information in the TIGRE databases is broken into low level components called atoms. The boundaries of each intellectual element and physical component are used to bound the atoms. A program called the atomizer breaks the SGML data into these atoms according to the needs of both structures and creates database records.

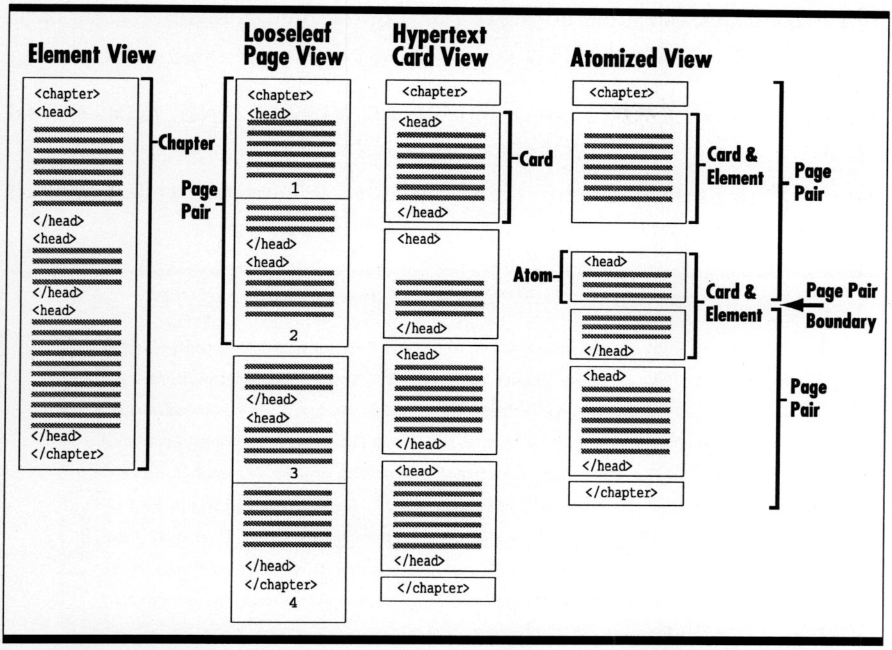

Figure 87. *Using Database Atoms to Resolve Conflicting Concurrent Structures*

The atoms can be assembled into any of the desired structures, page pairs or elements. Hypertext cards tend to use the same boundaries as elements, but in electronic delivery environments there are constraints on the size of addressable "cards" and TIGRE can be made to manage this additional structure in the same way the page pair physical structure is accessible.

What makes this schema work is the inclusion of information at each physical boundary on the current intellectual state, composition settings, page numbers. This information is called initial conditions and is used for database loading and extraction, setting pages, and even for verifying intellectual structure during editing. Tagging can be inserted to the chunk of text being extracted in according to a physical structure to make it parseable, and then removed again when the data is reloaded back into the database.

Why go to all this bother, you might ask, when a data managed in the intellectual structure can always be reprocessed into the pages and then published? There are efficiencies to be gained in maintaining concurrent structures, especially for loose-leaf publishing. Commercial loose-leaf publishing must keep the number of pages recomposed and published to a minimum to keep product costs down. Without absolute control over pages, and the ability for editors to work in pages structures, it is difficult to manage what is known as a page budget. (Note: The commercial system that was evaluated had a fairly good mechanism to manage pages, but it did not work 100% of the time, sometimes extra pages would wind up making it to print.)

ACCESS BY ELEMENT AND PHYSICAL VIEWS, AND RANGES OF EACH

Ranges of any of these structures can be accessed as a group as well as shown in the following screens:

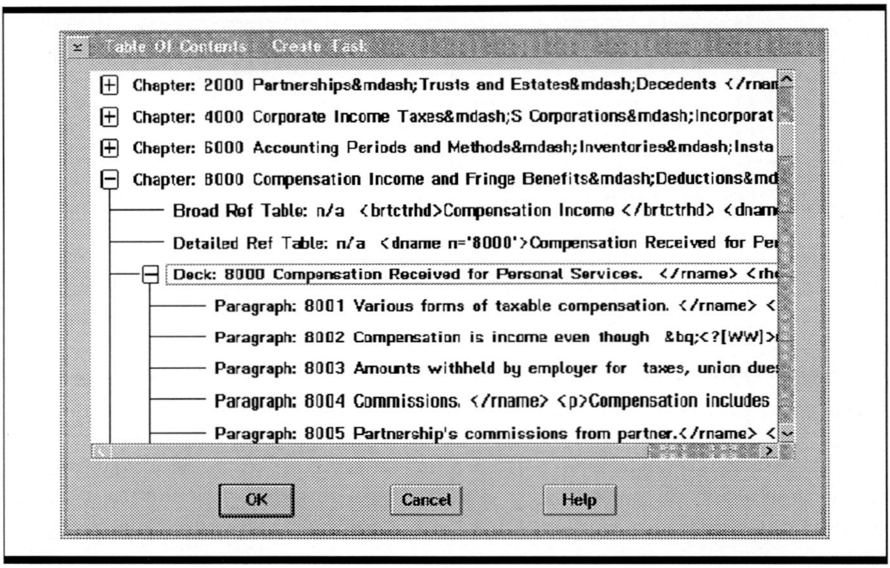

Figure 88. *TIGRE Table of Contents View*

TIGRE allows a user to access information through a table of contents view showing the structure of the information in the database. In RIA parlance, a subchapter is called a deck. Deck 8000 is selected in this example and a WIP task could be created for all of the deck, including all of the hierarchical paragraphs contained within it. The user could easily traverse the structure and select and intellectual hierarchical element and create a task. The name of the task, actually the first several characters of the `name` element's content, are available to aid in identification.

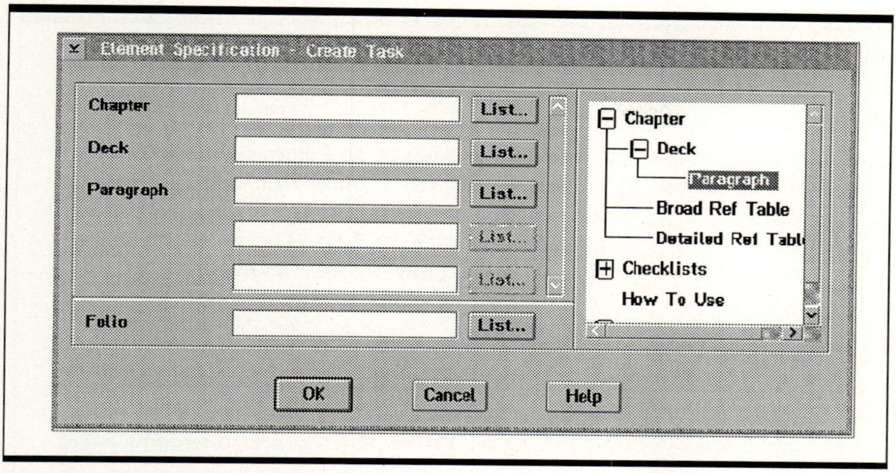

Figure 89. *TIGRE Element View Screen*

TIGRE also allows a user to access a list of all elements at a specific level in the database. In this instance the user may choose to have a list of hierarchical paragraphs listed for potential accessing.

The tree structure shown on the left of the screen is based upon the actual model of the database, and may be very different for other types of information with different logical structures. The user can traverse this tree structure or select from the main hierarchical elements that the administrators have determined were useful to list on the left (additional structural elements could be listed but two levels have been grayed out since this portion of the database only has three levels).

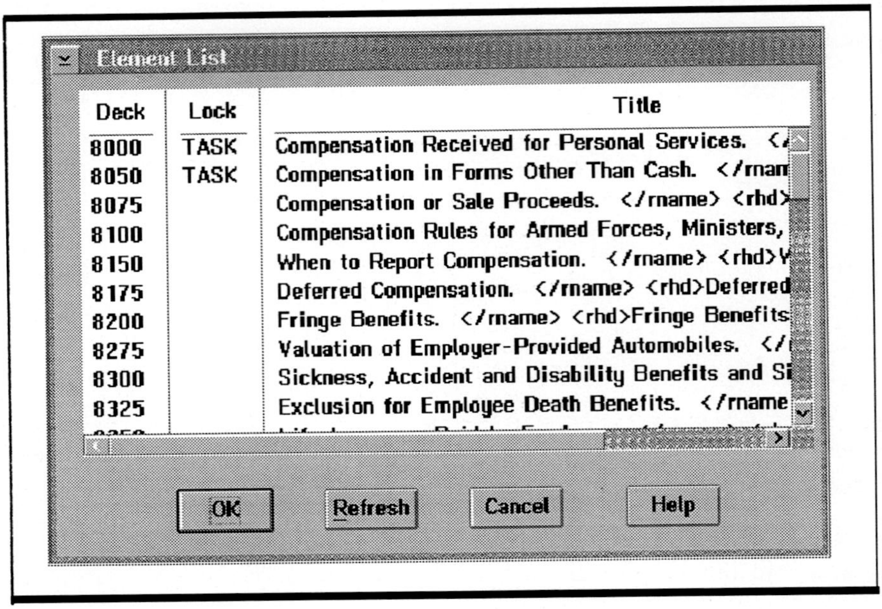

Figure 90. *TIGRE Element List Screen*

A user can list all of the structural elements at a given level on the Element View screen and select it for creating a WIP task. Note that there are two decks already locked since tasks have been created for them and they have not yet been checked back into the database.

MASTER DATABASES

At RIA, some information is created once and used many times in many different types of products. For instance, some or all of the Internal Revenue Code, the tax laws of the United States, appear in nearly every publication and CD-ROM product that RIA produces. A scheme was developed whereby this information could be maintained in a single "master" database and used in each of these publications. The dependencies are tracked to alert users of the information when the master database is updated.

An editorial person is charged with keeping the master code database completely up to date. Whenever a CD-ROM is reissued a complete copy of the code data can be included with the assurance that it is completely up to date.

There are timing issues related to using the master database approach for reusing material mixed with other materials in a publication that need to be managed. For example, there may be text surrounding a block paragraph containing tax code from the master database. If the code portion in the block quote is updated as soon as the master database from which it was taken is updated, then the surrounding text discussing it must also immediately be updated to reflect the new material. Otherwise, the surrounding text may be out of synchronization with the code material. TIGRE allows the user to track when changes are made to the code material and implement the changes where it is reused on their own schedule. RIA has developed several master databases and many publication databases. The interdependency can become very complex.

BATCH COMPOSITION

An early goal of the TIGRE development project was to reduce composition costs and to achieve what has been called 100% batch composition. Typical composition processes require that each page be inspected and any areas where the composition failed be resolved manually. Bad line breaks, errors in line spacing, orphans, and more severe errors have to be resolved by a human operator using an interactive workstation. Most composition systems can achieve up to 95% perfectly composed pages, but that still leaves 5% that need to be fixed by hand.

A significant problem with performing page correction on composed files is that it may be difficult to have these changes reflected in the SGML data. Either the data is managed separately from where the page correction is performed, or the SGML data would need to be polluted with composition-specific coding. Through the use of a batch composition system integrated into the TIGRE server, RIA has achieved 100% successful composition of all pages without interactive clean-up. If a composition problem does arise, and they do occasionally, the format developers enhance the composition programs rather than fix the page. If the page was corrected, the error would continue to show up in similar situations until the composition programs were fixed.

TIGRE eliminates the need for page inspection and correction by nipping the problem in the bud. If a composition problem is complex and will cause delays to the production schedule, the author can either leave the error on the page (if it is minor) and republishing the page later (remember, this is loose-leaf), or change the content a little to eliminate the problem. Since the system is connected to many laser printers throughout the company, an author can send the file they are editing to print, and within minutes see a laser printed copy of the page that looks exactly as it will after final composition.

Pages, by the way, can be composed on any PostScript device. Currently, many pages are composed on 600dpi laser printers since higher resolution devices supporting PostScript are still too slow to handle the volume of pages produced by RIA each year.

WORKFLOW AND WORK-IN-PROGRESS

An essential feature of the TIGRE system is the ability to create "tasks" of work to be assigned to users for updating, passed along to the next person in the work flow, perhaps a reviewer, and to track to progress of all active tasks through the entire process. These active tasks are maintained in a Work-in-progress (WIP) database. Once a chunk of text is checked out of the database, access to it is not allowed until it is checked back in.

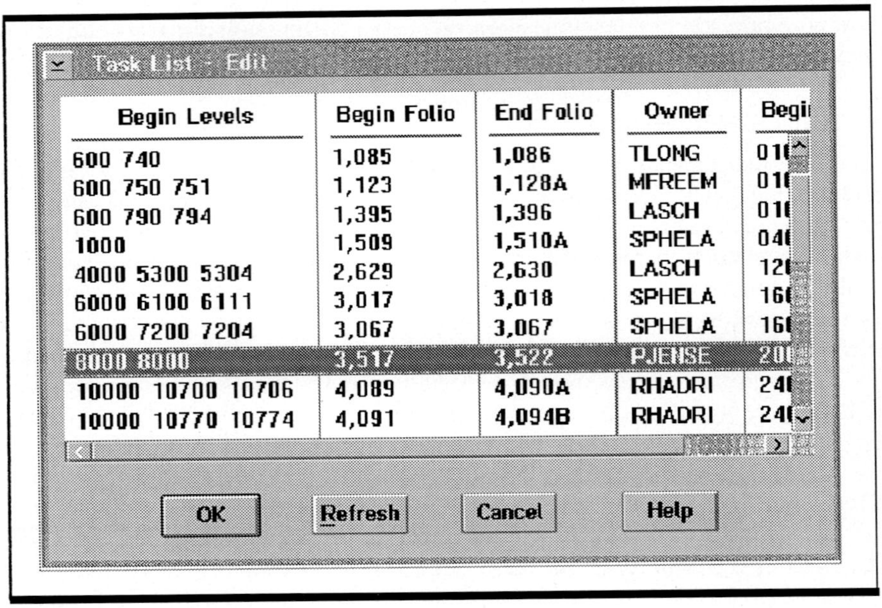

Figure 91. *WIP Task List Screen*

Tasks stored in the WIP database can be viewed in the WIP Task screen. Information about tasks are available, including the element number and level (first column), folio (page) numbers, and the person who checked the task out. Care is taken to ensure proper task management to prevent tasks being lost in the master database. The WIP process enforces strict control over each task.

SGML-SMART EDITING

Users are presented with a formatted view of the information when editing, as shown in the WriterStaion/PM session below:

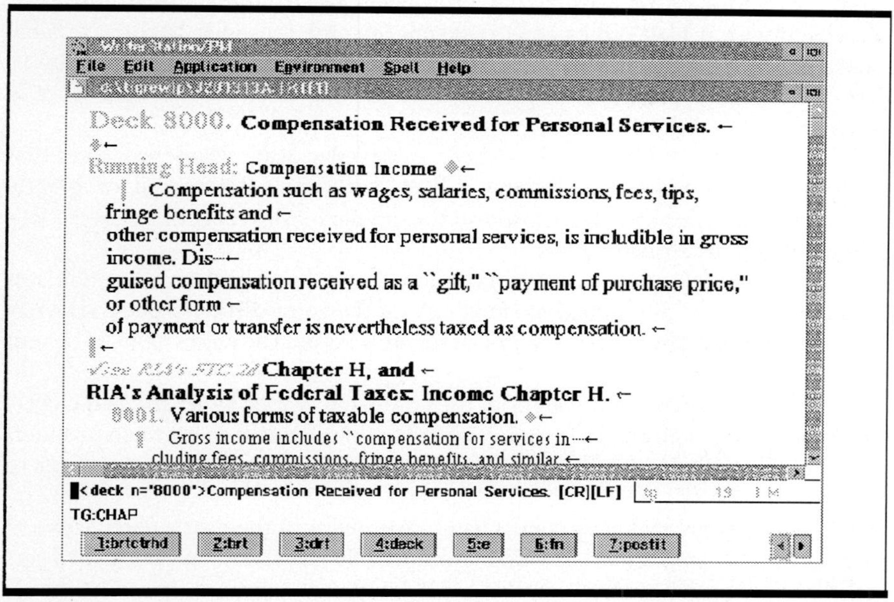

Figure 92. *TIGRE Editing Session Showing Formatted SGML Text*

As with other formatting SGML editors, the information is processed on the fly when opened to provide graphical feedback to the user to assist in identification of the information elements contained within. In this case, the user has edited Deck 8000, the heading for which is at the top of the screen. Other elements that are highlighted include cross-references, generated text, and structural elements. Near the bottom of the screen is a line showing the actual coding of the text on the where the cursor is currently located. The bottom of the screen shows buttons for placing elements that are allowed in this context. There are many pop-up and pull-down menus also available that assist the user in the proper placement and construction of the SGML coding. A validation function can be executed to double check that the DTD is being complied with and errors can be resolved during the interactive editing session.

Successes and Difficulties

TIGRE has successfully met the design goals stated in the functional requirements documents prepared at the beginning of the project, although many of the specific functions were hard won and some took longer than expected to make work properly. But, from a purely financial perspective, after nearly two years of conversion and system development, RIA is beginning to get the return on their investment.

The process of reusing data has been greatly streamlined and costs associated with it have either been reduced, or some reuse has become feasible where it was cost prohibitive before under the old system. Data is more up to date. The production of alternate versions such as CD-ROM has been greatly enhanced.

Technological benefits have been achieved as well. Many processes that were performed manually are now either completely automated or greatly assisted by the computer due mostly to the detailed SGML encoding and SGML-smart utilities developed by RIA.

The composition process has been streamlined and made much less expensive. Authors get immediate feedback on the composition process and may continue to edit right up to the very last seconds before the pages need to be sent to the printer.

Work is managed throughout the company. WIP tasks are tracked closely and managed by the system. Interdependencies of information between products are carefully tracked and tasks can be initiated by the completion of updates to other databases.

The last area where benefits were expected is in the user's perspective of whether the system is an improvement or not. The jury is still out, but most users feel that life is more difficult working in a structured environment. The development and leadership team did everything they could to anticipate and alleviate user difficulty. Extensive user familiarization and training was performed throughout the project.

The system also features workflow management and notification facilities to assist managing the complex workflow that is part of the new system. This workflow requires that the Editorial Department take responsibility for the entire publishing process, where before other departments handled many other tasks. The new responsibilities are largely automated or assisted, but they still represent new concepts and a sense of "ownership" that was never held before by Editorial. The cultural change required by the new system is slowing beginning to take hold and user acceptance is beginning to improve, but still requires constant attention in the form of training and extensive support.

Many of the benefits that were stated during the design and implementation phases of the project were not fully understood by non-technical personnel. For instance when functions were described as automated and streamlined by technical people, they were believed to promise simplification of tasks and reduction of costs, but were interpreted by non-technical people as deprofessionalization and even job elimination. Needless to say, this perception raised a lot of concern in the Editorial staff. Ironically, most processing that was automated was not in the authoring and editing areas where work is performed that requires human thinking, but rather in production areas such as the composition department.

The general feeling in Editorial is that their workload has increased somewhat and that some of the tools are unforgiving. But, as more information about new processing opportunities, reduction in costs, and other benefits are shared with this department, the user acceptance has improved gradually. What finally made a significant improvement in user acceptance was the successful introduction of a new product in record time and low cost. The new product was based on reused information from other products and was produced in about one third the amount of time it traditionally takes to introduce a new product to market. In fact, this product was inspired by an announcement by a competing publisher to attack a weakness in the RIA product line, and the quick introduction of the new product not only eliminated this weakness, but allowed RIA to deliver to market a product that filled that niche after that same competitor had advertised they intended to do so. The concrete realization of the marketing and strategic product development benefits of an SGML-based system was the first real significant benefit that the users could see as benefiting their department directly.

This new product was produced, though, with considerable support from the technical staff. All the legacy products that have been migrated have also required much more support directly to the end user, where before, the technicians in the composition department would shield the end user from these issues. Reduction in support will only be achieved through reduction of the "customized" look and organization of each different product, and the development of standards styles and processing and formatting applications used for entire classes of documents and data types. For instance, little nuances that were once felt to provide a distinctive look and feel to each product, must now be evaluated for value or they will be eliminated in order that a more consistent product line can be produced and programming and application development can be simplified.

Sucesses are beginning to trickle down to the end users. The financial analysis is clear that the system delivered costs savings in the areas of composition and some processing costs, and new products are possible due to processing that was previously unfeasible. Technical development is becoming simpler and the production tools have stabilized. Even though these benefits are now clearly recognized, it has been nearly two years since the first prototype product was converted and produced under the new system. A payback schedule of two years is not uncommon for a project that has a scope as wide as the TIGRE implementation at RIA.

CRITICAL SUCCESS FACTORS

The implementation of TIGRE was hard won. It is no trivial task to totally re-engineer an entire publishing company. A project the size and scope of TIGRE is not for the feint of heart. What made TIGRE happen was:

- strong leadership skills,
- a sustained focus on solving the business problems identified in the beginning of the project,

- the pragmatic adoption of leading edge (not bleeding edge) technologies, and
- the detailed definitions possible from the implementation of SGML.

The TIGRE implementation, in retrospect, embodied many of the same aspects of a fairly complex computer system development

APPENDIX • TWO

Case Study: Kodak Technical Information Documentation

Introduction

This case study represents an example of a small-scale implementation of SGML that was completed on a budget that just about any company can afford. This implementation resulted in improvements in processing time, cost, and complexity and served as a test of the technology to determine a future course for document processing within the group. Kodak has begun the second phase of this project including expansion into other document types, delivery formats, and system functionality, and will eventually expand this system so that it can serve as a centralized collection and distribution repository for marketing information.

Background

Eastman Kodak Company is a major manufacturer of photographic materials including sensitized materials such as films and papers. Technical Information documents, or TIs, are produced to provide users of sensitized products with necessary information. These documents contain information pertinent to the use of the product. Every product that Kodak sells has a corresponding TI that is distributed in various forms to provide a high level of product information to the customer.

The distribution vehicles include hard copy and several internal and a file format used for external on-line services (called CMS), including Compuserve, America Online and the Internet. TIs may be altered slightly for internal use versus external consumer use, the latter being a shorter and less technical version of the same information. Internal users include Kodak marketing and sales representatives as well as product developers and manufacturing staff. The advent of the Internet and HTML provided the stimulus for Kodak to explore new ways to distribute this type of information, and many other types, of information in electronic form and to determine the best method for creating and maintaining the information prior to preparing it for distribution in the various formats. Kodak will provide increasing amounts of information via the Internet in addition to the many electronic delivery services they employ.

Scope and Goals

Kodak conducted a prototype test to determine whether SGML could enable their system to easily transform text to each of the distribution formats while providing an effective means for creating and maintaining it. A subset of the documents was chosen, as was three output forms; paper composition, and internal on-line service format, and HTML. The goal of the system was to demonstrate how data preparation could be simplified while easing the transformation to these formats.

Since this was a prototype intended to provide a proof-of-concept, the scale of the project was fairly small. The limited scope allowed the development and implementation to progress very quickly and at lower costs. Due to the frugal economic climate, funding would not likely have been available for a larger project with additional risks. The prototype was conducted and designed with an eye on future expansion in both content and distribution formats. People from other related departments, who might some day adopt the system for their information, were included in the planning and design sessions to ensure scalability.

The Project

Results came in a matter of weeks. The first couple meetings were used to familiarize all the participants in SGML concepts and to describe the relationship of SGML to HTML. After the first meeting, it became clear that HTML would be used as a distribution format and not as the model in which the information would be created and managed. A richer DTD that meets a broader range of needs was subsequently developed. TIs are fairly structured and consistent, so the document analysis and DTD development required only four meetings and a few hours of independent analysis by the SGML Analyst. Kodak hired Dale Waldt and Information Architects, Inc. for SGML analysis and data conversion programming development. The conversion of a small select group of TIs was performed by Kodak employees using the OmniMark programs developed specifically for their data and for parsing.

The source documents are currently stored as flat files in a networked MS-DOS environment. During the conversion processing, minor changes were made to the DTD to support constructs found in existing documents. Some documents needed minor modification and enhancement to make them more consistent and compliant with the emerging DTD. Simultaneously, Information Architects, Inc. developed three down-translate programs to be used to convert the SGML source files to the three delivery formats. These formats needed to support simple linking, some content generation, and subtle nuances for composition. These down translate modules were designed to run 100% batch and not require manual modification after processing to make the output suitable for delivery. Data management, version control, and work flow management may be included in later phases of development.

The print output translator produces RTF-encoded files which will be composed using Microsoft Word for review and print distribution. A style guide is applied to the RTF files to complete the printed page. The in-house on-line service is an ASCII-based keyword file system that utilizes simple proprietary generic coding and a series of menu hierarchies for navigation and access to the text. Graphs of key photographic products parameters, such as spectral sensitivity, MTF, and D*log*E curves, were prepared in Excel and are assembled on demand when called from the text via a reference. The HTML output is created in batch and delivered to the department that is responsible for building and enhancing their HTTP server.

The Marketing Technical Support department in Kodak had made a commitment to use Microsoft Word as their text editor several years earlier and felt that advantages could be realized by continuing to use Word for document creation. Users were already trained in its use and little or no investment in editing software would be needed if Word could be used. About the same time this project started, Microsoft announced the upcoming release of their SGML offering, Microsoft Author for Word. But, at the time of this writing SGML

Author for Word was still in limited beta testing and work with SGML Author has just begun.

Even with acquisition of either of these add-on SGML tools for word, the purchase of OmniMark and development and conversion costs, the entire project will cost less than US$25,000. Expansion of the system would require incremental costs in the areas of data conversion, additional delivery format translation development, and additional licenses of either editing tool. The very small investment in this system replaces many hours of manual labor related to converting the original documents using less sophisticated tools and manual processes. Kodak expects to be able to increase the volume of data processed by existing employees using this new SGML-based system, and to create additional output and delivery formats very easily and cost effectively as part of a larger information distribution and management scheme.

Expansion of the system is expected to eventually include upstream and downstream processing environments and other departments. This project will serve as a model and proof of the approach's effectiveness, in order to facilitate the approval process for future development projects.

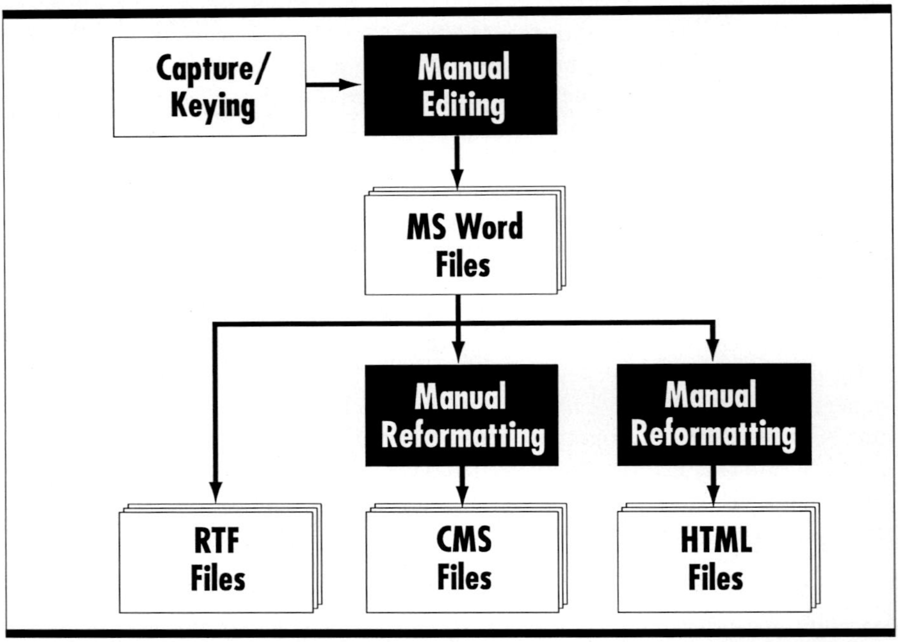

Figure 93. *Data flow of legacy Kodak TI document creation and processing system dependent on manual reformatting steps (manual steps are in black).*

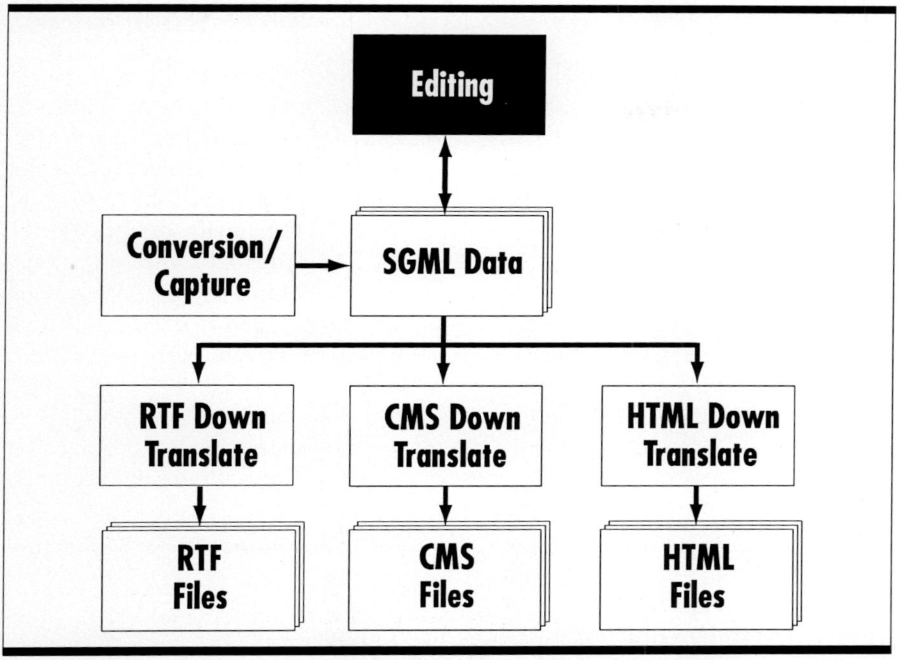

Figure 94. *Data flow of new SGML-based Kodak TI document creation and processing system eliminating manual reformatting steps.*

Future

The Marketing Technical Support department at Kodak has found sufficient savings in the limited implementation of the SGML-based TI creation and editing system to warrant expansion to other document types. Each document type, such as marketing specification sheets, press releases, and technical information documents, have their own unique features and constraints. For instance, the product specification sheets have been carefully formatted and ways of retaining this formatting information are being explored. The expansion of this project may include using Adobe Acrobat as an alternative distribution format. Also, additional auto-tagging and data capture processes may be needed since these materials will be fed from other sources in formats not supported under the initial system.

The expansion of the system will include evaluating how the information can be easily processed and stored in a repository to facilitate additional distribution formats and channels. Long range plans might eventually include demand printing, fax-back, and additional electronic delivery formats. This system is carefully being built with an eye on adding data management functionality and additional translation capability to support future needs.

APPENDIX • THREE

Case Study: Douglas Aircraft Company

Introduction

The Douglas Aircraft Company has adopted SGML to better meet customer's information needs and for the significant benefits it promises for their own processing requirements. This case study is an ideal example of how to implement an SGML-based publishing system in a complex commercial environment where the publications support a manufacturing process, in this case large commercial aircraft. The benefits, development history and strategy, and the lessons learned are discussed.

The Need for SGML at Douglas Aircraft

Douglas Aircraft Company (DAC), the commercial aircraft division of McDonnell Douglas Corporation, has a long history of producing well-known aircraft for the commercial airline industry. Several models of jetliners in use today throughout the world that are produced by DAC include the MD-80, the MD-90, the MD-11, and the planned MD-95.

Each aircraft produced by DAC must be accompanied by information that is vital to the operation and maintenance of that aircraft. Because of the intense economic pressures on airlines to reduce costs and maximize utilization of resources, this information is as vital to the airline or maintenance facility as the aircraft itself. The quality and timeliness of information delivered to the airlines by DAC plays a significant role in ensuring both the long-term viability of DAC products and the profitability of the companies that operate them.

This information is extremely important to DAC itself and is viewed as one of their most significant products. DAC devotes millions of dollars and hundreds of thousands of hours each year to generate and maintain information deliverables for their customers. This information must be exceedingly accurate and must comply with strict standards.

Because of the complexity inherent in aircraft documentation, large volumes of information and hundreds of people are involved in producing the information provided to customers. DAC felt the need to employ modern methods and tools to efficiently and effectively perform this function.

In response to this mission, DAC chartered the Electronic Data Distribution (EDD) project to enable efficient and effective publication of DAC's information deliverables in the Air Transport Association (ATA) 2100 compliant digital formats. There are three primary goals to this project:

- Meet modern ATA requirements
- Improve customer satisfaction
- Improve DAC operations

Since the EDD project began in early 1994, the first two document management modules have been completed in DAC's company-wide information management and publishing system. This new system produces both traditional print and electronic deliverables.

Meeting Modern ATA Requirements

The ATA created the ATA 2100 documentation information interchange standard, a new way of creating, providing, and using information that helps both aerospace manufacturers and airlines. ATA 2100 applies international standards to meet many immediate needs of the industry. It also provides a foundation for even more robust interchange of information in the future, including timely on-line availability of information and a common database across the industry.

It is felt by DAC that the ATA 2100 standard benefits DAC and its customers. Prior to the availability of this standard, manufacturers were forced to maintain electronic information in proprietary forms. The valuable life of DAC's information is much longer than that of most software and hardware products. Under the EDD project, information will be free of the need for expensive conversion between proprietary formats and will outlive various system components.

The EDD system uses SGML for text encoding that provides the added benefit of supporting easy translation to multiple output formats from a single source file. This markup allows multiple uses and presentations of the information and is a means of extracting information elements, including composition for printed deliverables, electronic formats, and the DTDs for interchange with airlines. SGML is both a long-term means for preserving information and a robust means of interchanging and utilizing information.

IMPROVE CUSTOMER SATISFACTION

DAC expends a tremendous amount of resources converting information into printed paper. The airlines must take this paper and extract the information contained within the pages and prepare it in a variety of different ways to support various internal operations. The airline's goal is to provide the right information at the right time in the right place, primarily to increase aircraft utilization and reduce costs. Unfortunately, paper is poorly suited for this need. Paper deliverables are less valuable to customers due to the expensive requirement to convert paper-bound data into a form that can be easily reformatted and reused. The means of rendering and electronically displaying information by airline operators is extremely varied. By providing ATA 2100 compliant data to their customers, DAC is providing a robust source of information that may be incorporated into an operator's automated systems.

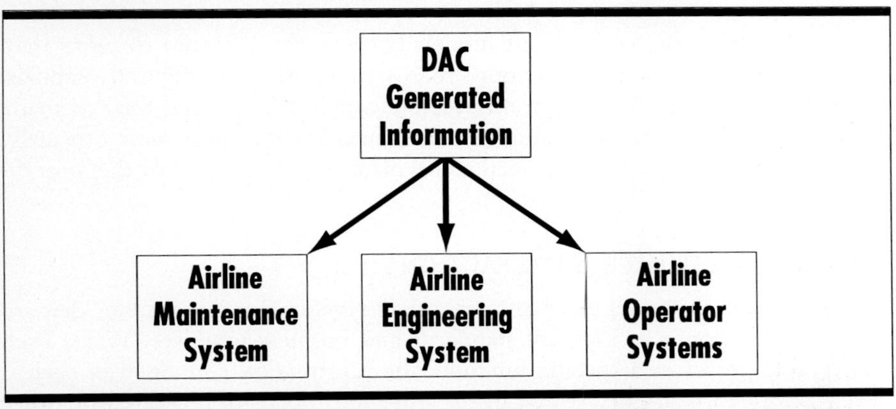

Figure 95. *Data in DAC aircraft document deliverables is reformatted for use by airlines to support a variety of internal systems.*

Information produced by DAC may be distributed in very complex configurations that involve several aircraft models in use at many airlines and delivered in the form of many document types. A small sample of this configuration is illustrated below:

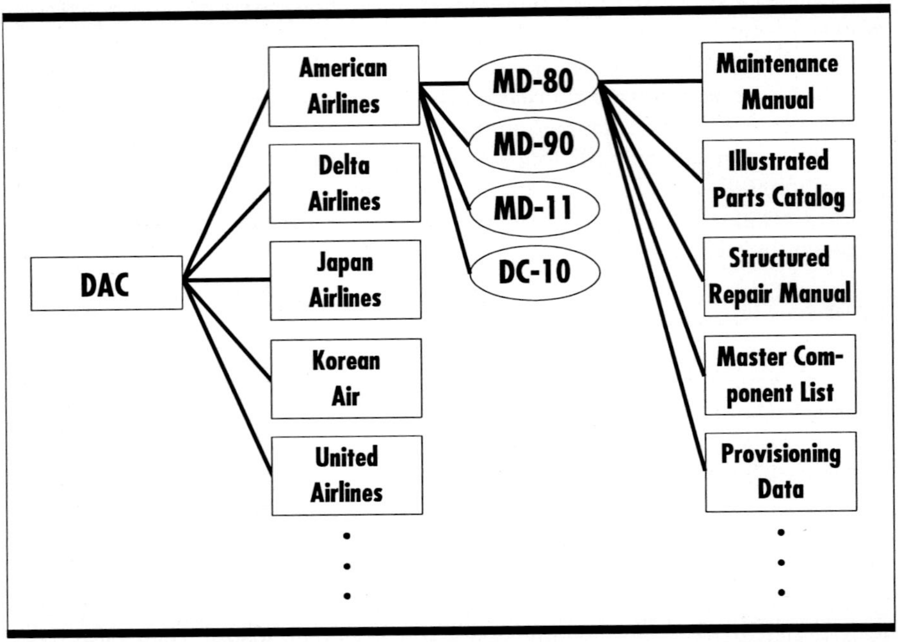

Figure 96. *Illustration of complexity of configuration of DAC information. Each airline may have unique requirements for each aircraft configuration. Also, each aircraft model will have many different information deliverables (these are displayed for the MD-80 model).*

DAC information on four aircraft models is currently delivered to more than ninety airlines in the form of more than fifty separate configured manuals, totaling more than 18,000 customizable deliverables. The need for this many information deliverables is a daunting data management requirement, especially considering that the data may need to be managed for the life of the aircraft, generally more than two decades.

Improve Customer Satisfaction

For every aircraft model there are more than seventy-five deliverables that are created in response to industry standards and business practices. While each deliverable performs a specific function, the information contained in each is often compiled from, or created in response to, information created by other DAC organizations or subcontractors. Sharing information between organizations is, therefore, very important both for reasons of efficiency and to ensure that data deliverables do not conflict with each other.

DAC has many internal systems in use in several internal organizations and also relies on several outside agencies to supply information. Even though the publishing tasks necessary to produce aircraft documentation are some of the most challenging in any industry, many of these systems are several generations behind "state-of-the-art". There is perceived tremendous benefit to operating efficiency and costs to be achieved through adoption of SGML and the ATA 2100 DTD under the EDD project.

There are several external factors that DAC hopes to take advantage of, including:

- Rapidly increasing computing hardware performance
- Emergence of standards
- Dramatic increase in the availability and power of "off-the-shelf" software
- Broader range of automation potential enabled by improved network and system tools.

DAC's EDD project is leveraging these dramatic improvements to provide a result that only a few years ago would not have been possible.

Accomplishments To Date

The EDD project began in early 1994 and progressed rapidly to meet aggressive goals. The need for the EDD system was considered critical due to the intense economic pressures faced by DAC and the airlines. Since that time, the project has been on-time, within budget, and has provided more features than originally planned for.

Requirements Gathering

Initially, functional requirements were gathered from major DAC organizations that produce documentation in support of DAC products. This was an important step since the EDD system was intended to be adopted company-wide and was not intended to be specific to a single organization within DAC. Because of the diversity of information produced, a wide variety of requirements were compiled, some very challenging.

DAC's information requirements are extensive. While some information is common to all aircraft of a given model, most require custom publishing to reflect the unique configuration of a single aircraft. Many of these documents must be updated periodically throughout the life of the aircraft to reflect improvements implemented after leaving the aircraft (DAC still provides supporting documentation for its DC-3, a fifty-nine year old aircraft). In addition, DAC must retain a highly accurate and comprehensive history of original and revised publications to support internal and FAA (Federal Aviation Administration) requirements.

System Architecture and Design

The EDD system architecture was designed to allow for extensive scalability in order to support the need to phase the system in across the entire company. An advanced client/server architecture with the followng features was chosen:

- Standards-based hardware and software enabling broad flexibility and straight-forward integration of disparate products.
- Open Software Foundation (OSF) Distributed Computing Environment (DCE) and Distributed File System (DFS) to provide growth potential, enable integration with other DCE/DFS products, allow the use of multiple servers, balance network and processing loads, and enable distribution of computing devices.
- Redundant disk arrays for secure data storage.

The EDD project is being implemented in phases to manage the complexity and minimize risk. The EDD system is being jointly developed by DAC and Integrated System Solutions Corporation's Publishing, Consulting and Services Group (ISSC PC&S), a subsidiary of IBM corporation.

The architecture of the system is modular to allow flexibility and independent development. Standards (official and *de facto*) are utilized where possible to provide inter-operability and include SGML.

Commercially available software is used where possible to reduce development costs and allow DAC to take advantage of vendor experience and upgrades. Functions of these packages have been extended where needed through product configuration, vendor-supported upgrades, the product's scripting language, and integrated development tools.

The EDD system appears to users as a single, integrated system, but is, in fact, comprised of a tightly coupled set of nearly two dozen software products bound together with a minimum amount of custom integration software.

Proof-of-Concept System

A prototype was developed to demonstrate the system's ability to match the most challenging user requirements. The prototype demonstrated selected features and represented the architecture to be demonstrated throughout DAC. The EDD system provides the following features:

- Creation of an electronic work order for a document to be created or changed.
- Electronic assignment and routing of work orders to the author.
- Instant notification to users of tasks to be performed.
- Production of multiple configurations of the same document via a common configuration database.
- On-line validation during editing.
- Importing existing SGML data for use in a new document.

- Ability for reviewers to "redline" illustrations (annotate the illustration without modifying the data itself).
- Capability to manage a document as multiple objects and store them in a central repository.
- Reuse of data without duplicating it.
- On-line notification to an author that data they are using has been modified.
- Ability to output either an entire document or only pages that have been revised.
- A security system that enables specific functions to be performed based on the user's job function.
- Automatic generation of "boilerplate" text containing standardized text and text from the work order.
- Secure storage and retrieval of work-in-progress data (text, illustrations, and work orders) and completed data.
- Locking of completed approved documents to prevent alteration.
- Ability to output documents on paper or in an electronic form on a disk.
- Ability to track jobs and report their status.
- Ability to search and retrieve text and illustrations based on attributes (aircraft model, date created, Service Bulletin number, etc.) associated with the data object.

IMPLEMENTATION OF PRODUCTION SERVICE BULLETIN SYSTEM

In November, 1994, DAC implemented a majority of functions from the proof-of-concept prototype system to produce Service Bulletins. All new Service Bulletins produced by DAC are now created and output on the EDD system and are available in ATA 2100 compliant form. The next module, which will be implemented in early 1995, will make selected documentation available on-line via the Internet's World Wide Web. Other near-term modules will further expand capabilities of the system and enable advanced publication of selected documentation.

Lessons Learned

The EDD Project Manager, Douglas Alberg, described the implementation effort in a session at the Documation '95 conference in Long Beach, California, in early March, 1995. The aggressive schedule of this implementation project led to a very rapid system development, less than a year. Alberg, was initially focused on technology issues, but soon learned that human issues were often more difficult to solve. While some individuals welcomed the major changes associated with implementing this complicated system, others were threatened and resisted change. Because of the tight schedule, user involvement in the project was generally limited to a few key users from each organization, though more thorough involvement was desired. Constant, effective communication of the goals and progress of the project, along with flow-down of information from the key users to all users of the system, created an overall smooth transition to the new system.

Strong leadership and system development management skill were also cited by Alberg as contributing factors in the project's success. The project champion kept the project focused on business objectives articulated early on in the project planning.

SGML was cited as being a particularly enabling technical feature due to the ability to easily translate SGML data into simpler distributable forms. When more than one distribution form is required, managing data in SGML alleviates expensive conversion costs for transforming data between proprietary formats. Alberg also contends that, while converting data from a proprietary format to SGML during implementation may be expensive, it is less expensive than the proprietary conversion they were facing on an on-going basis.

Alberg also stressed the need for new implementors to learn from experienced SGML implementors. Success is more likely when a project benefits from experienced implementors who have found the difficulties in implementing a system that is as complex as EDD.

Finally, Alberg cited the phased implementation that allowed for learning from each step as they were implemented and adjusting future steps accordingly as a factor in EDD's success. Contracted work was designed to be deliverable oriented as well, as opposed to hiring contractors on an hourly services basis. This allowed the project leaders to measure progress and success better than if clearly defined deliverables had not been specified.

Future

System components that are planned for the near future as part of the EDD system include:

- Delivery of selected materials via the Internet's World Wide Web to allow customers to access information from anywhere in the world via an Internet access provider and local access charges.
- Development and roll out of the DAC on-line library for use by internal personnel to improve data sharing and reduce research time.
- Completion of a common database containing information supporting engineering, product support, and other functions within DAC.
- Completion of an illustration management system that will allow DAC to more effectively produce ATA-compliant CGM and TIFF illustrations for inclusion in a variety of documents and search and retrieval of these illustrations against the attribute information to be maintained for each.

- Expansion of EDD for use in preparation and management of selected documentation for many DAC aircraft models.

Summary

While DAC has many important reasons for developing the EDD system, an overriding factor is that it must do so to remain competitive in the highly challenging commercial aerospace marketplace. Their customer's requirements for effective, accurate, and flexible information support have spawned this highly successful project and provided benefits to both DAC and DAC's customers. The challenging requirements of the EDD system could not have been accomplished without SGML, a standard embraced by DAC as a vital tool for the company.

DAC has developed the EDD system for survival. In the intensely competitive airline and aerospace industry, competitive advantage is constantly sought. Significant investments in new products and services require effective, accurate, and flexible information support in a variety of deliverables. SGML is a key component of the EDD system, which DAC management feels will be an important contributor to the continued survival of the company.

APPENDIX • FOUR

Colophon: How this Book was Produced

This book was created using the concepts and techniques discussed in the book. We thought that it would be appropriate to use the tools and share the development experience in this case study.

Data Gathering

When we decided to write this book, we gathered years worth of notes, slides, presentation materials, notes, DTDs, programs, and everything else we could find that would remind us what it was like to learn about SGML.

This exercise helped us focus, not only on material for the book, but also on the reader. Our data gathering process was similar to what most organizations go through in order to begin their document analysis and system implementation.

We ended up with material created on every conceivable computer platform, from mainframes to palmtops, and in practically every authoring environment we had including text programming editors, presentation software, spreadsheets and databases.

Initial Authoring

We are almost reluctant to say that we used Microsoft Word for Windows to do bulk entry and initial structural organization. There were several reasons for this decision:

1. Microsoft Word is readily available wherever we go. We both have it on our home machines and travel portable machines. Plus, the program imports many different file formats.
2. Word is the greatest editing environment ever created[1]. The simple yet powerful interface and outlining capabilities made it a pleasure to use.
3. Illustrations could be imported easily into Word, or created and edited inline on the same platform. This helped us to keep our thoughts while we sketched out a diagram. We created tables in the same way.
4. Word outputs a clear text file format called rich text format (RTF). We knew that we could eventually use RTF to translate into SGML.
5. We were still working on the format of the DTD. Working without a DTD was preferable as we flushed out the final structure.

We never expected to use Word for final production editing because we needed even more power than Word could give us. We wanted to do complex indexing and cross-referencing that Word did not provide. It was a case of personal productivity versus production capability. We put off the production for a while, but not without a cost.

We created several private drafts for our own review using Word. Then, when the book was ready for outside review, we swallowed our pride and printed copies for a select group of SGML professionals who generously offered their time and criticism.

---

1 Vendors who make SGML-smart editorial workstations would be advised to study the reasons behind the success of Microsoft Word.

SGML Conversion

When the books came back from the reviewers, it was clear that major reorganization would need to be done for the final product. At that point, we were ready to convert the documents to SGML and use SGML-smart editors for the final re-arrangement and editing.

First we saved all Microsoft Word files as RTF. Then Travis wrote an OmniMark program to read the clues in these files and create rough SGML. We knew we would eventually convert the Word files to SGML, so we made very consistent use of styles to give the conversion program hints about structural items.

We then used a combination of ASCII text editors and some Exoterica Corporation OmniMark programs to clean up and validate these rough SGML files. There are tools available that could have made the process faster, but we felt comfortable with the tools we had been using, and the whole conversion only took about 15 hours.

SGML Production

Once the files were tagged to a particular DTD, we could concentrate on making editorial changes and re-arranging the content. We used InContext, Author/Editor, and Vedit, each of that had strengths and weaknesses for the task. Vedit is a programming editor that doesn't know anything about SGML. The editor was used in conjunction with some Windows NT batch programs and OmniMark programs developed to show document structure and table of contents organization. Old habits die hard.

Ventura Publisher Used for Output

Springer-Verlag agreed to accept PostScript files as our deliverable for the book. This allowed us complete control over the presentation of the book.

We considered using Microsoft Word as the composition engine. Although Word does not have the ability to do some of the complex cross-referencing we wanted to do, our application could do these things and pass to Word what it could do, such as page number referencing.

When our book designer came back with a very nice design, it became apparent that Word would have trouble with the basic formatting. It probably could be done, but we chose Adobe PageMaker instead because of its superior page-layout ability. Our production designer created a set of PageMaker styles to carry out the design, then created a chapter by hand using our SGML files. She exported the text, which formed a basis for the next step.

After designing the templates and programs for PageMaker, we found a serious shortcoming in PageMaker that rendered it unusable. PageMaker does not support internal page references. We thought that any serious composition program would do this, but after looking for the coding to produce references and spending hours on the phone to Adobe, we found that the feature was just not there.

We switched to Corel Ventura Publisher version 5.0, since it does handle internal cross-references. We thought.

Travis developed OmniMark programs to create tagged Ventura files that were flowed into the book. A final visual pass was made before final printing to clean up widows and minor anomalies.

After creating a Ventura publication and putting twelve chapters, ten appendices, a table of contents, and an index, we had problems with Ventura during the renumbering phase. The program bombed when we had the page cross-references in the file. Corel engineering sent us an interim release that fixed the problem.

We used Ventura Publisher to create PostScript files for the book, which we put on a CD-ROM and sent, along with laser-printed proof pages, to Springer-Verlag in Germany for printing.

Tables

Tables usually pose a problem for the SGML implementor. For this book, we considered and discarded using several different table methodologies:

1. Use a row-and-column style table DTD structure. This type of structure is common in SGML implementations for various reasons. It is fairly easy to implement, and provides control over the look of each cell. We discarded this right away because it conflicts with our philosophy of separating format and structure; a row-and-column DTD is totally format-oriented.
2. Use a relational database to store tabular information, then access it via a query. Format the results and send to the output device. This would have required too much programming effort for such a small number of tables.
3. Use a spreadsheet to store two-dimensional table images. This would work similarly to the database approach, in that the data would be stored and maintained outside of the scope of the SGML document. We discounted this plan because of the same considerations of programming effort as databases.
4. Create a content-oriented structure for each table. This plan had some merit because it defined tables in terms of their content, not their presentation. The problem was that the number of elements required for such an approach made it unworkable given the time constraints.

We settled on an approach that recognized that tables contain data that has meaning, but that they are also inherently format-oriented. The table section of Brian and Dale's Excellent DTD (See Appendix 5, *Brian and Dale's Excellent DTD* on page 411) defines tabular data in terms of its columns, instead of rows. While this might seem to be just a transposition of the format-oriented approach, it is actually more than that, since databases are generally stored in a column-oriented fashion, with each column defining the data type and meaning.

The table portion is shown below:

```
<!DOCTYPE table [
<!ELEMENT table          - -            (field+, caption)          >
<!ATTLIST table          id             ID                #REQUIRED>
<!ELEMENT (title | caption)
                         O O            (#PCDATA)                  >
<!ELEMENT field          - O            (title, cell*)             >
<!ATTLIST field          id             ID                #REQUIRED
                         field-name     CDATA             #REQUIRED
                         relative-wid   CDATA             #IMPLIED
                         contained-in   IDREF             #IMPLIED
                         depends-on     IDREFS            #IMPLIED
                         type           (char |
                                        date |
                                        dollar |
                                        signed-int |
                                        unsigned-int |
                                        floating |
                                        formula |
                                        function |
                                        verbatim |
                                        integer)          'char'   >
<!ELEMENT cell           - O            (#PCDATA)                  >
<!ATTLIST cell           id             ID                #REQUIRED>
]>
  ...
<cell id='i693'>Inclusion
<caption>Exceptions
</table>
```

Table 13, Exceptions on page 238 was tagged as follows:

```
  ...
<table id='i691'>
<field id='i692' field-name='Exception'
relative-wid='2'>Exception

<cell id='i693'>Inclusion
```

```
<cell id='i694'>Exclusion

<field id='i695' field-name='Description'
relative-wid='5'>Description

<cell id='i696'>The elements listed can occur anywhere in the
element being defined, or in any of its descendants.

<cell id='i697'>The elements listed cannot occur anywhere in the
element being defined, or in any of its descendants.

<field id='i698' type='verbatim' field-name='Exception Example'
relative-wid='3'>Example

<cell id='i699'>+(footnote)

<cell id='i700'>-(note)
<caption>Exceptions
</table>
```

Notice the `field-name` attribute. This can be used by search engines to retrieve semantic information about the data contained in the column. This provides a pragmatic compromise between content-tagging each individual table and creating a strictly format-oriented approach.

The `relative-wid` attribute is used to indicate to the application how wide to make each column. Since all tables are as wide as the page column, this ratio is divided into that width to come up with an absolute measure. This is our only concession to a format-oriented approach.

The `contained-in` and `depends-on` attributes are used for spanning heads and row stubs. This book does not contain any tables that use spanning[1].

Graphics

Graphical material was created and gathered over a period of months from whatever source was available. Product screen shots were usually done from our

---

1 The methodology for doing spanning, and one inspiration for the table methodology used in this book, comes from an article in <TAG>, The SGML Newsletter, Volume 8, Number 2, February, 1995, titled "Representing Table Structure and Content" by Lloyd L. Harding.

system running Windows NT, but some were supplied by vendors or implementors.

All line-art was re-created using Adobe Illustrator for Windows to assure a consistent look. We planned to import the EPS files that Illustrator created directly into Ventura. However, the EPS filter in Ventura lost the font information, so we ended up converting the Illustrator graphics to the Windows Metafile format. These were placed in the Ventura chapter files.

Wherever there was a graphic in the SGML data, we placed a Ventura "anchor" so the graphics would find their locations easily. This enabled us to flow the text into the Ventura chapters as many times as we needed, and the graphics would always end up in the correct spot.

Valid SGML Examples

A book about SGML would not be much good if it contained SGML errors. We took very seriously the effect of an error in our examples. Early on, we endeavored to parse each example before putting it in the book. We would laboriously create a DTD and instance, even if all we wanted to do was to show how a particular markup looked.

After getting the DTD and markup correct, we would paste the appropriate lines into the document.

During the editing cycle, the examples would change (for example, to correct a typographical error, or to make tag names more readable). This would cause us to go through the manual process of parsing, correcting, and pasting the examples back in.

Why not use our application to do the work for us? We developed a DTD for writing DTDs, and tagged all examples to this structure. In the case that we wanted to show less than an entire SGML document (with the `DOCTYPE` declarations and such), every declaration element has an attribute called `print` that could be set to `noprint` for those lines we did not want to appear in the book. If an element was set to `noprint`, an ellipsis (...) was put in its place to show the omission.

All SGML code examples are in a tag called `<sgml-code>`. Travis included into the OmniMark down-translate programs routines to create a temporary SGML document file whenever the program encountered the `<sgml-code>`tag. The free parser, SGML-S[1] was invoked against this temporary file, and the return-code interrogated. If the return code indicated a problem with the parsing run, a flag was put in the output file for correction.

1 Actually, the parser used was NSGML-S (also called SP), a new version of SGML-S written by James Clark.

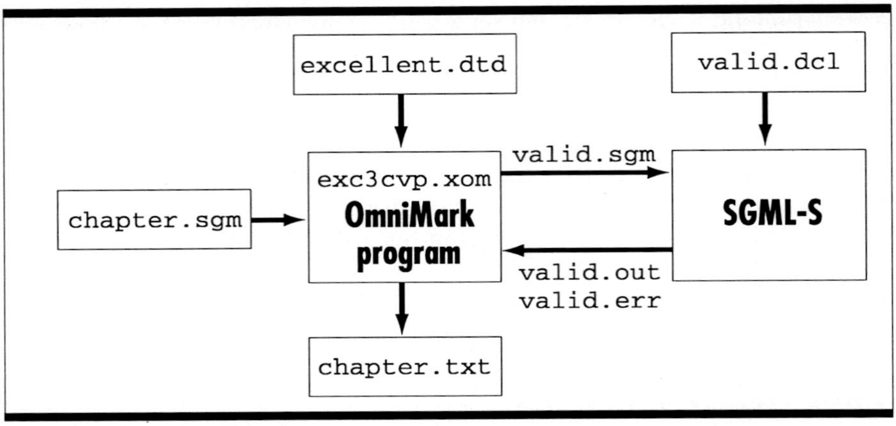

Figure 97. *"Hot" Validation of SGML Examples*

There are several examples in the book where the markup is incorrect. The <sgml-code>element has an attribute called errorok that allowed the markup to be incorrect without putting a flag in the output file. Every example of this is clearly marked in the copy.

In places where we want to show the output of the parser, there is an element called <parser-output>that has an attribute type that will print out the input, output, or error streams from the most recent parsing run. These examples are in the book.

This process enabled us to make corrections to the examples as necessary, but still ensured that all examples in the book are correct. This small example showed a big advantage of SGML for publishing. That is, we treated the document as more than just a collection of words that were to be printed. The rich tagging allowed us to validate that some of the words were technically correct (as in the above example). Other tagging allowed for easy creation of an on-line version of the book. There are many other things we can do with this data, because we know its underlying structure.

World Wide Web Access

The DTD describes a structure that requires an introduction element consisting of a paragraph or two. Travis wrote an OmniMark program to extract this information from each chapter and create an HTML document for publishing on the World Wide Web. It took about three hours to write the program, test it, and extract the data.

The url is

```
http://www.sgml.com/SGMLImplementationGuide/abstract.html
```

Another program was written to translate the entire contents of Chapter 1 into HTML. The url for this is

```
http://www.sgml.com/SGMLImplementationGuide/Chapter1.html
```

Text as Data

Creating the documents using this approach enabled us to do things that would not be possible any other way without a lot of work. Hot validation of SGML examples and derivative outputs are just some examples of the advantages of treating text as data.

1. Travis wrote a program to extract all resources in Appendix 8, *SGML Resources* on page 445 and create pages to send to the appropriate vendors for verification.
2. As part of the book validation, a list of all acronyms in the book were gathered and compared to the list of definitions in the glossary. We used this list to add undefined acronyms to the glossary, and remove entries that were not mentioned in the book. The program also sorted all of the entries alphabetically
3. During the final editing phase, we kept referring to an outline that was created with a program to extract all titles and their unique identifiers. This allowed us to see the overall structure of the book at a high level, and enabled us to insert the proper cross-references.
4. Ventura did not provide the rich indexing we wanted, so Travis wrote an OmniMark program to generate an index while it built the rest of the file. This gave us ultimate control over the look of the index. We could have done the same with a Table of Contents, but Ventura did fine, here.
5. There is an element called "product" that is used to indicate a vendor-provided software tool. The production programs verified that all products are listed in the index, and that they are all listed in the resource guide. When an electronic version of this book is created, this will probably be a hot link to the vendors World Wide Web page.

There is no doubt that we will use this database in the future to do other things.

Production Credits

The body type of the book is Adobe Janson. Running headers and footers are set in ITC Copperplate. SGML keywords, SGML coding examples, and other verbatim material is done with a TrueType version of Courier New that has been compressed to 70% of its original size using Altsys Fontographer, version 3.5.

Illustrations for the part title pages are original artwork created by Jared Camp. Book design was provided by Donna Wickes. Production design and Adobe Illustrator illustrations were created by Deni Travis.

APPENDIX • FIVE

Brian and Dale's Excellent DTD

Introduction

This appendix contains the DTD that was used for this book. As we developed the book, the DTD changed slightly. We wanted to take a snapshot of the DTD at the time the book was printed, so we actually placed the document in this appendix from the living file.

The following tagging was used to create the example:

```
<!DOCTYPE verbatim SYSTEM "excellen.dtd" [
<!ENTITY     excellent   PUBLIC
         "-//SIG//DTD Brian and Dale's Excellent DTD//EN"      >
]>
<verbatim>
 &excellent;
```

```
</verbatim>

<!-- Brian and Dale's Excellent DTD

     Public identifier:

     DOCTYPE PUBLIC
     "-//SIG//DTD Brian and Dale's Excellent DTD//EN"
                                                                -->

<!-- General entity declarations                                -->
<!ENTITY mdo     SDATA "<!"                                      >
<!ENTITY pero    SDATA "%"                                       >
<!ENTITY mdc     SDATA ">"                                       >
<!ENTITY ero     SDATA "&"                                       >
<!ENTITY com     SDATA "--"                                      >
<!ENTITY nullcom SDATA "<!>"                                     >
<!ENTITY stago   SDATA "<"                                       >
<!ENTITY percnt  SDATA "%"                                       >
<!ENTITY tagc    SDATA ">"                                       >
<!ENTITY pio     SDATA "<?"                                      >
<!ENTITY pic     SDATA ">"                                       >
<!ENTITY MSC     SDATA "]]>"                                     >
<!ENTITY MSO     SDATA "<!["                                     >
<!ENTITY lt      SDATA "<"                                       >
<!ENTITY gt      SDATA ">"                                       >
<!ENTITY amp     SDATA "&"                                       >
<!ENTITY second  SDATA '"'                                       >
<!ENTITY inch    SDATA '"'                                       >
<!ENTITY foot    SDATA "'"                                       >
<!ENTITY apos    SDATA "[apos  ]"                                >
<!ENTITY sub2    SDATA "[sub2  ]"                                >
<!ENTITY mdash   SDATA "[mdash ]"                                >
<!ENTITY bullet  SDATA "[bullet]"                                >
<!ENTITY emdash  SDATA "[emdash]"                                >
<!ENTITY ldq     SDATA "[ldq   ]"                                >
<!ENTITY rdq     SDATA "[rdq   ]"                                >
<!ENTITY lsq     SDATA "[lsq   ]"                                >
<!ENTITY rsq     SDATA "[rsq   ]"                                >
<!ENTITY TAG     SDATA "[TAG   ]"                                >

<!-- Parameter entity declarations                              -->
<!ENTITY % exceptions "(inclusion | exclusion)"                  >
```

```
<!-- print attribute controls printing of sgml-code elements -->
<!ENTITY % print "print (print | noprint) print"              >
<!ENTITY % id    "id     ID     #IMPLIED"                      >
<!ENTITY % paragraph-inclusions "footnote | quote | list |
           table | illustration | example | xref | foreign |
           verbatim | sgml-code | emphasis | currency |
           start-tag | end-tag | entity-reference | cite |
           parser-output | reserved-word"                      >

<!ENTITY % table-attributes
           "contained-in    IDREF     #IMPLIED
            depends-on      IDREFS    #IMPLIED"                >

<!-- Get ISO public identifier set                           -->
<!ENTITY % iso-reference PUBLIC
                        "-//SIG//ENTITIES Reference//EN">
<!-- !!! %iso-reference;-->


<!-- Notations, (these don't do anything)                    -->
<!NOTATION MSWord SYSTEM "noprog.exe"                          >
<!NOTATION Pict   SYSTEM "noprog.exe"                          >


<!ELEMENT book          - O  (front-matter, body-matter,
                              rear-matter)
                              +(index-item | product | acronym) >
<!ATTLIST book          isbn        CDATA    #IMPLIED          >

<!ELEMENT front-matter  - O  (title-recto, title-verso?,
                              foreword, preface,
                              acknowledgements?, contents?)    >

<!ELEMENT (foreword | preface | acknowledgements)
                        - O  (title-group | paragraph)+        >

<!-- Contents are placed here. level tells application how
     many levels to include                                  -->
<!ELEMENT contents      - O  EMPTY                             >
<!ATTLIST contents      level       NUMBER   3                 >


<!ELEMENT title-recto   - O  (title, subtitle?, author+)       >
<!ELEMENT title-verso   - O  (paragraph+)                      >
```

```
<!ELEMENT title        O O  (#PCDATA) +(quote | reserved-word |
                              start-tag | end-tag)              >

<!ELEMENT subtitle     O O  (#PCDATA)                           >

<!ELEMENT author       - O  (surname, first-name, position?)    >
<!ELEMENT (surname | first-name | position)
                       - O  (#PCDATA)                           >

<!ELEMENT body-matter  - O  (part+)                             >
<!ELEMENT part         - O  (title, object?, chapter+)
                                                                >
<!ATTLIST part         %id;                                     >

<!ELEMENT appendicies  - O  (title, object?, appendix+)
                                                                >

<!ELEMENT chapter
                       - O  (title, introduction,
                             (paragraph | section |
                             title-group)+)
                                            +(reserved-word)    >
<!ELEMENT appendix
                       - O  (title, (paragraph | section |
                             title-group)+)
                                            +(reserved-word)    >
<!ATTLIST (chapter | appendix)
                       %id;                                     >

<!ELEMENT introduction - O  (paragraph+, related-topics)        >
<!ELEMENT related-topics
                       - O  (xref*)+                            >

<!ELEMENT section      - O  (title, (paragraph |
                             title-group)+)                     >
<!ATTLIST section      %id;                                     >

<!-- Title groups can contain other title groups, in effect
     creating an endless number of hierarchical levels
     applications will only support the first three title
     groups in a unique manner. Four on will look the same    -->
<!ELEMENT title-group  - O  (title, (paragraph | title-group)+)
                                            +(illustration)     >
```

```
<!ATTLIST title-group   %id;                                    >
<!ELEMENT paragraph     O O  (#PCDATA |
                                   %paragraph-inclusions;)+ >

<!-- acronyms are validated against the glossary terms        -->
<!ELEMENT acronym       - -  (#PCDATA)      -(acronym | xref) >

<!-- SGML code declarations start here
     DISCLAIMER: This DTD was created for the purpose of
     validating SGML examples for Brian and Dale's Excellent
     Book. It was not designed as a DTD parser; it is possible
     to tag a DTD or instance to this DTD and not have the
     resulting data parse                                     -->

<!ELEMENT sgml-code     - -  (doctype-declaration, markup)
                                      +(comment | break) >
<!ATTLIST sgml-code     errorok (errorok | noerrorok) noerrorok
                        %id;                                    >

<!ELEMENT doctype-declaration
                        - O  (element-declaration |
                              entity-declaration |
                              attlist-declaration |
                              shortref-declaration |
                              marked-section-declaration |
                              usemap-declaration |
                              comment |
                              notation-declaration)*

                                     +(entity-reference) >

<!-- doctype declaration attributes:
     id        unique identifier
     refid     use the specified DTD (no lookahead; must be
               previously specified in the instance) This is a
               #CONREF attribute, so specifying it renders the
               element EMPTY
     gi        generic identifier
     print     print or don't print the doctype-declaration. If
               refid is specified, the value of this attribute
               overrides the one in the original DTD.
     type      puts PUBLIC or SYSTEM in the declaration. external
               should be specified also
```

```
    external contains the external identifier (system or
             public)
    name     contains a filename that is to be used as the
             DTD (like using SYSTEM "usr/identifier.dtd")
                                                          -->
<!ATTLIST doctype-declaration
                        id   ID              #IMPLIED
                        refid IDREF          #CONREF
                        gi   NAME            #REQUIRED
                        %print;
                        type      (public | system)  #IMPLIED
                        external  CDATA              #IMPLIED
                        name      CDATA              #IMPLIED  >


<!ELEMENT markup        O O  (#PCDATA |
                             start-tag |
                             end-tag |
                             marked-section-declaration |
                             processing-instruction |
                             entity-reference)+             >

<!ELEMENT comment       - -  CDATA                          >
<!ATTLIST comment       %print;                             >

<!ELEMENT entity-reference
                        - O  EMPTY                          >

<!-- type=parameter makes it a parameter entity           -->
<!ATTLIST entity-reference
                        name NAME            #REQUIRED
                        %print;
                        type (parameter | general) general  >

<!ELEMENT start-tag     - O  (attr)*                        >
<!ATTLIST start-tag     gi   NAME            #REQUIRED
                        %print;                             >
<!ELEMENT attr          - O  EMPTY                          >
<!ATTLIST attr          name NAME            #REQUIRED
                        %print;
                        quote    (squote | dblquote) squote
                        minimize (minimize | nominimize)
                                             nominimize
                        value  CDATA         #REQUIRED      >
```

```
<!ELEMENT end-tag        - O  EMPTY                                >
<!ATTLIST end-tag        gi   NAMES           #REQUIRED
                         null (null | nonull) nonull
                         %print;                                   >

<!ELEMENT element-declaration
                         - O  (content-model, inclusion?,
                              exclusion?)                          >

<!ELEMENT marked-section-declaration
                         - -  ANY                                  >
<!ATTLIST marked-section-declaration
                         keyword   CDATA    "include"              >

<!ATTLIST element-declaration
                         gi   NAMES           #REQUIRED
                         %print;
                         stm  (s- | so)   so
                         etm  (e- | eo)   eo                       >
<!ELEMENT content-model O O  (#PCDATA)                             >

<!ELEMENT %exceptions;  - O  EMPTY                                 >
<!ATTLIST %exceptions;  gi   NAMES           #REQUIRED
                         %print;                                   >

<!ELEMENT attlist-declaration
                         - O  (attribute*)                         >

<!ATTLIST attlist-declaration
                         gi   NAMES           #REQUIRED
                         %print;                                   >

<!ELEMENT attribute      - O  EMPTY                                >
<!ATTLIST attribute      attr-name      NAME  #IMPLIED
                         declared-value CDATA #IMPLIED
                         type (notation | fixed) #IMPLIED
                         default-value  CDATA #IMPLIED             >

<!ELEMENT processing-instruction
                         - O  CDATA                                >

<!ELEMENT notation-declaration
                         - -  CDATA                                >
```

```
<!ATTLIST notation-declaration
                        name    NAME        #REQUIRED
                        %print;
                        type    (system | public) #IMPLIED     >

<!ELEMENT replacement-text
                        - O  RCDATA                            >
<!ATTLIST replacement-text
                        external  CDATA              #CONREF
                        quote     (squote | dblquote | none)
                                  squote
                        type      (system | public | cdata |
                                  sdata | pi | starttag | ndata |
                                  endtag | ms | md)  #IMPLIED  >

<!ELEMENT entity-declaration
                        - O  (replacement-text)                >
<!ATTLIST entity-declaration
                        name   NAME              #IMPLIED
                        default (default | nodefault) nodefault
                        %print;
                        type   (general | parameter | cdata)
                                               general         >

<!ELEMENT shortref-declaration
                        - O  (shortref-literal+)               >
<!ATTLIST shortref-declaration
                        map-name  NAME    #REQUIRED
                        %print;                                >

<!ELEMENT usemap-declaration
                        - O  EMPTY                             >
<!ATTLIST usemap-declaration
                        map-name     NAME   #REQUIRED
                        element-type NAME   #REQUIRED
                        %print;                                >

<!ELEMENT shortref-literal
                        - O  EMPTY                             >
<!ATTLIST shortref-literal
                        literal CDATA          #REQUIRED
                        name    NAME           #REQUIRED
                        %print;                                >
```

```
<!-- inserts one of three files from most recent sgml-code
     parsing run (input, output, or error log). setting lines
     attribute to 'lines' causes the line number to precede
     each output line
                                                              -->

<!ELEMENT parser-output - O  EMPTY                             >
<!ATTLIST parser-output type (input | output | error) output
                        lines  (lines | nolines)  nolines      >

<!ELEMENT rear-matter   - -  (appendicies+, glossary*,
                             resources?, index?)               >

<!-- indicates to the application where to put the index    -->
<!ELEMENT index         - O  EMPTY                             >

<!ELEMENT glossary      - O  (title, glossary-item+)
                                 +(index-item | acronym) >
<!ATTLIST glossary      generated  CDATA            #CONREF
                        type       (term | acronym)  #REQUIRED >

<!ELEMENT index-items   O O  (index-item+)                     >
<!-- index items. Attribute values:
    type:
        base      item gets page reference
        sub-item  will be nested under item
                  item does not get page reference
        see       will be nested under item prepended
                  with 'See:'
                  item does not get page reference
        see-also  will be nested under item prepended
                  with 'See also:'
                  item gets page reference

    print:
        print     contents are output to page
        noprint   contents are suppressed from page

   it is a semantic error to omit text when type != base

   <index-item>error</index-item>
        error, 123
   <index-item sub-item='recovery'>error</index-item>
        error
```

```
            recovery, 124
     <index-item see='boo-boos'>error</index-item>
         error
            See: boo-boos
     <index-item see-also='boners'>error</index-item>
         error, 125
            See also: boners
                                                                   -->
<!ELEMENT index-item    - -  (#PCDATA)           -(index-item) >
<!ATTLIST index-item    type (sub-item | see | see-also | root)
                                               root
                        %id;
                        text        CDATA    #IMPLIED
                        print       (print | noprint) print    >

<!ELEMENT product       - -  (#PCDATA)                          >
<!ATTLIST product       index-text  CDATA    #IMPLIED
                        print       (print | noprint) print    >

<!ELEMENT (term | definition | acro)
                        - O  (#PCDATA)      +(acronym | quote) >
<!ELEMENT resources     - O  (title, paragraph+,
                             resource-group+, addresses)
                                                +(index-item) >
<!ATTLIST resources     %id;                                    >
<!ELEMENT resource-group
                        - O  (title, entry+)                    >
<!ATTLIST resource-group
                        addl-info-type  CDATA  #REQUIRED        >

<!ELEMENT entry         - O  (resource, description,
                             addl-information?, cost?)         >
<!ATTLIST entry         where-to-get  IDREFS  #REQUIRED
                        id   ID    #REQUIRED                    >
<!ELEMENT (resource | description | addl-information | cost)
                        O O  (#PCDATA)
                                +(quote | currency | verbatim) >

<!ELEMENT addresses     - O  (address+)                         >

<!ELEMENT address       - O  (company, address-line*,
                             phone*, e-access*)                 >

<!ELEMENT (company | address-line | phone | e-access)
```

```
                         - O  (#PCDATA)                             >
<!ATTLIST e-access       type (url | e-mail) e-mail                 >
<!ATTLIST phone          type (voice | fax | modem)  voice          >
<!ATTLIST company        %id;                                       >

<!ELEMENT break          - O  EMPTY                                 >
<!ATTLIST break          tab  NUMBER   #IMPLIED                     >

<!ELEMENT example        - -  RCDATA                                >
<!ELEMENT caption        O O  (#PCDATA)
                            +(footnote | quote | reserved-word |
                            verbatim | start-tag | end-tag)         >
<!ELEMENT emphasis       - -  (#PCDATA)                             >

<!ELEMENT illustration   - -  (object+, caption)                    >
<!ATTLIST illustration   %id;                                       >
<!ELEMENT object         - O  EMPTY                                 >
<!ATTLIST object         %id;
                         name         CDATA   #REQUIRED
                         type         (wmf | pict | bmp | eps)
                                              #REQUIRED             >
<!ELEMENT glossary-item - O  (term & acro? & definition?)           >

<!-- foreign words are generally italicized                        -->
<!ELEMENT foreign        - -  (#PCDATA)                             >

<!ELEMENT cite           - -  (#PCDATA)                             >

<!-- currency is indicated so automatic conversions can be
     done by the application                                       -->
<!ELEMENT currency       - -  (#PCDATA)                             >
<!ATTLIST currency       type (us-dollar | bp | yen) us-dollar      >

<!-- reserved-word is generally set in monospaced font             -->
<!ELEMENT reserved-word - -  (#PCDATA)                              >

<!-- verbatim is generally set in monospaced font. "keep"
     attribute indicates to application that all text is to
     be kept together on the page.                                 -->
<!ELEMENT verbatim       - -  RCDATA                                >
<!ATTLIST verbatim       %id;
                         keep   (keep | nokeep)   nokeep
                         block  (block | inline)  block             >
```

```
<!-- xref attributes:
     refid    points to id
     see      generates the word "See"
     refer    generates the words "Refer to"
     autotext generates the words saved by id holder
     page     generates the words "on page"
                                                          -->
<!ELEMENT xref          - 0  EMPTY                         >
<!ATTLIST xref          refid       IDREFS    #REQUIRED
                        see      (see | nosee) see
                        refer    (refer | norefer) norefer
                        number   (number | nonumber) number
                        autotext (autotext | noautotext)
                                                  autotext
                        page     (page | nopage) page      >

<!-- table is in columnar form for better semantics. keep
     attribute indicates that the entire table is to be kept
     together on the page                                 -->
<!ELEMENT table         - -  (field+, caption)             >
<!ATTLIST table         %id;
                        keep   (keep | nokeep)   nokeep    >
<!ELEMENT field         - 0  (title, cell*)                >
<!ATTLIST field         %id;
                        %table-attributes;
                        relative-width  NUMBER  #IMPLIED
                        type   (char | date | currency |
                               signed-int | unsigned-int |
                               floating | formula | function |
                               verbatim | integer)  char   >
<!ELEMENT cell          - 0  (#PCDATA |
                             %paragraph-inclusions;)+      >
<!ATTLIST cell          %id;
                        %table-attributes;                 >

<!ELEMENT footnote      - -  (#PCDATA | %paragraph-inclusions;)+
                                              -(footnote) >

<!ELEMENT quote         - -  (#PCDATA | paragraph |
                             %paragraph-inclusions;)+      >

<!-- applications can expect to support up to four levels of
     nested lists. titles in list items are run-in        -->
<!ELEMENT list          - -  (title?, list-item+)          >
```

```
<!ATTLIST list             type (ordered | bulleted | simple)
                                              ordered          >
<!ELEMENT list-item        - 0  (title?, paragraph+)           >
```

APPENDIX • SIX

Fully Commented SGML Declaration

Introduction

This appendix contains two commented versions of SGML declarations. The first is sort of a default declaration that, when used, does absolutely nothing. That is, it contains all of the default values specified by the standard. This is available electronically at `http://www.sgml.com/SGMLImplementationGuide/sgml.dcl`

The second example is also an SGML declaration that contains all of the default values, but each value is declared explicitly, so you can see what kinds of parameters can be changed in order to customize SGML for your application. This is available at `http://www.sgml.com/SGMLImplementationGuide/verbose.dcl`

Default SGML Declaration

This declaration represents a common SGML Declaration with the reference concrete syntax. A declaration similar to this is what most parsers use as defaults if no SGML declaration appears in the document.

```
<!SGML "ISO 8879:1986"
    CHARSET
        BASESET "ISO 646-1983//CHARSET
            International Reference Version (IRV)//ESC 2/5 4/0"
        DESCSET
            0 9 UNUSED
            9 2 9
            11 2 UNUSED
            13 1 13
            14 18 UNUSED
            32 95 32
            127 1 UNUSED

        CAPACITY
            SGMLREF
            TOTALCAP 35000  -- must have at least one capacity
                               defined --
        SCOPE
            DOCUMENT

        -- reference concrete syntax starts here --

        SYNTAX
            SHUNCHAR
            CONTROLS
                0 1 2 3 4 5 6 7 8 9 10 11 12 13 14 15 16 17
                18 19 20 21 22 23 24 25 26 27 28 29 30 31
                127 255
            BASESET "ISO 646-1983//CHARSET
                International Reference
                Version (IRV)//ESC 2/5 4/0"
            DESCSET 0 128 0
            FUNCTION
                RE 13
                RS 10
                SPACE 32
                TAB SEPCHAR 9
            NAMING
                LCNMSTRT ""
```

```
            UCNMSTRT ""
            LCNMCHAR "-."
            UCNMCHAR "-."

            NAMECASE
                GENERAL YES
                ENTITY NO
        DELIM
            GENERAL SGMLREF
            SHORTREF SGMLREF
            NAMES SGMLREF
        QUANTITY SGMLREF

    -- reference concrete syntax ends here --

    FEATURES
        MINIMIZE
            DATATAG NO
            OMITTAG YES
            RANK NO
            SHORTTAG YES
        LINK
            SIMPLE NO
            IMPLICIT NO
            EXPLICIT NO
        OTHER
            CONCUR NO
            SUBDOC NO
            FORMAL YES
            APPINFO NONE

>
```

Fully Defined SGML Declaration

This fully defined SGML declaration can be used as a template to create variant concrete syntaxes. Beware that, in order to demonstrate how the reserved names field works, SGML names have all been mapped to other names. In order to have a useful declaration, you may comment this area out, or just the names that you don't want to change.

```
<!SGML "ISO 8879:1986"

    CHARSET
```

```
--
    Base character set for the document.
    In this case, ISO 646, or standard ASCII
--
BASESET
    "ISO 646-1983//CHARSET
        International Reference Version
        (IRV)//ESC 2/5 4/0"

--
    Described character set portion. Indicates which
    character numbers are to be recognized by the parser
--

DESCSET
      0   9   UNUSED
      9   2    9
     11   2   UNUSED
     13   1   13
     14  18   UNUSED
     32  95   32
    127   1   UNUSED

--
    Capacity set. Indicates to the application how much
    memory should be required in order to parse the
    document. This area is ignored by most parsers
    today.
--

CAPACITY  -- PUBLIC "ISO 8879:1986//CAPACITY
             Reference//EN"--
    SGMLREF
    TOTALCAP   35000
    ELEMCAP    35000
    ENTCAP     35000
    IDREFCAP   35000
    ENTCHCAP   35000
    EXGRPCAP   35000
    EXNMCAP    35000
    ATTCHCAP   35000
    GRPCAP     35000
    IDCAP      35000
```

```
    ATTCAP     35000
    LKNMCAP    35000
    LKSETCAP   35000
    AVGRPCAP   35000
    MAPCAP     35000
    NOTCAP     35000
    NOTCHCAP   35000

--
    Concrete syntax scope. Can be DOCUMENT, which means
    the declared concrete syntax is used throughout the
    document, or INSTANCE, which means the reference
    concrete syntax is used in prologues, and the
    declared concrete syntax is used in the document
    instance.
--

SCOPE
    DOCUMENT

SYNTAX

--
    Shuuned character number identification. This is a
    list of all characters that the parser is to report
    as unsupported. Shunned characters numbers should
    not be used to represent ordinary data characters.
--

    SHUNCHAR
        CONTROLS
        0 1 2 3 4 5 6 7 8 9 10 11 12 13 14 15 16 17
        18 19 20 21 22 23 24 25 26 27 28 29 30 31 32
        127 255

--
    Syntax-reference character set
--

BASESET
    "ISO 646-1983//CHARSET
    International Reference Version (IRV)//ESC 2/5 4/0"
DESCSET
    0 128 0
```

```
--
    Function character identification. Record end (RE),
    record start (RS) and space (SPACE) must be defined,
    plus whatever else is a function for the concrete
    syntax.
--

FUNCTION
    RE                   13
    RS                   10
    SPACE                32
    TAB       SEPCHAR     9

--
    Naming Rules. Indicates name characters and name
    start characters allowed in addition to the defaults
    (letter for name start and letter or digit for
    name). Add to this if your tag names have other
    characters.
--

NAMING
    LCNMSTRT  ""
    UCNMSTRT  ""
    LCNMCHAR  "-."
    UCNMCHAR  "-."

--
    Name case. Indicates whether upper- and lower-case
    letters are equivalent (YES) or not (NO). The values
    below differentiate in SGML names (element,
    attribute, and other names) and entities. With
    the defaults, <title>, <Title>, and <TITLE> are
    equivalent, while &mouth;, &Mouth;, and &MOUTH;
    are all different.
--

    NAMECASE
        GENERAL  YES
        ENTITY   NO

DELIM
```

```
--
    General delimiters. Be careful when changing
    delimiters to assure that there is not a
    conflict.
--

GENERAL
    SGMLREF
        AND        "&"
        COM        "--"
        CRO        "&#"
        DSC        "]"
        DSO        "["
        DTGC       "]"
        DTGO       "["
        ERO        "&"
        ETAGO      "</"
        GRPC       ")"
        GRPO       "("
        LIT        '"'
        LITA       "'"
        MDC        ">"
        MDO        "<!"
        MINUS      "-"
        MSC        "]]"
        NET        "/"
        OPT        "?"
        OR         "|"
        PERO       "%"
        PIC        ">"
        PIO        "<?"
        PLUS       "+"
        REFC       ";"
        REP        "*"
        RNI        "#"
        SEQ        ","
        STAGO      "<"
        TAGC       ">"
        VI         "="

--
    Short Reference Delimiters. These can be changed
    as appropriate. The standard deprecates short
    reference strings longer than a single
```

```
        character, unless the string is a common
        keyboarding convention or coding sequence.
    --

    SHORTREF
      SGMLREF
        "&#TAB;"
        "&#RE;"
        "&#RS;"
        "&#RS;B"
        "&#RS;&#RE;"
        "&#RS;B&#RE;"
        "B&#RE;"
        "&#SPACE;"
        "BB"
        '"'
        "#"
        "%"
        "'"
        "("
        ")"
        "*"
        "+"
        ","
        "-"
        "--"
        ":"
        ";"
        "="
        "@"
        "["
        "]"
        "^"
        "_"
        "{"
        "|"
        "}"
        "~"
--

     Reserved Name Use. To change a name, enter the
     desired name in the right- hand column next to the
     appropriate name. A new name cannot be the same as
     the one it is re-defining, nor can it be more than
```

```
    NAMELEN characters in length.

    The values in this example are not very useable. For
    example, an element declaration would look like
    this:

    <!THINGEE elem - MINOK (content | model | #WORDS)+>

    Comment out this area if you want the default
    values.

--


NAMES
    SGMLREF
        ANY         XANY
        ATTLIST     XATTLIST
        CDATA       XCDATA
        CONREF      XCONREF
        CURRENT     XCURRENT
        DEFAULT     XDEFAULT
        DOCTYPE     XDOCTYPE
        ELEMENT     THINGEE
        EMPTY       XEMPTY
        ENDTAG      XENDTAG
        ENTITIES    XENTITIS
        ENTITY      XENTITY
        FIXED       XFIXED
        ID          XID
        IDLINK      XIDLINK
        IDREF       XIDREF
        IDREFS      XIDREFS
        IGNORE      XIGNORE
        IMPLIED     XIMPLIED
        INCLUDE     XINCLUDE
        LINK        XLINK
        LINKTYPE    XLINKTYP
        MD          XMD
        MS          XMS
        NAME        XNAME
        NAMES       XNAMES
        NDATA       XNDATA
        NMTOKEN     XNMTOKEN
```

```
        NMTOKENS   XNMTOKNS
        NOTATION   XNOTATON
        NUMBER     XNUMBER
        NUMBERS    XNUMBERS
        NUTOKEN    XNUTOKEN
        NUTOKENS   XNUTOKNS
        O          MINOK
        PCDATA     WORDS
        PI         XPI
        POSTLINK   XPOSTLNK
        PUBLIC     XPUBLIC
        RCDATA     XRCDATA
        RE         XRE
        REQUIRED   XREQUIRD
        RESTORE    XRESTORE
        RS         XRS
        SDATA      XSDATA
        SHORTREF   XSHORTRF
        SIMPLE     XSIMPLE
        SPACE      XSPACE
        STARTTAG   XSTARTAG
        SUBDOC     XSUBDOC
        SYSTEM     XSYSTEM
        TEMP       XTEMP
        USELINK    XUSELINK
        USEMAP     XUSEMAP

--
    Quantity Set. Indicates quantities that the parser
    monitors. The most-often changed values are NAMELEN
    (length of tag names) and LITLEN (length of entity
    replacement text).

--

QUANTITY
    SGMLREF
        ATTCNT       40
        ATTSPLEN    960
        BSEQLEN     960
        DTAGLEN      16
        DTEMPLEN     16
        ENTLVL       16
        GRPCNT       32
```

```
        GRPGTCNT     96
        GRPLVL       16
        LITLEN      240
        NAMELEN       8
        NORMSEP       2
        PILEN       240
        TAGLEN      960
        TAGLVL       24

--
    Feature use
--

FEATURES

--
    Markup Minimization Features.
--

    MINIMIZE
        DATATAG  NO          -- YES or NO --
        OMITTAG  YES         -- YES or NO --
        RANK     NO          -- YES or NO --
        SHORTTAG YES         -- YES or NO --

--
    Link Type Features.
--

    LINK
        SIMPLE   NO          -- YES or NO --
        IMPLICIT NO          -- YES or NO --
        EXPLICIT NO          -- YES or NO --
--
    Other Features
--

    OTHER
        CONCUR   NO          -- YES or NO --
        SUBDOC   NO          -- YES or NO --
        FORMAL   YES         -- YES or NO --

--
    Application-specific Information. Indicates
```

```
        information that is independent of the document
        type an link process definitions. Could be used
        to specify an architecture to which the document
        conforms, HyTime, for example.
     --

        APPINFO NONE

>
```

APPENDIX • SEVEN

Glossary of Terms and Acronyms

AAP American Association of Publishers .

ACM Association for Computing Machinery .

AIIM Association for Information and Image Management .

ANSI American National Standards Institute .

API Application Programming Interface .

ARC Almaden Research Center.

ASCII American Standard Code for Information Interchange .

ATA-100 or ATA-2100 Air Transport Association/Airline Industries Association (Industry SGML Data Interchange Standard) .

ATM Adobe Type Manager .

Auto-tagging The process of locating and applying markup to textual information using an automated, programmatic utility. May be based on content interrogation or visual recognition concepts.

BBS Bulletin Board System .

BLOBS Binary Large Objects.

CALS Continuous Acquisition and Lifecycle Support (U.S. Department of Defense initiative) .

CANDA Computer Aided New Drug Application .

CApH Conventions for Application of HyTime .

CCITT Consultative Committee for International Telephony and Telegraphy

CD-ROM Compact Disk Read-Only Memory .

CDA Compound Document Architecture .

CGA Color Graphics Adapter .

CGM Computer Graphics Metafile .

Client/Server Architecture An approach to designing and constructing systems that separates functions between distributed clients, usually workstations, and one or more centralized servers or hosts. Dependent on clear separation of functions and a modular approach to system component design with clearly defined inter-operability functionality.

COBOL COmmon Business-Oriented Language .

Conceptual Design Design based on visionary or conceptual ideas about system functionality that will need further refinement and testing during the implementation process.

Content Interrogation The process of interrogating textual information to find information components by parsing through the content character by character. Uses clues found in the content or natural language portion of text, not the available coding or position.

Content-oriented Markup Encoding in text designed to impart the information identification independent of structural relationship and format rendering.

CPU Central Processing Unit .

Cumulative Net Benefit Quantitative benefit of a system implementation that takes into account the cumulative costs and benefits across the entire life of the system, usually on an annual basis.

DARPA Defense Advanced Research Projects Agency .

Data Cleansing The process of correcting data encoding errors through repeated parsing and addition of coding to make the data conform to a specific DTD.

Database Management System (DBMS) A system for managing data using data storage, processing, accessing functionality, usually with a strong application programming interface (API) for integration with other system components.

DBMS See Database Management System.

DCA Document Content Architecture .

DCE Distributed Computing Environment.

DEN Document-Enabled Networking (Novell Xerox document management standard) .

Desktop Publishing Systems (DTP) Document composition and layout systems involving interactive operator functionality available in desktop computing environments.

Detailed Design Design that has incorporated detailed analysis and rigorous definition of requirements during the implementation process.

DFS Distributed File System (OSF).

DIS Draft International Standard (OSF).

DLL Dynamic Link Library (MS-Windows) .

Document Analysis The process of identifying all of the components of information needed to support an organization's document information processing requirements and defining a markup language to be used in encoding information.

DOS Disk Operating System .

Downward Translation The process of pragmatically interpreting a more detailed form of markup into a less detailed, or lower, form of markup. Usually SGML markup is held to be a higher form when translating into a specific rendering markup such as composition coding.

DPI Dots Per Inch .

DSSSL Document Style Semantics and Specification Language (ISO 10179) .

DTD Document Type Definition .

DTP Desktop Publishing .

DTP See Desktop Publishing Systems.

EBCDIC Expanded Binary Coded Decimal Interchange Code .

EDI Electronic Data Interchange .

EPS Encapsulated PostScript .

EPSIG Electronic Publishing Special Interest Group .

ESIS Element Structure Information Set .

FAA Federal Aviation Administration (U.S.).

FAX Facsimile .

FCC Federal Communications Commission .

Federated Publishing Systems Systems that support publishing information across a heterogeneous and/or distributed environment. Based upon Federated Database systems principles where information may be managed and processed in a variety of formats and operating systems and may be stored in distributed systems conforming to a generalized data storage schema.

FIPS Federal Information Processing Standard .

Format-oriented Markup Encoding in text designed to impart the formatting appearance of the text after rendering by a composition system.

FOSI Format Output Specification Instance .

FTP File Transfer Protocol .

GCA Graphic Communications Association .

GCARI Graphic Communications Association Research Institute.

GEF Graphic Exchange Format (public domain GIF/ replacement) .

Generic Markup Coding in text that is generic or independent of specific processes. May be based on formatting, structure, or content identification.

GIF Graphic Interchange Format (Unisys/CompuServe bitmap format) .

GLTP General Language Transformation Process (DSSSL).

GML Generalized Markup Language (IBM) .

GOSIP Government OSI/ Protocols .

Granularity The level of detail of a data model design or the level of detail needed to support specific processes and identification requirements.

GUI Graphical User Interface .

H&J Hyphenation and Justification .

HPGL Hewlett-Packard Graphics Language .

HPPCL Hewlett-Packard Printer Command Language .

HTML HyperText Markup Language .

HTTP HyperText Transfer Protocol .

HyTime Hypermedia/Time-Based Structuring Language (ISO/ 10744) .

I/O Input/Output .

ICADD International Committee for Accessible Document Design .

IEEE Institute of Electrical and Electronics Engineers .

IETF Internet Engineering Task Force .

IETM Interactive Electronic Technical Manual .

Internet A worldwide collection of interconnected networks. Forms the backbone for the electronic mail and the World Wide Web.

IRS Internal Revenue Service (U.S.).

ISDN Integrated Services Digital Network (144 Kbps) .

ISO International Standards Organization .

JCALS Joint Continuous Acquisition and Lifecycle Support (US DoD) .

LAN Local Area Network .

Loose-leaf, Loose-leaf Publishing Printed products that allow for issuance of changed pages that must be inserted by the user organization, publishing systems that provide functionality to produce, manage, and control loose-leaf products.

MIME Multipurpose Internet Mail Extension .

MIPS Millions of Instructions Per Second .

MIS Management Information System .

NCSA National Center for Supercomputing Applications (Univ Illinois) .

NIST National Institute of Science & Technology (was NBS/) .

NOS Network Operating System .

OCR Optical Character Recognition .

ODA Office Document Architecture (ISO/ 8613) .

ODBC Open Database Connectivity (Microsoft) .

OEM Original Equipment Manufacturer .

OOPS Object-Oriented Programming System .

OS Output Specification (MIL/-M-28001) .

OSF Open Software Foundation .

PC Personal Computer.

PDF Portable Document Format (Adobe) .

PIA Printing Industries of America, Inc..

Procedural Markup Coding in text that describes processes to be applied to the text during rendering or processing.

QA Quality Assurance .

Qualitative Benefits Benefits to be derived from a system implementation that are not easily expressed in quantitative form, also known as soft benefits.

Quantitative Benefits Benefits to be derived from a system implementation that can easily be expressed in quantitative form, such as cost and or time savings.

RAM Random-Access Memory .

RAST Reference Application for SGML/ Testing .

RBOC Regional Bell Operating Company .

RCS Revision Control System .

RDBM Relational Database Manager .

Re-engineering Process of system design that based upon process-based design. Re-engineering may involve dramatic redesign to change from one processing paradigm to another.

RFC Request for Comments .

RFI Request for Information.

RFP Request for Proposal .

RIA Research Institute of America.

RTF Rich Text Format (Microsoft) .

SFQL Structured Full-text Query Language .

SGML Standard Generalized Markup Language (ISO 8879:1986).

SGML The Standard Generalized Markup Language (ISO 8879 1986). A standard for describing markup languages independent of specific processing systems, operating systems, and document models, designed for data longevity and portability.

SIG Special Interest Group.

SLIP Serial Line Internet Protocol (RFC/ 1055) .

SPDL Standard Page Description Language .

SQL Structured Query Language .

STAIRS Storage And Information Retrieval System (IBM) .

STEP Standard for Exchange of Product Data (ISO) .

Structure-oriented Markup Encoding in text design to impart the hierarchical and structural relationship of information independent of formatting and rendering considerations.

SVGA Super Video Graphics Array (display standard).

TCIF Telecommunications Industry Forum .

TCP/IP Transmission Control Protocol/Internet Protocol .

TEI Text Encoding Initiative .

TIFF Tagged Image File Format .

TMS Text Management System .

TOC Table of Contents.

Tree-to-tree Transformation The process of programmatically translating textual information from one hierarchical markup scheme by associating one structure to another using pre-defined relationships.

Uniform Resource Locator (url) A network address that is unique enough to assure that it addresses a particular site, document, or pre-defined point in a document. Used on the Internet and the World Wide Web.

url See Uniform Resource Locator.

UTF Universal Text Format (Newspaper Assoc. of America).

Validation The process of using a parser to check the conformance of a data instance against a specific DTD and reporting of errors where the instance does not conform.

VGA Video Graphics Array (display standard) .

Visual Recognition The process of identifying information components by programmatically analyzing the appearance of the information after rendering and then applying markup.

WAIS Wide Area Information Server .

WAN Wide Area Network .

WIP Work in Process, Work in Progress.

World Wide Web (WWW) A collection of Internet sites providing information to the public. Each World Wide Web site runs a software server that allows a user running a "Web Browser" program to access the information specified by the site administrator.

WWW See World Wide Web.

WYSIWYG What You See Is What You Get .

APPENDIX • EIGHT

SGML Resources

The comments included in the product and services descriptions below are intended to clarify and may include what is purely the opinion of the authors. Every attempt was made for currency and accuracy, but within every vital industry there is much change. A frequently updated version of this listing is available at `http://www.sgml.com/SGMLImplementationGuide/resource.html`. Comments and updates should be sent to `resources@sgml.com`.

The items within each classification are not listed in any particular order.

PARSERS

ARC Parser

WHERE TO GET

Public Domain
International SGML Users' Group (ISUG)

DESCRIPTION

Charles Goldfarb, the pioneer of SGML, wrote this parser as the standard was being written. The main purpose was to see if features they were putting in the language were implementable. Contains an interface to REXX.

COST

Free

OPERATING SYSTEM

MS-DOS, Macintosh (source available)

SGML-S

WHERE TO GET

Public Domain

DESCRIPTION

Based on the ARC parser, with many improvements and bug fixes. Outputs ESIS directly for inclusion into other processes. It is widely used and supported. A re-write of the SGML-S parser is called SP (for"SGML Parser").

COST

Free

OPERATING SYSTEM

Unix, MS-DOS, Macintosh (source available)

Mark-it

WHERE TO GET

Sema Group Systems, Ltd.

DESCRIPTION

Parser that uses the SGML LINK feature to control output during processing.

COST

US$1,000 up

OPERATING SYSTEM

Unix, MS-DOS, Mainframe

ASP

WHERE TO GET

Public Domain

DESCRIPTION

Developed at Vrije Universiteit in Amsterdam as an educational adventure.

COST

Free

OPERATING SYSTEM

Unix (source available)

XGML Validator

WHERE TO GET

Exoterica Corp.

DESCRIPTION

Uses Exoterica Corporation's SGML Engine to validate documents to a DTD. Does not provide ESIS, only an error stream.

COST

US$65

OPERATING SYSTEM

MS-DOS

HyMinder

WHERE TO GET

TechnoTeacher, Inc.

DESCRIPTION

A HyTime engine available as a C++ class library. Includes an SGML parser.

COST

Contact vendor for pricing.

OPERATING SYSTEM

Unix, MS-Windows

Project YAO

WHERE TO GET

Public Domain
International SGML Users' Group (ISUG)

DESCRIPTION

A free HyTime engine designed by the inventors of HyTime to promote the standard.

COST

Free

OPERATING SYSTEM

Source code

XGML Kernel

WHERE TO GET

Exoterica Corp.

DESCRIPTION

Consists of a C language function library that contains Exoterica Corporation's fast and accurate parsing technology. Available only for commercial applications with a royalty arrangement.

COST

Contact vendor for pricing.

OPERATING SYSTEM

Unix, Macintosh, MS-DOS

EDITORS

Adept•Editor

WHERE TO GET

ArborText Inc.

DESCRIPTION

Native SGML formatting editor with a TeX kernel for page makeup. Good table and equation editors. Highly customizable with good API. Main editorial workstation for billion-dollar JCALS project.

COST

US$1,500 up

OPERATING SYSTEM

Unix, MS-Windows

Author/Editor

WHERE TO GET

SoftQuad, Inc.

DESCRIPTION

The first real SGML "Quasi-WYG" editor. Powerful Applications Builder available for creating applications using a particular DTD. Good table editor. Works well with SoftQuad Publishing System (based on troff). Allows users to easily create SGML documents using built-in templates, and full context-sensitive markup assistance.

COST

US$995

OPERATING SYSTEM

Macintosh, Unix, MS-Windows

FrameMaker and FrameMaker+SGML

WHERE TO GET

Frame Technology Corp.

DESCRIPTION

A structured text editor. FrameMaker does not use SGML per se, but allows for editing structured documents. FrameMaker+SGML which supports import of DTDs and SGML instances and integrates authoring and editing with publishing capabilities.

COST

US$1,495 up.

OPERATING SYSTEM

Unix, Macintosh, MS-Windows.

Intellitag

WHERE TO GET

Novell Corp.

DESCRIPTION

WordPerfect's entry into the SGML editing market which includes import and export conversion functionality.

COST

US$495

OPERATING SYSTEM

Unix, MS-DOS

WordPerfect SGML Edition

WHERE TO GET

Novell Corp.

DESCRIPTION

WordPerfect SGML Edition layers SGML tagging and validation, along with a layout generation process, on top of WordPerfect 6.1 for MS-Windows. Combines interactive parsing with a WYSIWYG editing environment.

COST

US$249

OPERATING SYSTEM

MS-DOS

SGML Tag Wizard

WHERE TO GET

NICE Technologies

DESCRIPTION

A wizard add-in for Microsoft Word 6 for MS-Windows. Includes a parser as a MS-Windows .DLL. Manifests itself as a toolbar in Word. Allows mapping of element names to character attributes for a formatted view.

COST

Contact vendor for pricing.

OPERATING SYSTEM

MS-Windows

Microsoft Author for Word

WHERE TO GET

Microsoft Corp.

DESCRIPTION

Add-in for Microsoft Word for Windows that assists in structured document authoring. Does not use SGML, but does import and export SGML files via style coding and specialized comments. Includes structure checking function. Avalanche Development Company and SoftQuad will market add-ons for Author.

COST

US$400/seat

OPERATING SYSTEM

MS-Windows and Word for Windows version 6

HoTMetaL

WHERE TO GET

SoftQuad, Inc.

DESCRIPTION

HTML editorial software with spell-checking, thesaurus, search and replace. Similar to Author/Editor with HTML DTD hard-coded. HoTMetaL is free and available bundled with Spyglass' Enhanced Mosaic2.

HoTMetaL Pro is an enhanced version and is available for purchase from SoftQuad.

COST

Free (Pro version is US$200)

OPERATING SYSTEM

X-Windows, Sun Motif (HoTMetaL), MS-Windows, Macintosh, SGI/IRIX, HP-UX, AIX/RS6000, Solaris, DEC Alpha OSF/1 (HoTMetaL Pro).

Interleaf

WHERE TO GET

Interleaf, Inc.

DESCRIPTION

With version 5, Interleaf has integrated some aspects of SGML into their editing, formatting, and document management platforms. The company provides several tools to build SGML-based applications

COST

Contact vendor for pricing.

OPERATING SYSTEM

MS-DOS, Unix

InContext

WHERE TO GET

InContext Corp.

DESCRIPTION

Structured editor. Provides dual view of structure and content. Also part of the Xerox XSoft SGML package. Also available is the InContext software developer kit supporting integration of the editor with other software applications.

COST

US$995

OPERATING SYSTEM

MS-Windows

EASE

WHERE TO GET

E2S

DESCRIPTION

Character-based editor, similar to Markup, except with an SGML parser built-in. Multi-language support

COST

US$1,250 (MS-DOS) US$6,500 (Unix)

OPERATING SYSTEM

MS-DOS, Unix

WriterStation

WHERE TO GET

Frame Technology Corp.

DESCRIPTION

Editor with SGML parser front-end. Has tools to build applications. Very customizable. Works well with Frame DL Pager. Strong API.

COST

US$1,500 and up

OPERATING SYSTEM

MS-DOS, OS/2 Presentation Manager, MS-Windows

GRIF SGML Editor

WHERE TO GET

Grif S.A.

DESCRIPTION

Formatting SGML structured document editor. Recently chosen by IBM France as their internal SGML editor.

COST

Contact vendor for price.

OPERATING SYSTEM

Unix, MS-Windows, Macintosh.

GRIF SGML Notes

WHERE TO GET

Grif S.A.

DESCRIPTION

A "slimline" version of the Grif SGML Editor. Does not support display of images.

COST

Contact vendor for price.

OPERATING SYSTEM

MS-DOS, MS-Windows

SARA

WHERE TO GET

Oxford University Press

DESCRIPTION

SGML Aware Retrieval Application (SARA).

COST

Contact vendor for price.

OPERATING SYSTEM

MS-DOS, MS-Windows

Write-It

WHERE TO GET

Zandar Corporation

DESCRIPTION

Contact Vendor

COST

OPERATING SYSTEM

MS-DOS

SEMA Smart Editor

WHERE TO GET
Auto-Graphics, Inc.

DESCRIPTION
A database SGML editor from Auto-Graphics. Includes audit trails, editor notes, graphics support, and database reference (auto update). Includes a parser.

COST
Contact vendor for pricing.

OPERATING SYSTEM
Unix, MS-Windows, Windows NT.

Edit Time

WHERE TO GET
TimeLUX

DESCRIPTION
A fast editor that does not concern itself with fancy displays. All markup is shown, along with indications of error conditions. A good editor for production personnel who are not afraid of looking at markup. Also handles Unicode character sets.

COST
Contact vendor for pricing.

OPERATING SYSTEM
MS-Windows

Near&Far Author

WHERE TO GET
Microstar Software Ltd.

DESCRIPTION
An add-in for Microsoft Word. Shows structure and content concurrently using the same technology as that used in Microstar's document modelling tool Near&Far. Provides interactive parsing while using Microsoft Word as the editing environment.

COST
US$249

OPERATING SYSTEM
MS-Windows

DOCUMENT MODELING TOOLS

DTD Viewer

WHERE TO GET

ZIFTech Computer Systems, Inc.

DESCRIPTION

A graphical browser for DTDs. The product shows all aspects of a DTD including content models, attribute lists, notations, entities and so on. This is just a viewer, and cannot be used to create DTDs.

COST

US$110

OPERATING SYSTEM

MS-Windows

SGMLCompanion

WHERE TO GET

Publishing Development AB

DESCRIPTION

A stand-alone DTD creation and maintenance tool. Displays element tree graphically.

COST

US$400

OPERATING SYSTEM

MS-Windows

Near&Far

WHERE TO GET

Microstar Software Ltd.

DESCRIPTION

Designed for the user who must analyze, create, or modify document structures. Allows the modeling of a document graphically and creates a DTD on demand. Can be used with CADE (Computer Aided Document Engineering) Groupware. Strong reporting features for use in documentation development.

COST

US$795 (MS-Windows version), US$995 (Unix version).

OPERATING SYSTEM

MS-Windows, SunOS, Solaris, HP-UX.

Near&FAR Lite

WHERE TO GET

Microstar Software Ltd.

DESCRIPTION

Companion product to Near&Far. Allows users to visualize document models created in Near&Far. Can be used for teaching and communicating document structures.

COST

US$195 (MS-Windows version).

OPERATING SYSTEM

MS-Windows (others upon request).

CADE Groupware

WHERE TO GET

Microstar Software Ltd.

DESCRIPTION

Environment for collaborative document analysis and design, based on Lotus Notes. Companion product to Near&Far. Allows stored objects to be managed in a central repository and access by multiple users.

COST

US$995 (per server).

OPERATING SYSTEM

Platforms supported by Lotus Notes.

DTD2HTML

WHERE TO GET

Public Domain

DESCRIPTION

COST

OPERATING SYSTEM

Unix

RulesBuilder

WHERE TO GET

SoftQuad, Inc.

DESCRIPTION

Part of the Author/Editor package. Allows administrator to map tag names and context into on-screen formats, and users to edit and compile DTDs, and make them available to Author/Editor.

COST

US$995

OPERATING SYSTEM

Unix, MS-Windows, Macintosh

Document•Architect

WHERE TO GET

ArborText Inc.

DESCRIPTION

Used to create FOSIs and DTDs. Has interactive FOSI interface, so the user can see what effect each <e-i-c> will have when created.

COST

US$1,500 up

OPERATING SYSTEM

Unix, MS-Windows.

BROWSERS

DynaText

WHERE TO GET

Electronic Book Technologies, Inc.

DESCRIPTION

Compiles SGML files into electronic books and creates index for fast retrieval. Provides comprehensive hyperlink support. Supports various graphics standards.

COST

Contact vendor for pricing.

OPERATING SYSTEM

MS-Windows, Unix, Macintosh

Helmsman

WHERE TO GET

Northern Telecom

DESCRIPTION

Build function created indexed files from PostScript input. No direct SGML support. PostScript file must be created using a formatter.

COST

Contact vendor for pricing.

OPERATING SYSTEM

MS-Windows, Macintosh, Unix

BookManager

WHERE TO GET

IBM Corp.

DESCRIPTION

Part of the IBM publishing solution suite. Creates indexed file from formatted SGML files. Provides full text retrieval with hot links.

COST

Contact vendor for pricing.

OPERATING SYSTEM

VM, MVS, OS/2

Folio Views

WHERE TO GET

Folio Corporation

DESCRIPTION

Electronic publishing software family which produces Folio Views infobase files for distribution on CD-ROM, floppy disk, local-area networks, or using the Folio Infobase Web Server, via the World Wide Web.

COST

US$295 to US$3,995

OPERATING SYSTEM

MS-DOS, MS-Windows, Macintosh

Folio Views 3.1 SGML Toolkit

WHERE TO GET

Folio Corporation

DESCRIPTION

A toolkit for converting SGML documents to Folio infobase format. Includes Exoterica OmniMark and the Folio VIEWS 3.1 SGML Driver which validates SGML files and automates their conversion. Driver is available separately.

COST

Toolkit: US$2,995, Driver alone: US$495.

OPERATING SYSTEM

MS-DOS, MS-Windows, Macintosh

GUIDE Professional Publisher

WHERE TO GET

InfoAccess Corp

DESCRIPTION

A Suite of software tools and services that accept SGML data including CALS, J20008, AIA, and SEMI DTDs.

COST

Contact vendor for price.

OPERATING SYSTEM

MS-Windows

Grif SGML ActiveViews

WHERE TO GET

Grif S.A.

DESCRIPTION

WYSIWYG viewing of native SGML data, including complex tables and math. Provides hypertext navigation tools and a multi-view interface for rapid information access. Designed to support distribution of data in electronic products such as CD-ROMs.

COST

Contact vendor for price.

OPERATING SYSTEM

Unix, MS-Windows

InContext Spider

WHERE TO GET

InContext Corp.

DESCRIPTION

HTML editor which allows creation of Web pages.

COST

US$99

OPERATING SYSTEM

MS-Windows

HyperWriter

WHERE TO GET

Ntergaid, Inc.

DESCRIPTION

An environment for delivering electronic SGML documents electronically. Has OmniMark integrated to allow for full SGML support and hypertext capabilities.

COST

Contact vendor for pricing.

OPERATING SYSTEM

MS-DOS, MS-Windows

Lector

WHERE TO GET

Open Text Corp.

DESCRIPTION

A fast SGML browser with limited formatting capabilities.

COST

Contact vendor for pricing.

OPERATING SYSTEM

Unix, MS-Windows

OLIAS

WHERE TO GET

HaL Software Systems, Inc.

DESCRIPTION

Electronic delivery system that offers access to both SGML and World-wide Web (WWW) documents via an Internet connection.

COST

Contact vendor for pricing.

OPERATING SYSTEM

Unix

SGML Darc

WHERE TO GET

Synex Information AB

DESCRIPTION

Now called SoftQuad Explorer.

COST

OPERATING SYSTEM

Unix, MS-Windows

SoftQuad Explorer

WHERE TO GET

SoftQuad, Inc.

DESCRIPTION

An SGML document archiving and electronic delivery tool. A browser with full support of SGML. Allows "SGML Searches" , another way of saying the product can access text in a context-sensitive manner.

COST

US$995 (entire application), client application depends on volume.

OPERATING SYSTEM

MS-Windows

SuperBook System

WHERE TO GET

Bellcore

DESCRIPTION

A hypertext electronic document delivery system that allows client-server access to document databases. They are working on SGML support.

COST

Contact vendor for pricing.

OPERATING SYSTEM

Unix, MS-Windows, Macintosh, OS/2

WorldView

WHERE TO GET

Interleaf, Inc.

DESCRIPTION

Viewer for documents created using various tools: Word, WordPerfect, Postscript, FrameMaker, and Interleaf. Will also accept certain SGML documents if formatted using Interleaf 5 <SGML>.

COST

Contact vendor for pricing.

OPERATING SYSTEM

MS-DOS, Unix

TRANSLATORS

Exoterica OmniMark

WHERE TO GET

Exoterica Corp.

DESCRIPTION

Conversion, translation, and SGML data enrichment programming tool. Uses Exoterica's XGML Engine incorporating the XGML Kernel. Provides four types of translations and has a powerful pattern-matching and processing language. Integrated parser eases development of automated traditional and electronic product production.

COST

US$2,495 and up

OPERATING SYSTEM

MS-DOS, Windows NT, Unix, OS/2, Macintosh, VMS, MVS, others

Balise

WHERE TO GET

AIS Berger-Levrault

DESCRIPTION

An SGML application programming environment based around a validating parser. Main use of Balise is for SGML-to-SGML transformation, SGML instance enrichment, parsing and validation, database loading, and formatting. Designed with performance in mind and is useful as an integration tool.

COST

Contact vendor for pricing.

OPERATING SYSTEM

Unix, VMS, MS-DOS, Windows NT.

DynaTag

Where to Get

Electronic Book Technologies, Inc.

Description

A conversion environment using the Rainbow DTD as a guide for converting word-processing and other formatted documents to SGML.

Cost

Contact vendor for pricing.

Operating System

Unix, MS-Windows

PowerPaste

Where to Get

ArborText Inc.

Description

An interactive or batch conversion environment using the Rainbow DTD as the start for converting word-processing and other formatted documents to any arbitrary DTD.

Cost

Contact vendor for pricing.

Operating System

Unix, MS-Windows.

MetaMorphosis

Where to Get

MID Information Logistics Group

Description

A tool for converting any valid SGML instance to one of several popular word processor file formats or into another valid SGML instance.

Cost

Contact vendor for price.

Operating System

Unix, VMS, MS-DOS, and others upon request.

i2c

WHERE TO GET

MID Information Logistics Group

DESCRIPTION

Utility to convert tables structured according to ISO TR 9573-11:1992 into the CALS tables DTD; i2c is a runtime application of Balise.

COST

Contact vendor for price.

OPERATING SYSTEM

Unix, MS-DOS

Copenhagen SGML Tool (COST)

WHERE TO GET

Public Domain

DESCRIPTION

Freeware conversion tool. Uses publicly available language, Tool Command Language (TCL), to create downward translations. Distributed in source code form under the GNU public license provisions.

COST

free

OPERATING SYSTEM

Unix

Avalanche FastTag

WHERE TO GET

Avalanche Development Company

DESCRIPTION

Conversion tool that recognizes elements visually and provides objects to programmer for processing. Includes output specification language. Standard conversion packages available. The Visual Recognition Engine works well in recognizing tables.

COST

US$2,450 (MS-DOS, US$3,100 (Unix)

OPERATING SYSTEM

MS-DOS, Unix

Avalanche SGML Hammer

WHERE TO GET

Avalanche Development Company

DESCRIPTION

Translates from SGML to any other format. Uses same output language as FastTAG. Can be used for SGML-to-SGML conversion.

COST

US$1,500 (MS-DOS) US$2,100 (Unix)

OPERATING SYSTEM

MS-DOS, Unix

AAP2ISO

WHERE TO GET

NICE Technologies

DESCRIPTION

A translator for converting documents adhering to the AAP document standard to the ISO version of the AAP standard, ISO 12083.

COST

Contact vendor for pricing.

OPERATING SYSTEM

Unix, MS-Windows

Integrated Chameleon Architecture

WHERE TO GET

Public Domain

DESCRIPTION

A toolset for generating data translators. Developed by the Ohio State University Department of Computer and Information Science. Can be used to generate translators to and from a constrained subset of instances of DTDs.

COST

free

OPERATING SYSTEM

Unix

Rainbow-Makers

WHERE TO GET

Public Domain

DESCRIPTION

Applications used to create SGML files adhering to the Rainbow DTD from common word-processor and page-layout programs.

COST

free

OPERATING SYSTEM

Unix, MS-DOS

IBM SGML Translator

WHERE TO GET

IBM Corp.

DESCRIPTION

Part of IBM's BookMaster series of documentation tools.

COST

Contact vendor for pricing.

OPERATING SYSTEM

IBM

SGML ExportFilter for FrameMaker

WHERE TO GET

MID Information Logistics Group

DESCRIPTION

Converts any structured FrameMaker document or selected structural elements thereof to SGML instances including graphics and tables (using the CALS table model).

COST

US$3,100 for firstUS$600 additional

OPERATING SYSTEM

Unix

SGML2TEX

WHERE TO GET

Public Domain

DESCRIPTION

General-purpose translator for converting certain SGML documents to TeX

COST

OPERATING SYSTEM

MS-DOS

TagWrite

WHERE TO GET

Zandar Corporation

DESCRIPTION

A stand-alone data conversion utility without a parser.

COST

Contact vendor for pricing.

OPERATING SYSTEM

MS-Windows

qwertz/FORMAT

WHERE TO GET

Public Domain

DESCRIPTION

SGML to LaTeX and nroff/troff translator. Contains DTD emulating LaTeX document styles, BibTeX bibliographies and Unix manual pages.

COST

Free

OPERATING SYSTEM

Unix (source available)

FORMATTERS/PAGINATORS

BookMaster

WHERE TO GET

IBM Corp.

DESCRIPTION

The anchor of IBM's publishing suite. BookMaster consists of an SGML translator, a formatter (DCF), and other tools for creating, managing and publishing documents.

COST

Contact vendor for pricing.

OPERATING SYSTEM

VM, MVS

CAPS

WHERE TO GET

XSoft, a division of Xerox

DESCRIPTION

Composition software for structured document publishing. CAPS features SGML page composition, automated batch pagination, and distributed network printing. Can be used separately or as part of the Xerox XSoft publishing system.

COST

Starter package: US$24,995

OPERATING SYSTEM

SunOS 4.3 and Solaris 2.3

LaTeX

WHERE TO GET

TeX Users' Group

DESCRIPTION

LaTeX is a set of macros written on top of TeX that allows for the creation of documents that use generic tags. LaTeX version 3 is being developed. It will work more closely with SGML

COST

Free

OPERATING SYSTEM

All

Composer

WHERE TO GET

Frame Technology Corp.

DESCRIPTION

A batch composition engine that takes SGML and FOSI input and produces PostScript pages. Has SGML parser front-end and very good loose-leaf support. Uses FOSI for output specification.

COST

Contact vendor for pricing.

OPERATING SYSTEM

Unix, VMS

Adept•Publisher

WHERE TO GET

ArborText Inc.

DESCRIPTION

Turnkey native SGML publishing system that combines Adept•Editor and FOSI-driven composition engine (TeX-based).

COST

US$1,500 up

OPERATING SYSTEM

Unix, MS-Windows soon

SGMLEnabler

WHERE TO GET

SoftQuad, Inc.

DESCRIPTION

A Quark Xpress extension that allows translation of files from SGML to Quark Xpress. Allows users to import SGML documents into Quark and refine their layout using Quark's formatting tools.

COST

US$495

OPERATING SYSTEM

Macintosh

Corel Ventura Publisher

WHERE TO GET

Corel Corporation

DESCRIPTION

Desktop publishing package that can be fed with tagged files. SGML capabilities to be offered in version 6.

COST

US$595

OPERATING SYSTEM

MS-Windows

Interleaf 5 <SGML>

WHERE TO GET

Interleaf, Inc.

DESCRIPTION

Turn-key publishing system with SGML tacked-on. Has good support for graphics and paper output.

COST

Contact vendor for pricing.

OPERATING SYSTEM

Unix

DATA MANAGEMENT SYSTEMS

Astoria

WHERE TO GET

XSoft, a division of Xerox

DESCRIPTION

An SGML document component manager which allows users to access, search, and reuse their documents and components in a graphical, iconic environment. Ca be used separately or as part of XSoft's SGML publishing system.

COST

Not available

OPERATING SYSTEM

Expected support for Unix and PCs.

Parlance Document Management (PDM)

WHERE TO GET

Xyvision, Inc.

DESCRIPTION

Manages document modules in a production environment. Stores documents or document fragments as objects that can be combined for publishing in multiple documents with output to different media types. Also has revision control, and workflow features. Can be integrated with Xyvision publishing system and third-party products.

COST

Contact vendor for pricing.

OPERATING SYSTEM

Unix (server and client), MS-Windows (client)

Texcel Information Manager

WHERE TO GET

Texcel (UK) Ltd.

DESCRIPTION

An integrated set of tools surrounding an SGML-smart object-oriented database called Repository Manager. Texcel Information Manager tools include workflow management, electronic review, browsing, document assembly, and a link to outside databases and other applications.

COST

Approx US$32,000 for six-user configuration

OPERATING SYSTEM

SunOS, Solaris, HP-UX, RS6000, AIX (server and client), MS-Windows (client only).

DynaBase

WHERE TO GET

Electronic Book Technologies, Inc.

DESCRIPTION

A Client-server object-oriented database system that understands SGML natively. Can be integrated into a DynaText book-building environment.

COST

Contact vendor for pricing.

OPERATING SYSTEM

Unix and Windows NT Server, Unix and MS-Windows clients.

SGMLserver

WHERE TO GET

Information Dimensions Inc.

DESCRIPTION

Provides front-end for the company's full-text database product, BASISplus. Allows data to be defined at any level of granularity and stored intelligently. Provides a parser for verification as part of database load process.

COST

Contact vendor for pricing.

OPERATING SYSTEM

Unix, VMS, MVS, VM

SGML/Store

WHERE TO GET

AIS Berger-Levrault

DESCRIPTION

SGML database load and access toolkit designed to support large document editorial revision. Server runs under Unix under a client/server architecture and may be integrated with a variety of SGML editorial applications.

COST

Contact vendor for pricing

OPERATING SYSTEM

Unix, MS-DOS

Search Server, Ful/Text

WHERE TO GET

Fulcrum Technologies

DESCRIPTION

Two separate products that allow intelligent SGML storage of data based on Fulcrum's SQL database knowledge. Ful/Text is an SGML-smart database kernel, and SearchTools provides a full-text front-end.

COST

Search Server, Ful/Text: US$795 per user

OPERATING SYSTEM

Unix, MS-DOS, MS-Windows, Windows NT, VMS, others.

Fulcrum Surfboard

WHERE TO GET

Fulcrum Technologies

DESCRIPTION

Fulcrum Surfboard combines Fulcrum's powerful retrieval engine with Internet access protocols to allow World Wide Web and other Internet users to search and navigate effectively through the corporate publications and information put on the Internet.

COST

Fulcrum Surfboard: US$15,000 per server

OPERATING SYSTEM

Sun/OS 4.1.3, Solaris 2.3, HP/UX, Windows NT, others.

PAT

WHERE TO GET

Open Text Corp.

DESCRIPTION

A fast SGML-smart search and retrieval engine. Works in conjunction with LECTOR, an SGML viewer.

COST

Contact vendor for pricing.

OPERATING SYSTEM

Unix

SARA

WHERE TO GET

British National Corpus

DESCRIPTION

SGML Aware Retrieval Application

COST

Contact vendor for pricing.

OPERATING SYSTEM

Unix, MS-Windows

Polytron Version Control System (PVCS)

WHERE TO GET

Intersolv, Inc.

DESCRIPTION

Commercial version control system. Multi-user and network architecture eases workgroup project management. Third-party add-ons available.

COST

Contact vendor for pricing.

OPERATING SYSTEM

Unix, MS-Windows HP-UX, IBM RS/6000, SCO, Sun, OS/2, SCO, Windows NT, QNX, VMS.

GNU Revision Control System (rcs)

WHERE TO GET

RCS Information

DESCRIPTION

Free revision control system available from the GNU Software Foundation. Works in conjunction with other GNU software.

COST

Free

OPERATING SYSTEM

Unix, MS-Windows, Windows NT, source-code available.

Microsoft SourceSafe

WHERE TO GET

Microsoft Corp.

DESCRIPTION

General-purpose source code management and version control system. SourceSafe provides for true project level configuration control. Rather than using numbers to branch, such as version 2.3.6.1, a logical release or customer name can be used to implement the same construct.

COST

Contact vendor for pricing.

OPERATING SYSTEM

MS-DOS, Macintosh, MS-Windows, Windows NT

Relational Document Manager

WHERE TO GET

Interleaf, Inc.

DESCRIPTION

Consists of three modules: Library Manager provides access and security to SGML objects and fragments. Configuration Manager controls and maintains revision levels for objects. Workflow Manager routes information throughout workgroup.

COST

US$40,000

OPERATING SYSTEM

Unix, VMS, Macintosh, MS-Windows

WORLD WIDE WEB APPLICATIONS

DynaWeb

WHERE TO GET

Electronic Book Technologies, Inc.

DESCRIPTION

Server for World Wide Web (WWW) site. Provides intelligent front-end to create HTML files on-the-fly from a DynaText database based on a request from a client browser.

COST

Contact vendor for pricing.

OPERATING SYSTEM

Unix, Windows NT (soon).

Folio Infobase Web Server

WHERE TO GET

Folio Corporation

DESCRIPTION

Commercial hypertext transfer protocol (http) server with translation layer connecting Folio's proprietary infobase format. Product provides on-the-fly translation of infobase data into HTML format for publishing information on the World Wide Web.

COST

US$6,500

OPERATING SYSTEM

Windows NT

Panorama, Panorama Pro

WHERE TO GET

SoftQuad, Inc.

DESCRIPTION

Browser for SGML documents on the World Wide Web. Uses output specification language, DSSSL Lite to format documents adhering to arbitrary DTDs on the Web. Panorama Pro offers style sheet editor and advanced linking functions to base product. Users can view SGML documents on the World Wide Web. Panorama is bundled with Spyglass'

Enhanced Mosaic 2. An Enhanced version, Panorama Pro, is available for purchase from SoftQuad.

COST

Panorama bundled with Spyglass' Enhanced Mosaic 2. Panorama Pro is US$139.

OPERATING SYSTEM

MS-Windows

HoTMetaL, HoTMetaL Pro

WHERE TO GET

SoftQuad, Inc.

DESCRIPTION

Authoring environment for creating HTML documents for delivery on the World Wide Web. HoTMetaL Pro adds spell- and grammar-checkers, and other advanced features, to the base product.

COST

HoTMetaL available free. HoTMetaL Pro is US$495

Microsoft Internet Assistant

WHERE TO GET

Microsoft Corp.

DESCRIPTION

Add-in for Microsoft Word for Windows 6 allowing users to view and create HTML documents for delivery on the World Wide Web.

COST

Contact vendor for pricing. Available at www.microsoft.com

OPERATING SYSTEM

Add-in for Microsoft Word for Windows 6

WORKFLOW PRODUCTS

InConcert

WHERE TO GET

XSoft, a division of Xerox

DESCRIPTION

Document-based workflow management software for distributed computing environments. Can be used separately or as part of XSoft's SGML publishing system.

COST

US$23,000 (includes InConcert server, developer's and desktop kit, and 1 client license.)

OPERATING SYSTEM

SunOS, Solaris, AIX, HP-UX (server and clients), MS-Windows (client only)

WorkSMART

WHERE TO GET

InfoDesign Corporation

DESCRIPTION

Defines and manages work by defining "jobs" in terms of the logical sequence of "tasks" required to accomplish a specific goal. Allows easy graphic programming of workflows and jobs. Uses SGML internally to track objects.

COST

US$2,500 per seat

OPERATING SYSTEM

Unix

PassagePRO

WHERE TO GET

Passage Systems, Inc.

DESCRIPTION

Document management and workflow system.

COST

Contact vendor for pricing.

OPERATING SYSTEM

Unix

CONSULTING SERVICES

Information Architects, Inc.

WHERE TO GET

Information Architects, Inc.

DESCRIPTION

An independent SGML consulting and system-integraion group. Senior SGML consultants provide high-level information infrastructure analysis, document analysis, and DTD development. Analysts and programmers create and maintain documentation systems based on SGML, including systems analysis, integration, and conversion. Training in all aspects of SGML implementation is available. Information Architects is a sub-contractor on the billion-dollar JCALS project.

ATLIS Consulting Group

WHERE TO GET

ATLIS Consulting Group

DESCRIPTION

Provides document analysis, DTD development, SGML user training, conversion training and management overview.

Database Publishing Systems, Ltd.

WHERE TO GET

International SGML Users' Group (ISUG)

DESCRIPTION

System integrators specializing in the application of SGML. Also, provides legacy data conversion consulting and services.

InfoDesign Corporation

WHERE TO GET

InfoDesign Corporation

DESCRIPTION

An independent SGML consulting group and system integration company. The company also developed, markets, and integrates WorkSmart, a task management and workflow tool.

Exoterica

WHERE TO GET

Exoterica Corp.

DESCRIPTION

Developers of OmniMark and other SGML products. Exoterica provides consulting to their clients, mostly integrating their software into existing environments. Exoterica specializes in creating custom languages to solve their clients problems.

ArborText

WHERE TO GET

ArborText Inc.

DESCRIPTION

Sellers of SGML-based editing and composition tools, TeX formatters, and other publishing tools. ArborText offers, training, integration and general SGML consulting to their clients.

Pindar plc

WHERE TO GET

Pindar plc

DESCRIPTION

System integrators specializing in the application of SGML. Also, provides legacy data conversion consulting and services.

CONVERSION SERVICES

Data Conversion Laboratory

WHERE TO GET

Data Conversion Laboratory

DESCRIPTION

Scanning and conversion service bureau designed to support documentation and publishing requirements. Performs conversion to SGML from many formats.

COST

Contact vendor for pricing.

Innodata

WHERE TO GET

Innodata

DESCRIPTION

Large data conversion and capture service bureau with bulk keying facilities. Experienced in SGML encoding and conversion.

COST

Contact vendor for pricing.

Saztec Phillipines, Inc.

WHERE TO GET

Saztec Phillipines

DESCRIPTION

Large volume legacy conversion, keying, scanning, and CD-ROM service bureau with SGML experience.

COST

Contact vendor for pricing.

Gateway Conversion Technologies

WHERE TO GET

Accura Innovative Services

DESCRIPTION

Provides conversion of documents between different electronic formats, including SGML.

Database Publishing Systems, Ltd.

WHERE TO GET

International SGML Users' Group (ISUG)

DESCRIPTION

System integrators specializing in the application of SGML. Also, provides legacy data conversion consulting and services.

Pindar plc

WHERE TO GET

Pindar plc

DESCRIPTION

System integrators specializing in the application of SGML. Also, provides legacy data conversion consulting and services.

PERIODICALS

<TAG>, The SGML Newsletter

WHERE TO GET

SGML Associates, Inc./<TAG> The SGML Newsletter

DESCRIPTION

Premier periodical covering topics of interest to SGML users and developers. Published monthly, <TAG> is the only regular source of SGML news, technical features, information, and reviews. <TAG> enjoys an international subscription base, and strives to cover the world of SGML.

COST

US$180 per year. User Group, bulk-purchase, and institutional rates available.

FREQUENCY

Monthly

ISUG Bulletin

WHERE TO GET

International SGML Users' Group (ISUG)

DESCRIPTION

The International SGML Users' Group publishes a quarterly newsletter containing technical articles, news, and reports from the standards-making fronts.

COST

included with ISUG membership

FREQUENCY

Occasionally

EPSIG News

WHERE TO GET

EPSIG

DESCRIPTION

EPSIG publishes a quarterly newsletter devoted to topics of interest to EPSIG members, not just SGML.

COST

included with EPSIG membership

FREQUENCY

Quarterly

SGML Resource Guide

WHERE TO GET

Graphic Communications Association (GCA)

DESCRIPTION

A regularly updated loose-leaf publication covering worldwide resources for SGML implementors and users.

COST

US$54.95

FREQUENCY

Frequently

CALS Journal

WHERE TO GET

CALS Journal

DESCRIPTION

The CALS Journal is the most widely known periodical serving the CALS market..

COST

US$60 per year

FREQUENCY

Quarterly

USER COMMUNITY

comp.text.sgml newsgroup

WHERE TO GET

comp.text.sgml

DESCRIPTION

A usenet newsgroup dedicated to issues relating to SGML. The group attracts everyone from the novice user to seasoned pros, and has a self-moderated feeling.

COST

Free

ADDITIONAL INFORMATION

Usenet Newsgroup

Usenet access

WHERE TO GET

International SGML Users' Group (ISUG)

DESCRIPTION

local user groups

COST

Contact vendor for pricing.

ADDITIONAL INFORMATION

Dozens of Users' Groups dedicated to SGML are being formed all over the world. These groups offer new or potential SGML users local access to other users and sometimes present experts and vendors of SGML products.

ifi.uio.no

WHERE TO GET

Public Domain

DESCRIPTION

This is an ftp site accessible via anonymous ftp (ftp ifi.uio.no, login: anonymous, password: <your e-mail address>). Most SGML resources are available here, including a complete archive of messages from `comp.text.sgml`.

COST

Free

ADDITIONAL INFORMATION

ftp

STANDARDS PUBLICATIONS

SGML (ISO 8879:1986)

WHERE TO GET

International Standards Organization (ISO)
Graphic Communications Association (GCA)

DESCRIPTION

The actual SGML standard. Full title: Information Processing —Text and Office Systems—Standard Generalized Markup Language (SGML)

COST

US$38

FORM

Paper

DSSSL (ISO IEC DIS 10179:1991)

WHERE TO GET

International Standards Organization (ISO)
Graphic Communications Association (GCA)

DESCRIPTION

Text Composition—Document Style Semantics and Specification Language (DSSSL) is an SGML application devoted to describing how an SGML file should be represented, such as on paper or to a database.

COST

Contact vendor for pricing.

FORM

Paper

HyTime (ISO/IEC 10744:1992)

WHERE TO GET

International Standards Organization (ISO)
Graphic Communications Association (GCA)

DESCRIPTION

Information Technology—Hypermedia/Time-based Structuring Language (HyTime) is a standard neutral markup language for representing hypertext, multimedia, hypermedia, and time- and space-based documents in terms of their logical structure.

COST

Contact vendor for pricing.

FORM

Paper

SPDL (ISO/IEC DIS 10180:1991)

WHERE TO GET

International Standards Organization (ISO)
Graphic Communications Association (GCA)

DESCRIPTION

Information Processing—Text Composition—Standard Page Description Language (SPDL) Defines a standard method for describing the contents of a page. This is essentially enhanced PostScript.

COST

Contact vendor for pricing.

FORM

Paper

Many others

WHERE TO GET

International Standards Organization (ISO)
Graphic Communications Association (GCA)

DESCRIPTION

There are ISO standards for character set representation, registration of public entities, music definition, and others, all related to SGML. These are generally very dry reading, but essential for developing systems that comply with international stand

COST

Contact vendor for pricing.

FORM

Paper

CONFERENCES

SGML Conference

WHERE TO GET

Graphic Communications Association (GCA)

DESCRIPTION

SGML '94, SGML '95, etc. Popular North American SGML conference. SGML is featured, along with its new uses and advanced theories. Includes an "Up-to-Speed" tutorial on the day before.

COST

US$600-800

WHEN

Late Fall (Northern Hemisphere)

SGML Europe

WHERE TO GET

Graphic Communications Association (GCA)

DESCRIPTION

Previously called Markup '93, Markup '94, etc. This is the European equivalent to the annual SGML conference.

COST

US$600-800

WHEN

Late Spring (Northern Hemisphere)

Documation

WHERE TO GET

Graphic Communications Association (GCA)

DESCRIPTION

Graphic Communications Association (GCA)'s replacement for the long-running TechDoc conferences. Will broaden from SGML to all aspects of documentation including technical documentation, imaging, and multi-media.

COST

US$600-800

WHEN

Mid-Winter (Northern hemisphere)

CALS(several)

WHERE TO GET

SGML Associates, Inc./<TAG> The SGML Newsletter
CALS Journal

DESCRIPTION

Many conferences all over the world devoted to CALS.

ORGANIZATIONS

Graphic Communications Association (GCA)

WHERE TO GET

Graphic Communications Association (GCA)

DESCRIPTION

The premier group for SGML information and support. Graphic Communications Association (GCA) is an affiliate of the Printing Industries of America (PIA). The GCA conducts conferences, seminars, and tutorials on SGML topics.

COST

Contact vendor for pricing.

SCOPE

International

International SGML Users' Group (ISUG)

WHERE TO GET

International SGML Users' Group (ISUG)

DESCRIPTION

Group of standards makers, suppliers, technical managers, writers and other users of ISO 8879 SGML formed to facilitate sharing experiences and expertise on methodology. Members receive a newsletter and discounts on books, ISO standards, and conferences. More than 20 regional affiliates have chapters world wide.

COST

Individual: US$62 per year, corporate: US$125 per year.

SCOPE

International

International Organization for Standardization (ISO)

WHERE TO GET

International Standards Organization (ISO)

DESCRIPTION

Based in Geneva, Switzerland, ISO is the home of standards efforts worldwide. The SGML standard, and many of the related standards, are developed under the auspices of and published by ISO.

COST

Voluntary participation in standards activities.

SCOPE

International

SGML SIGhyper

WHERE TO GET

SGML SIGhyper

DESCRIPTION

A special interest group organized under ISUG for the promulgation of information about HyTime and DSSSL.

COST

Contact vendor for pricing.

SCOPE

International

Electronic Publishing Special Interest Group (EPSIG)

WHERE TO GET

EPSIG

DESCRIPTION

EPSIG is a collaboration between the Association of American Publishers (AAP) and the Graphic Communications Association Research Institute (GCARI). EPSIG offers a quarterly newsletter and other information about electronic publishing.

COST

Varies depending upon the type of membership: US$25, US$200, US$500 per year

SCOPE

North America

PUBLICATIONS

The SGML Implementation Guide

WHERE TO GET

SGML University
Graphic Communications Association (GCA)

DESCRIPTION

By Brian E. Travis and Dale C. Waldt. The first book on SGML implementation. This is the book the authors needed when they were first getting started in the SGML business. Contains information about building the business case, conversion, databases, SGML, document analysis, and implementation.

COST

US$50

PAGES

525

The SGML Handbook

WHERE TO GET

SGML University
Graphic Communications Association (GCA)

DESCRIPTION

By Charles Goldfarb, the father of SGML. This book is essential for implementing SGML. It contains the full text of ISO 8879, annotated by the author. It has a unique push-button access system that provides paper hypertext linking.

COST

US$95

PAGES

688

Practical SGML (Second Edition)

WHERE TO GET

SGML University
Graphic Communications Association (GCA)

DESCRIPTION

By Eric van Hervijnen. Described as a practical SGML survival kit for SGML users rather than developers. The book provides a practical and painless introduction to the essentials of SGML and an overview of some SGML applications.

COST
US$45

PAGES
288

Making Hypermedia Work: A User's Guide to HyTime

WHERE TO GET
SGML University
Graphic Communications Association (GCA)

DESCRIPTION
by Steven J. DeRose and David G. Durand. The first book on the HyTime standard. Authors do a good job of explaining the complex subject matter.

COST
US$68

PAGES
384

SGML: The Users' Guide to ISO 8879

WHERE TO GET
SGML University
Graphic Communications Association (GCA)

DESCRIPTION
By Joan Smith. The first book on SGML is a cross-referenced guide to the standard. It contains 200 syntax productions, a subject index, graphic representations for ISO 8879 character entities, and a list of SGML keywords.

COST
US$50

PAGES
173

SGML: An Author's Guide to the Standard Generalized Markup Language

WHERE TO GET

SGML University
Graphic Communications Association (GCA)

DESCRIPTION

By Martin Bryan. A highly detailed manual explaining and illustrating features of ISO 8879. Aimed at technical and non-technical authors, publishers, typesetters and users of desktop publishing systems. It assumes no prior knowledge of computing.

COST

US$40

PAGES

380

Annotated Bibliography and List of Resources

WHERE TO GET

SGML Associates, Inc./<TAG> The SGML Newsletter

DESCRIPTION

Robin Cover's comprehensive publication covering all articles, publications, and other resources about SGML over the years.

COST

US$30

PAGES

36

SGML Primer

WHERE TO GET

SGML University
Graphic Communications Association (GCA)

DESCRIPTION

Developed by SoftQuad, this small publication gives a 15-minute introduction to SGML.

COST

US$13.50

PAGES

25

SGML and Related Standards

WHERE TO GET

SGML University
Graphic Communications Association (GCA)

DESCRIPTION

By Joan Smith. The book covers standards for document description and processing languages developed by ISO.

COST

US$50

PAGES

151

SEMINARS

Implementing an SGML Publishing System

WHERE TO GET

University of Wisconsin-Madison/Extension

DESCRIPTION

Sponsored by the University of Wisconsin-Madison Department of Engineering Professional Development. A four-day course in practical SGML implementation techniques. Includes a diskette with The SGML Control Center, a tool to make it easier to develop and debug SGML applications, and sample documents and DTDs. Continuing education units are earned.

COST

US$1000

Implementing an SGML Publishing System

WHERE TO GET

University of Wisconsin-Madison/Extension

DESCRIPTION

Sponsored by the University of Wisconsin-Madison Department of Engineering Professional Development. A two-day version of the course above delivered over the NTU satellite network. Continuing education units are earned.

COST

US$350.

GCA Tutorial Series

WHERE TO GET

Graphic Communications Association (GCA)

DESCRIPTION

Sponsored by the Graphic Communications Association, these seminars provide generalized and specific information for the SGML implementor. Courses include SGML Basics, SGML Management Strategies, SGML Syntax, DTD Design, HyTime, and tutorials for the authoring and drug industries.

COST

Contact vendor for pricing.

MISCELLANY

SGML Tutorial

WHERE TO GET

Electronic Book Technologies, Inc.

DESCRIPTION

A hypertext-based product derived from Eric van Herwijnen's book Practical SGML. The tutorial uses EBT's DynaText product to provide interactive lessons on MS-Windows-based workstation. Includes parser.

COST

US$95

ADDITIONAL INFORMATION

MS-Windows 3.0 or higher

Industry Initiatives

WHERE TO GET

SGML Associates, Inc./<TAG> The SGML Newsletter

DESCRIPTION

There are many instances where companies in a particular industry will form a consortium to determine requirements for sharing data using SGML. Examples are CALS, the Air Transport Association's ATA-2100, and many others.

COST

Not applicable.

ADDITIONAL INFORMATION

Contact industry group

Conformance Testing Initiative Test Suite on CD-ROM

WHERE TO GET

Exoterica Corp.

DESCRIPTION

Exoterica Corporation's effort in developing a suite of documents to test conformance to the SGML standard is published in a CD-ROM containing

2,500 conforming SGML documents and 700 non-conforming documents. In addition, the disc contains a hypertext viewer.

COST

US$95

ADDITIONAL INFORMATION

Most operating systems

SGML: The Movie

WHERE TO GET

SGML University
Graphic Communications Association (GCA)

DESCRIPTION

A light-hearted introduction to SGML for managers. The movie provides an overview of the benefits of SGML via a trip to a future world.

COST

US$95

ADDITIONAL INFORMATION

VHS

SGML Content Modeller

WHERE TO GET

SGML University
Graphic Communications Association (GCA)

DESCRIPTION

Created by Tommie Usdin of ATLIS Consulting Group, this is a set of paper dolls that users can put together to form content models of their documents. Each piece only fits where it should, resulting in syntactically correct models.

COST

US$50

ADDITIONAL INFORMATION

Cardboard

Public DTDs

WHERE TO GET

Public Domain

DESCRIPTION

There are many DTDs that are available for public use. Sometimes these can be used as-is, but, more often, they are used by DTD authors to learn new ways to develop their own applications.

COST

Free

ADDITIONAL INFORMATION

electronic or paper

APPENDIX • NINE

Addresses of SGML Companies

Accura Innovative Services
500 Aerial Parkway
Morrisville NC 27560
USA
Voice: +1 919-941-0050
Fax: +1 919-941-1051

AIS Berger-Levrault
35, rue du Pont
F-92200 Neuilly-sur-Seine
France
Voice: +33 (1) 46-40-84-00
Fax: +33 (1) 46-40-84-10

ArborText Inc.
1000 Victors Way, Suite 400
Ann Arbor, MI 48108
USA
Voice: +1 313-996-3566
Fax: +1 313-996-3573

ATLIS Consulting Group
6011 Executive Blvd.
Rockville MD 20852
USA
Voice: +1 301-816-4311

Auto-Graphics, Inc.
3201 Temple Avenue
Pomona, CA 91768
USA
Voice: +1 909-595-7204
Fax: +1 909-595-3506
e-mail: `info@autographics.com`

Avalanche Development Company
947 Walnut Street
Boulder, CO 80302
USA
Voice: +1 303-449-5032
Fax: +1 303-449-3246
e-mail: `sales@avalanche.com`

Bellcore
8 Corporate Place - Room 3A184
Piscataway, NJ 08854
USA
Voice: +1 908-699-5800
Fax: +1 908-336-2559
e-mail: `idoreg@ims.bellcore.com`
url: `http://www.belcore.com`

British National Corpus
Oxford University Computing Services
13 Banbury Road
Oxford, OX2 6NN
United Kingdom
Voice: +44 (865) 273280
Fax: +44 (865) 273275
e-mail: `natcorp@oucs.ox.ac.uk`

CALS Journal
14407 Big Basin Way
Saratoga CA 95070
USA
Voice: +1 408-867-8600
Fax: +1 408-867-9800

comp.text.sgml
comp.text.sgml
Usenet newsgroup

Corel Corporation
The Corel Building
1600 Carling Avenue
Ottawa, Ontario
Canada K1Z 8R7
Voice: +1 613-728-8200
Fax: +1 613-761-9176

Corena A/S
Askerveien 61
P.O.Box 470
N-1371 Asker
Norway
Voice: +47-66 79 45 00
Fax: +47-66 79 45 90
e-mail: `toralf@corena.no`

Data Conversion Laboratory
184-13 Horace Harding Expressway
Fresh Meadows, NY 11365
USA
Voice: +1 718-357-8700
Fax: +1 718-357-8776

E2S
Voice: +32 91 21.03.83
Fax: +32 91 20.31.91

Electronic Book Technologies, Inc.
One Richmond Square
Providence, RI 02906
USA
Voice: +1 401-421-9550
Fax: +1 401-421-9551

EPSIG
c/o GCARI
P.O. Box 25707
Alexandria VA 22313
USA
Voice: +1 703-519-8184
Fax: +1 703-548-2867

Exoterica Corp.
1545 Carling Avenue, Suite 404
Ottawa, Ontario
K1Z 8P9
Canada
Voice: +1 613-722-1700
Fax: +1 613-722-5706
e-mail: `info@exoterica.com`

Expert Software Systems
Building de Schelde
Moutstraat 100
B-9000 Gent
Belgium
Voice: +32 91 21.03.83
Fax: +32 91 20.31.91
e-mail: `e2s@e2s.be`

Folio Corporation
5072 North 300 West
Provo UT 84604
USA
Voice: 800-543-6546
Voice: 801-229-6700
Voice: 801-229-6790
e-mail: `sales@folio.com`

Frame Technology Corp.
333 West San Carlos Street
San Jose, CA 95110
USA
Voice: +1 408-975-6000
Fax: +1 408-975-6600

Fulcrum Technologies
785 Carling Avenue
Ottawa Ontario K1S 5H4
Canada
Voice: +1 613-238-1761
Fax: +1 613-238-7695
e-mail: `info@fultech.com`
url: `http://www.fultech.com`

Graphic Communications Association (GCA)
100 Daingerfield Road
Alexandria VA 22314
USA
Voice: +1 703-519-8160
Fax: +1 703-548-2867

Grif S.A.
Immeuble Le Florestan
2, boulevard Vauban
B.P. 266
F-78053 St. Quentin en Yvelines
France
Voice: +33 1-30-12-14-30
Fax: +33 1-30-64-06-46

HaL Software Systems, Inc.
3006A Longhorn Blvd., Suite 113
Austin, TX 78758
USA
Voice: +1 512-834-9962
Fax: +1 512-834-9963
e-mail: `jps@hal.com`

IBM Corp.
400 Columbus Avenue
Valhalla, NY 10595
USA
Voice: +1 914-749-3409

InContext Corp.
2 St. Clair Ave. West, Suite 1600
Toronto
M4V IL5
Canada
Voice: +1 416-922-0087
Fax: +1 416-922-6489

InfoAccess Corp
e-mail: `guide@halcyon.com`

InfoDesign Corporation
One Prince Street
Alexandria VA 22314
USA
Voice: +1 703-519-9656
Fax: +1 703-519-9775

Information Architects, Inc.
6360 S. Gibraltar Circle
Aurora CO 80016
USA
Voice: +1 303-766-1336
Fax: +1 303-680-4906
e-mail: `info@sgml.com`
url: `http://www.sgml.com/iai`

Information Dimensions Inc.
5080 Tuttle Crossing Blvd
Dublin, OH 43017-3569
USA
Voice: +1 614-761-8083
Fax: +1 614-761-7290

Innodata
Brooklyn, NY
USA
Voice: +1 718-625-7750

Interleaf, Inc.
Prospect Place
9 Hillside Avenue
Waltham, MA 02154
USA
Voice: +1 617-290-0710
Fax: +1 617-290-4943

International SGML Users' Group (ISUG)
c/o MS. Gaynor West
Database Publishing Systems Ltd
PO Box 361
Swindon
Wiltshire SN5 7BF
United Kingdom
Voice: +44 793-512-515
Fax: +44 793-512-516
e-mail: dpsllgew@visionware.co.uk

International Standards Organization (ISO)
Central Secretariat, Geneva
Voice: +41 22-24-12-40
Fax: +41 22-33-34-30

Intersolv, Inc.
1700 NW 167th Place
Beaverton, OR 97006
Voice: +1 503-645-1150
url: http://www.intersolv.com

Microsoft Corp.
One Microsoft Way
Redmond, Washington 98052-6399
USA
Voice: 206-882-8080
url: ftp://ftp.microsoft.com
url: http://www.microsoft.com

Microstar Software Ltd.
34 Colonnade Rd N
Nepean, Ontario
K2E 7J6
Canada
Voice: +1 613-727-5696
Fax: +1 613-727-9491
e-mail: cade@msl.isis.org

MID Information Logistics Group
Ringstrasse 19
69115 Heidelberg
Germany
Voice: +49 6221-166091
Fax: +49 6221-23921
e-mail: post@mid-heidelberg.de
url: http://www.mid-heidelberg.de

NICE Technologies
Chemin des Hutins
Veraz
F-01170 Gex
France
Voice: +33 50-42-49-40
Fax: +33 50-42-49-40
e-mail: evh@altern.com

Northern Telecom
200 Athens Way
Nashville TN 37228
USA
Voice: +1 615-734-4000

Novell Corp.
1555 N. Technology Way
Orem, UT 84057
USA
Voice: +1 801-225 5000
Fax: +1 801-225 5077

Ntergaid, Inc.
60, Commerce Park
Milford, CT 06460
USA
Voice: +1 203-783-1280
Fax: +1 203-882-0850
e-mail: 75160.3357@compuserve.com

Open Text Corp.
180 King Street South, Suite 550
Waterloo, Ontario
N2L 1P8
Canada
Voice: +1 519-888-7111
Fax: +1 519-888-0677

Oxford University Press
Walton Street
Oxford
OX2 6DP
UK
Voice: +44 (865) 267979
Fax: +44 (865) 267990

Passage Systems, Inc.
465 Fairchild Dr., Suite 201
Mt. View, CA 94043
USA
Voice: +1 415-390-0911

Pindar plc
Reydale Building, First Floor
60 Piccadilly
York
YO1 INX
United Kingdom
Voice: +44 (0)1904 613040
Fax: +44 (0)1904 613110
e-mail: `pindar@cix.compulink.co.uk`

Public Domain
url: `ftp://ftp.ifi.uio.no:/pub/SGML`
url: `ftp://sgml1.ex.ac.uk`

Publishing Development AB
Torpvagen 10
S-175 43 Jarfalla
Sweden
Voice: +46 (8) 580-37579
Fax: +46 (8) 580-37579
e-mail: `christian@pubdev.se`

RCS Information
url: `http://www.eecs.nwu.edu /cgi-bin/info/rcs.info`
url: `ftp://cs.purdue.edu/pub/RCS`
url: `ftp://pub/pc/win3/nt`

Saztec Phillipines
Saztec Building, Pascor Drive
Sto. Nino, Paranaque 1700
Metro Manila, Phillipines
Voice: +632 831-1396
Fax: +632 831-0279
e-mail: `sazphil@mozcom.com`

Sema Group Systems, Ltd.
AG Building
Place du Champ de Mars 5
Bte 40
B-1050 Bruxelles
Belgium
Voice: +32 2 508 5323
Fax: +32 2 512 1499

SGML Associates, Inc./<TAG> The SGML Newsletter
6360 S. Gibraltar Circle
Aurora CO 80016
USA
Voice: +1 303-680-0875
Fax: +1 303-680-4906
e-mail: `tag@sgml.com`
url: `http://www.sgml.com/TAG`

SGML SIGhyper
Director: Erik Naggum
PO Box 1570
VIKA
0118 Oslo
Norway
Voice: +47-2295-0313
e-mail: `erik@naggum.no`

SGML Open
Mary Laplante, Executive Director
218 Parliament Drive
Coraopolis PA 15108
USA
Voice: +1 412-264-4258
url: `http://www.sgmlopen.org`

SGML University
Fax: +1 303-680-4906
url: `http://www.sgml.com/sgmlu`

SoftQuad, Inc.
56 Aberfoyle Crescent, Suite 810
Toronto, Ontario
M8X 2W4
Canada
Voice: +1 416-239-4801
Fax: +1 416-239-7105

Synex Information AB
Kallforsv. 24
S-124 32 Bandhagen
Sweden
e-mail: `haitto@nada.kth.se`

TimeLUX
L-1611 Avenue de la Gare
Luxembourg 1611
Luxembourg
Voice: +35 240 53 224
Fax: +35 240 50 09
e-mail: `timelux@mail.interpac.be`

TeX Users' Group
Fax: +1 401-751-1071
e-mail: `tug@math.ams.org`

Texcel (UK) Ltd.
Fountain Court
28-32 Frances Road
Windsor Berkshire SL4 3AA
UK
Voice: +44 01753 833111
Fax: +44 01753 854090

TechnoTeacher, Inc.
3800 Monroe Avenue
Pittsford, NY 14534-1330
USA
Voice: +1 716-389-0961
Fax: +1 716-389-0960
e-mail: hyminder@techno.com

University of Wisconsin-Madison/ Extension
Engineering Professional Professional Development
College of Engineering
702 Langdon Street
Madison, WI 53706
Voice: +1 800-462-0876
Voice: +1 608-262-1299
Fax: +1 800-442-4214
Fax: +1 608-265-3448

Westinghouse Electric Corp.
P.O.Box 746
Baltimore, MD 21298-6451
USA
Voice: +1 410-993-2214

XSoft, a division of Xerox
10875 Ranhco Bernardo Road, Suite 200
San Diego, CA 92127
USA
Voice: +1 619-676 7700
Fax: +1 619-676 7710
e-mail: info@xsoft.xerox.com
url: http://www.xsoft.com

Xyvision, Inc.
101 Edgewater Drive
Wakefield, MA 01880
USA
Voice: +1 617-245-4100
Fax: +1 617-246-6209

Zandar Corporation
R.R.2 Box 962 (Hanley Lane)
PO Box 467
Jericho, VT 05465
USA
Voice: +1 802-899-1058

ZIFTech Computer Systems, Inc.
120 Herchmer Crescent
Kingston, Ontario
K7M 2V9
Canada
Voice: +1 613-531-9226
Fax: +1 613-531-8003
e-mail: 70444.126@compuserve.com

APPENDIX • TEN

Index

!

#CONREF
change processing, 357
default value, 244, 246
end-tag an error, 221
table processing, 352
#CURRENT
default value, 244
easing entry, 362
#FIXED
default value, 244
#IMPLIED
default value, 244
#PCDATA
defined, 234
#REQUIRED
default value, 244
100% batch composition, 379
<TAG>, The SGML Newsletter
description, 485

A

AAP2ISO
description, 467
Access, 374
element view, 377
intellectual structure, 376
accumulated benefit, 137
accumulated costs, 137
Accura Innovative Services
address,
Acrobat
in case study, 389
Add-ins
SGML, 51
Adept•Editor
in database environment, 200
loose-leaf environment, 357
public entity mapping, 329
Adept•Editor
description, 449
Adept•Publisher
composition engine, 52

composition engines, 111
Adept•Publisher
description, 471
Adobe
acrobat, 389
Illustrator, 407
PageMaker, 38, 403
advertising, 40
Aging System, 9
aircraft
maintenance documentation, 392
aircraft document deliverable, 393
AIS Berger-Levrault
address, 503
Balise, 177
Ambiguity
using for maximum benefit, 341
ambiguous content model
avoiding, 315
analyst
skills, 104
Annotated Bibliography and List of Resources
description, 496
API
customizing applications, 117
programmers, 104
toolkits, 110
application, 60, 61, 101
analysts, 104
browsers, 110
capture, 105
composition engines, 111
conversion, 106
databases, 110
defined, 102
development, 203
development team, 103
editorial workstation types, 106
editorial workstations, 106
format development, 141
FOSI, 114
glue, 118
implementation factors, 105
integration issues, 118, 119
manager, 103
owner, 103
parser, 102
programmers, 104
SGML, 44, 60
SGML-smart, 50
system tools, 143
translators, 111
users, 105
vendor-supplied, 117
ArborText, 111, 482
address, 503
AdeptEditor, 357
AdeptPublisher, 52
description, 482
PowerPaste, 167
ARC Parser
description, 446
architectural forms, 57, 117
ASP
description, 447
Astoria
description, 58
screen, 58
Astoria
description, 473
ATA, 392, 397
ATLIS Consulting Group
address, 503
ATLIS Consulting Group
description, 481
attribute, 299
See also: attribute list declaration
capturing essential information, 348
in start-tag, 221
name omission, 319
specifying semantic information, 363
vs. element, 304
vs. elements, 66
Attribute Definition List
declaration, defined, 224
omitted attribute specification, 319
attribute definition list declaration (ATTLIST)
defined, 240
attribute list declarations
organizing, 280
author
professional, 39, 40
role, 39
Author/Editor, 50, 451
book production, 403
description, 449
public entity mapping, 329
screen shot, 49
authoring, 8
opportunities, 19
Auto-Graphics, Inc.
address, 503
auto-taggers, 47
Auto-tagging, 21,
automated processes, 4
automation, 5
Avalanche Development Company
address, 504
FastTag, 373
SGML Author add-ins, 451
Avalanche FastTag
description, 466
Avalanche SGML Hammer
description, 466
AWK, 154, 177

B

Balise, 466
conversion tool, 106, 177, 178
basic document elements,
Bellcore
address, 504
benefit, 7
qualitative, 135
quantifying, 134
quantitative, 135
stated in business terms, 8
BLOBS
database considerations, 202
BookManager
description, 459
BookMaster
description, 470
box diagrams, 79
branch
reconciliation, 188
Brian and Dale's Excellent DTD
cross-references, 293
in the flesh, 293
indexing, 299
tables, 405

British National Corpus
 address, 504
browsers, 52, 110
 HTML, 56
business
 case, making the, 7
 issues, 5, 8
 needs
 objectives, 124, 123, 124
by-product, 78, 90
 conversion through attrition, 167
 process, 31

C

CADE Groupware
 description, 457
CALS Journal
 address, 504
 description, 486
CALS Conference
 description, 490
CAPACITY
 explained, 226
Capitalization, 26
CAPS
 description, 470
Capture, 43, 45
Capturing, 8
 See also: conversion
Cautions
 common elements, 300
CD-ROM, 53, 55, 372
 development, 113
CDATA
 declared value, 241
 defined, 236
CGM
 graphic format, 16
 in ATA documents, 398
change
 communication, 127
 managing, 127
character architectures, 119
character reference
 defined, 223
 in markup, 220
check-out/check-in, 186
citation
 database, 306
 directive 10-289, 307
cleansing process, 164
client/server architecture, 373, 396
COBOL, 177
code analysis, 73
Collection process, 31
Comment
 declaration, defined, 225
 defined, 222
 in DTD, 278
 in markup, 220
 null, 262
 protecting from parser, 350
communicate
 structure, 79
comp.text.sgml newsgroup
 address, 504
 description, 487
Compatibility, 119
Composer
 description, 470
composition, 32, 52, 8
 See also: information delivery
 automated, 30
 issues, 379
composition engine, 52
computer-based editing, 12
conceptual design, 133
Concurrent Structures, 374, 375
conditional processing, 365
conformance
 testing, 46
conformance test suite, 46
Conformance Testing Initiative Test Suite on CD-ROM
 description, 499
connectors, 82
 table, 231
consistency
 costs, 16
consultant
 document analysis, 68
containment, 80
content, 78
 document, 87
 extraction and generation process, 174
Content extraction/generation, 171
content identification, 76
content model, 82, 83
 examples, 232
 explained, 231
 mixed content, 313
content tagging, 15, 89
content-overdose, 90
context-sensitive searching, 52
contractors, 147
conversion, 45, 47, 109, 145, 154
 against proprietary coding, 176
 application, 106
 application languages, 106
 clean-up, 347
 cleansing, 164
 cleansing through attrition, 166
 code analysis, 73
 content interrogation, 178
 context, 179
 costs, 165
 data, 151
 data capture, 171
 definition, 153
 difficulties, 108
 errors, 109
 interactive assisted, defined, 176
 manual, defined, 175
 phases, 161
 pre-conversion testing, 168
 process, 154, 163
 process flow, 158
 processing, 154, 163
 processing log, 158
 production feeds, 172
 program, 61
 programs, 156, 168
 project, 154
 Rainbow, 109
 resolution of issues, 170
 service bureaus, 169
 skills, 170
 specification, 156, 157
 specifications, 169
 strategies, 165
 through attrition, 166
 tools, 153
 tracking, 159
 types of, 175
 validation, 164
 verification, 155
 visual recognition, 179

conversion service bureau, 73
conversions
 standardized coding, 179
converters, 47
Copenhagen SGML Tool (COST)
 description, 466
Corel Corporation
 address, 504
Corel Ventura Publisher, 471, 111, 404
 description, 471
Corena A/S
 address, 504
cost evaluation, 133
cost/benefit analysis, 137
costs
 conversion, 145
 system, 145
Creation, 43, 45, 8
 See also: authoring
cross reference, 96
cross-reference
 common elements, 260
 generating text automatically, 294

D

data
 conversion, 4, 45, 151, 153, 154
 database, 45
 enhancing, 153
 extraction, 174
 inconsistency, 9
 ownership, 77, 203
 reuse, 13, 112, 397
 verification, 155
data capture, 171
 See also: conversion
 opportunities, 20
Data Conversion Laboratory
 address, 504
 description, 483
Data Gathering, 401
Data Inconsistency, 9
data integrity, 204
data interchange
 difficulties, 4
data management, 14, 17, 183
 requirements, 77
data model, 77
Data Organization, 18
data processing
 concepts, 5
data server, 55
data sharing, 398
data tag
 defined, 273
database, 43
 access, 77
 atoms, 374
 document, 65
 full-text, 193
 granularity, 202
 implementation, 192
 object-oriented, 58
 opportunities, 16
 textual, 86
 user authorities, 211
 version control, 186
database management, 11
 using file system as, 186
 opportunities, 17
Database Publishing Systems, Ltd., 481, 483
 description, 481, 483
Datalogics Corporation
 See: Frame Technology Corp.
DBMS, 14, 15, 19, 20, 37
 publishing integration, 37
DCE, 396
DTD2HTML
declaration
 element, 229
Deductive reasoning
 in document analysis, 342
defining data, 14
defining information structures, 15
Delivery, 51
design
 benefits, 77
 document analysis, 69
desktop publishing, 19, 25, 36, 38, 40
 benefits, 38
 drawbacks, 39
 issues, 37
 selection, 41
 suitability, 41
DFS, 396
DL Composer
 composition engine, 52
Documation
 description, 490
document, 66
 analysis, 65
 analyst, 68
 assembly, 201
 configuration, 396
 definition, 75
 fragments, access, 18
 hierarchy, 81
 inconsistency, 13
 instance, 67, 218
 model, 67, 75
 revision number, 187
 skills, 68
 structure, 78, 87
 tracking, 13
 version number, 187
document analysis, 65
 consultant, 68
 deductive reasoning, 342
 design issues, 75
 design questions, 74
 document model, 75
 exercise, 92
 flow, 74
 goal, 76
 goals, 70
 preliminary analysis, 73
 process, 70
 railroad diagrams, 83
 report, 71
 representation, 69
 sample marked-up pages, 81
 table of contents, 343
 team, 67, 69, 73
 typographic clues, 78
 work flow issues, 75
document analyst, 67
 described, 66
 skills, 68
document design, 66
Document Models
 document analysis, 44
document structure
 box diagrams, 79
 containing elements, 79
 diagraming, 78
Document Type
 declaration, defined, 224
document type definition, 218
 See also: DTD
 defined, 229

Document•Architect
description, 458
documentation
DTD, 218
Documentation Analysts, 104
Douglas Aircraft Company, 391
down translation, 181
DSSSL (Document Style Semantic Specification Language, ISO IEC DIS 10179:1991)
database considerations, 201
description, 488
legacy conversion, 141
related standards, 60
related-standards, 115
DSSSL-Lite, 52, 56
DTD, 57, 61, 73
See also: document analysis
advanced features, 283
application overview, 287
change, 145
change strategy, 284
commenting, 278
development, 59
development time, 69
documentation, 72, 216, 287
format-oriented, 89
fragments, managing, 308
industry-specific, 113
informal part, 218
managing change, 163
managing multiple internal structures, 359
naming conventions, 276
ordering, 279
organizing, 216
preliminary analysis, 73
Rainbow, 167
specific vs. general, 216
system issues, 91, 92
tables, 87
testing, 286
version control, 284
white space, 281
DTD Viewer
description, 456
DynaBase
database considerations, 202
description, 474
in action, 200
DynaTag
and Rainbow, 167
description, 464
DynaText
database considerations, 202
description, 459
electronic delivery, 53, 110
screen, 53
with DynaBase, 200
DynaWeb
description, 478

E

e-i-c, 114
E-mail
workflow, 212
E2S
address, 504
EASE
description, 452
EBT
See: Electronic Book Technologies, Inc.
EDD, 392
editions, 189
editors
formatting, 48
Non-SGML-smart, 107
SGML-smart formatting, 107
structured, 51
editorial workstation
implementing, 106
Electronic Book Technologies, Inc.
address, 504
DynaBase, 200
DynaTag, 167
DynaText, 53, 110
electronic delivery, 31, 51, 52, 110
electronic product, 41
electronic product production issues, 173
electronic products, 4
add-on production process, 37
electronic publishing, 8
See also: information delivery
Electronic Publishing Special Interest Group (EPSIG)
description, 493
electronic work order, 396
element, 24
content model, 83
declaration, defined, 224
name length, 277
relationships, 73
vs. attribute, 304
element content
vs. mixed content, 312
element declaration
defined, 229
element declarations
grouping, 280
organizing, 280
element structure information set, 46
element-in-context, 114
elements
common, 91, 288
floating, 344
tracking information about, 340
vs. attributes, 66
EMPTY
defined, 236
empty element
end-tag not allowed, 221
uses, cross-references, 322
uses, external graphics, 321
uses, formatting information, 324
uses, part numbers, 323
enabling technologies, 12, 372
end-tag
defined, 221
in markup, 220
Enthusiometer, 148
ENTITIES
declared value, 241
Entity
declaration, defined, 224
declared value, 241
protecting from parser, 351

entity management, 185
Entity references, 221
See also: general entity reference
environment
database, 44
editing, 50
features, 14
SGML, 44
unstructured, 50
EPSIG, 286, 485, 493
address, 504
EPSIG News
description, 485
equations
common elements, 292
executing, 292
error
fatal, 46
reporting, 46
ESIS, 46
evaluation criteria, 129
Exoterica Corporation, 54, 447, 464, 481, 482, 499
address, 504
description, 481
OmniMark, 177, 373, 403, 464
XGML Kernel, 448
Expert Software Systems
address, 504
export
SGML, 110
External system interconnect, 204
extraction, 8
See also: information delivery

F

FastTag, 466, 467
conversion tool, 373
feature
composition, 38
features
optional, 228
professional publishing systems, 39
table, 228
federated system, 35
file system, 186
filtering
definition, 153
filters, 156
Floating Elements, 344
Folio
and OmniMark, 352
screen-ready tables, 353
SGML Toolkit, 54
Views, screen, 54
Folio Corporation
address, 504
Folio Infobase Web Server
description, 478
Folio Views, 54
CD-ROM Delivery, 113
database considerations, 202
screen shot, 54
Folio Views
description, 459
Folio Views 3.1 SGML Toolkit
description, 460
footnote
common elements, 298
recursion, 312
rendering in electronic documents, 356
format
document, 87
system-specific, 45
Format Development Checklist, 142
Format tagging, 87, 88
formatted view, 24
formatter, 111
formatting, 28
formatting application, 142
formatting development, 141
formatting editors, 48
FOSI, 114
composition engine, 52
composition engines, 111
database considerations, 201
example, 114
hints, 111
legacy conversion, 111
pre-processing, 115
pre-processing for, 318
Frame Technology Corp.
WriterStation, 373
address, 505
DL Composer, 111
DL Pager, 52, 373
FrameMaker, 109
SGML Add-in, 51
FrameMaker
description, 449
Rainbow Makers, 109
FrameMaker+SGML, 107
Fulcrum Surfboard
description, 475
Fulcrum Technologies
address, 505
full-text
adoption, 6
full-text database
query, 195
full-text databases, 192
functional evaluation, 127
functional requirements, 128
evaluation, 127, 129

G

Gateway Conversion Technologies
description, 483
GCA (Graphic Communications Association), 490, 492
description, 492
GCA Tutorial Series
description, 498
general entity reference, 98, 157
in markup, 220
defined, 221
generic markup, 27, 28, 33
global information management, 35
GLTP, 115
glue, 119
convert prologues, 317
entity management, 318
normalize instances, 317
pre-process SGML instances, 318
using in an SGML environment, 119
GNU Revision Control System (rcs)
description, 476
goals
system, 10, 11

grain, 202
granularity, 76, 110
 database considerations, 201, 152
Graphic Communications Association
 See: GCA
 address, 505
Graphics, 15
 common elements, 260
GRIF, 453, 460
Grif S.A.
 address, 505
Grif SGML ActiveViews
 description, 460
GRIF SGML Editor
 description, 453
GRIF SGML Notes
 description, 453
GUIDE Professional Publisher
 description, 460

H

HaL Software Systems, Inc.
 address, 505
head, 187
Helmsman
 description, 459
hierarchical structures, 196
hot-lead, 32
HoTMetaL
 description, 451
HoTMetaL Pro
 description, 479
HTML, 55, 56
hub file, 185
 managing documents, 324
humans
 expensive manual labor, 10
HyMinder
 description, 447
hypertext, 30, 52, 117
HyperWriter
 description, 461
HyTime
 architectural forms, , 277
 defined, 117
 Panorama, 57
HyTime (ISO/IEC 10744:1992)
 description, 488

I

i2c
 description, 465
IBM, 194, 453, 459, 468, 470
 OS/2, 373
IBM Corp.
 address, 505
IBM SGML Translator
 description, 468
ID
 declared value, 241
 on DOCTYPE, 345
 when deleting documents, 357
ID Link Set
 declaration, defined, 225
IDREF
 declared value, 242
 in cross-references, 293
IDREFS
 declared value, 242
ifi.uio.no
 description, 487
implementation
 phased, 145
 planning, 121
 project, 121, 122
 resources, 146
 small-scale, 385
Implementation Factors
 determining, 111
Implementation Planning, 69
Implementation Tasks
 cost areas, 140
Implementing an SGML Publishing System
 description, 498
import
 SGML, 110
InConcert
 description, 480
inconsistent
 documents, 13
InContext, 50
 book production, 403
 screen shot, 49
InContext
 description, 452
InContext Corp.
 address, 505
InContext Spider
 description, 461
increase accuracy
 See: goals
increase sales
 See: goals
indexed term
 identified, 299
Indexing, 17
 common elements, 299
 opportunities, 17
indicators, 82
Industry Initiatives
 description, 499
InfoAccess Corp
 address, 505
infobase
 Folio, 352
InfoDesign Corporation, 481
 address, 505
 description, 481
information
 access, 14, 41, 376
 analysis, 66, 76
 business objectives, 77
 business requirements, 76
 capture, 8, 45
 consistency, 16
 control, 77
 conversion, 151
 creation, 8, 45
 database, 45
 delivery, 8, 51
 describing the structure, 86
 document, 66
 elements, 76
 extraction, 30
 interchange, 5, 113
 logical form, 29
 management, 8, 68
 modeling, 85
 output processing, 45
 ownership, 77
 physical representation, 78
 product-specific, 34
 reuse, 10
 reuse difficulties, 9
 structural, 45
 structure, 7
 system-independent, 45
 tabular, 87
 textual, 86, 87
 work flow, 77
Information Access
 limitations, 9

information analysis, 66
  See also: document analysis
Information Architects, Inc., xxiv, 387, 481
  address, 505
  description, 481
information conversion, 140
  See: conversion
Information Dimensions Inc.
  address, 505
Information Dimensions, Inc., 373
information elements, 29
Information Management, 11
initial conditions, 375
Innodata, 483
  address, 505
  description, 483
installation, 145
instance
  validation, 46
Integratability, 118
Integrated Chameleon Architecture
  description, 467
integration, 13, 34
integration issues, 119
Intellitag
  description, 450
interchange, 29
Interleaf, 107, 452, 472
  description, 452
  Rainbow Makers, 109
Interleaf 5 <SGML>
  description, 472
Interleaf, Inc.
  address, 505
International Organization for Standardization (ISO)
  description, 492
International SGML Users' Group (ISUG), 485, 492, 493
  address, 505
  Bulletin
  description, 485, 492
international standard, 29
International Standards Organization (ISO), 60
  address, 506
Internet, 55, 386
Intersolv, Inc.
  address, 506
ISO 10179, 115
ISO 10744:1992, 117
ISO 8879:1986, 29
ISO 9000, 121
ISO Standards Model, 60
ISUG,
  See: International SGML Users' Group

J

James Clark
  SGML-S, 407
job tracking, 9

K

keying
  See: conversion
  production, 50
Kodak, 385

L

language translation, 20
LaTeX
  description, 470
leaf
  loose-leaf, 373
Lector
  description, 461
legacy data, 78
  See also: conversion
  document analysis, 78
linear production process, 172
linear publishing process, 38
link, 113
Link Set
  declaration, defined, 225
Link Set Use Declaration
  declaration, defined, 225
  defined, 223
  in markup, 220
Link Type
  declaration, defined, 225
links, 52, 91, 172, 174
LISP, 177
LIT
  in attribute, 346
LITA
  in attribute, 346
Longevity, 91
loose-leaf, 34, 39, 41, 372

M

Making Hypermedia Work: A User's Guide to HyTime
  description, 495
Manage process, 31
management issues, 5
Mandated Deliverable, 113
Mark-it
  description, 446
marked section
  cautions in ignored, 335
  declaration, defined, 225
  defined, 223
  hiding information from customer, 336
  in DTD, 264
  in markup, 220, 223
  using parameter entities, 336
markup, 15, 24, 25, 32, 33, 46, 47, 155
  application process, 77
  complexity, 38
  content, 14
  content-oriented, 15
  defined, 219
  device-specific, 27
  editors, 47
  error, 46
  generic, 15, 30
  specific, 37
  structural, 15
  systems, 24
  tools, 75
master database, 19, 37, 378
Mead Data Central
  LEXIS/NEXIS, 55
MetaMorphosis
  description, 465
Microsoft, 451, 479
  SGML Add-in, 51
  SourceSafe, 191

Microsoft Author for Word
 at Kodak, 387
 screen shot, 51
Microsoft Author for Word
 description, 451
Microsoft Corp.
 address, 506
Microsoft Internet Assistant
 description, 479
Microsoft SourceSafe
 description, 477
Microsoft Word
 as typesetter, 387, 403
 at Kodak, 387
 book production, 402
 formatted view, 25
 Rainbow Makers, 109
 SGML-smart enhancement, 109
 unstructured text, 107
Microstar Software Ltd., 59
 address, 506
 Near&Far, 59, 279, 281
MID Information Logistics Group
 address, 506
migration strategy, 144
minimization
 omitted tag, 230
 reduce keyboarding costs, 353
mixed content
 defined, 313
model groups, 232
Mosaic, 56
multiple access, 37

N

NAME
 declared value, 242
name start character, 230
NAMES
 declared value, 242
Near&Far
 description, 456
 DTD development, 279
 screen, 59
Near&Far Lite
 description, 456
nesting
 See: recursion

Netscape
 screen, 56
newsletter, 41
NICE Technologies
 address, 506
NIST, 47
NMTOKEN
 declared value, 242
NMTOKENS
 declared value, 242
nomenclature, 77
normalized, 119
Northern Telecom
 address, 506
Notation
 declaration, defined, 225
 declared value, 242
Notes
 common elements, 300
Novell Corp.
 address, 508
Ntergaid, Inc.
 address, 506
NUMBER
 declared value, 242
NUMBERS
 declared value, 242
NUTOKEN
 declared value, 243
NUTOKENS
 declared value, 243

O

object model, 196
object-oriented databases, 192, 195
 definition, 195
objectives, 124
 document analysis, 76
objects, 110, 195
 definition, 195
occurrence, 29
 illustrated, railroad diagrams, 83
occurrence indicators, 82
 table, 232
OLIAS
 description, 462
OmniMark, 403, 404, 407, 408, 409, 460, 461, 464, 482
 and Folio, 54
 book production, 111, 403
 code sample, 155
 conversion tool, 106, 177, 178, 373, 387
 public entity mapping, 328
 table translation, 352
 User's Group, 6
on-line, 55
On-line services
 development, 113
Open Text Corp.
 address, 506
opportunities
 business, 4
order, 29, 78
 illustrated, railroad diagrams, 83
organization
 change, 12, 77
Output, 43
Oxford University Press
 address, 506

P

page
 images, 32
 marked-up, 81
page budget, 375
page layout
 complexity, 40
 interactive, 40, 41
 looseleaf, 41
page pair, 375
PageMaker
 book production, 403
 desktop publishing, 38
Pager
 composition engine, 52
Panorama, 56
Panorama Pro
 description, 478
parameter entities, 338
 See also: entities
 in the DTD, 338
 using, 307
Parameter Entity References
 naming, 256, 303
 using, 302

parameter separators
complex content models, 238
Parlance Document Management (PDM)
description, 473
parser, 46, 50, 154
errors, 46
validating, 46
validation, 46
parsing, 164
Passage Systems, Inc.
address, 506
PassagePRO
description, 480
PAT
description, 475
pattern-matching, 177
paving over the cow path, 8
See also: process re-engineering
payback period, 137, 138
PERL, 177
phototypesetting, 32
physical boundary
initial conditions, 375
physical data structures, 16
physical structure
page pair, 375
Pindar plc, 482, 484
address, 506
description, 482, 484
plan
conversion, 161
politics
corporate, 343
Polytron Version Control System (PVCS)
description, 476
PowerPaste
and Rainbow, 167
description, 465
Practical SGML (Second Edition)
description, 494
pratfall
See: tipnique
Presentational Markup, 26, 179
Procedural markup, 26, 27
process
automated, 70
flow, 8
re-engineering, 8, 125
process re-engineering, 12, 125
processes
publishing, 31, 45
streamline, 13
Processing, 31
CD-ROM, 113
conversion, 156, 163
Processing instruction
adding level information, 334
defined, 222
in editorial workstation, 334
in markup, 220
in typesetter, 335
inter-application communication, 348
the right way, 333
processing instruction entity
special processing instruction, 223
Produce process, 31
production
costs, reduced, 30
feeds, 171
linear process, 16, 36
ongoing feeds, 173
outdated processes, 9
productivity, 38
increase, 136
professional publishing, 39
selection, 41
suitability, 41
professional publishing system, 40
professional system, 39
programmability
database considerations, 201
project
benefits, 123
scope, 123
project manager,
project planning, 398
Project Scope, 123
Project YAO
description, 448
prologue, , 427
See also: SGML declaration
conditional processing, 367
converting, 316
defined, 217
glue considerations, 317
parameter entities, 336
proof-of-concept, 386
proprietary markup, 154
prototype, 396
Public Domain
address, 507
Public DTDs
description, 500
public entities
mapping files, 328
publishing
desktop, 37
loose-leaf, 375
process, 31
stand-alone, 32
Publishing Development AB
address, 507
publishing environment
limitations, 4
publishing process, 31
Publishing Process Flow, 36
publishing system, 23, 30
broken, 3
concepts, 5
federated, 35
integrated, 33, 34
linked, 33
problems, 8
professional, 37
Stand-alone composition systems, 32
Punctuation, 26

Q

quantities
table listing, 226
Quark XPress
desktop publishing, 38
QuasiWYG, 48
query, 194
database considerations, 202
full-text database, 195
quote
typographical, 295
using short references for, 330
Quotes
common elements, 295
nested, 357
qwertz/FORMAT
description, 469

R

railroad diagrams, 82
Rainbow, 109, 167
 and the Holy Grail, 109
 conversion, 167
 Rainbow Makers, 109, 167
Rainbow-Makers
 description, 467
rank
 defined, 273
RCDATA
 defined, 237
rcs, 189
RCS Information
 address, 507
re-engineering, 8
 See also: process re-engineering
reasoning
 deductive, 342
 inductive, 342
recursion
 See: nesting
 unintentional, 311
redline, 397
reduce costs
 See: goals
reference concrete syntax.
 defined, 226
rekeying
 conversion, 181
Related Standards, 4
relational databases, 192
Relational Document Manager
 description, 477
Repositories, 58
Request for Information, 136
Requests for Quotations, 136
requirements, 124, 395, 396
 evaluation grid, 131
 granularity, 128
 weighting, 130
requirements analysis, 123, 373
resources
 conversion, 161
Reusability, 90
reuse, 10, 15, 16, 35, 112
revenue opportunities, 30
revision, 19, 187
 branching, 188
 cycle, 13
 deltas, 189
 editions, 189
 head, definition, 187
 history, 189
 number, 187
 opportunities, 19
 packages, 45
revisions, 78
rich text, 24
risk
 evaluation, 139
roles, 12, 125, 126
 changing, 12, 126
 document analysis, 69
RTF, 25
rules
 illustrating model rules, 83
RulesBuilder
 description, 457

S

sample marked-up pages, 73, 80
SARA
 description, 454, 476
Saztec Phillipines
 address, 507
 description, 483
scanning
 See: conversion
Search Server, Ful/Text
 description, 475
security
 tool development, 143
Sema Group Systems, Ltd.
 address, 507
SEMA Smart Editor
 description, 454
Service Bulletins, 397
SGML
 advanced features, 283
 application, 4
 benefits, 7
 composition engines, 111
 conversion, 152, 156
 customization, 285
 databases, 110
 declaration, 217
 declaration, defined, 224
 defined, 5
 environment, 4, 44
 evangelist, 67
 export, 110
 implementation, 121
 import, 110
 publication-specific development, 111
 quinquennial review, 219
 system, 101
 translation, 111
 understanding, 215
 versions, 219
 workstations, 106
 WYSIWYG editor, 48
SGML (ISO 8879:1986)
 description, 488
SGML and Related Standards
 description, 496
SGML Associates, Inc./<TAG> The SGML Newsletter
 address, 507
SGML Conference
 description, 490
SGML Content Modeller
 description, 500
SGML Darc
 description, 462
SGML Declaration
 common, 426
 defined, 225
 fully defined, 427
SGML Europe
 description, 490
SGML ExportFilter for FrameMaker
 description, 468
SGML Open
 address, 507
 public entity mapping technical resolution, 328
SGML Primer
 description, 496
SGML Resource Guide
 description, 485
SGML SIGhyper
 address, 507
 description, 493
SGML Tag Wizard
 description, 450
SGML Tutorial
 description, 499
SGML University
 address, 507
SGML-S
 description, 446

SGML-smart editor, 19, 47
SGML-smart workstations, 5
SGML/Store
description, 474
SGML2TEX
description, 468
SGML: An Author's Guide to the Standard Generalized Markup Language
description, 495
SGML: The Movie
description, 500
SGML: The Users' Guide to ISO 8879
description, 495
SGMLCompanion
description, 456
SGMLEnabler
description, 471
SGMLOpen
public identifier mapping, 260
SGMLserver
description, 474
Short Reference Mapping
declaration, defined, 224
Short Reference Use
declaration, defined, 224
in markup, 220
Short references
capturing essential information, 349
SHORTREF, 330
See also: short reference minimization
using in quotes, 330
using in tables, 331
skills
changing, 12
smart data, 44
SNOBOL, 177
SoftQuad, 56, 451, 462, 496
Explorer, 110
PanoramaPro, 57
Publishing System, 449
SoftQuad Explorer
description, 462
SoftQuad, Inc.
address, 507
sorting, 8
See also: information delivery
SourceSafe
illustrated, 191
Spacing, 26
SPDL (ISO/IEC DIS 10180:1991)
description, 489
special characters, 94
specific markup
difficulties, 10
speed production
See: goals
SSP, 115
Standardized Markup, 28
validation, 28
start-tag
attributes, 221
defined, 221
in markup, 220
omission, 308
status codes, 20
structural hierarchy, 50
structure, 76, 78
defining, 76
document, 87
Non-SGML, 107
relationships, 73
tree diagram, 79
Structure tagging, 88
structured concepts
benefits, 5
structured editor, 107
structured editors
SGML-smart, 107
structured information, 5
style sheets, 27
sub-elements, 70
sunk costs, 129
SuperBook System
description, 463
Synex Information AB
address, 507
system
architecture, 396
degree of automation, 92
evaluation, 132
evaluation and design, 122
evaluation, 373
functional evaluation, 127
goals, 10, 372
integration, 4
limitations, 92
limitations of an unstructured, 4
modular, 396
objectives, 67
open, 13
performance, 91
problems, 13
proprietary, 13
publishing, 31
requirements, 122
selection, 41
SGML, 43
text processing, 45
System Development Checklist, 143
systems analysis, 66
Systems Analysts, 104

T

Table
common elements, 288
electronic delivery considerations, 291
format tagging, 87
format vs. content, 288
format-oriented, 87
using short references in, 331
<TAG>, The SGML Newsletter
description, 485
tagging
content, 89, 174
tagging assistance, 128
TagWrite
description, 469
task management, 380
tasks, 13, 379
assigment, 209
concurrent, 21
TCP/IP, 373
technical documentation, 35
problems, 11
technology
adoption, 5, 6
advanced, 5
benefits, 6, 7
changes, 5
database, 11
document processing, 385
emerging, 7
enabling, 11, 372
evolution, 7
information, 137
restructuring processes, 124

TechnoTeacher, Inc.
address, 507
test suite
conformance, 47
TeX, 27
TeX Users' Group
address, 507
Texcel, 473
database considerations, 202
Texcel (UK) Ltd.
address, 507
Texcel Information Manager
description, 473
Text
concepts, 5
text processing, 5
The SGML Handbook
description, 494
The SGML Implementation Guide
description, 494
Thomson Corporation
RIA Case Study, 371
TIFF
graphic format, 16
in ATA documents, 398
use in empty element, 322
TIGRE, 374, 376, 377, 381
tipnique
See: pratfall
Titles
multi-part objects, 360
tom-foolery
See: whiz-bangery
tool
workflow, 205
toolkits
API, 110
tools, 61
assisted markup, 5
CD-ROM delivery, 113
conversion, 153
conversion programming, 177
database management, 143
delivery, 45
desktop publishing, 38
DTD development, 59
evaluation, 5
functionality, 13
selection, 122
SGML, 43, 45
SGML database management, 184
SGML-smart enhancements, 110
structured, 36
structured editing, 9
visual recognition, 178
workflow, 57, 58
training, 143, 145, 146
developers, 144
developing, 144
end-user, 144
SGML, 144
training topics, 144
transaction processing
database considerations, 201
transformers, 47
translating, 8
See also: information delivery
translation, 7, 112
definition, 112, 153
downward, 181
indstry interchange application, 114
language, 20
tree-to-tree, 47, 180
translations
language, 14
translator, 47
tree diagram, 78, 79
tree-to-tree translation, 180
tree-transformation, 114
trunk, 187
typesetting, 51, 52
development, 112

U

University of Wisconsin-Madison/Extensio
address, 507
unstructured information, 9
unstructured text
difficulties, 4
unstructured tools, 4
upward transformation, 179Usenet access
description, 487
user acceptance, 127, 382
User Authorities, 211

V

validating parser, 46, 154
validation, 29, 36
difficulties, 28
unstructured editors, 107
variant concrete syntaxes
defined, 226
Vedit
book production, 403
Ventura Publisher, 404
as typesetter, 52
book production, 111, 404
verification, 155
definition, 155
version, 75, 187
definition, 187
number, 187
reconciliation, 189
Version control, 186, 189
branching, 188
definition, 186
editions, 189
implementation factors, 191
networking, 192
part of SGML environment, 45
reconciliation, 188
reporting, 189
version management
database considerations, 201
versions, 14, 20, 78
visual clues, 78
Visual recognition, 179
vocabulary
information elements, 76

W

walkthrough, 163
Warnings
common elements, 300
Westinghouse Electric Corp.
address, 508
whiz-bangery, 3
See also: tom-foolery

WIP, 379
word processor, 107
WordPerfect, 25, 450, 463
  and Folio Views, 54
  Rainbow Makers, 109
  SGML Add-in, 51
  SGML-smart enhancement, 109
  underlying codes, 24
  unstructured text, 107
WordPerfect SGML Edition
  description, 450
work flow
  issues, 16
  opportunities, 18
work in progress, 8
  See also: workflow
work load
  workflow, 13
work process
  fragmentation, 13
Work-in-progress, 379
workflow, 183, 379
  application considerations, 105
  automated tools, 58
  described, 58
  in action, 206
  in case study, 374
  information elements, 77
  integration, 107
  management tools, 57
  part of SGML environment, 45
  task, 205
  tool development, 143
workflow management tools, 205
workflow management system
  implementation, 211
workflow manager, 57
WorkSMART
  description, 480
workstation
  integration, 110
  power, 9
  SGML editorial, 48
  SGML-smart, 49
  SGML-smart enhancements, 109
  user interaction, 107
World Wide Web (WWW), 55
WorldView
  description, 463
Write-It
  description, 454
WriterStation, 373
WriterStation
  description, 453
WYSIWYG, 24, 48
  rich text, 25

X

XGML Kernel
  description, 448
XGML Validator
  description, 447
XSoft
  Astoria, 58
XSoft, a division of Xerox, 452, 470
  address, 506
Xyvision, 473
Xyvision, Inc.
  address, 508

Z

Zandar Corporation
  address, 508
ZIFTech Computer Systems, Inc.
  address, 508

Printing: Mercedesdruck, Berlin
Binding: Buchbinderei Lüderitz & Bauer, Berlin